Red Brotherhood at War

Red Brotherhood at War

Vietnam, Cambodia and Laos
since 1975

—————————◆—————————

GRANT EVANS
AND
KELVIN ROWLEY

VERSO
London · New York

First published by Verso 1984
This revised edition published 1990
© Grant Evans and Kelvin Rowley 1984
All rights reserved

Verso
UK: 6 Meard Street, London W1V 3HR
USA: 29 West 35th Street, New York, NY 10001-2291

Verso is the imprint of New Left Books

British Library Cataloguing in Publication Data
Evans, Grant, *1948–*
    Red brotherhood at war: Vietnam, Cambodia and Laos since
    1975. – 2nd ed.
    1. Indo-China. Political events, 1949–
    I. Title   II. Rowley, Kelvin, *1948–*
    959.704

    ISBN 0–86091–285–X
    ISBN 0–86091–501–8 pbk

US Library of Congress Cataloging-in-Publication Data
Evans, Grant, 1948–
    Red brotherhood at war: Vietnam, Cambodia, and Laos since 1975/
    Grant Evans and Kelvin Rowley. – Rev. ed.
        p.   cm.
    Includes bibliographical references.
    ISBN 0–86091–285–X — ISBN 0–86091–501–8 (pbk.):
    1. Indochina – Politics and government.   I. Rowley, Kelvin, 1948–
    II. Title.
    DS550.E94   1990
    959—dc20

Typeset by BP Integraphics, Bath, Avon
Printed in Finland by Wemer Söderström Oy

Contents

Maps   vii

Preface to the Second Edition   xvii

  1   Nationalism Painted Red   1

  2   Vietnam: The Myth of Post-war Expansionism   35

  3   Laos: The Eclipse of 'Neutralist' Communism   59

  4   Cambodia: The Politics of Perfect Sovereignty   81

  5   China: The Pedagogy of Power   115

  6   Indochina: Federation or Alliance?   147

  7   ASEAN: The Dominoes Push Back   181

  8   Coalition of Lost Causes   201

  9   The Great-Power Triangle and Indochina   231

10   Towards the Golden Peninsula?   263

11   Red Brotherhood in War and Peace   301

Bibliography   309

Index   313

Maps

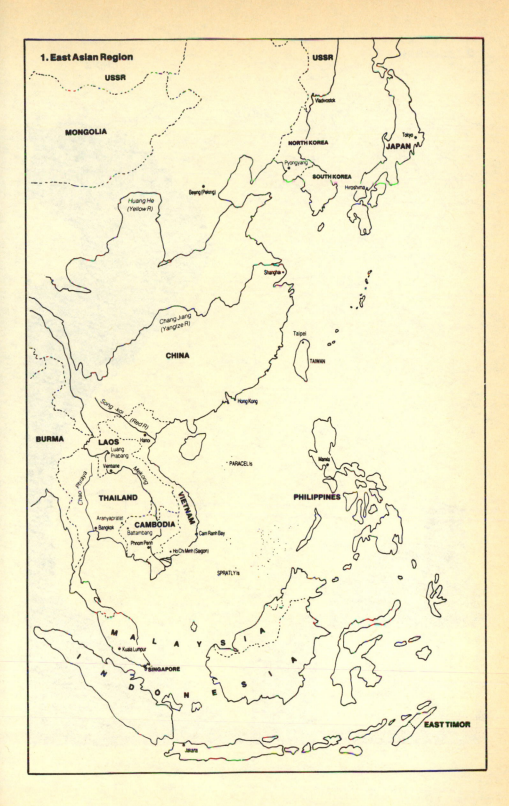

1. East Asian Region

USSR

USSR

MONGOLIA

Vladivostok

NORTH KOREA

Tokyo

JAPAN

Pyongyang

SOUTH KOREA

Beijing (Peking)

Hiroshima

Huang He
(Yellow R)

Shanghai

Chang Jiang
(Yangtze R)

Taipei

CHINA

TAIWAN

Hong Kong

Song Koi (Red R)

BURMA

LAOS

Hanoi

Luang
Prabang

Manila

Vientiane

PARACEL Is

Chao Phraya

Mekong

THAILAND

VIETNAM

PHILIPPINES

Aranyaprater

CAMBODIA

Bangkok

Battambang

Cam Ranh Bay

Phnom Penh

Ho Chi Minh (Saigon)

SPRATLY Is

M A L A Y S I A

Kuala Lumpur

SINGAPORE

I N D O N E S I A

EAST TIMOR

Jakarta

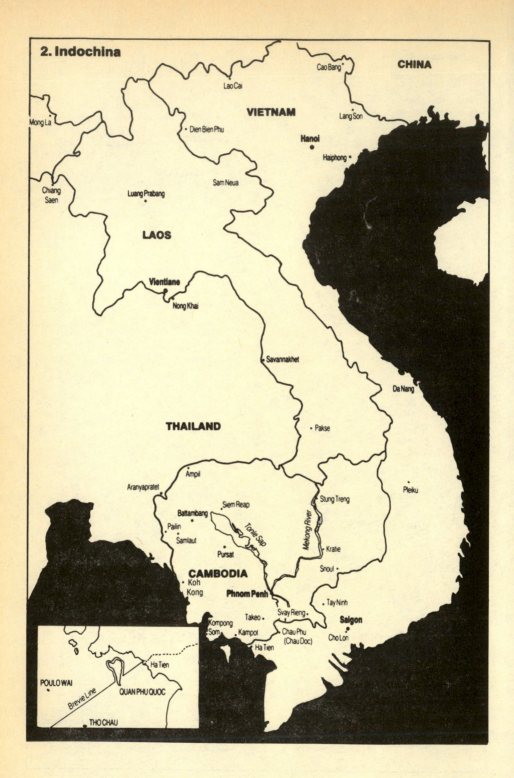

2. Indochina

CHINA

VIETNAM

Cao Bang

Lao Cai

Lang Son

Mong La

Dien Bien Phu

Hanoi

Haiphong

Sam Neua

Chiang Saen

Luang Prabang

LAOS

Vientiane

Nong Khai

Savannakhet

Da Nang

THAILAND

Pakse

Ampil

Aranyapratet

Pleiku

Siem Reap

Stung Treng

Battambang

Pailin

Tonle Sap

Mekong River

Samlaut

Kratie

Pursat

Snoul

CAMBODIA

Koh Kong

Phnom Penh

Tay Ninh

Takeo

Svay Rieng

Saigon

Kompong Som

Kampot

Chau Phu (Chau Doc)

Cho Lon

Ha Tien

POULO WAI

Ha Tien

Brevie Line

QUAN PHU QUOC

THO CHAU

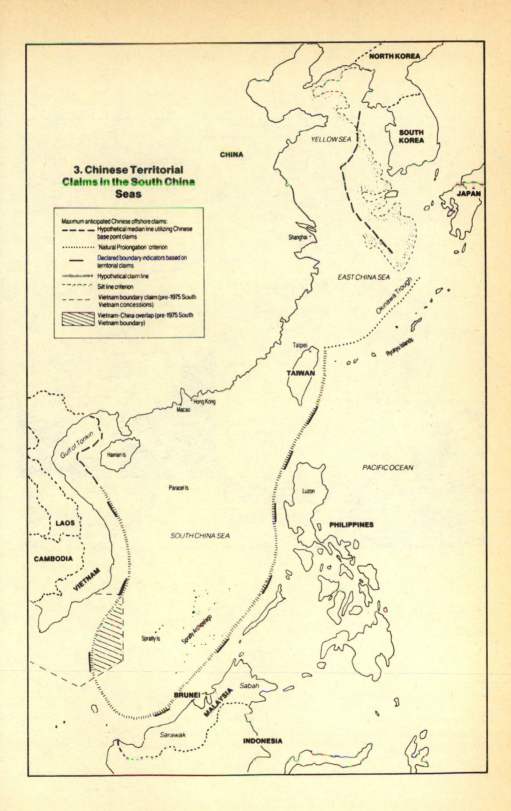

3. Chinese Territorial Claims in the South China Seas

Maximum anticipated Chinese offshore claims:

- – – – Hypothetical median line utilizing Chinese base point claims
- ········ 'Natural Prolongation' criterion
- ——— Declared boundary indicators based on territorial claims
- ⊶⊶⊶⊶ Hypothetical claim line
- –·–·–· Silt line criterion
- – – – Vietnam boundary claim (pre-1975 South Vietnam concessions)
- ▨▨▨ Vietnam-China overlap (pre-1975 South Vietnam boundary)

NORTH KOREA

CHINA

YELLOW SEA

SOUTH KOREA

JAPAN

Shanghai

EAST CHINA SEA

Okinawa Trough

Taipei

Ryukyu Islands

TAIWAN

Hong Kong

Macao

Gulf of Tonkin

Hanan Is

PACIFIC OCEAN

Paracel Is

Luzon

LAOS

PHILIPPINES

CAMBODIA

SOUTH CHINA SEA

VIETNAM

Spratly Is

Spratly Archipelago

Sabah

BRUNEI

MALAYSIA

Sarawak

INDONESIA

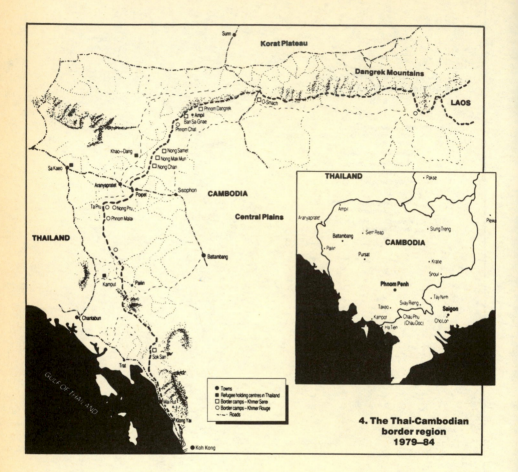

Main map labels:

Sum

Korat Plateau

Dangrek Mountains

O-Smach

LAOS

Phnom Dangrek
Ampil
Ban Sa-Gnae
Phnom Chat

Khao-I-Dang

Nong Samet
Nong Mak Mun
Nong Chan

Sa Kaeo

Aranyaprathet

CAMBODIA

Sisophon

Poipet

Ta Pru   Nong Pru

Phnom Malai

Central Plains

THAILAND

Battambang

Kamput   Pailin

Chantabun

Trat   Sok San

GULF OF THAILAND

Mai Rut

Klong Yai

Koh Kong

Legend:
● Towns
■ Refugee holding centres in Thailand
□ Border camps – Khmer Serei
○ Border camps – Khmer Rouge
-·-· Roads

Inset map labels:

THAILAND

Pakse

Aranyaprathet   Ampil

Battambang   Siem Reap   Stung Treng

Pailin   **CAMBODIA**

Pursat   Kratie

Snoul

Phnom Penh

Takeo   Svay Rieng   Tay Ninh

Kampot   **Saigon**

Chau Phu (Chau Doc)   Cho Lon

Ha Tien

Pleiku

4. The Thai-Cambodian border region 1979–84

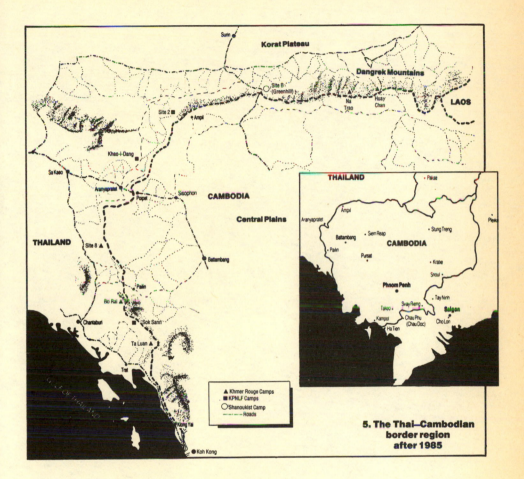

5. The Thai–Cambodian border region after 1985

Patriotism is useful for breaking the peace, not for keeping it.

THORSTEN VEBLEN, *An Inquiry into the Nature of Peace*

All nationalists have the power of not seeing resemblances between similar sets of facts. The nationalist not only does not disapprove of atrocities committed by his own side, but he has a remarkable capacity for not even hearing about them.

GEORGE ORWELL, 'Notes on Nationalism'

Preface to the Second Edition

After thirty years of war, peace came to Indochina in 1975. Because the victorious parties in Indochina were all Communist, it was generally expected that relations between them would be 'fraternal' and peaceful. But, unknown to most of the world, strains and fractures had already appeared in the 'militant solidarity binding the three peoples in friendship and brotherhood'. The peace was short-lived, and a new war erupted between Pol Pot's Democratic Kampuchea regime and Vietnam, then between China and Vietnam. This was the Third Indochina War. The first two had been 'wars of national liberation'. But now the victorious 'liberators' had turned on each other.

For some, these events spelled the end of the ideas of socialist internationalism. The *New York Times* ran an editorial entitled 'The Red Brotherhood at War' in which it announced, gloatingly: 'They are singing "The Internationale" on all sides of the Asian battlefields this week as they bury the hopes of the Communist fathers with the bodies of their sons.' The 'hopes of the Communist fathers' had been that, since war was caused by capitalist imperialism, international socialism would bring peace. These ideals now lay shattered by the new conflicts in Indochina. It is scarcely surprising that many on the western Left were confused and disorientated by these developments.

The late 1970s was the era of what Fred Halliday called the Second Cold War. Everywhere in the West, it was the Right which was in the ascendancy both politically and intellectually. Inevitably, perceptions of developments in Indochina were widely viewed through the ideological spectacles of militant anti-Communism. The anti-Communists saw Moscow as the source of all evil, and seized on the Vietnam–Democratic Kampuchea war as proof of the brutal, expansionist nature of Soviet-backed 'socialist internationalism'. This also provided a retrospective vindication for the US intervention in Vietnam.

Yet this perspective provided its adherents with more emotional satisfaction than insight. There were many inconvenient facts that did not
fit, but the mood of the time was such that these were usually overlooked.
In their unthinking zeal, the anti-Communist militants entered an open
alliance with the Communism of Deng Xiaoping, and a furtive one with
the Communism of Pol Pot, against Vietnamese Communism. Liberals
bowed to the prevailing intellectual tide, as can be seen by comparing
the two books William Shawcross wrote on Cambodia (the first published
in 1979, the second in 1984).

The first edition of this book was written in 1982–83, when the political–
intellectual climate was at its most foul. In both Washington and Moscow
aged politicians shouted insults and recycled stale slogans from the 1940s.
In writing this book we were consciously seeking to transcend the standard
clichés, and explain why Communist states had gone to war with each
other in Indochina. What, exactly, had happened in Indochina after 1975?
What happened to 'socialist internationalism' in the paddyfields and
forests of Indochina? What explains the strange ideological bedfellows
that were prompted by this conflict? How could right-wing Republicans
in the USA come to some accord with the Chinese Communists, but
not with the Vietnamese? The answer was not provided, in our view,
by Soviet–Vietnamese 'socialist internationalism' – as claimed by western
anti-Communists, and the supporters of the Chinese and the Khmer
Rouge. Nor was it provided by the betrayal of these principles by rene-
gades and 'deviationists' – as the Soviets said of the Chinese, and the
Vietnamese said of the Khmer Rouge.

The view we develop in this book is that, at least in Asia, Communism
was always strongly nationalistic. In contrast to Eastern Europe after
World War II, it did not come to these countries on the back of Soviet
tanks. In Asia Marxism–Leninism was seized upon by politicized intellectuals searching for a way of inspiring and mobilizing their people to
expel western colonialism. Other political ideologies could perform this
task too, and in much of Asia independence came under the banner of
non-Communist nationalism. In the part of the world we are concerned
with, however, Communist nationalism played a decisive role. Sociologi-
cally, Asian Communism had little to do with the working class. To the
extent it developed an internationalist perspective, it was the internationalism of intellectuals and bureaucrats. It is of course a well-known fact
that in Europe 'internationalism' served as a vehicle for particular national
interests. In Asia the internationalist veneer was even thinner.

Nationalism, Tom Nairn once wrote, has been the great failure of
Marxist analysis in the twentieth century. We agree, although it must
be said that liberal and conservative analysts have not fared much better.

The tendency has been to delegate 'the Study of Nationalism' to its own little academic sub-specialization, divorced from wider historical, political and sociological concerns. If this book has any use to those whose interests lie beyond events in Indochina since 1975, it will probably be as an attempt to bridge some of these gaps.

Nationalist assumptions are deeply embedded not only in the rhetoric of all sides to the conflict in Indochina, but also in the writings of many journalists and academics about these events. Like most powerful ideologies, nationalism exists at the level of a set of assumptions that are taken for granted, rather than explicitly argued. In reading reviews of the first edition of *Red Brotherhood at War* we were struck by the extent to which country specialists absorbed the particular nationalism to which they are habitually exposed. Cambodia experts considered us to be not sympathetic enough to the aspirations of Cambodian nationalism; similarly, China experts found us too harsh on Beijing; while Vietnam experts found us taking insufficient account of Vietnam's particular problems; and experts on Laos discovered we were insensitive to Lao nationalism.

Sometimes they had interesting points to make, but few seemed to realize that this book is not about the teleological unfolding of any national *Geist*. It is about the interaction, the conflicts, between contending nationalisms – the points at which the subjective 'truth' of each nationalism collides, often painfully, with external realities. What is distinctive about this book among recent publications on Indochina is its region-wide focus. No other book attempts to put all the players in the drama into the picture: the inclusion of Laos as a revealing point of comparison with Cambodia, for example, provides a perspective on the politics of the region not found elsewhere.

In a world bursting with nationalist passions, we think there is a lot to be said in favour of the internationalist standpoint of classical liberalism and socialism. Such a standpoint is not without problems, however, and in this second edition we have attempted some more general theoretical reflections on the prospects for internationalism in our closing pages. But this is not a book about internationalism. It is one about nationalism – or rather, about nationalisms.

As the leaders of nationalistic states, victorious Communists quarrelled with each other over clashes of interest both real and symbolic. They looked for friends, formed alliances to strengthen their own hand and to isolate their opponents, much as non-Communist nationalists do. The political behaviour that results was, we thought, best explained in terms of the classical 'realist' view of international relations, in which sovereign states pursue their national interests as best they can by forming alliances and coalitions. In this context, the relations between local states and the great powers is of central importance. The years after the victory of Communist nationalism in Indochina were especially turbulent because of the impact of Communist China on the international power balance.

However the classical version of 'realist' analysis of international relations is complicated by the fact that even the most 'monolithic' state has a variety of interests, and internal conflicts often arise over these. Policies have often been shaped by economic as well as purely power-political concerns, for example. The nature of dissension within the ruling elite over such matters, and the way in which it is handled by leaders, often impacts decisively on foreign policy. Pol Pot's regime was ultimately brought to ruin by Vietnamese military intervention, but this was – we argued – a response to the extraordinarily destructive and reckless way the Cambodian dictator dealt with these questions.

That sets out the bare bones of the analysis we developed, and in the pages that follow we flesh it out with historical detail. All this might seem like a statement of the obvious, but it is not. It certainly cut across the grain of the conventional Cold War wisdom on these matters. We showed that, far from relentlessly pursing expansionist goals in the post-1975 period, Hanoi was struggling to overcome internal crises and reacting to unanticipated external pressures, especially from Pol Pot's regime. While Hanoi was capable of responding with considerable ruthlessness to this situation, it was not out to absorb its neighbours into an 'Indochina Federation'. Despite the claims of some authors, Laos is better understood as an ally rather than an annexe of Vietnam; and the same holds for post-1979 Cambodia as well. We also showed that China and the USA played a more active role than is usually realized. This led some reviewers to describe us as being 'pro-Hanoi', but events since publication in 1984 have only vindicated our argument. It was suggested that we were being hopelessly naive to suggest that, under favourable circumstances, Hanoi might withdraw its troops from Cambodia and Laos. But it was not us who were being credulous: today, Vietnam no longer has troops in either Cambodia or Laos.

Probably no issue has been more misunderstood, on both the Right and the Left, than China's emergence as a great power, and its impact on Southeast Asia. The fog of incomprehension was so dense that we felt it necessary to devote a considerable amount of space (in chapter 5) to unravelling it and examining its roots. Little has improved in this regard since the early 1980s. One might have expected that in the wake of the Tiananmen Square massacre in June 1989 and the international outcry against Beijing, some fundamental reappraisal of China's foreign policy would have occurred. It has not, and one can only reluctantly admire the ability of the masters of Beijing to manipulate western opinion on Indochinese matters.

Thus we have not felt it necessary to revise the basic argument of our book in preparing this second edition. Indeed the predictions and interpretations have stood the test of time as well as one could hope. We argued in the final chapter of the first edition that a Sino-Soviet *rapprochement* would open up the possibility for a settlement in Cambodia, and it has. We argued against ideas of Vietnamese expansionism and claims about an 'Indochina Federation' and have been proven correct. We argued that the regime in Phnom Penh established by the Vietnamese would be the core of any future administration and that ASEAN would have to search for a face-saving way of coming to terms with this fact. While Cold War ideologues have been carrying out a vigorous rearguard action, ASEAN now seems set on this course. Matched against the thousands and thousands of words written over the last decade by journalists and academics about the 'true' nature of Vietnamese ambitions, or the 'puppet' governments in Phnom Penh or Vientiane, our analysis in retrospect looks very sober and reasonable.

However, the first edition was an interim report, drawn up in the midst of the conflict. In updating it, we have condensed some sections of the book, and added new material to update the story to October 1989. When the first edition appeared there were few other books dealing with these events. Since then a number of useful books have appeared. We have drawn on their researches, and have criticized their arguments where appropriate. While they are often invaluable on particular countries or periods, none of them gives the comprehensive and up-to-date overview that *Red Brotherhood at War* provides.

Throughout this book we have often written of countries, cities and governments as if they were one and the same thing ('Vietnam', 'Hanoi', 'the Socialist Republic of Vietnam'; 'America', 'Washington', 'the United States', and so on). This is, of course, no more than a literary convenience. Since in most cases we are actually referring to the handful of people responsible for the management of a state's external relations, we should perhaps apologize to all those citizens of countries and cities who have no responsibility for the decisions made in their names. Even in the most democratic states, foreign policy is the area of government most removed from popular control.

The Pol Pot government insisted that the correct translation into English of the name of the country it ruled was 'Kampuchea'. However 'Cambodia' remained the most widely used and familiar term for most westerners, and this is the name we have used here. However, in discussing Pol Pot's party we have used its own chosen rendering of 'Communist Party of Kampuchea' (CPK). We have done the same with the regime it established, 'Democratic Kampuchea' (DK). However 'Peking' has been effectively displaced by 'Beijing' as the most familiar rendering of the name of the Chinese capital.

We have tried to discharge our debts to published sources in our notes and in the bibliography, while keeping the book as readable as possible. Since we first began work on this book in 1979 we have been given generous assistance by various people in Vietnam, Cambodia, Laos, Thailand and Australia. In this second edition we would also like to thank Peter Cox, Ben Kiernan and Carlyle Thayer for their encouragement and assistance. Elizabeth Astbury and Archara Rowley continued to tolerate our obsession with events in Indochina. We are happy to take responsibility for the opinions expressed in this book.

Grant Evans, *Hong Kong*
Kelvin Rowley, *Melbourne*
October 1989

Nationalism Painted Red

Two explanations are commonly put forward in the West for the new round of war in Indochina after 1975. One, espoused particularly by the right wing in the United States, is that it was due to the aggressive 'internationalism' of the Vietnamese Communists and to the failure of the American intervention. In their view, no sooner had the Communists conquered South Vietnam than they turned their energies to the subjugation of neighbouring Laos and Cambodia, doubtless at the behest of Moscow. The USA, paralysed by misplaced guilt, stood helplessly by and did nothing to save the latest victims of Communist aggression.

Few Indochina experts would agree that things were as simple as this, and we shall show how wrong this interpretation is in chapter 2. In this chapter we will focus on the second explanation, which is more influential among specialists on the region and western liberal commentators. This explains the new conflicts in terms of the triumph of ancient and deep-rooted national antagonisms over the ideological bonds of internationalist Communist solidarity.

Such an interpretation certainly has some basis in the rhetoric of the antagonists themselves, who have not hesitated to find an ancient pedigree for contemporary quarrels. In September 1978 the Pol Pot regime produced a *Black Paper* depicting the current conflict as the culmination of five centuries of Khmer struggles against relentless expansion by the Vietnamese. Almost devoid of Marxist-Leninist rhetoric, it explained the conflict in purely nationalist – indeed, essentially racist – terms. It was, according to the *Black Paper*, the 'true nature' of Vietnam to be an 'aggressor, annexationist and swallower of other people's territory'. This was indignantly rejected by Hanoi as a 'crude falsification' of history, but faced with the Chinese invasion of February 1979, the Vietnamese leaders responded by invoking, in less crude but distinctly similar terms,

Vietnam's 'two thousand years of struggle against Chinese domination'.

Ancient Traditions or Colonial Transformation?

Such a line of explanation is accepted by many commentators who other-wise rarely find themselves in agreement with the Communists. For exam-ple, Elizabeth Becker, a leading American commentator on Cambodia, sees the war between Vietnam and Pol Pot's regime as the result of cultural antagonisms rooted in Cambodia's origins as an 'Indianic' state and Viet-nam's origins as a 'Sinitic' state. The Cambodian–Vietnamese border is thus 'one of the great cultural divides of Asia', marking 'the frontiers of Asia's two great cultures, China and India'. This she compares to the divide between the 'artistic Latin culture' and the 'industrious northern temperament' which supposedly occurs on the Franco-German border.[1]

Becker proceeds to illustrate this with a discussion of matters such as clothing, cooking and Khmer dancing. But she does not try to argue that the Vietnamese invaded Cambodia in 1979 because they wanted to stop a fun-loving Pol Pot enjoying his dances. Indeed, she does not succeed in making any connection between the cultural factors she lists and the outbreak of the war. The European parallels she draws surely show only how superficial and far-fetched this line of reasoning is. No serious histor-ian of, let us say, the origins of World War II has wasted time pontificating about the clash between 'artistic' and 'industrious' temperaments in Alsace-Lorraine. They have found it more useful to analyse the problems, ambitions and actions of the governments of the time.

Milton Osborne has presented a much more focused and persuasive version of the culture clash argument. Cambodia is an ancient empire which has been whittled down over the centuries by the expansion of states to its east (Vietnam) and to its west (Thailand). As Thailand was also an 'Indianic' state, defeat at Thai hands did not bring about any real changes in the Cambodian political system. The Cambodians there-fore did not think of the Thai as incorrigible enemies. But defeat at the hands of the Vietnamese meant the imposition of a fundamentally alien system of goverment. Thus, argues Osborne:

The differences between these cultures had very practical implications. When the Vietnamese absorbed Cambodian territory they sought to transform it into something that was 'standard' Vietnamese. They sought to do this behind clearly demarcated frontiers. The Cambodians, even when they had been power-ful, had not thought in these terms, neither had the Thais. For the Thais and Cambodians, both beneficiaries of Indian ideas on statecraft, frontiers were regarded as porous and shifting and new populations that might come under the control of the state as the result of conquest were not of necessity to be moulded into some pale imitation of the conqueror.[2]

The alien methods of rule imposed by Vietnamese conquests meant that the Khmer thought of the Vietnamese, in contrast to the Thai, as 'fundamentally and irretrievably racial enemies'. It was, according to Osborne, this deep-rooted traditional conflict that re-emerged after 1975 and destroyed Communist solidarity. With the Vietnamese invasion of 1978, the Pol Pot government experienced 'the ultimate proof of their countrymen's traditional fears' of the Vietnamese.

But there are serious problems even with this version of the argument. Despite their common culture, as Khien Theeravit, of Bangkok's Chulalongkorn University, has observed, 'the Siamese and the Khmer kingdoms were often at war with one another.'[3] As Khien remarks, when the Thai and the Khmer went to war they 'observed no rules of warfare and espoused no martial modes of conduct. More often than not, they demonstrated savagery in the conduct of warfare.' Marauding armies sacked and pillaged villages. The victors executed defeated kings, massacred their followers, sacked their capitals, and enslaved their subjects.[4]

The Cambodian empire lost more territory to the Thai than to the Vietnamese – a fact that is known and resented by many modern Cambodian nationalists (even if those who are in alliance with the Thai against the Vietnamese find it expedient not to dwell on it). The same is true for Laos, despite the much vaunted cultural similarities, while the greatest military threat to the Thai kingdom – its real 'historic enemy' – was another Buddhist kingdom, Burma.

Incredible amounts of romantic nonsense have been written about Asia's 'gentle Buddhist kingdoms'. If more observers had been aware of the real historical record, they might have been better prepared for what happened when Cambodia came apart in the 1970s. But for the moment, the relevant point is that we think it unlikely that the Khmer found being sacked, pillaged or executed by the Thai any more congenial than suffering such actions at the hands of the Vietnamese. We suspect that their aspirations were either to be left in peace, or to be the ones doing the sacking, pillaging and executing. And techniques of administration are more likely to concern officials than peasants.

Anti-Vietnamese Khmer nationalism is a product of the colonial era, rather than of 'traditional animosities' stretching back to antiquity. As Benedict Anderson has noted, there is a striking contradiction between the 'objective modernity' of nations and their 'subjective antiquity' in the eyes of nationalists.[5] Osborne is right in saying that in pre-colonial times the boundaries of the Cambodian and Thai states were 'porous and shifting'. But this was not because they were 'beneficiaries of Indian ideas on statecraft', in contrast to the Vietnamese and the Chinese. In both cases, states were based on the ability of rulers to command obedience and loyalty from their subjects, rather than sovereignty over fixed territory. The domains of powerful states were separated by 'frontier zones' of loose and uncertain loyalties, rather than carefully defined territorial borders. The latter is a concept imported by Europeans in the colonial era, who attempted to impose a legal–bureaucratic rationality on their conquests.

Rhetoric about the 'sacred soil' of the nation is thus characteristic of modern times. In pre-colonial Asia as in medieval Europe it was a person (the supreme ruler) rather than soil which was pronounced 'sacred'. In any case, as we shall see in chapter 4, Pol Pot's regime did not adopt the rather casual approach to border questions that might be expected from a 'beneficiary of Indianic ideas on statecraft'. Moreover, the vicissitudes of politics and war in modern times simply do not coincide with the enduring patterns of cultural differences. Why, for example, did China support 'Indianic' Cambodia against 'Sinitic' Vietnam in the conflict of 1977–78? To answer this question, we have to analyse the modern political conjuncture, not traditional cultures.

Answers in terms of the latter usually take 'tradition' as a kind of historical *deus ex machina* which explains everything and does not itself need to be explained. However, traditional culture is not the spontaneous emanation of mysterious racial instincts but the product of concrete historical experiences and institutions. It is maintained by constant efforts, and serves the interest of specific groups.

This general point has been made by Barrington Moore in terms that can hardly be bettered:

> The assumption that cultural and social continuity do not require explanation, obliterates the fact that both have to be created anew in each generation, often with great pain and suffering. To maintain and transmit a value-system, human beings are punched, sent to jail, thrown into concentration camps, cajoled, bribed, made into heroes, encouraged to read newspapers, stood up against a wall and shot, and sometimes even taught sociology. To speak of cultural inertia is to overlook the concrete interests and privileges that are served by indoctrination, education, and the entire complicated process of transmitting culture from one generation to the next ... We cannot do without some conception of how people perceive the world and what they do or do not want to do about what they see. To detach this conception from the way people reach it, to take it out of its historical context and raise it to the level of an independent causal factor in its own right, means that the supposedly impartial investigator succumbs to the justifications that ruling groups generally offer for their most brutal conduct. That, I fear, is exactly what a great deal of academic social science does today.[6]

These remarks are particularly relevant when we find 'tradition' cited to explain the behaviour of the Pol Pot group. Nevertheless this interpretation remains popular. It appeals to the common belief that 'nations' are 'natural' political communities (based perhaps on race or traditional culture) of great antiquity, yearning for political expression. But it denies the fact that in pre-modern Europe and elsewhere, 'nations' did not exist in the contemporary sense at all. Affairs of state were the exclusive preserve of a ruling aristocracy and the mass of the common people were wholly excluded from 'the political community'. They were subjects rather than citizens. It was only with the onset of those sweeping changes loosely summed up as 'modernization' that a belief in the principle of nationality took root in Europe. As Hans Kohn puts it: 'Modern nationalism originated in the seventeenth and eighteenth centuries in north-west Europe and its American settlements. . . . It became a general European movement in the nineteenth century.'[7] And, in the twentieth century, it has spread to the non-European world, largely as a result of the disruption of traditional systems of political domination by European expansion.

Nations are political communities created historically by successful nationalist movements. There are two basic elements in the process. The first is the creation of a modern state – a sovereign power with a centralized bureaucracy, uniform and impersonal laws, and a monopoly of the legitimate use of force, ruling a territory and population strictly defined in law. The second element is the incorporation of the lower classes into this system of political domination. This is facilitated by a common language and culture (which may or may not be associated with common racial features). But these ingredients are neither necessary nor sufficient – 'actually existing nations' have been shaped as much by political expediency as by theoretical formulae.

We should also add that nationalist changes can be bought about 'from above', as rulers adapt and reform existing states, or 'from below', as revolutionary forces mobilize the population behind their struggle to create a new state. As we shall see in the case of the three nations of Indochina, the disintegration of a traditional system of domination may result in both processes occurring simultaneously. The result is competing nationalisms. Nationalism arises, therefore, not from traditionalism but from its breakdown. Arguments and interpretation based on 'antiquity of nations' merely pander to the mythology of modern nationalism, the mythologies by which the rulers of nation-states seek to gain legitimacy and mobilize popular support. There are thus no such things as 'true nationalism' and 'false nationalism' – though such claims are favourite rhetorical devices among political propagandists of all sides. The reality is just conflicting varieties of nationalism, some of which emerge victorious, and some of which prove unsuccessful.

Triumphant nationalists, as a rule, like to see history written in terms that show the justice and the inevitability of their victory, and the correctness of their political line: in short, successful nationalism uses history as a legitimating myth. Unfortunately, much contemporary scholarship is devoted to elaborating the mythology rather than analysing the anatomy of nationalist politics. Nevertheless, the Indochinese present is conditioned by the past, and an awareness of the historical background is essential to an unravelling of the tangled web of events since 1975.

At the core of the explanation of the Vietnam–Cambodia war in terms of 'historical animosities' is the assumption that the conflicts of the post-colonial era are a resumption of the rivalries of the traditional states of pre-modern Indochina. There is no doubt that Angkor (ancient Cambodia), Champa (in what, more recently, was South Vietnam) and Lane Xang (in what is now Laos and northeastern Thailand) were among the main casualties of these conflicts. Nor is there any reason to dispute that the Vietnamese state was one of the most successful participants in these conflicts.

This success reflected the superior ability of Vietnam's centralized bureaucratic state to assess and mobilize resources. It is presumably to the application of legal–bureaucratic norms that Osborne was referring when he spoke of the transformation of conquered territory into 'standard' Vietnamese. In the so-called 'Indianized' states, political authority was, in Max Weber's terminology, 'patrimonial' rather than bureaucratic. Although legitimized by custom and religion (Therevada Buddhism), authority was exercised by dignitaries who depended for their position wholly on the personal favour of an autocratic king. Authority over subordinates was in principle arbitrary at every level, although it was in practice constrained by respect for custom. The system as a whole was held together by chains of patron–client relations.

The most visible sign of the success of the Vietnamese state was the great 'march to the south', begun in the fifteenth century. This movement was a result of a combination of peasant migration precipitated by population pressures in the heartland of Vietnamese civilization, the Red River Delta, and the superior strength of the Confucian state. By the seventeenth century the Vietnamese had destroyed the kingdom of Champa – with, it should be noted, the help of the Cambodians, who also benefited from the destruction of the Cham state. In the wake of this, Vietnamese settlers began moving into the lower Mekong Delta, now a thinly populated area of the Cambodian empire.[8]

Many commentators neglect to mention that the counterpoint to the growth of Vietnamese power in the east was the rise of the kingdom of Thailand in the west. Although Champa lost out principally to the Vietnamese, both Angkor and Lane Xang lost more territory to the Thai than to the Vietnamese. Thus, when it produced a White Paper on Thai–Cambodian relations in 1983, the Heng Samrin government was able to produce a chronicle of 'expansionist acts' by the Thai that is every bit as valid and impressive as that produced by Pol Pot to indict the Vietnamese. Such chronicles of past aggressions do much to mobilize nationalist indignation. But they do nothing to explain what contemporary conflicts are about.

By the late eighteenth century both Cambodia and Laos had been reduced to 'tributary states' subordinate to both Vietnam and Thailand. The outcome was that, especially as a king's reign drew to a close, ambitious princes would try to strengthen their hand in the local court by seeking Thai or Vietnamese patronage. In the 1840s the Thai king, Rama III, described the consequences: 'The Cambodians always fight among themselves in the matter of succession. The losers in these fights go off to ask for help from a neighbouring state; the winner must then ask for forces from the other.'[9]

The result was a destructive cycle of court intrigue and foreign intervention – in which attempts by individual players in the power game to improve their individual position further weakened the position of the state as a whole. In the light of these shifting alliances, attempts to claim that traditional alignments created 'natural enemies' (or 'natural allies') in the region do not stand up to serious examination.

This cycle had its greatest impact on the relatively accessible lowland country. By the mid-nineteenth century the Cambodian kingdom had declined to the point where many observers thought its complete dismemberment by the Thai and the Vietnamese was inevitable. The Lao kingdom lost virtually all its lowland territory to the Thai. Driven into the mountain hinterland, it became little more than a loosely connected collection of principalities which survived more because of their inaccessibility than because of their political capacity.

These developments of the pre-colonial era certainly helped set the stage for more recent developments. But the most important development shaping modern Indochina has been the experience of European colonialism, rather than the pre-colonial heritage. It was French rule that finally shattered traditional patterns of political domination in Vietnam, Laos and Cambodia alike. The French both dismembered Vietnam (into Cochin China, Annam and Tonkin) and joined it with Laos and Cambodia. The *imperium* that resulted – France's 'Indochina Federation', was without precedent in the traditional political institutions of the region.

French rule also brought about a major transformation of society in Indochina. Once their control was reasonably secure – in the first decade of the twentieth century – the French embarked on a programme of 'rational exploitation' of the colonies that would gladden the heart of any

1980s New Rightist. They shed 'white man's burden' rhetoric in favour of a user-pays, export-orientated approach. In the colonies, the 'economic rationalists' of the day felt no obligation to pander to claptrap about popular welfare, which was irritatingly persistent in the metropolis (where the common man, but not woman, had won the vote). The result was development in the colonies, but of such a sort as to provoke revolt among its victims.

The most fundamental change was the commercialization of agriculture: under French rule the Mekong Delta became a major exporter of rice. French capital also poured in to establish plantations, mines and railways. From the statistics that are available, it seems clear that economic development accelerated under the French; but it was a very lopsided process, and its benefits were distributed very unevenly. Few, if any, filtered down to the ordinary people – Vietnamese peasants and coolie labourers were among the poorest in all Asia – but a commercial middle class grew up in the main towns, especially Saigon. A numerically small working class, centred on the towns, the plantations and the mines, also emerged.[10]

The impact of French colonialism was extraordinarily uneven in its geographic impact. Development was concentrated in Vietnam, where it wrought immense changes, whereas the traditional social and political structure of Cambodia remained basically intact, and Laos was left to stagnate as a backwater of the Federation staffed by no more than a hundred French officials (there were tens of thousands in Vietnam).

French colonialism destroyed the traditional Confucian system of rule in Vietnam. Although the Confucian examination system was allowed to linger on until 1919 as an alternative route into the bureaucracy, the French quickly introduced their own western-style education system to train Vietnamese officials. It need hardly be added that they were assigned to lowly tasks, under the watchful eyes of their French superiors.

Both Cambodia and Laos had been acquired by the French for primarily strategic reasons. They became 'protectorates', intended to serve as a buffer, protecting the more valuable coastal provinces of French Indochina from hostile powers. The French were also competing with the British for a southern route to China, which they hoped control of the Mekong valley would provide. Inevitably, this brought them into conflict with the Thai, outraged by their loss of influence in Cambodia and Laos, and distressed by the success of the French in rolling back the territorial gains Thailand had made in happier times. But the Thai king was also hard pressed by the British in the west, and it took all his skill to juggle the British against the French to avoid an outright annexation of his kingdom.

Thailand lost territory to both the British and the French. Nationalist ideologues would subsequently present this defeat on two fronts as a victory. In relative terms, they do have a point. Thailand came through the colonial era as an independent state, and it was the only country in the region to do so. In Cambodia the traditional social and political structure was still largely intact in 1945. Private titles to land had been established, but French commercial penetration was limited. Rubber plantations were established in the east of the country, but the French preferred to work them with Vietnamese coolie labour. The French also used Vietnamese to staff their colonial bureaucracy. They did little to provide the Khmer with a western-style education. As a result, unlike Vietnam, there was virtually no indigenous working class or intelligensia until the 1930s.

In Vietnam the French conquest dismembered a powerful state, apparently in a phase of regional, ascendancy. In Cambodia they proclaimed a protectorate over a kingdom already in decline. The standing of the traditional monarchy probably suffered in both countries as a result. But the blow was heavier in Vietnam. Vietnamese nationalists would soon turn against a humiliated emperor as a 'puppet' of France. In Cambodia the traditional monarch survived as a diminished, but credible, focus of political life. As nationalism developed in Vietnam, its cadres had no doubts that the French were responsible for national humiliation.

Their Cambodian counterparts took a more ambiguous position from the start, both on the monarchy and on the French. They reflected not only on the humiliation of their king at the hands of the French, but also on the losses Cambodia suffered at the hands of its immediate neighbours before French intervention. French rule disrupted life even less in Laos than it did in Cambodia. Since the break-up of Lane Xang, Laos was really a confederation of small principalities, with regionally based aristocratic families wielding political power. The king, based in the royal capital of Luang Prabang, exercised little real power; symptomatically, the French established their administrative capital elsewhere, in Vientiane. Peasant life was barely touched. Only the merest handful of Lao aristocrats were given any education by the French. The principal headache of the French in colonial Laos was fractious hill tribes who resented French attempts to bring them under the control of lowland authorities.

French rule also brought an end to Chinese hegemony over the states of Indochina. In the face of French annexations, Tu Duc, the last traditional ruler of Vietnam (more strictly, of its surviving northern rump, Tonkin) had turned increasingly to the Chinese for support. But when, in keeping with long-established precedent, he sent a formal mission of tribute to Beijing in 1880, the French seized on this as an intolerable act of defiance and used it as their excuse for the conquest of Tonkin. In 1885 the French forced the Vietnamese ceremonially to melt down the seal of investiture granted by the Chinese emperors to the rulers of Vietnam. The Chinese invaded in protest, but were quickly defeated, and in 1885 signed a treaty with the French by which they formally renounced suzerainty over Vietnam. This was a dramatic instance of the general process by which European imperialism shattered the traditional Sino-centric pattern of relations between states in Southeast Asia.

The various borders of Indochina were for the first time given precise legal demarcation as a result of the assertion of French power. The borders of Laos and Cambodia with Thailand were determined in various treaties between the French and the Thai from 1867 to 1925. The borders between China and Vietnam and Laos were laid down in Sino-French negotiations in the 1880s and 1890s. On the other hand, the boundaries between Laos, Vietnam and Cambodia were decided simply as internal administrative divisions within French Indochina, and they were adjusted on several occasions for official convenience; only after World War II were they accorded the status of international borders. As a result of the colonial experience, therefore, the Indochinese countries found themselves with borders to whose determination none of them had been a party. This was to prove an explosive legacy in the era of victorious nationalism.

Vietnam: Anatomy of Nationalist Revolution

Modern nationalism emerged in the Indochinese countries as a response to colonial rule. The earliest and the strongest movement emerged in Vietnam. There was already in Vietnam that loose sense of national identity that could be termed 'proto-nationalism': and it was here that the transforming impact of colonialism was greatest. The basic anatomy of modern nationalism can be seen most clearly in Vietnam.[11]

Vietnamese resistance to French rule went through several distinct stages of evolution. With some variations, a similar pattern can be found in many colonial nationalist movements. Opposition began immediately after conquest, as a movement of traditionalist royalism. Members of the old ruling class felt the immediate impact of French conquest most fully, for it was they and not the common people who experienced political dispossession. Many of them sought salvation through a restoration of the full power of the Vietnamese throne, a vigorous reassertion of traditional Confucian values, and the expulsion of disruptive foreign influences. From the 1860s onwards, local mandarins organized military resistance to the French in many parts of the country. At times they succeeded in tying up tens of thousands of French troops, but by 1895 the movement had basically been beaten.

The second phase was one of westernization. As early as the 1870s, some members of the Vietnamese upper class were consciously rejecting the Confucian tradition in favour of western culture. This trend was

strengthened by the defeat of traditionalists, which seemed to prove con-
clusively the practical superiority of European civilization, and by the
growth of a semi-westernized merchant class in the port towns. Educated
Vietnamese drank deeply of western culture, looked to western political
models for the future of their own country and, at least before 1914,
submitted to western tutelage. Those who sought reforms couched their
demands in moderate and respectful terms, and accepted the timetable
decided on by the French.

This phase ended with World War I. Within Europe and beyond it,
the war shattered the confidence in the superiority of European civilization
that had provided the intellectual and emotional underpinning of imperialism. After the war, the colonial reformers turned in more radical directions. In Vietnam, fewer and fewer were willing to follow French
timetables.

Vietnamese opposition to French rule entered its third phase with the
birth of modern nationalist movements after World War I. These were
at first narrowly based, drawing their support from the urban, educated
classes, and they were profoundly influenced by events outside Vietnam
– not only World War I, but also the Chinese (1910) and Russian (1917)
revolutions. The Russian revolution, in particular, seemed to offer a way
forward to those who wished for the benefits of modernization but
opposed western imperialism. By the 1930s the two main groups contending for the leadership of the Vietnamese nationalist movement were the
Vietnam Quoc Dan Dang (VNQDD), which modelled itself on Chiang
Kai-shek's Guomindang in China, and the Indochinese Communist Party
(ICP), which was led by Ho Chi Minh and looked to the Soviet Union
for its political model.

This third stage can be termed that of 'elite nationalism'. Subjection
to alien rule had implanted the idea that the Vietnamese were one people,
a nation with a common past and a common destiny – and that it should
take this destiny into its own hands, against French resistance if need
be. Greg Lochart has recently emphasized that the crucial linguistic shifts
– from terms denoting people as 'subjects of the king' to denoting them
as citizens, and from patriotism as loyalty to the person of the king to
loyalty to the cause of the people – took place only in the twentieth
century.[12] But this idea remained restricted for the time being to the better-
off classes. In terms of their social backgrounds, there was little to choose
between the leaderships of the Communists and the anti-Communist
nationalists. Both drew heavily on the children of middle- and lower-
ranking Confucian officials, educated and westernized by the French,
and usually employed as minor civil servants or school teachers until
they became professional political agitators. The social gulf between them
and the peasant majority remained vast, and their mass following minimal.

Attempts by these elite groups to pressure the French into granting independence by means of propaganda and persuasion failed dismally, and by the end of the 1920s many of their members were in prison. When persuasion failed, the nationalists tried force, the VNQDD in particular proving adept at terrorist tactics. But while the nationalist groups were small and politically isolated they could be dealt with effectively by police repression. Vietnamese elite nationalism, even when it took a violent turn, presented no serious immediate threat to French rule in Indochina.

Given the intransigence of the French, the only way the nationalists could defeat them was by rallying wide popular support. Here again, European experience provided the model for those out to overthrow European rule. The nineteenth and early twentieth centuries in Europe witnessed the emergence of mass political movements and the democratization of political life. Whereas previously the only opinions that had counted in politics were those of various groups in the ruling classes, now the views and interests of the common people – the peasants, the working class and the middle classes – had to be taken into account as well. Liberal democracy, Communism and fascism all emerged in Europe as different responses to this entry of the common people on to the political stage. And despite their divergences, they all seemed to point to one fact of central importance – success in the new arena of mass politics depended on building an effective party organization propagating an ideology with popular appeal. The era of mass politics has been one of party politics and ideology, and this has proved as true in the colonies as in Europe itself.

Thus the fourth stage in the development of nationalism in Vietnam was the transition from elite nationalism to 'mass nationalism'. It was a stage of party-building and popular mobilization against colonial rule, which took place in the 1930s and 1940s against the background of the Great Depression and World War II. It also witnessed the development of a struggle between the Communists and the non-Communists for the loyalties of the common people.

The anti-Communists won a sizeable following among the mercantile classes in the port towns, particularly Saigon, and among the commercial landlords who dominated the rural economy of Cochin China, closely interconnected as they were with mercantile interests in Saigon. While they succeeded in attracting many prominent Vietnamese into their ranks, the anti-Communists remained essentially a conservative party of the well-to-do minority. Their great failure was that they made little effort to win the support of the peasantry, the largest class in Vietnamese society. It is not unreasonable to describe these groups as 'bourgeois nationalists'.

If their social base was narrow, they also lacked a coherent ideology and the organizational discipline necessary for success in modern mass politics. The political ideas of the bourgeois nationalists ranged from liberal democracy to overt fascism. Most wanted the French to go, or at least to hand over power to them, but beyond that they basically wanted to change the status quo as little as possible. Even their anti-French stance underwent revision as conflict with the Communists intensified, and by the 1950s many of them were looking to the French for protection from the Communists, while the French found them a congenially moderate alternative to Communism. But this *rapprochement* with the French in the middle of the war of independence only served to weaken further the already dubious patriotic credentials of the bourgeois nationalists. They also suffered from chronic factionalism, and were unable to establish a stable political organization that could sink enduring roots. In many ways, they simply did not progress beyond the amateurish politics of the elite nationalism of the 1920s.

Their Communist rivals, on the other hand, did make this transition. They succeeded in building and maintaining a disciplined organizational structure of cells and branches, which effectively linked the rank-and-file members in villages and factories to the national party leadership. They also possessed the advantage of having a leader of outstanding personal capabilities, Ho Chi Minh. And unlike the traditional Confucian state, to which it is sometimes compared, Communist organization penetrated deep into the lowest levels of the social structure. The Communists were also notable in the ruthlessness with which they dealt with rivals and opponents. In the state to which this movement gave eventual birth, a highly centralized government would be linked to a strong grassroots organization by a tightly disciplined party apparatus.

The Communists had considerable success in mobilizing working-class support. But, in terms of its social composition, the Indochinese Communist Party was hardly the 'party of the proletariat' it claimed to be. The industrial working class was still very much a minority group in Vietnamese society; and the Communists achieved their key success where the bourgeois nationalists failed, in the countryside. By exploiting agrarian grievances – landlordism, usurious moneylenders, corruption and the abuse of power by local officials – they succeeded in gaining a following among the peasants in many areas of the Vietnamese countryside: while in many others they were, if not supported, at least feared and respected. While the urban working class did play some role, the Communist revolution in Vietnam was basically a peasant uprising organized by intellectuals from a middle-class (and even aristocratic) background.

In the early 1930s the Communist movement was ravaged by police repression, and it was their leading role in the resistance to the Japanese occupation of Indochina during World War II that brought the Communists to the forefront of the nationalist movement. A similar pattern can be detected in a number of European countries that underwent fascist occupation, with the result that this was the period of fastest growth in the history of the international Communist movement. In May 1941, the Communist Party formed the 'Vietnam Doc Lap Dong Minh' (League for the Independence of Vietnam), better known as the Viet Minh, whose objective was Vietnamese independence, and launched an armed struggle against the Japanese – in other words, it was aiming at the expulsion of the French as well as the Japanese. As the most effective anti-Japanese force in Indochina during World War II, the Viet Minh managed to attract the support not only of many Vietnamese nationalists, but also of Free French forces and even the American Office of Strategic Services (OSS), who at one point provided Ho Chi Minh's forces with weapons.[13]

When the Japanese surrendered in August 1945 the Viet Minh seized power in Hanoi and proclaimed the Democratic Republic of Vietnam (DRV). The puppet emperor retained by the French, Bao Dai, agreed to abdicate in favour of the DRV. The French, however, were unwilling to accept the loss of Indochina. They returned in force in 1946, and the First Indochina War began. The French aimed at securing all of Indochina, and tried to rally anti-Communist forces in Cambodia and Laos as well as Vietnam to their cause. The war between the French and the Viet Minh thus ranged through all of Indochina until the French defeat at Dien Bien Phu in May 1954.

The French had been by no means alone in their struggle against the Communist-led nationalist movement in Indochina. While there were many Vietnamese who supported the Viet Minh, there were many others who were mortally afraid of them. Thus the remaining traditional monarchists, many bourgeois nationalists and most Catholics rallied to the French-sponsored Bao Dai government. The 'war of national liberation' between the Viet Minh and the French was also, to a significant degree, a civil war between left-wing and right-wing Vietnamese; and when the French left Indochina that conflict had not been resolved.

The French had another ally in the United States of America. Alarmed at the spread of Communist influence in Asia, the USA had early turned against the Viet Minh. Immediately after the outbreak of the war in Korea in 1950, it began providing large-scale military assistance to the French forces in Indochina, and from then until 1954 the US Treasury paid 80 per cent of the cost of France's war in Indochina.

The battle of Dien Bien Phu took place on the eve of a minor international conference at Geneva to settle the Indochina and Korea crises. All the major powers, including the USA and Communist China, attended. The Viet Minh delegation, led by Pham Van Dong, was eager to taste the fruits of victory, but was persuaded to accept a compromise by its Soviet and Chinese allies. Instead of the authority of the DRV being accepted throughout the whole of Vietnam, the Viet Minh accepted the 17th parallel as a temporary demarcation line, Viet Minh forces regrouping to the north and pro-French forces to the south. Elections were to be held within two years to decide the future of the country. But the elections were never held; the reunification of Vietnam was delayed twenty years, and only achieved by war.

The Second Indochina War

The origins and nature of this Second Indochina War are often misunderstood.[14] It was certainly not, as the US government claimed in the 1960s, an external attack by Communist forces on the 'independent state of South Vietnam' established at the Geneva Conference, for no such state was established at Geneva. Although they had withdrawn their military forces to the north of the 17th parallel, the Viet Minh had been a genuinely nation-wide movement, and many of its civilian cadres and supporters had remained behind in the south.

Nor was it simply a popular uprising against an unrepresentative and repressive government in South Vietnam, as many liberal critics of the Americans argued. The insurgency in the south was not autonomous, but fully supported by the Communist north. In reality, the war was a struggle between the two streams of nationalism that had developed in Vietnam, under the French – bourgeois nationalism centred on Saigon, and the mass nationalism of the Viet Minh, which had created the regime in Hanoi.

From 1954 to 1959 the leadership in Hanoi had looked to peaceful methods of reunification, but these were spurned by the government in Saigon. This led to some tension with the Communist cadres in the south, who were faced with a mounting campaign of repression by the Saigon regime and wanted to go over to a policy of armed opposition. In 1959, the Hanoi leadership decided to back armed struggle in the south. At the 3rd National Congress of the Vietnam Workers' Party – the name then being used by the Communist Party – in 1960, a number of southern cadres were promoted to leading positions. Among them was Le Duan, who had been pushing the southerners' case for a change of tactics since 1957. He was elected to the crucial position of general secretary of the party.

The National Liberation Front of South Vietnam (NLF) was formed in December 1960 to lead the struggle. A popular front organization modelled on the Viet Minh, it became popularly known to western readers as the Viet Cong. From that point on the fighting in the south escalated rapidly into full-scale war.

The creation of a separate state in the south was primarily an American strategy to prevent the Communists from consolidating the gains they had won on the battlefield at Dien Bien Phu and at the negotiating table at Geneva. Recognizing that Bao Dai was a discredited figure, the Americans threw their weight behind his last prime minister, Ngo Dinh Diem. A conservative Catholic of Confucian background, he was an elitist of strongly authoritarian convictions. He disliked the disorder of liberal democracy and rejected in principle the idea of government based on 'mere numbers'. 'Society', he told Bernard Fall, 'functions through personal relations among men at the top.'[15] This was not the man to lead bourgeois nationalism successfully into the era of mass politics.

At first, Diem had surprising success. In the first two years of his rule, he succeeded in breaking the power of the Cao Dai and Hoa Hao sects, which controlled much of Saigon and the southern countryside. Then he turned to the more difficult task of eradicating the Viet Minh infrastructure. In doing this he relied on straightforward police-state methods, for which he was roundly criticized by western liberals. But Diem's real problem was not his reliance on dictatorial methods – the Vietnamese Communists were not squeamish about the methods they used – but the fact that his dictatorship had a precariously narrow base of support. It was a dictatorship of Catholics, many of them pro-French refugees from the north, over a predominantly Buddhist population. Even within the Catholic community, all effective power lay within one family clique. Even more importantly, it began as and remained an urban-based regime, closely tied to commercial interests in Saigon: as time went on, and much of the southern countryside effectively passed into the hands of the NLF, it became more and more dependent on external economic, political and military support.

The Americans were caught in an insurmountable dilemma in Vietnam in the early 1960s. Their presence in the country was already more blatant than the French presence had ever been, and Communist propaganda was tellingly exploiting this to depict Diem as a 'puppet' of American imperialism. To deepen their involvement would be to undercut further the credentials of the 'nationalist alternative' to Communism. But when they gave Diem his head, he pursued policies based on such narrow interests that he actively alienated support and drove people into the Communist camp. After a wave of Buddhist demonstrations against his regime, with American collusion, Diem was murdered in a military coup in 1963. But the subsequent military regimes in Saigon were never able to overcome the heritage bequeathed by Diem.

The rapid deterioration of the military situation in South Vietnam after Diem's death led to an escalation of the American involvement. This wrought immense destruction in both North and South Vietnam, but it did nothing to solve the fundamental political problems of the Saigon regime and in key ways it compounded them. Massive reliance on the USA undermined its nationalist credibility, and the torrent of dollars led to spreading corruption that sapped the morale of government supporters. The rise of the 'PX millionaires', as one-time President Nguyen Cao Ky called them, made the war into a blatantly self-serving enterprise for the wealthy in Saigon. The result was that many people who loathed the Communists were simply unwilling to fight for the southern regime when it came to the crunch.

And, of course, the crunch did come, in the early 1970s. The illusion that American military power would smash the Communists and bring about a quick and easy victory was shattered by the Tet offensive in 1968.[16] After that, the Americans began to negotiate seriously for a withdrawal: having undermined the nationalist credentials of their Vietnamese allies by massive intervention, they now gambled everything on 'Vietnamization' of the war. The American presence was scaled down progressively, and a complete withdrawal of their forces was negotiated in 1973 – an agreement hailed as 'peace with honour' in Washington and 'treachery' in Saigon. Once the Americans were out, the ceasefire in South Vietnam collapsed almost immediately, and in early 1975 the whole political–military structure of the Saigon regime was unravelled with such speed and completeness that even the Communists were taken by surprise.[17] Essentially, the bourgeois nationalists of Saigon had never been able to progress beyond the elite politics of the 1920s. In 1975 they were finally overwhelmed by the mass nationalism forged by the Viet Minh in the 1940s.

Cambodia: Royalists versus Republicans

In Vietnam, the development of a modern nationalist movement in response to colonialism can be seen in relatively 'pure' form. It took place over a lengthy period of time and, though overlapping to some extent, the different phases stand out as chronologically distinct. In Cambodia and Laos, the impact of colonialism was milder, and modern nationalism emerged later. When it did develop, the different phases of the process were 'telescoped' together in a confusing fashion, and heavily influenced by the course of events in Vietnam.

In Cambodia, the French were initially content to declare a protectorate over the throne, and set up a skeletal colonial administration. Since few Cambodians had the education or clerical skills needed to fill the bottom ranks of the colonial bureaucracy, the French brought in Vietnamese to fill these positions. By the early twentieth century, they had imposed French property laws and taxes, and expanded corvée labour. But Cambodia was peripheral to France's colonial venture in Indochina and traditional patterns of life and political authority were relatively undisturbed. Subordination to the French probably reduced the status of the king, but until World War II the country's political life consisted almost exclusively of court intrigue in Phnom Penh.

In 1941 the king died, and the French installed the youthful Prince Norodom Sihanouk on the throne. An only child, Sihanouk was shy and introverted, and thus presumed to be suitably malleable by French officials. In appointing him they passed over the Sisowath branch of the royal family, which had expected to inherit the throne. Norodom–Sisowath rivalry continued for decades after this.

The French made little effort to educate the Cambodians. In the racialist doctrines that guided colonial practice, they thought that there was little point. It was easier to bring in 'superior' Vietnamese to do the job. It was not until 1933 that the first high school in Cambodia was opened. Even in the 1950s there were only a couple of thousand Cambodians with a secondary education. Educated Cambodians found their path to influence and status blocked as much by the Vietnamese the French appointed to the colonial bureaucracy as by the French themselves.

The first stirrings of Cambodian nationalism appeared in the late 1930s. Given the intimate relation between the monarchy and the French, the first nationalists were of necessity also anti-monarchist. And given French policies favouring the Vietnamese, they were anti-Vietnamese as well. When the Japanese decided to eliminate French rule in 1945, they installed a prominent nationalist, Son Ngoc Thanh, as prime minister. A bitter rivalry soon broke out between the new king and the new prime minister. But, with the help of the returning French, Sihanouk was able to depose Thanh and send him into exile.

Thanh had a considerable following in Phnom Penh, among the students in particular. When the French introduced reforms establishing an elected National Assembly in Cambodia, they formed a Democratic Party. Its opponents were little more than cliques of conservative bureaucrats and landowners, who wanted little or no change. The Democrats wanted to drive the French out and establish a Cambodian government.

To Sihanouk's dismay, the Democrats won a majority of the seats in the National Assembly in the first elections, in 1946. Control of the National Assembly gave the Democratic Party position and status but not real power, as it soon discovered when it tried to restrict royal and French power. The Democratic Party began to splinter into factions. It could still rally huge crowds to greet Thanh when he returned triumphantly from exile in 1951. But it was unable to protect its hero, and within six months Thanh was forced to flee the capital.[18]

The Democratic Party was essentially an urban phenomenon, the Cambodian version of bourgeois nationalism. Given the French assumption of the inferiority of even educated Cambodians to the Vietnamese, it was fuelled by anti-Vietnamese resentment, as well as by hostility to French rule. It was these French attitudes and policies which created the 'traditional hostility' towards the Vietnamese, about which so much was written in the 1970s and 1980s.

As soon as they returned, the French tried to restore their control over rural Cambodia, but by 1946 disorganized armed resistance had developed in many rural areas. Many of the Khmer Issaraks ('Independent Khmer') looked to Thanh for leadership. When Son Ngoc Thanh fled Phnom Penh in 1951, it was to areas on the Thai–Cambodian border under the control of pro-Thanh Issaraks. From there he directed anti-French and anti-Sihanouk guerrilla warfare for several years.

By this time the Issarak movement had grown considerably. But it was divided. As the war in the Vietnamese parts of French Indochina intensified, the French, through Sihanouk, recruited Cambodians to fight against the Viet Minh; and the Viet Minh began to encourage and organize Issarak groups in Cambodia. By the early 1950s one wing of the Issaraks, led by Son Ngoc Minh, was strongly pro-Viet Minh. The other wing, which looked to Son Ngoc Thanh, became increasingly antagonistic to the Vietnamese. They were united only in their hostility to Sihanouk and his French masters.

As the military situation in Indochina turned in favour of the Viet Minh, the strength of their Issarak allies grew rapidly. By 1954 they had about 5,000 men under arms, supported by some 2,200 Viet Minh troops, and controlled large areas of the countryside. They faced 6,000 French troops and a Royal Khmer Army which had been built up by the French to a total strength of 33,000, but which still depended on the command of French officers.[19]

By this time the pro-Thanhist Issarak movement had collapsed, its followers going to either the Sihanouk side or the pro-Vietnamese side. Sihanouk rallied many of the anti-Vietnamese Issaraks, and many urban Democratic Party supporters, by making a dramatic reversal. Although earlier an opponent of Cambodian independence, in 1953 he launched himself as the champion of a 'Crusade for Independence'. He quickly became a master of the arts of manipulating the international mass media and outmanoeuvring his domestic opponents. After some hesitation, the French decided that he was a more congenial prospect than the Issaraks, and hastened to grant independence to his government.

At the Geneva Conference of 1954, Son Ngoc Minh's followers, not to mention the Thanhists, were denied representation. Most were forced to go into exile in Vietnam. Sihanouk, originally appointed to the throne because of his pliability, thus emerged as the man who had won Cambodian independence from the French. In contrast to Bao Dai in Vietnam, he succeeded in focusing emergent Cambodian nationalism on the throne and the traditional political system.

Sihanouk consolidated his dominance in 1955 by holding the elections promised at Geneva. He formally abdicated from the throne in favour of his father. Sihanouk then established his own political party, the Sangkum. To conservative Cambodians, he was still the god-king. To radical Cambodians, he was the democrat who had won independence and given up the throne.

The chief opposition to Sihanouk came from the Democratic Party. The surviving rump of Son Ngoc Minh's movement formed the Pracheachon. Several Democratic Party and Pracheachon candidates were jailed, and some were killed, during the election campaign. Shortly afterwards the leading Democrats fled the country, and Sihanouk's police began hunting down the remaining left-wing Issaraks (the 'Khmer Viet Minh', as he called them) in the countryside. Despite this, the International Control Commission (established at Geneva to oversee the implementation of the agreements) certified the 1955 elections in Cambodia as 'correct'.[20]

Following this triumph, Sihanouk re-established an effective monopoly over Cambodian political life, and systematically inculcated monarchist sentiments into his subjects. As Elizabeth Becker summed up the period that followed:

> Sihanouk put his royal stamp on everything. The monarchy remained one of the pillars of the country in the constitution. The royal palace remained the center of society.... And Sihanouk heavily subsidized the symbols of the throne – the royal palace and court, the royal museum and antiquities, the heavy royal hand at every turn. The prince enjoyed a status that would have been the envy of his immediate royal predecessors – total control over the country without the domineering protection of a foreign power.[21]

Sihanouk had outmanoeuvred the early leaders of both bourgeois nationalism and radical mass nationalism in Cambodia. But these forces went underground, or were absorbed into Sihanouk's own Sangkum ('People's Community') party. Sihanouk began espousing a 'Buddhist socialism' so vague that both religious conservatives like Lon Nol and young radicals like Khieu Samphan were able to find something in it that they could support.

The continuity of traditional monarchic political and religious institutions linked pre- and post-colonial Cambodia, and after the departure of the French Sihanouk interpreted regional politics in terms of the rivalries between the old kingdoms. He pointed to the contrast between the glories of Angkor and the sad state into which Cambodia had fallen in modern times. This he explained, not in terms of the socio-economic or political weaknesses of the Khmer Empire, but in terms of its geographic position and the evil designs of its enemies. As proof of this analysis, he took border disputes with both Thailand and South Vietnam.

Immediately after the Geneva Conference, Sihanouk had flirted with the idea of aligning himself with the West. But this effectively meant joining the Southeast Asia Treaty Organization (SEATO). He feared that this would mean the subordination of Cambodia to its more powerful anti-Communist neighbours with (as he saw it) designs on Cambodian territory – South Vietnam and Thailand. The USA was willing to defend Cambodia's territorial integrity against Communist forces but not against right-wing regimes. On the other hand, Sihanouk found that the Communist bloc was willing to give him unequivocal assurances on this point, Communist China in particular coming to the support of his government. Sihanouk therefore opted for a policy of neutralism, and found that, while the USA was not willing to tolerate such a policy, especially in the light of its growing commitment to South Vietnam, it was positively welcomed by the Communist countries. Sihanouk thus found himself pushed in a 'pro-Communist' direction in his foreign policy, although he feared and detested Communism.

Combined with the populist trappings he adopted, this had led to much confusion about the basic nature of Sihanouk's regime. Sihanouk's main purpose was to perpetuate the monarchy that had ruled his country for centuries, and the ideological and socio-economic forces that sustained it.

Analysis of Cambodian politics has been hopelessly confused by the widespread notion that Sihanouk was (and still is) a 'charismatic' figure. The term derives from the writings of Max Weber, but is grossly misused in this context. Many commentators seem to use it as a synonym for 'enjoying popular support'. But Weber used the term to refer to the extraordinary characteristics of a leader who gathers disciples, by force of character and conviction, to overthrow traditional or legal–bureaucratic rulers. The charismatic leader is a revolutionary, a popular demagogue, or a military hero – not a traditional monarch. Under Weber's typology, Sihanouk's regime should be classified as one based on patrimonial traditionalism.[22] The basis of his popular support was not personal magnetism but the strength of royal institutions in a strongly traditionalist society. Sihanouk clung to the ideal of the benevolent despot worshipped by the peasants (to whom he liked to refer as 'my little people'). Bureaucrats, businessmen, generals and politicians always filled him with suspicion; they represented 'vested interests', not 'the people'. Their existence was tolerated, as a rule, but Sihanouk took every opportunity to restrict their influence in Cambodian politics.

To see Sihanouk's rule in perspective, it may be useful to compare it with the reign of King Chulalongkorn in Thailand (1868–1910). Chulalongkorn was basically successful in carrying through a 'revolution from above'. He transformed a traditional patrimonial regime, essentially similar to Sihanouk's, into a centralized bureaucratic state, taking the British colonial administration in Burma as his model. Of course, this transformation was by no means total, and even today the Thai bureaucracy is riddled with networks of patronage rooted in the traditional pattern – but this should not obscure the central reality of the transformation he brought about.

Chulalongkorn also actively promoted commerce and capitalist development within his kingdom. Ultimately, the modernization of state and society in Thailand proved incompatible with the patrimonial regime that initiated it. The autocratic power of the monarchy was destroyed in the revolution of 1932. This gave military, bureaucratic and business groups in Bangkok a strong voice in the government, while the monarchy, with vastly diminished powers, was retained to integrate the traditionalist peasantry into the new political system. This arrangement proved durable enough to service all the subsequent political upheavals in the region.

Aware of the dangers of backwardness, Sihanouk made considerable efforts to modernize Cambodian society. Making up for the neglect of the French, he oversaw the development of a modern educational system. By the end of the 1960s, primary school enrolments had reached one million, secondary school enrolments more than 100,000 and tertiary enrolments 10,000. He sought foreign aid to foster urbanization and the growth of commerce. This led to considerable growth of the middle class in Phnom Penh. By the late 1960s 10 per cent of the population of the whole kingdom lived in Phnom Penh.

But Sihanouk did not bring about a political 'revolution from above' in Cambodia. After 1954 he continued to deal with the new bourgeois politicians in Phnom Penh in the way absolute kings usually deal with court intrigue – by a judicious combination of patronage, manipulation, espionage and repression. At first he favoured the Right, and persecuted the Left; then, in 1963, when he thought that the Right was growing strong, he turned to the Left; and then in 1966, just when the Left appeared to be consolidating its position, he dropped it to reinstate the Right once more.

Furthermore, as Michael Vickery emphasizes, much of the demand for education was fuelled by a desire for status and privilege rather than by the country's economic needs. By the mid-1960s, most of the available positions in the public service had been filled. Nor could the growing pool of educated Khmer youths be absorbed into an expanding business sector. Business was largely in the hands of ethnic Chinese and Vietnamese, and after 1963 the economy was in recession anyway. The result was an expanding stratum of restless and frustrated young would-be bourgeois, the driving force behind many nationalist and radical movements.

While their parents remained attached to the pomp and ceremony of royalty and the consolations of traditional religion, many of these young people had become, as one observer put it, 'de-tribalized'. They 'no longer identified with their cultural context, their hierarchy and their political symbolism', and were increasingly alienated from Sihanouk's government. Furthermore, as Vickery also points out, this whole process of urban expansion imposed increasing burdens on the rural sector. Even if Vickery's account exaggerates the parasitical character of urban expansion, this must have put serious strains on the agricultural sector. Cambodia had one of the most backward, low-productivity agricultural sectors in Asia.[23]

By the late 1960s attempts at both capitalist and socialist modernization had been enveloped in a system of royal patronage, favour-swapping and increasingly blatant corruption. But the frustrations of the would-be modernizing elites were concealed beneath a veneer of obligatory king-worship, and thick layers of tourist brochure clichés about the 'kingdom of smiles' from romantic western observers. The world was, therefore, quite unprepared for the ferocity with which these frustrations finally erupted after the Sihanoukist system collapsed in 1970.

In the end, Sihanouk's position was undermined by the escalation of the war in Vietnam, rather than by indigenous social forces. One of his main concerns in the 1960s, amply justified by what followed in the 1970s, had been to keep his country out of the war. To this end, Sihanouk had been willing to turn a blind eye to the Communist infiltration of troops and supplies into South Vietnam via the 'Ho Chi Minh trail' through the forests of Laos and eastern Cambodia, provided that the Vietnamese kept away from populated regions. He also allowed them to purchase rice supplies in Cambodia. Sihanouk was also willing to turn a blind eye when the Americans began secretly bombing Vietnamese forces in eastern Cambodia in 1969, but publicly protested when they began bombing Khmer villages as well.

However, this destabilized Sihanouk's government internally. In 1966, Sihanouk had reinstated the Right, and driven the Left out of government. Lon Nol, a right-wing general who Sihanouk had long entrusted with the suppression of Cambodian Communism, became prime minister. Left-wing politicians and students disappeared from Phnom Penh, and joined the small bands of Communist guerrillas in the mountains. Sihanouk denounced the 'Khmers Rouges', and sought to crush their movement.

The right wing in Phnom Penh applauded this, but were thoroughly alarmed by what they saw as Sihanouk's pro-Communist and pro-

Vietnamese foreign policy. Then when American bombing of their border sanctuaries pushed the Vietnamese deeper into Cambodia in 1969, the Right was panic-stricken. In any case, the right wing had its own agenda, and Sihanouk was not part of it. Lon Nol joined with Sirik Matik, a prince in the Sisowath line of the royal family, to organize a coup against Sihanouk in March 1970. They proclaimed a Khmer Republic.

This was greeted with enthusiasm in Phnom Penh, but it caused consternation in the provinces. Traditional loyalty to the monarchy remained strong in rural Cambodia in 1970, and where it had broken down the peasants had turned to alternatives more radical than the bourgeois republican nationalism that was in the ascendancy in Phnom Penh.

Lon Nol's coup of March 1970 was analogous with the 1932 revolution in Thailand. But Sihanouk's 'enlightened despotism' had been weaker and less effective than that of Chulalongkorn. The weakness of both state and bourgeoisie meant that the outcome was very different. The backwardness of Cambodia virtually ensured that bourgeois nationalism would be a débâcle.

Sihanouk, furious at his 'betrayal' by Lon Nol and Sirik Matik, joined with his erstwhile enemies on the Left to form the National United Front of Kampuchea (NUFK). This sealed the fate of the Lon Nol regime. A bourgeois revolution was opposed by an alliance, ideologically implausible but effective in practice, between monarchism and radicalism. It was a war between town and countryside in an overwhelmingly agrarian society.

Lon Nol tried to build support for his government by encouraging an anti-Vietnamese frenzy. In Phnom Penh and other towns, many Vietnamese residents were slaughtered in brutal pogroms. Lon Nol dispatched his army to drive the Vietnamese Communists out of their sanctuaries. They responded by inflicting a series of devastating defeats on the ill-prepared army of the Khmer Republic, from which it never recovered. Then, to make matters worse, attacks by the South Vietnamese and US armies drove the Vietnamese Communists deep inside Cambodia. This relieved Communist pressure on South Vietnam, but only temporarily. Years later, a American ex-army officer explained US actions by saying that they had had to draw the wolves off South Vietnam by throwing them another carcass. Lon Nol's Cambodia was that carcass.

The Lon Nol government thus started out badly, and soon went on to much worse. Within a matter of months it controlled only enclaves around Phnom Penh and the provincial capitals, and territory along the main roads linking these enclaves. By 1972 it was already clear that the government was doomed unless major changes took place. Lon Nol was driven by what one of his own military commanders later characterized as 'fairyland ambitions to see the [Cambodian army] transformed into a grand armed force, made in the image ... of the US armed forces, bypassing all of the fundamental principles of development and operation'.[24] As his dreams collapsed Lon Nol withdrew increasingly into mystical reveries. And as the Khmer Republic turned into a chaotic and incompetent military dicatorship, many middle-class Cambodians who had welcomed Sihanouk's downfall now waited apprehensively for the inevitable fall of the new regime.

As in the First Indochina War, the policy of the Vietnamese Communists in the areas they occupied in Cambodia was to keep a low profile, to encourage and arm local insurgents, and to withdraw when these groups appeared capable of standing on their own. In 1970–71, much of the main-force fighting against Lon Nol's army was carried out by the Vietnamese, but from 1972 it was mainly in the hands of the Khmer Rouge. The Vietnamese happily assumed that because of their shared 'anti-imperialist' objectives and the 'fraternal bonds' between Communists in Vietnam and Communists in Cambodia, there would be no serious conflict between their interests and those of the national liberation movement they were encouraging in Cambodia.

Sihanouk soon found out that the Khmer Rouge leaders of the 1970s were not as easy to manipulate and outmanoeuvre as their predecessors had been in the days of Son Ngoc Thanh and Son Ngoc Minh. The Khmer Rouge leaders welcomed Sihanouk's followers into the ranks of the NUFK, but they kept Sihanouk out of the country as head of a 'government in exile' in Beijing, and progressively stripped him of his political influence inside Cambodia. By 1974–75, Pol Pot was organizing purges of active Sihanoukists from the ranks of the NUFK. Between them, Lon Nol and Pol Pot smashed the institutional structure of the traditional monarchy and wiped out many of its key personnel. Stripped of power, Sihanouk lost his divine status and much of his popular support as well.

The overthrow of Lon Nol's government in 1973 was only averted by American saturation bombing of Khmer Rouge forces closing in on Phnom Penh. However, with US disengagement from Indochina from 1973, aid to the Phnom Penh regime was scaled down in 1974. The final downfall came in April 1975, and the NUFK came to power in Phnom Penh. The exiled Sihanouk was head of state, but power lay in the hands of the Khmer Rouge.

Laos: The Paradox of Extreme Backwardness

For all its backwardness, Cambodia had both a centralized state and a relatively homogeneous population living in an area with a distinct

geographical identity as a basis for nationalism. By contrast, in Laos
the population consisted of a diversity of ethnic groups scattered across
a rugged mountain terrain. Even today, less than half the population
are Lao; the majority of the population thus consists of 'national minori-
ties'. The mountainous topography tends to divide Laos into a number
of separate geographical (and economic) zones, and internal communications were largely non-existent until recently. On the eve of the French
conquest, the royal family in Luang Prabang exercised little real control
and effective political power lay in the hands of regionally based aristocratic families. This 'feudal' fragmentation of power in Laos was preserved
by the French, and gave rise in due course to the most anarchic of the
modern nationalist movements. If in Cambodia the Khmer race seemed
to provide a 'natural' basis for the nation, in Laos the central problem
was that the construction of a nation required the integration of the
most diverse ethnic groups, and Lao nationalism had to avoid at all costs
the xenophobic inflection taken on by Khmer nationalism.

As in Cambodia, the growth of nationalism in Laos stems from 1945,
when the Japanese overthrew the French and installed a Lao government.[25] Here, even more than in Cambodia, politics still consisted exclusively of the rivalries between members of aristocratic families. Only a
handful of Lao (mostly from the aristocracy) received any higher education, even in the post-independence period, and the middle-class intellectuals who played such an important role in the Vietnamese and
Cambodian revolutions were almost non-existent.

But Laos too soon found itself a battleground for the French and
Viet Minh forces during the First Indochina War. As a consequence,
it underwent the whole evolution from a traditionalist royalism to a mass
nationalism modelled on the Viet Minh within a single generation. This
resulted in a situation where the competing streams of nationalism, primarily royalists and Communists (bourgeois nationalism being for all
practical purposes non-existent in Laos), were all lead by rival members
of the royal family. The mystique of royalty in a Therevada Buddhist
society, monopolized by Sihanouk in Cambodia, was in Laos shared
among different groups, including the Communists.

The main problems they confronted did not arise out of the modernization of Lao society – that process lying almost wholly in the future –
but out of the traditional dilemma faced by Lao rulers (and other rulers
of weak states with more powerful neighbours). The question was whether
to turn to Vietnam for support and some kind of political model, or
to Thailand, or to opt for a neutralist course of balancing one carefully
against the other. But with the Communists gaining control of North
Vietnam and Thailand aligned with the United States, these questions
turned Laos into a battleground of the Cold War.

The first nationalist movement was the Lao Issara ('Free Lao') movement created in August 1945 by the premier of the Japanese-installed government, Prince Phet Sarath, along with his brother, Prince Souvanna Phouma, and their half-brother, Prince Souphannavong. In September, in the wake of the 'August Revolution' in Hanoi, they declared the complete independence of Laos from the French, and placed the king under house arrest when he objected. But the Lao Issara were capable of putting up only scattered resistance when the French returned, and its leaders were soon forced to go into exile in Bangkok. But Souphannavong tried to rebuild his forces, and he soon developed contacts with the Viet Minh.

In 1949, the French granted nominal independence to the royal Lao government. Many of the exiles were satisfied with this, and returned to Vientiane. But Souphannavong and the more radical members of the nationalist movement retreated into the mountains of Laos to continue armed resistance. In August 1950 Souphannavong, along with a number of hill-tribe leaders, such as the Hmong chief Faydang Lobliyao, formed what came to be called the Pathet Lao ('Nation of Laos') to fight for complete independence, and in the following year they formalized their alliance with the Viet Minh.

In Laos, the Geneva Conference provided for a neutralist government under Prince Souvanna Phouma, for regroupment zones for the Pathet Lao forces in Phong Saly and Sam Neua provinces, and for the peaceful reunification of the country along lines similar to that envisaged for Vietnam. The agreement ran into difficulties because of the antipathy between the rightists in the Royal Lao Government (RLG) army, who had fought with the French, and the Pathet Lao, but the general expectation was that, notwithstanding the Pathet Lao, these could be integrated into a national coalition government.

But Laos was by now a battlefield in the Cold War. As with South Vietnam and Cambodia, the USA wanted Laos to become part of its anti-Communist SEATO alliance. There were anti-Communists in Laos who wished for the same thing, and the Americans were soon given the opportunity they wanted. Shortly after the formation of SEATO, Souvanna Phouma's defence minister was assassinated, precipitating a cabinet crisis that led to the government's resignation. This was followed by a right-wing government which quickly opened the door to American economic and military aid for the RLG. Under these circumstances, negotiations with the Pathet Lao stalled, and armed clashes between the RLG and Pathet Lao forces became common.

In the teeth of American opposition, Souvanna Phouma returned to power in 1956, committed to a policy of neutralism and reconciliation with the Pathet Lao. After long negotiations he formed a coalition government in 1957. But the USA was adamantly opposed to this coalition, viewing it as a thinly disguised Communist takeover (along the lines of Eastern Europe in the late 1940s). It forced Souvanna Phouma to resign by withholding the economic assistance on which the RLG had become dependent, and by instigating the closure of the Thai border. A new rightist government was formed, but it proved unable to consolidate its position in the face of opposition from the neutralists and the Pathet Lao.

A period of political chaos ensued, ended by a reconvened Geneva Conference in 1961. This bought Souvanna Phouma back as the head of a tripartite coalition. But the USA refused to stop supplying the CIA-funded 'Secret Army' of Hmong leader 'General' Vang Pao, which continued to operate behind Pathet Lao lines. The neutralists split over the issue, the Pathet Lao leaders abandoned Vientiane, and Souvanna Phouma and the other neutralists who remained in Vientiane became the captives of the Right, led by Phoumi Nosovan. From 1963, after teetering on the brink on many occasions, Laos slid into full-scale civil war.

The extreme backwardness of Laos did not provide Phoumi Nosovan with a bourgeois social base enabling him to play the role of a Ngo Dinh Diem, or even a Lon Nol, in Laos. Nor was it possible for the RLG to exploit traditional religious loyalties to the throne in the manner of Sihanouk. Whereas the appeals of sanctified royalty covered the great majority of Cambodians, the political reach of specifically Lao culture hardly extended beyond the lowland population. Over half the population fell outside this cultural universe and were hostile to its encroachments. Such narrowly based nationalism only served to perpetuate the alienation of the hill tribes from the Lao government. Nosovan thus found himself as little more than a local strong-arm man whose power was dependent on external patronage.

The USA threw its weight solidly behind the right wing controlling the RLG from 1963. Secret bombing of Pathet Lao areas commenced in 1964, and over the next decade, every town, and most villages, in the Pathet Lao-controlled zone were destroyed. But the extreme factionalism and disunity of the rightists meant that the USA took over more and more RLG administrative functions, to the point where the American ambassador was popularly known as the 'second prime minister', and there were many who thought that in reality he was the first prime minister. But this did not transform the RLG into an operational government; it simply undermined its legitimacy, to the point where its own military commanders refused to accept the 'interference' of the central authorities in their regional domains. The RLG thus reproduced the fragmentation of power characteristic of traditional Laos.

Unlike the Lao Right, the Pathet Lao had been operating in the mountains since 1949. Since they had no chance of building up a broad movement in this environment unless they transcended narrow tribal loyalties, they appreciated the vital importance of ethnic integration for nation-building in Laos. Since at least 1950 they had been at pains to incorporate a wide spectrum of tribal leaders into their power structure and in the end this foresight paid off handsomely. While the top leadership of the Pathet Lao always consisted predominantly of lowland ethnic Lao, the majority of their troops were recruited from minority groups. It makes sense to say that the Pathet Lao leaders finally defeated their opponents by forging a Lao national coalition to overwhelm an ethnically Lao government.

This, of course, would be an oversimplification. Naturally, control of tribal groups did not always fall the Pathet Lao's way. The Hmong around the Plain of Jars, under Touby Ly Fong, for example, supported the French and later provided the main recruitment base for Vang Pao's 'secret army'. But his traditional Hmong rival, Faydang, became a founder of the Pathet Lao. And the way they incorporated their Hmong followers was a good practical illustration of the differences between the two sides. Vang Pao's followers gave their loyalties to him and the Hmong people; few of them cared less what happened to the RLG. On the other hand, Faydang's followers became members of ethnically mixed Pathet Lao regular units, where much energy was devoted to building up a multi-racial 'national' spirit.

While the Lao Right turned to Thailand and the USA for support in the civil war, the Pathet Lao turned to Hanoi and the Communist bloc. The main Pathet Lao base areas were close to the Vietnamese border, and they were given both logistic and political support by the Vietnamese. While they were under the protection of the North Vietnamese army, these bases could never be militarily destroyed by the RLG. The Viet Minh also provided an organizational and ideological model for the Pathet Lao. Since the Vientiane regime had done little to establish a national educational system, many Pathet Lao cadres received their first education in party schools, and if they went on to higher education, they went to Hanoi, Beijing or Eastern Europe. Pathet Lao nationalism was thus not bred of the extreme isolation that one might at first expect. It was always tempered by a degree of Communist cosmopolitanism, and never degenerated into the backwoods chauvinism that was soon to emerge in Cambodia.

In one sense, it is impossible to overstate Vietnamese influence on the Pathet Lao; yet, in another sense, this is done all the time. The Pathet Lao modelled itself on the Viet Minh, and accepted Vietnamese assistance, but it was a Lao national movement under the leadership of a member of the Lao royal family. For all its failings, the Pathet Lao administrative apparatus was run by Lao nationals for Lao nationals, which was more than could be said for the RLG. It was never an instrument of Vietnamese 'colonialism' in Laos, as is often alleged. If the Vietnamese had really wanted to colonize Laos, the best way would have been to annex it militarily and administer it directly – most of the population, after all, probably objected to lowland Lao control as much as they would have to Vietnamese control. Instead, the Vietnamese provided support and encouragement, and waited patiently while the Pathet Lao movement got off the ground.

While it took the Pathet Lao many years to build up a fighting force capable of seriously threatening the RLG, it could never topple it as long as the USA was fully committed to the RLG. The outcome of the war in Laos thus depended less on success in the battlefield – although the war was increasingly going the way of the Pathet Lao after 1968 – than on the ability of the Vietnamese to negotiate an American withdrawal from Indochina. As soon as this was achieved, the civil war in Laos came to an end, and as the USA scaled down its assistance the anti-Pathet Lao forces disintegrated.

While international political forces have played a vital role in all three Indochinese countries, this has been especially the case in the weakest of them. The forces of modernization that produced a revolutionary upheaval in Vietnam and a collapse of the traditional political order in Cambodia had hardly been felt in Laos. The civil war that resulted from the collapse of Souvanna Phouma's second coalition government was almost wholly the result of external forces rather than of any internal social and political explosion. The lowland peasantry remained largely indifferent to both sides, and it was the Pathet Lao's ability to mobilize more successfully among the minority groups that was finally decisive.

When a ceasefire was signed in 1973, the Pathet Lao controlled 80 per cent of the countryside. A new coalition was formed under Souvanna Phouma, and in 1974 Souphannavong returned to the capital to take up his government post. From this point on the Pathet Lao steadily assumed control of the government as the right wing disintegrated. Vang Pao's 'secret army' continued the war against the Pathet Lao in the countryside, but suffered a major defeat in April 1975. Coinciding with the fall of Phnom Penh and Saigon, this threw the remaining rightists in Vientiane into a panic, and many fled the country. By June, almost the entire wartime RLG leadership had debarked to Thailand. The RLG army, which had still been controlled by the Right, disintegrated, and was officially disbanded in June, followed by the complete demise of the RLG in December 1975, when King Savang Vatthana signed a letter of abdication in favour of 'the people's democratic system'.

At Souphannavong's suggestion, both the ex-king and Souvanna Phouma were appointed as advisers to the government – a conciliatory gesture designed to promote national accord that was in striking contrast to the policies being pursued in Cambodia. But then, in Laos the leap into political modernity had been so compressed that the transition from monarchism to Communist mass nationalism had taken place under the leadership of a member of the traditional royal family. The unification of the country under the Pathet Lao was thus in a real sense a family reunion as well.

Nation-building and Communism in Indochina

Liberals in nineteenth-century Europe believed that when oppressed nationalities were freed from foreign domination, when the principles of national self-determination were applied throughout the world, sovereign nation-states would live in peace and harmony. This optimistic vision of international peace has been badly battered by the bloody torrent of imperialism, chauvinism and militarism that has so far constituted the international politics of the twentieth century – so much so that one recent historian of nationalism has likened it to a fairy-tale in which the Sleeping Beauty is transformed into Frankenstein's monster.[26] However, this optimistic vision has lived on in socialist and Communist theories of international relations. According to Marxist theorists, the clash of sovereign nation-states is due to the competitiveness and the imperialism of capitalism. It is a product of the self-interest of ruling classes, not of the working classes. When socialism replaces capitalism, therefore, the promise of international harmony will be realized.[27] In Indochina, the promised day arrived in 1975.

Ultimately, this view rests on the premiss that states are essentially instruments of class rule. It neglects the extent to which state power is actually used to create political communities, and to defend them against external attack, irrespective of the class nature of the state. We have argued here that nationalism is essentially a movement for the creation of a modern state based on such a community. It aspires to a government based on notions of popular sovereignty rather than authority sanctified by time and tradition, or divine will.

Looked at from one angle, nationalism is an empty rhetorical vessel, given a concrete social and political content by the successful nationalists themselves. The institutions of the nation-state can serve a variety of social ends, and nationalists have conflicting visions of the national community they attempt to build. Nationalism thus comes in a variety of forms – left-wing and right-wing; pluralistic, dictatorial and totalitarian. Thus, paradoxically, we have seen that in Indochina the spread of the ideal of 'national unity' ushered in a period of civil war. Both sides insisted that they alone were the 'true' nationalists; it was a matter of which side was able to mobilize the population and, finally, impose its particular view. In Indochina, the groups capable of doing this were the Communists.

Communism did not come to power in Indochina as a party of working-class socialism but as the radical wing of the nationalist reaction to colonial rule, as a movement of middle-class and peasant nationalism. This was typical of the successes Communism experienced elsewhere in Asia (and other Third World countries as well). The Indian ex-Communist M.N. Roy wrote in 1951:

> Communism in Asia is essentially nationalism painted red. ... The Leninist program was to regard nationalism as an ally; now communism plays the role of nationalism, and appears in its most extreme form, having a corresponding share of all its vices – racism, cultural revivalism, intolerance, jingoism and resistance to western bourgeois influence. This nationalist degeneration is a general feature of postwar communism, and assumes its most pronounced form in Asia.[28]

Roy is in error here only in describing nationalism as a 'degeneration' of Communism. In Asia, Communism was rooted in nationalism from the start. And since nationalism meant above all the political mobilization of the masses for purposes of state, it is not surprising that the triumph of nationalism has added a further element of popular passion to clashes between states. In this regard, there is no good reason to expect that Communist states would be basically different from non-Communist ones. Events in the Indochinese countries since 1975 seem to bear out such pessimistic reflections.

Notes

1. Elizabeth Becker, *When the War Was Over*, New York 1986, p. 337.
2. Milton Osborne, *Before Kampuchea: Preludes to Tragedy*, Sydney 1979, pp. 165–6; see also his article 'Cambodia and Vietnam: A Historical Perspective', *Pacific Community*, vol. 9, 1978.
3. Khien Theeravit, 'Thai–Kampuchean Relations: Problems and Prospects', *Asian Survey*, vol. 22, 1982, p. 562. Despite these pertinent observations, Khien's overall perspective is closer to Osborne's than to ours.
4. Of the Khmer kingdom in the early nineteenth century, David Chandler has written: 'It would be difficult to overstress the atmosphere of threat, physical danger, and random violence.... The sources are filled with references to torture, executions, ambushes, massacres, village burnings, and the forced movement of populations.... [Invaders] and defenders destroyed the villages they came to, killed or uprooted anyone they met, and ruined the landscape they moved across' (*A History of Cambodia*, Boulder 1983, p. 122). See also Trevor Ling, *Buddhism, Imperialism and War*, London 1979, which focuses on the military contest between Burma and Thailand.
5. Benedict Anderson, *Imagined Communities: Reflections on the Origins and Spread of Nationalism*, London 1983, p. 14.

6. Barrington Moore, Jr, *Social Origins of Dictatorship and Democracy*, London 1967, pp. 486–7.

7. Quoted in K.R. Minogue, *Nationalism*, Baltimore 1970, p. 17. In a recent survey Corneilia Navari writes: 'The pre-nineteenth century state did not serve nations; it did not even serve "communities". It served God, the Heavenly Mandate, the Law of Allah; it served hereditary rulers – the dynasts and the dynasties who were portrayed as God's vicars and whose appointed task was to carry out that mandate. . . . The fact of what language any dynast's subjects spoke was irrelevant to that task, and the particular cultures of his people only mattered to the degree to which they impeded that mandate.' Navari emphasizes that it was not until the nineteenth century that the idea that states ought to be based on nations was widely accepted in Europe and 'it was only in 1918 that any government made being a nation-state the basic criterion of political legitimacy and the basic condition of treating with other governments' ('The Origins of the Nation-State', in Leonard Tivey, ed. *The Nation-State: The Formation of Modern Politics*, Oxford 1981, p. 14). For recent Marxist and anti-Marxist essays see respectively Anderson, *Imagined Communities*, and Ernest Gellner, *Nations and Nationalism*, London 1983.

8. For a serious discussion of a topic that has provoked much overheated rhetoric, see M.G. Cotter, 'Towards a Social History of the Vietnamese Southward Movement', *Journal of Southeast Asian History*, vol. 9, 1968.

9. Quoted by Chandler, p. 116.

10. The most recent account of the economic and social impact of colonialism on Indochina is Martin J. Murray, *Development of Capitalism in Colonial Indochina 1870–1940*, Berkeley 1980. Murray tries to show – rather unconvincingly in our opinion – that French exploitation led to the stagnation rather than the development of the Indochinese colonies. We would also note that it is a book about Vietnam rather than Indochina as a whole – Cambodia and Laos are hardly mentioned. For an earlier account, painted in rose-coloured hues that contrast sharply with Murray's account, see Charles Robequain, *The Economic Development of French Indochina*, London 1941.

11. The best overall account is William J. Duiker, *The Rise of Nationalism in Vietnam 1900–1941*, Ithaca 1976.

12. Greg Lochart, *Nation in Arms: Origins of the People's Army of Vietnam*, Sydney 1989, pp. 41–51.

13. The head of the OSS's Indochina mission has provided an informative account of these events: Archimedes Patti, *Why Vietnam? Prelude to America's Albatross*, Berkeley 1980.

14. The literature on this period is immense. Much of it deals with American experiences and American problems. William J. Duiker, *The Communist Road to Power in Vietnam*, Boulder 1981, focuses on the other side. Gabriel Kolko's *Vietnam: Anatomy of a War, 1940–1975*, London 1985, seeks systematically to cover both sides.

15. Bernard B. Fall, *The Two Vietnams: A Political and Military Analysis*, London 1963, p. 237.

16. This is a judgement hotly disputed by many supporters of the US intervention, who argue that Tet was a victory for the US and Saigon. But Nguyen Van Loc, Prime Minister in the Saigon government at the time, later said: 'We lost the battle for the South in 1968. . . . By 1975 the Communists had to push only in a few chosen areas to gain total victory' (quoted by V.G. Kulkarni, *Far Eastern Economic Review*, 2 June 1983).

17. For a detailed account, cf. Arnold R. Isaacs, *Without Honor: Defeat in Vietnam and Cambodia*, Baltimore 1983.

18. Chandler, pp. 175–82.

19. Ben Kiernan, *How Pol Pot Came to Power*, London 1985, pp. 130–34.

20. Ibid., pp. 157–62.

21. Becker, p. 99.

22. Cf. 'The Social Psychology of the World Religions', in Hans H. Gerth and C. Wright Mills, eds, *From Max Weber: Essays in Sociology*, New York 1958, pp. 296–9. Those who hope to salvage the conventional wisdom may also care to peruse Section 3 of Weber's essay on 'The Sociology of Charismatic Authority' (Gerth and Mills, pp. 251–2). Here

he discusses 'charismatic kingship'. But this relates to the early phase of kingship, when 'the king is everywhere primarily a warlord'.

23. Cf. Michael Vickery, *Cambodia 1975–1982*, Sydney 1984, pp. 19–24. The quote comes from Jacques Nepote, in Kiernan, p. xiv.

24. General Sak Sutsakhan, quoted by Becker, p. 138.

25. The best account is MacAlister Brown and Joseph J. Zasloff, *Apprentice Revolutionaries: The Communist Movement in Laos 1935–1985*, Stanford 1986.

26. Minogue, pp.7–8.

27. See, for example, the Second International's famous Stuttgart Declaration of 1907 on 'Militarism and International Conflicts': 'Wars are ... inherent in the nature of capitalism; they will cease only when the capitalist economy is abolished, or when the magnitude of the sacrifice of human beings and money, neccessitated by the technological development of warfare, and popular disgust with armaments, leads to the abolition of this system. That is why the working classes, which have primarily to furnish the soldiers and make the greatest material sacrifices, are the natural enemies of war, which is opposed to their aim: the creation of an economic system based on socialist foundations, and which will make a reality out of the solidarity of nations' (quoted by James Joll, *The Second International 1889–1914*, 2nd edn, London 1974, pp. 206–7).

28. Quoted by Rupert Emerson, *From Empire to Nation: The Rise to Self-Determination of Asian and African Peoples*, Cambridge, Mass. 1960, pp. 373–4.

2

Vietnam: The Myth of
Post-war Expansionism

Following the fall of Phnom Penh to Vietnamese forces in January 1979 the London *Economist* wrote: 'This invasion by Vietnam will not reassure the Asian neighbours of Vietnam's burgeoning little communist empire. The Vietnamese are Southeast Asia's Prussians; a people whose aggressive insecurity, or maybe plain aggression, creates insecurity around them.' The editorial comment, entitled 'Ho's will is done', claimed that the invasion fulfilled 'the lifelong goal of the dead leader'. Thus *The Economist* saw the invasion as a long-premeditated action spurred on by an aggressive Vietnamese foreign policy and national psychology. A similar opinion was expressed by former US Secretary of State Henry Kissinger in the 1982 instalment of his memoirs, *Years of Upheaval*:

> The Vietnamese ... outlasted French occupation, all the time nurturing the conviction that it was their mission to inherit the French empire in Indochina. Lacking the humanity of their Laotian neighbours and the grace of their Cambodian neighbours, they strove for dominance by being not attractive but single-minded. So all-encompassing was their absorption with themselves that they become oblivious to the physical odds, indifferent to the probabilities by which the calculus of power is normally reckoned. ... Our misfortune had been to get between these leaders and their obsessions. Our Indochinese nightmare would be over; Hanoi's neighbours were not as fortunate. Propinquity condemned them to permanent terror.[1]

The premise of all this rhetoric was that once the war in the south was over, Hanoi, unilaterally and without provocation, adopted policies of expansion and aggression towards its neighbours and other countries in the region. Only defeat for Hanoi could save Southeast Asia from 'permanent terror'.

Before seeing whether Hanoi's post-war policies justified such claims, we should clear up the matter of Ho Chi Minh's 'will' referred to by *The Economist*. This has been claimed by a number of right-wing authors to be a call for the establishment of an 'Indochina Federation' ruled from Hanoi and embracing Laos and Cambodia as well as South Vietnam. This is simply untrue. On 10 May 1969 Ho signed a 'Last Will and Testament', written, he explained with distinct Confucian overtones, 'in expectation of the day when I shall go to rejoin the venerable Karl Marx, Lenin, and our revolutionary elders'. It was a call for unity, discipline and a high standard of morality in the Vietnamese Communist Party (VCP), and for a continuation of the struggle to reunite Vietnam. On international affairs, he addressed himself to the Sino-Soviet split:

> Having dedicated my life to the service of the revolution, I am all the more proud to see the international Communist and workers' movement expand, and I suffer all the more because of the dissension that at present divides the Communist powers. I want our party to do its best to contribute efficaciously to the re-establishment of good relations between the Communist powers, on a Marxist-Leninist and international proletarian basis, always in conformity with the demands of the mind and heart. I firmly believe that the fraternal parties will one day be reunited.

And he concluded: 'My ultimate desire is that all our party and all our people, closely united in combat, will raise up a Vietnam that is peaceful, unified, independent, democratic and prosperous. Thus we will make a worthy contribution to world revolution.' There was no mention at all of Laos and Cambodia, or of the 'Indochina Federation' which this veteran anti-French leader allegedly wished to create. Consistent with this, Le Duan was able, at the VCP's 4th Congress in 1976, to boast that Hanoi had already 'succeeded brilliantly' in fulfilling Ho's will by bringing about the unification of Vietnam – without mentioning Cambodia or Laos in this context.[2]

Vietnamese Foreign Policy after the War

For a more realistic perspective we must recognize, first of all, that the end of the war in Vietnam had considerable implications for regional politics. Even if it had no designs on its neighbours, a Vietnam that was no longer pouring its energies into civil conflict promised to be a major new power in the region. With a population in excess of 50 million, Vietnam was the most populous state in mainland Southeast Asia and the third largest Communist state in the world. With a regular army of 680,000 troops, hardened by decades of warfare, Hanoi was a military power to be respected. Whatever its professed intentions, therefore, it is not surprising that the governments of Southeast Asia viewed Hanoi with some apprehension after its victory in 1976 – especially those who had backed the USA in Indochina.

However, it was soon apparent that the Vietnamese government's main concern was not military adventures abroad but the rebuilding of its war-shattered country. The need was overwhelming. Forty years of war had left Vietnam with a per capita income that was about a quarter of that of Thailand, and about a thirtieth of that of the developed capitalist countries. Furthermore, the cutting of American aid to the south precipitated an immediate crisis. Colonial Vietnam had been an important exporter of rice (this came mainly from the fertile provinces of the south; the densely populated north had itself relied on imports from the south). Years of war had destroyed this capacity, and the rapidly growing population had become increasingly dependent on outside supplies of food – from the West in South Vietnam, from China in North Vietnam. The country's economy was clearly fragile, and would have to be handled with care if it was to be nursed back to health. But the leadership was optimistic. Le Duan declared that the working people of Vietnam would have 'a better life in five or ten years', and even 'a radio set, a refrigerator, and a TV set for each family'.[3] Party delegates were in a euphoric mood as they assembled for the 6th Congress of the VCP in December 1976. It had been sixteen years since the previous Congress. But now the country was unified and at peace, and the party could turn its attention to socialist construction.

Half the membership of the previous Central Committee was not re-elected. At the apex of power the Politburo was expanded from thirteen to seventeen members. The new members included prominent southern Communist leaders – Nguyen Van Linh, Vo Chi Cong and Vo Van Kiet. Only one surviving veteran leader, Hoang Van Hoan, was dropped. Le Duan was re-elected general secretary. These personnel changes were later subjected to conflicting interpretations. Hoang Van Hoan later claimed that a third of the Central Committee was purged as a pro-Soviet faction led by Le Duan usurped power and eliminated its pro-Chinese rivals. This conformed to a long-standing interpretation of Vietnamese politics in terms of 'pro-Soviet' and 'pro-Chinese' factions. No doubt Hoan himself was dropped because of his opposition to the VCP's tilt towards Moscow. But he was the exception rather than the rule. Carl Thayer has argued that most of the changes in the Central Committee were the result of the retirement of the aged, the ill and the incompetent, rather than of a power struggle between entrenched factions.[4]

The government's policies after the war were summed up in the Political Report, delivered at the 4th Congress by Le Duan. Vietnam had been reunified, and Communist political power had been consolidated. The greatest task facing the leadership now was economic reconstruction. The Congress adopted Vietnam's Second Five Year Plan, which aimed at making the country self-sufficient in food once more by the end of 1980. Surplus labour from the towns would be absorbed into productive employment on state farms in New Economic Zones (NEZs) to be opened up in the western Mekong basin, near the Cambodian border, and in the Central Highlands. Rice production was expected to rise to 21 million tonnes of paddy, and the process of industrialization would get under way. Overall, the planners expected a growth rate of 15 per cent per annum in Vietnam's gross national product as the country recovered from the ravages of war. But since, as Le Duan put it in announcing the plan, 'accumulation from internal sources is non-existent', the whole strategy depended on an influx of foreign aid to finance investment. Partly in recognition of the need to attract foreign capital, it was decided to soft-pedal on the issue of 'socialist transformation' in the south.

Subsequent developments have shown the 1976 plan to have been excessively optimistic. But the key point is that it was geared towards peaceful economic development, not military preparations. As one writer put it:

> The Second Five Year Plan, which was principally a development plan, had discounted defence development. ... Vietnam certainly expected a long period of peace after the liberation of Indochina in 1975, and it assumed that defence would no longer need the priority that it had during the previous three decades, and thus allow the unfettered pursuit of economic goals of reconstruction and development.[5]

The army was not demobilized, but it was largely redirected to peacetime tasks. Troops were employed on rebuilding transport and communications infrastructure, as well as clearing land.[6] The Vietnamese plan of 1976, therefore, did not anticipate 'expansion' into Cambodia or conflict with any of the country's neighbours.

The section of Le Duan's report dealing with foreign policy was comparatively brief. Imperialism, he said, was a declining force, while the socialist camp was growing stronger day by day, as were the struggles of national liberation and working-class movements around the world. These factors added up to an 'irreversible trend' which meant that Vietnam would be able to undertake the construction of socialism under 'new and favourable conditions'. In his analysis, nationalism, socialism and internationalism were harmoniously fused. Victory in the 'war for national liberation' had removed obstacles to national reunification and 'takes the whole country towards socialism'. At the same time, he affirmed the international significance of the national revolution:

> The Vietnamese revolution is part and parcel of the world revolution. Our people's victory in the patriotic war of resistance against US aggression is closely associated with the wholehearted support and great assistance of our brothers and friends from all continents. ... Our people's victory is a worthy contribution to the common victory of the world revolutionary forces.

Elaborating on this 'internationalist' foreign policy, Le Duan called for a strengthening of relations between Vietnam and 'all the fraternal socialist countries'. In this context, he judiciously balanced praise for the Soviet Union with praise for the People's Republic of China, which, he said, 'is rapidly building a powerful socialist country'. He made no mention of the Sino-Soviet split, but said that Vietnam was committed to 'restoring and consolidating solidarity, and promoting mutual support and assistance' among socialist countries. He warmly praised the 'great historical victories' in Laos and Cambodia, and called for a strengthening of the 'special relationship' between these countries. This emphasis on international solidarity certainly contrasts with the Maoist espousal of national 'self-sufficiency', but there is no justification for reading it as a policy of foreign expansion.

Towards the non-Communist countries of Southeast Asia, Le Duan's position was one of studied ambiguity. On the one hand, he sought to promote peaceful coexistence among Communists and non-Communists in the region. Vietnam was, he declared, 'ready to establish and develop relations of friendship and cooperation with other countries in this area'. On the other hand, he also spoke of Vietnamese support for the 'just struggles of the peoples' for democracy, independence, peace and 'genuine neutrality' (this he specified as meaning 'without military bases and troops of the imperialists on their territories'). This implied threat to back local Communist insurgents was not inspired by a doctrinal commitment to the 'export' of revolution. It was aimed at frightening Southeast Asian governments into minimizing the military presence of Hanoi's recently defeated antagonist, the USA.

These hints from Hanoi were particularly alarming for Thailand and the Philippines: they had been members of the US-sponsored Southeast Asia Treaty Organization (SEATO) along with the now-defunct Saigon regime; they had committed troops to the struggle against Communism in Indochina, and allowed US airstrikes in Vietnam, Cambodia and Laos from their soil. However, the other main states of the region – Malaysia, Singapore and Indonesia – were hardly less vigorous in their hostility towards Communism. It is not surprising that Hanoi viewed all of them with some suspicion, and was inclined to view the Association of Southeast Asian Nations (ASEAN), which brought them all together, as a covert military alliance directed against Vietnam.

However, Le Duan's report made it clear that the VCP leadership assigned first priority to national reconstruction, not international objectives. The party, people and government of Vietnam should, he said,

> make the most of the favourable international conditions so as to rapidly heal the wounds of war, restore and develop the economy, develop culture, science and technology, consolidate national defence, [and] build the material and technical basis of socialism in our country.

The foreign ministers of ASEAN responded to the changed situation in Indochina at their annual conference held in Kuala Lumpur on 13–15 May 1975 by expressing their desire 'to enter into friendly harmonious relations with each nation in Indochina'. On 24 July President Marcos of the Philippines and Prime Minister Kukrit Pramoj of Thailand re-affirmed this position in a joint statement which said that foreign military bases in the region were temporary and agreed in principle that SEATO 'had served its purpose' and should be phased out. Already, on 5 May, the Thai foreign ministry had announced the cessation of US operations from Udon airbase in northeastern Thailand and a programme for the scaling down of the US military presence in the country. These moves smoothed the way for talks on establishing diplomatic relations between Thailand, the Philippines and Vietnam.

Interestingly, all the ASEAN states had recognized the new Cambodian government on 18 April, the day after the fall of Phnom Penh, but took no common action on the new South Vietnamese regime – the Provisional Revolutionary Government (PRG). This presumably reflected the (accurate) belief of Thai intelligence that the Khmer Rouge was not a puppet of Hanoi and that immediate recognition could keep Phnom Penh from moving in Hanoi's direction.

Yet the ASEAN foreign ministers' conference showed that they were not unanimous about what approach ASEAN countries should take toward Communist Vietnam. Obviously feeling that Thailand and the Philippines may have been overreacting to events, Indonesia's Adam Malik cautioned that adjustments 'should not be inspired by negative notions of fear and uncertainty or of perceived "vacuums" in power relationships'. Singapore's Sinathamby Rajaratnam pointedly noted that it was wrong to assume that the USA was withdrawing from Asia, and warned that ASEAN should not give the impression that it was ready to do anything to win the favour of the Communist governments of Indochina.

While ASEAN was juggling with the consequences of the Communist victories in Indochina, it was Hanoi's nominal ally, China, which revealed itself to be the most alarmed. When President Marcos made the first visit to Beijing by an ASEAN head of state on 7 June, he was fêted by Deng Xiaoping, who warned him that an American withdrawal from the region would lead to increased Soviet activity, and praised the Philippines' 'unremitting effort to safeguard national independence and defend state sovereignty'. Deng urged the ASEAN countries not to overreact to developments in Indochina. He repeated his warning to the Thai prime minister at the end of June. The Chinese clearly did not wish to see an American military withdrawal from Thailand and the Philippines, as well as Indochina.

But Thailand and the Philippines persisted with their generally conciliatory policies toward Vietnam and continued to scale down their relations with the USA. No doubt their actions were influenced by the fact that the Soviet Union's policy towards ASEAN was generally sympathetic, seeing it as a laudable attempt at political and economic cooperation in danger of being pushed into playing a military role by the USA. Indeed, some ASEAN leaders were inclined to see the Soviet Union as a moderating influence on Vietnam, helping to allay the latter's fears that ASEAN was another SEATO.

From Hanoi's vantage point the regional situation had improved considerably by early 1976. Agreements to establish diplomatic relations with ASEAN states had either been reached or talks were progressing well, and SEATO had been formally abandoned in the previous September. Following the formal reunification of the north and south, Vietnam moved to consolidate its relationship with ASEAN. On 5 July the Vietnamese Foreign Minister, Nguyen Duy Trinh, said that his government was prepared to establish and develop relations of friendship and cooperation with other Southeast Asian countries on the basis of the following principles:

1. Respect for each other's independence, sovereignty and territorial integrity, non-interference in each other's internal affairs, and peaceful coexistence.

2. Not allowing any foreign country to use one's territory as a base for direct or indirect aggression and intervention against other countries in the region.

3. Establishment of friendly and good neighbourly relations, economic cooperation and cultural exchanges on the basis of equality and mutual benefit, together with settlement of disputes through negotiations in a spirit of mutual understanding and respect.

4. Development of cooperation among the countries in the region for the building of prosperity in keeping with each country's specific conditions and for the sake of independence, peace and genuine neutrality in Southeast Asia.

The deputy foreign minister, Phan Hien, set off on the same day to visit the capitals of all the ASEAN states, as well as Rangoon and Vientiane, in what was a generally successful effort at cultivating friendly relations. At a press conference in Singapore Phan Hien said he had taken note of assurances that ASEAN was not a military alliance, and was not influenced by any foreign country.

Post-war Relations with the United States

Until January 1977 the White House was occupied by the man who had presided over the end of the US débâcle in Indochina, Gerald Ford. Henry Kissinger, the architect of the American escalation of the war into Cambodia in 1970, the invasion of Laos in 1971 and the bombing of Hanoi in 1972, remained secretary of state. Neither man was known to hold the slightest sympathy for the Vietnamese government. When Saigon fell, they froze $150 million worth of Vietnamese assets in the USA, imposed a trade embargo on the country, and continued to veto Hanoi's admission to the United Nations. But Hanoi hoped that, with the war behind them, relations with the USA could be developed to offset Soviet and Chinese influence.

Vietnam made its first diplomatic move in September 1975. Prime Minister Pham Van Dong announced that Vietnam was ready to establish normal relations with the USA on the basis of the Paris Peace Agreement drawn up in 1973. For the Vietnamese, this entailed the fulfilment of promises made by President Richard Nixon in a letter to Dong on 1 February 1973, which offered aid to the value of $3,250 million for post-war reconstruction without any political conditions, in addition to other forms of aid to be agreed on between the two parties. In March 1976 Kissinger stated the US terms as being: first, accounting for US servicemen missing in action (MIAs); and second, 'the need for assurances of Hanoi's peaceful intentions towards neighbouring countries in Southeast Asia'. He said the Vietnamese could raise any issue they liked, including their demand for aid, although he 'would not hold out much prospect for that'.

Unofficial contacts had been made some months before in Paris between Vietnamese officials and American oil companies over the resumption of offshore oil exploration in the South China Sea, a move that would transgress the embargo on trade and business with Vietnam imposed by the US government following the fall of Saigon. The Vietnamese aim was clearly to play to powerful business interests in the hope of gaining some leverage within American political circles.

But 1976 was presidential election year in the United States. In the Republican Party, the right wing was out in force and the incumbent, Gerald Ford, was trying to hold on to his position in the face of the challenge from Ronald Reagan by beefing up his anti-Communist posturing. In March 1976, therefore, he was railing against the Hanoi leadership as 'a bunch of international pirates' to enthusiastic Republican crowds. This was hardly a promising atmosphere for Hanoi to make its bid for improved relations with Washington.

The US government's demand that the Vietnamese account for all 795 MIAs was impossible to fulfil. The Vietnamese replied that they would help in this project, but indicated that they could hardly be held responsible for all American MIAs in Vietnam. Privately, Kissinger said he had raised the MIA issue to force Hanoi to drop its demand for aid.[7] The MIA issue was a potent one in the hands of the right wing in Congress, particularly in an election year, and many Congressmen seemed to believe that Vietnam was still holding some of these MIAs prisoner. But this claim was rejected in a December 1976 report by a US House of Representatives Special Committee, which said that there was no evidence that any of the missing men were alive or being held prisoner. With this controversy apparently cleared up there were no major obstacles left to a normalization of US relations with Vietnam. But the real significance of the MIA issue soon became clear. The right wing intended to use it as a means of delaying *rapprochement* indefinitely. The MIA issue was used by the USA to veto Vietnam's application in November 1976 for UN membership because of its allegedly 'brutal and inhumane' attitude.[8]

The Carter administration took over the White House in January 1977, and it seemed at first to be offering a more conciliatory line. It dropped the US veto on admitting Vietnam to the UN, and relaxed its embargo on trade by permitting foreign ships or aircraft servicing Vietnam to refuel in the United States. The Secretary of State, Cyrus Vance, favoured normalizing US–Vietnamese relations. In March a presidential commission headed by Leonard Woodcock went to Hanoi to discuss this issue, the MIAs, and economic assistance.[9]

Carter had used the MIA issue against Ford during the election campaign. Now he was president, he wanted Woodcock to settle it once and for all. The Vietnamese had based their post-war planning partly on the assumption that the USA would fulfil Nixon's 1973 promise of aid, and they now pressed Woodcock hard on this issue. Carter had already rejected the idea that the USA had any legal or moral obligation to help the post-war reconstruction process in Vietnam. But a compromise seemed possible, and the prospects of normalization bright. The Vietnamese had set up an office to search for MIA remains. They provided Woodcock with twelve sets to take back to the USA, and promised full cooperation in the future. They demanded US aid for Vietnam as quid pro quo. However, they would be flexible about the form it took. Woodcock returned to Washington confident he had struck a reasonable bargain. Carter announced that he would 'respond well' to suggestions of US aid provided it was viewed as 'normal assistance' and not 'reparations'.

But after this Carter came under increasing pressure from right-wingers in Congress, and the administration retreated from the compromise Woodcock had brokered. Richard Holbrooke, Assistant Secretary of State for East Asian and Pacific Affairs dismissed Nixon's promise of aid as 'an outmoded historical curiosity that keeps arising and complicating the discussion'. In negotiations with the Vietnamese over the course of 1977, he insisted that Hanoi would have to accept recognition without conditions and without aid. Aid was a question which, Holbrooke told the Vietnamese, they could take up later. By December the Vietnamese wanted only an unofficial promise that the Americans would offer aid after normalization. 'You just whisper in my ear the amount you'll offer, and that is enough', Deputy Foreign Minister Phan Hien pleaded to Holbrooke. But this was still unacceptable to the Americans.[10]

The Vietnamese also urged Washington to end its embargo on trade and investment in Vietnam, even without diplomatic recognition. In April 1977 they announced a new, liberal, Foreign Investment Code, aimed at attracting western capital, US companies in particular. The few foreign businessmen who did venture to Hanoi found officials cooperative if inexperienced. But Washington refused to end the embargo and was not interested in allowing US companies to operate in Vietnam. Other countries followed the USA's lead. Pham Van Dong toured Western Europe seeking aid and investment. He returned with only a modest aid agreement from France, while the other Western Europeans indicated that they would not deal with Vietnam until Washington normalized relations with Hanoi. In the end, the Vietnamese National Assembly did not even bother translating the 1977 Investment Code into detailed legislation.

Washington's retreat from normalizing relations with Vietnam was part of a wider shift in US policy in 1977–78. The influence of militant right-wingers, led by National Security Adviser Zbigniew Brzezinski, grew rapidly. The policies of detente favoured by liberals like Cyrus Vance were abandoned for a more belligerent stance in policy over nuclear weapons, relations with Moscow and its allies, and military involvement in the Third World. The liberals were soon in full retreat, and in 1979–80 most quit the administration. It was thus under the Carter administration that the stage was set for Ronald Reagan's presidency and the New Cold War.[11]

The Right made much of Hanoi's 'inhumane' behaviour on the MIA issue and – with greater justification – its treatment of political prisoners. But these were not the main reason for refusing to recognize Hanoi. The Americans feared that such a move might jeopardize the USA's developing relations with China. Both the liberals and the right-wingers were agreed on this. Carter himself wrote in his memoirs: 'The China move was of paramount importance, so after a few weeks of assessment, I decided to postpone the Vietnam effort until we had concluded our agreement in Beijing.'[12]

By the middle of 1977, Vietnamese hopes of opening up to the West had been dashed. Accordingly, they turned back to their patrons in the Communist world, the Soviet Union in particular.

China and the Soviet Union: The End of Hanoi's High-wire Diplomacy

Both China and the Soviet Union had committed themselves heavily to North Vietnam before 1975. Vietnam had been the largest single recipient of Chinese foreign aid. But the Soviet Union was the most generous patron, and had supplied 70 per cent of Hanoi's foreign aid throughout the war. Ho Chi Minh's high-wire diplomacy had sheltered Vietnam from the stormier blasts of the Sino-Soviet dispute. After 1975 this became impossible, and the Vietnamese were steadily forced to take sides.

Following the fall of Saigon, Beijing's attacks on Moscow became more strident. In June 1975 Deng Xiaoping declared that the USSR was replacing the USA as the main threat to peace and security in Southeast Asia and that the Soviets 'insatiably seek new military bases in Asia'. It was an obvious warning to Vietnam. Le Duan travelled to Beijing in September and was received by Mao Zedong. From Beijing the Vietnamese leader went on to Moscow where he also signed an aid agreement covering the 1976–80 period. A joint communiqué was issued by the Vietnamese and Soviet delegates expressing agreement on all substantive issues. That no similar statement had been issued in Beijing was the first sign of serious differences between Vietnam and China.

Beijing was aiming at the total exclusion of Soviet influence from China's southern periphery. Unable to compete with Moscow in providing economic and technical assistance, Beijing demanded that the new governments in Indochina repudiate Soviet aid. Pol Pot's regime in Cambodia, pursuing a policy of 'self-reliance', agreed to do this, and was rewarded with Chinese backing. But Hanoi was pinning its hopes for economic reconstruction on international assistance. Thus Le Duan resisted Chinese pressure and signed an aid agreement in Moscow.

Without giving up Soviet aid, Vietnam did make concessions to Chinese demands in 1975–76. It refused to sign a treaty of friendship with the USSR, declined to join the Council of Mutual Economic Assistance (Comecon), and refused the Soviets access to the naval facility the USA had left behind at Cam Ranh Bay. Indeed, the Soviets were visibly irritated by Hanoi's stand-offish response to their generosity. Mikhail Suslov, who led the Soviet delegation to the 4th Congress, cut short his stay in Vietnam after Hanoi rejected his demands for a closer relationship. Over the following months Moscow showed its displeasure by delaying shipments of oil and spare parts to Vietnam.[13]

Following Le Duan's visit to Moscow in September 1975, Beijing began to publicize its territorial claims in the South China Seas, which overlapped with those of Hanoi. The 'territorial waters' claimed by the People's Republic of China stretched along almost the whole coast of Vietnam and to within twenty miles of the Malaysian state of Sarawak. China's claims overlapped with claims by Malaysia, the Philippines, Taiwan, and Indonesia as well. But it was Vietnam they affected most of all (see Map 3).

This dispute revolves around the control of some 127 tiny, scattered and largely uninhabited islands, in two groups – the Paracels, known by the Vietnamese as the Hoang Sa and by the Chinese as the Hsisha, and the Spratlys, known by the Vietnamese as the Truong Sa and by the Chinese as the Nansha. The Paracels are 240 kilometres southeast of China's Hainan Island in the north, and the Spratlys are 880 kilometres to the south of them.[14]

Control over these islands had been exercised by the South Vietnamese regime since the French exit from Indochina in the early 1950s. But Vietnamese sovereignty had never been accepted by either Taiwan or Beijing. Indeed, Woody Island in the Paracel group had been occupied by Chinese (Guomindang) forces since 1947. In late 1973, when President Thieu attempted to bolster his regime's nationalist credentials by provoking China in the Paracel Islands, China retaliated by forcefully expelling the Army of the Republic of Vietnam (ARVN) forces in January 1974 and occupying the whole group. During this action China staked its claim to 'indisputable sovereignty over these islands [both the Paracels and the Spratlys] and the seas around them'. With their struggle for unification still incomplete, the North Vietnamese and the PRG were forced to respond cautiously to the Chinese action: 'Disputes handed down by history,' said a northern official, 'often very complex ones, sometimes arise and need to be examined carefully. The countries concerned must settle these problems through negotiations.' The Chinese claims, however, were repeated by Beijing's delegate to the 3rd UN Law of the Sea Conference in June 1974. These assertions of Chinese sovereignty in the South China Sea foreshadowed the later Sino-Vietnamese conflict even before Saigon had fallen.

Shortly after the fall of Saigon the PRG announced the capture of 'beloved islands in the fatherland's waters', meaning the takeover of six islands in the Spratly group formerly occupied by southern Vietnamese soldiers. Beijing remained silent. However, following Le Duan's Moscow visit, the October issue of *China Pictorial* carried an illustrated article on Chinese exploration in the Paracels and reaffirmed its claim to islands in the South China Sea. The November issue of the Vietnamese army journal responded that whereas in the past 'our people's right to be its own master' had concerned only the north, it was now the armed forces' duty to protect the sovereignty and territorial integrity of the whole country, including 'the islands and continental shelf'. Later that same month the Beijing *People's Daily* set out China's most extensive and detailed claim to sovereignty in the South China Sea. Refraining from naming Vietnam, it noted that 'some of the islands still have not returned to the hands of the Chinese people', and it affirmed China's determination to recover them: 'We will absolutely not allow anyone to invade and occupy our territory on any pretext. The South China Sea islands are China's sacred territory. We have the duty to defend them.'

The issues went beyond nationalist irredentism on the part of either Hanoi or Beijing. Beijing was also involved in a similar situation in the East China Sea, where its claims overlapped not only with those of Taiwan and North and South Korea, but also with those of Japan, which in turn had overlapping claims with the USSR. At a global level this area was even more explosive than the South China Sea; and developments in the South China Seas could set precedents that would prove very costly to China.

China's growing assertiveness towards the offshore areas coincided with preparations for the first major working session of the UN Conference on the Law of the Sea in 1974. At this and subsequent conferences China has been one of the most militant supporters of extensive sovereignty over coastal waters. Its support for a 200-mile exclusive economic zone was vigorous from the outset. The tangled problems of the Law of the Sea were further complicated by exploration for offshore oil in both the South China and East China Seas. American companies had been conducting surveys for the Saigon regime (and Hanoi had wished to do likewise in the Tonkin Gulf) but by 1975 there had still been no substantial finds. Nevertheless, the area is considered to have good oil potential in the long term. Naturally both China and Vietnam would like these resources for their development efforts, but the fact that exploration and exploitation of them has not been pursued jointly in disputed areas indicates that there are deeper issues at stake. An expert on these questions wrote at the time: 'To put the oil factor into meaningful perspective, it should be viewed as one element in a more comprehensive Chinese effort to consolidate a position of regional primacy.'[15] Chinese maritime supremacy in the South China Sea would not only severely limit Hanoi's economic prospects but also make Vietnam very vulnerable to Chinese political pressure. Thus the dispute was not simply a crude two-sided grab for oil wealth (though in part it was just that), but also a Chinese demand for political submission on the part of the Vietnamese – and it was clearly understood as such in Hanoi.

If the Vietnamese had hoped that the ascendancy of moderates in Beijing after the fall of the 'Gang of Four' would soften China's stance over the South China Seas, they were swiftly disappointed. On 30 July 1977, eight days after Deng Xiaoping had been officially rehabilitated once more, China's foreign minister, Huang Hua, delivered an address which said that the issues in the South China Sea were non-negotiable:

> The territory of China reaches as far southward as the James Shoals, near Borneo, of Malaysia ... I remember that while I was still a schoolboy, I read about the islands in the geography books. At that time, I never heard anyone say that those islands were not China's. ... The Vietnamese claim that the islands belong to them. Let them talk that way. They have repeatedly asked us to negotiate with them on the [Paracels] issue; we have always declined to do so. ... As to the ownership of these islands, there are historical records that can be verified. There is no need for negotiations since they originally belonged to China. In this respect Taiwan's attitude is all right; at least they have some patriotism and would not sell out the islands. As to when we will recover the islands, this will have to wait until the time is ripe.[16]

Barring total capitulation to Vietnam to China's position, this statement set the stage for permanent tension between the two countries.

Vietnam's Ethnic Chinese and the Refugee Crisis

By 1977 tension between Hanoi and Beijing was also growing over Vietnam's 1.5 million ethnic Chinese (referred to as the Hoa). As in many other Southeast Asian countries, the overseas Chinese in Vietnam maintained a distinct Chinese culture and retained family links with China itself. Most had come as labourers or traders in the early stages of modern commercial expansion in Indochina, and by the mid twentieth century some Chinese played a prominent role in commerce and banking in many Southeast Asian countries. Before 1949 Beijing had insisted that the overseas Chinese were all Chinese citizens. If they took out citizenship in their country of residence, they were deemed to have taken out dual citizenship rather than to have renounced Chinese citizenship. Chinese governments claimed the right to intervene in other countries to protect China's overseas citizens.

With the coming of independence after World War II, nationalist governments throughout Southeast Asia often passed legislation deliberately favouring indigenous racial groups, or restricting the activities of the Chinese. In most countries they were obliged to renounce dual citizenship – they could become either a citizen of China or of their country of residence, but not both. In this context the Communists reappraised China's traditional posture of extra-territoriality. In the 1950s, at Zhou Enlai's initiative, the People's Republic of China formally renounced its claim to this right as part of its adoption of the principle of equality between nations.[17]

In Vietnam, China was able to reach agreement with Hanoi over the question of the ethnic Chinese in Vietnam, but not with the Saigon regime. In 1955 the central committees of the two Communist parties concluded that Chinese nationals in the north would be administered by Vietnam, would enjoy the same rights as Vietnamese citizens, and would be encouraged to adopt Vietnamese nationality voluntarily after 'sustained and patient persuasion and ideological education'. The agreement did not specify the time needed for the process of naturalization, though the Vietnamese have subsequently claimed: 'The Chinese ambassador in Vietnam in 1956, Kwei-po, said the time necessary for turning the Hoa into Vietnamese citizens was from eight to ten years or a little longer.'[18] Even this, the Vietnamese argued, was too long compared with practice elsewhere.

In the interim, the Chinese in North Vietnam were in a privileged position. In 1980 a 71-year-old Hoa refugee from the north recalled:

We had the best of both worlds. The Hoa in the north had all the rights and privileges of Vietnamese citizenship and none of its disadvantages. From about 1970 the Vietnamese had been trying to get us to become citizens, but few of us regarded it to be in our best interests. We would even vote in their elections. We were regarded as Vietnamese in all respects, except that we were not subject to the military draft.[19]

This was a valuable prerogative during the war and the Chinese were naturally not anxious to be assimilated.

Government pressure on the Hoa to assimilate increased in North Vietnam in the mid-1960s as a result of the Chinese Cultural Revolution, when some Hoa began their own 'Red Guard' activities. Worried about potential Chinese manipulation of the Hoa, in 1970 the North Vietnamese government began downgrading history and language lessons in Chinese schools; some years earlier Chinese signs had begun to disappear from shops in Hanoi and Haiphong. However, compared with the actions taken by Saigon, and to be taken throughout Vietnam after 1975, northern policy toward the Hoa before 1975 was moderate and tolerant.

In 1956 the Saigon regime of Ngo Dinh Diem had compelled the Hoa to take Vietnamese citizenship on pain of expulsion from Vietnam. Beijing protested against this in May 1957, saying that the Vietnamese measures were 'a brutal encroachment upon the legitimate rights of the overseas Chinese in South Vietnam'. Hanoi supported Beijing – though it is significant, certainly in retrospect, that this is the only statement Hanoi ever made with regard to the status of Chinese in the south before 1978. The National Liberation Front of South Vietnam, however, made a number of statements between 1960 and 1968 saying specifically that 'all decrees and measures of the US puppet regime regarding Chinese shall be abrogated', and that 'Chinese residents have the freedom and right to choose their nationality.'[20]

When the Vietnamese Communists marched into Saigon on 30 April 1975 the Hoa problem remained unresolved, a fact dramatized by the festoons of Chinese national flags and portraits of Mao Zedong which greeted them in Saigon's sister city Cholon. This was probably no more than an attempt by the Hoa to get on the good side of their new Communist rulers. Instead, it intensified Vietnamese Communist suspicions about the national loyalties of the Chinese in Vietnam.

In January 1976 the Vietnamese government ordered the Hoa in Cholon to register their citizenship. Most registered as Chinese, repudiating the citizenship forced on them by Diem. Dismayed, Hanoi ordered them to reregister, this time according to their status under the old Saigon government. Those who persisted in registering as Chinese were dismissed from employment and had their rations cut. Later in the year all Chinese newspapers in the south were closed down, followed by Chinese-run schools. Hanoi also began to tighten controls over the Chinese living in the north, mainly in Hanoi and Haiphong and along the Sino-Vietnamese border. As one refugee recalled: 'In 1977 the authorities tried to get the Hoa living on the border to adopt Vietnamese citizenship. Those who refused were forced to choose between returning to China or moving inland away from the border.'[21] Some 70,000 people chose to leave for China.

Beijing's *People's Daily* began to voice a revived interest in the overseas Chinese in February 1977, but it refrained from commenting on the Hoa until after Hanoi opted for an alliance with Moscow in the middle of the year. When Chinese Vice Premier Li Xiannian met Pham Van Dong in June, he gave him a dressing-down for 'not consulting China' on the issue and warned him that 'every country has the duty to protect the legitimate rights and interests of its nationals residing in other countries'. Li implied that he regarded all Hoa as Chinese citizens even where they had taken out Vietnamese citizenship.

There was more alarm in Hanoi when Beijing launched a new, active policy to enlist the support of overseas Chinese in late 1977. Outlining the new policy, the *People's Daily* of 4 January 1978 spoke of the overseas Chinese as 'part of the Chinese nation . . . with their destiny closely linked with that of the motherland' and declared Beijing's intent to 'work energetically among them ... to form a broad patriotic united front' to struggle against 'hegemonism'. Hanoi saw this as a declaration that the Chinese intended to use the Hoa as a fifth column against the Hanoi government. As Beijing also chose at this time openly to back Pol Pot's destructive border war against Vietnam, Hanoi believed it was faced with a Chinese campaign to disrupt Vietnam from within and without.

Internally, Hanoi's fears focused on the political loyalties of the Hoa community in the south. Its relations with the government were already tense. It held tremendous economic power, and considerable political clout. In August 1978 a VCP magazine gave the following analysis of the situation that had existed in the south:

> The bourgeois of Chinese descent ... controlled nearly all important economic positions, and especially firmly controlled three key fields: processing, distribution and credit. At the end of 1974 they controlled more than 80 per cent of the installations of the food, textile, chemical, metallurgy, engineering and electrical industries and nearly achieved a trading monopoly – wholesale trade 100 per cent, retail trade more than 50 per cent and export–import trade 90 per cent. They completely controlled the purchase of rice and paddy. ... Since they controlled the supply of goods to the market, they could manipulate prices ... through their import–export network and transport network and through the network of medium and small traders of Chinese origin. ... They built a closed world based on blood relations, strict internal discipline and a network of sects, each with its own chief, to aid the indigenous administration's direct interference. Each sect had its own budget, school, clinic, journal, headquarters and cemetery and a monopoly over a special branch of activity. This was truly a state within a state ...[22]

The Chinese oligarchy in the south controlled what one Vietnamese official described to Nayan Chanda as the 'strong capitalist heart beating inside the socialist body of Vietnam'.[23] Hanoi was now fearful that it could be won over to Beijing's cause.

On 5 February 1978 the VCP Central Committee made two strategically intertwined decisions: the first was to find a way of toppling the Pol Pot regime (see chapter 4); the second was to break the power of the Hoa oligarchy by accelerating the 'socialist transformation' of the south. The attack on 'bourgeois trade' in Saigon and Cholon was launched on a Friday (24 March) as many of the big traders were preparing to leave for a weekend at the beach resort of Vung Tau. As many as 30,000 businesses were nationalized; the young Communists who were mobilized to carry out the operation claimed they uncovered hoards of goods and gold bars. Thousands of other small businessmen and retailers were, however, allowed to continue operations. The measures were extended to the whole of the south in April. Then, on 3 May, the introduction of a new national currency to replace the formerly separate northern and southern denominations wiped out the savings of the wealthy, and tightened the government's grip on the economy. Those rendered unemployed by these measures were obliged to leave the cities for the NEZs on the Cambodian border: many preferred to leave the country.

In the north, there was no powerful Chinese business oligarchy. Here the Hoa worked in mines, ports or factories, or were small shopkeepers. However, many still had direct family and commercial ties with China itself. Hanoi's citizenship drive in the border regions had already produced an exodus to China, but the Hoa in Hanoi and Haiphong had not yet been confronted with the citizenship question. That changed abruptly a few weeks after the crackdown in the south. As one refugee related:

In early May Xuan Thuy (who had represented Hanoi at the peace negotiations in Paris) replied to a Radio Beijing broadcast accusing Vietnam of persecuting the Hoa. In his reply he noted that China and Vietnam had agreed after 1954 that the Hoa would gradually become Vietnamese. This announcement, which the Vietnamese radio repeated over and over, came as a shock to us. It had never before been made public. What worried us most was the draft, which we regarded as a sure road to death. It also meant those Hoa with relatives in China would no longer be able to visit them. This was important for economic as well as sentimental reasons. According to practice Hoa were able to visit China every three years. Those who went could bring Vietnamese goods to China and Chinese goods back to Vietnam for sale on the black market, so it meant an economic loss as well.[24]

At this point a vicious circle set in. The Hoa response only served to deepen Vietnamese suspicion of the ethnic Chinese who remained, which in turn made them more anxious to get out. The result was a rush of thousands of Hoa across the border to China.

The Hoa were also caught in a bitter tug-of-war between the Chinese and Vietnamese governments. As Hanoi saw it, its citizenship registration drive was a legitimate demand for loyalty from its citizens. But Beijing saw it as a challenge to its new policy towards the overseas Chinese. It denounced Hanoi for 'ostracizing, persecuting and expelling Chinese residents' and took on the role of champion of the overseas Chinese. In early 1978 Chinese diplomats began issuing Chinese passports to Hoa who wished to leave Vietnam, and in May Beijing announced that it was sending ships to pick up victimized Chinese residents of Vietnam. By now hundreds of thousands of Hoa were desperate to escape Vietnam, and applied for repatriation to China.

The Vietnamese announced that China could take back all the Hoa in Vietnam if it wished. But it refused to agree that they had been unjustly persecuted. But Beijing's motivations were political rather than humanitarian. Without such an acknowledgement from Hanoi, Beijing would not accept those who applied for repatriation. Then in July it blocked the overland outflow of Hoa by closing the Sino-Vietnamese border. By this time Hanoi was convinced that the whole affair was an attempt by China to destabilize Vietnam. It was at the height of this crisis that the VCP Politburo decided in June 1978 to 'clearly identify China as the main enemy of Vietnam'. It interpreted the closure of the border in July as an attempt to maintain 'a small Chinese nation in Vietnamese territory' in order to use it for 'trouble-making and disturbances'.

Previously, Hanoi had tried to pressure the Hoa into taking out Vietnamese citizenship. Now it was happy to see them leave the country. There was little prospect of them being accepted by other countries under regular immigration programmes so those seeking to leave Vietnam set out to sea in small boats, hoping that when they were either picked up by ships or had made it to a foreign shore they would be granted refugee status. From September 1978 Vietnamese officials began covertly cooperating with overseas Chinese syndicates operating from Hong Kong, Taiwan and Singapore to facilitate the departure of these 'boat people'. Since they had to buy their way out with bribes, there was considerable profit in the business for the officials involved.[25]

The Vietnamese government's participation in organizing the exodus naturally lifted the number of departures dramatically. There was a brief pause over December 1978 and January 1979, but following the Chinese invasion a surge of anti-Chinese sentiment throughout the country caused the number of departures from both the north and the south to skyrocket. Many of the Hoa left because they knew that in the mounting conflict between China and Vietnam, the Chinese in Vietnam would inevitably be the meat in the sandwich. Others were swept along in the panic. And large numbers of people – both Hoa and, to a lesser extent, ethnic Vietnamese – hoped to escape from deteriorating economic conditions. Whatever their reason for wanting to go, they all knew that emigration through official channels would be far too slow and protracted; they wanted to leave immediately, not in five years' time, and signed on with what journalists jokingly referred to as 'Rust Bucket Tours Inc.'.

But it was no joke. To get out as quickly as possible, the boat people were willing to take great risks. They were fleeced by unscrupulous entrepreneurs and corrupt officials, and the cost of their escape attempt did not end with payments of money and gold. They usually set out in small, overcrowded and dilapidated boats intended for coastal rather than deep-sea use. Few of them had any seafaring or navigational skills. They often ran out of food or water because of misjudgements of time and distance, and many of the boats broke down in mid-ocean. Many of those who sailed for Thai or Malaysian coasts died in brutal attacks by pirates operating in the Gulf of Thailand.

The exodus of boat people probably damaged Vietnam's international image more than its invasion of Cambodia. Even in 1978 it jeopardized Vietnam's developing relations with the ASEAN states who had to bear the main burden. All these countries had their own overseas Chinese problem and by 1979 many saw Vietnam's actions as an attempt to destabilize the rest of Southeast Asia. This sentiment was given its most forceful exposition by Singapore's foreign minister, Rajaratnam, in July 1979:

> once you go to the causes of [the exodus] you enter the secret world of wild Vietnamese ambitions and their even wilder dreams ... It is a military exercise to further the ambitions which the Vietnamese have concealed from us but not from their own people or their allies ... Their ambitions are hegemony in Southeast Asia ... In other words each junkload of men, women and children sent to our shores is a bomb to de-stabilize, disrupt, and cause turmoil and dissension in ASEAN states. This is a preliminary invasion to pave the way for the final invasion ... [26]

One major effect of the refugee crisis was to drive the ASEAN states into coordinating their policies towards Vietnam and Indochina. This undermined Vietnamese diplomacy in the region, which had taken full advantage of differences between the ASEAN countries.

By July 1979, when Rajaratnam was predicting that the worst was still to come, the refugee crisis had peaked. At the Geneva Conference that month the UN secretary general was able to say in his closing address that: 'the Government of the Socialist Republic of Vietnam has authorized me to inform you that for a reasonable period of time it will make every effort to stop illegal departures.' In the following three months the number of refugees leaving Vietnam fell dramatically – a fact that undermined the credibility of the Vietnamese government's protestations that it had no control over the exodus. Increasingly, they were leaving less for political reasons than to escape from Vietnam's poverty.

The Fateful Meridian

By mid-1977 Hanoi was in a bind. Its attempts to construct balanced relations with Moscow, Beijing and Washington had failed. Vietnam's economic situation was looking increasingly desperate. Insufficient aid from both East and West meant that the country's industrialization plans would have to be drastically scaled down. China had halted its wartime gift of 500,000 tonnes of rice per year, and cut its supply of consumer goods. Soviet oil and spare parts were in short supply. US policies meant that Vietnam had no prospect of an opening to the western world.

Meanwhile, agriculture suffered a series of setbacks. There were shortages of fertilizer and fuel, keenly felt in those areas of the south where modern farming methods, using high-yielding varieties of rice, had been established. Since the urban population was able to offer few goods in exchange for farm produce, and the official purchase price for rice was kept low, the peasants lacked market incentives to produce much beyond their own needs. Abnormal weather conditions worsened these problems, with drought followed by typhoons and floods.

Food shortages became acute. The monthly rice ration was cut to one kilogram, the rest of the month's ration being made up with wheat, flour, potatoes and other substitutes. The free-market price of rice spiralled to ten times the official price. Undernourished, the people were unable to maintain their working capacity, and labour productivity fell. Declining nutrition, coupled with shortages of imported drugs and medicines, led to a deterioration of public health. Many Vietnamese found that peace had bought a serious decline in their standard of living and, not unnaturally, they blamed the government.

In this context the Khmer Rouge launched its first full-scale attacks on Vietnamese border villages. These severely disrupted the NEZs in which the government had been hoping to absorb the urban unemployed into productive activity. Many people had been reluctant to go to the NEZs in the first place, their poor living standards leading some to refer to them as 'Vietnam's Siberia'. The Khmer Rouge attacks sent thousands of their inhabitants fleeing back to Saigon with tales of horror, making the urban population still more resistant to government pressures to move to the NEZs.

Hanoi had to make some hard choices. After the failure of his trip to Western Europe Pham Van Dong spent a month in talks with Soviet leaders, where he was joined by Le Duc Tho. They agreed to 'all-round Soviet–Vietnamese co-operation'. Hanoi's planners flew to Moscow, where they signed generous credit agreements. In July a Soviet military delegation flew to Vietnam, visiting, among other places, Cam Ranh Bay. Hanoi lavished gratitude on Moscow. 'When you drink water', declared Le Duan, 'you must not forget the source.'[27]

After years of resistance, the VCP leaders had finally made their choice between China and the Soviet Union. It was no doubt with considerable apprehension that they now waited to see how Beijing would respond. They may have hoped that the death of Mao and the swift demise of the 'Gang of Four' radicals in 1976 would lead to a new tolerance in Beijing. If so, they were soon disappointed.

Unable to compete with Moscow's largesse, China had sought to achieve its strategic objectives in Indochina after 1975 by pressuring Hanoi. Following Vietnam's decisive tilt towards the Soviets in mid-1977, Beijing decided to step up the pressure over a range of existing disputes. As the conflict with China and the domestic crisis in Vietnam intensified, so too did the fighting with Pol Pot's forces. In June 1978, when the VCP leadership decided to identify China clearly as the main enemy of Vietnam, they also decided that they would have to intervene in Cambodia to destroy Pol Pot's regime. Military preparations for the invasion began.

As insurance against Chinese retaliation, they moved to strengthen their ties with the Soviet Union. Hanoi finally became a member of Comecon on 29 July 1978. The following week China ended its remaining aid to Vietnam, withdrew all its technical personnel, and lashed out furiously at the Hanoi leadership for pursuing 'regional hegemonism', serving as the 'Cuba of the East' and 'junior partner' in a Soviet drive to win control of Southeast Asia. Vietnam also agreed to a military alliance with the Soviets. In June, General Giap flew secretly to Moscow to put a draft treaty and a shopping list of arms to the Soviet leaders. They readily agreed to Giap's proposal, and in August large shipments of Soviet arms were dispatched to Vietnam.[28] But the planned agreement was not signed just yet. In the meantime, Hanoi made a last, desperate effort to normalize relations with the USA.

On 11 July Phan Hien announced that Vietnam would drop all preconditions to normalization. After some delay, Holbrooke agreed to talks with the Vietnamese deputy foreign minister, Nguyen Co Thach, in New York in September. Thach made a play for American aid as part of the deal, but dropped this when Holbrooke objected. With the last obstacle removed, Thach proposed, US–Vietnamese relations should be normalized as soon as possible. Holbrooke promised to convey this to the president. But by this time Brzezinski rather than Vance was setting the pace on foreign policy in Washington. Brzezinski wanted to 'play the China card' against Moscow, but Beijing was playing hard to get. Brzezinski persuaded Carter that recognizing Vietnam would only add to American difficulties with China. Thach waited in New York for a month, but no response was forthcoming.

But Vietnam could not afford to wait. On 3 November 1978 Hanoi went ahead and signed the treaty of friendship with Moscow that had been drafted five months earlier. Brzezinski naturally pounced on this as justification of his stance, although it is arguable that Hanoi would not have gone ahead with it had it found Washington more responsive. When Holbrooke and Thach met again later that month, the USA had toughened its stance. Before normalization could proceed, Vietnam would have to guarantee not to attack Cambodia, and would have to desist from sponsoring illegal emigration and from provoking a Soviet-backed war with China. When Thach protested, the meeting came to an end.[29]

Vietnam also tried to build bridges to the anti-Communist ASEAN states. In July Phan Hien visited Malaysia and declared Vietnam's support for its proposal for a 'zone of peace and neutrality' in Southeast Asia. In September Pham Van Dong went on a goodwill tour of the ASEAN capitals, offering treaties of friendship to anyone who was interested, and trying to drum up support for Vietnam against China and Pol Pot. He apologized to his hosts because Hanoi had trained and supported guerrillas 'in the days when we needed to please the Chinese'. According to *The Economist*, Dong also spoke of 'possible cooperation with Malaysia and Thailand in providing intelligence against the guerrillas'. These overtures to ASEAN were unsuccessful. But such diplomatic setbacks could not stop the Vietnamese determination to deal with Pol Pot.

Hanoi's optimistic plans for peaceful post-war reconstruction lay in ruins by 1978. But, contrary to much propaganda, this was not due to fanatical Vietnamese 'expansionism'. Hanoi's priorities lay, at every point in these fateful years, in the economic development of a desperately poor country. In its negotiations with the West in the aftermath of the war, Hanoi was gambling for high economic stakes. It lost the gamble. But it was above all in its relations with 'fraternal' socialist countries that Hanoi's calculations went most seriously astray. Instead of enjoying the fruits of growing international cooperation among the socialist states of East Asia, Hanoi found itself embroiled in a fratricidal war with China and the Khmer Rouge. Only in Laos were Hanoi's post-war expectations more or less fulfilled.

Notes

1. Henry Kissinger, *Years of Upheaval*, London 1982, p. 12.
2. Communist Party of Vietnam, *Fourth National Congress: Documents*, Hanoi 1977, p. 11. The text of Ho's will has been reprinted in the appendices to Le Duan, *This Nation and Socialism are One*, ed. Tran Van Dinh, Chicago 1976.
2. Quoted by Vo Nhan Tri, 'Party Policies and Economic Performance', in David G. Marr and Christine P. White, eds, *Postwar Vietnam: Dilemmas in Socialist Development*, New York 1988, p. 88.
3. Carlyle A. Thayer, 'The Regularization of Politics: Continuity and Change in the Party's Central Committee, 1951–1986', in Marr and White. For the interpretation of Hanoi politics in terms of factional rivalries, cf. Thai Quang Trung, *Collective Leadership and Factionalism: An Essay on Ho Chi Minh's Legacy*, Singapore 1985.
5. D.R. Sar Desai, 'Vietnam's Quest for Security', in Sudershan Chawla and D.R. Sar Desai, eds, *Changing Patterns of Security and Stability in Asia*, New York 1980, p. 222.
6. William S. Turley, 'The Military Construction of Socialism: Postwar Roles of the People's Army of Vietnam', in Marr and White, pp. 205–9.

7. Nayan Chanda, *Brother Enemy*, San Diego 1986, p. 144.

8. For a good discussion, see Bill Herod, 'The Unfinished Business of America's MIAs', *Indochina Issues*, no. 17, June 1981.

9. Cf. Chanda, pp. 136–51, for a detailed account of Woodcock's mission.

10. Ibid., pp. 156–7.

11. Cf. Fred Halliday, *The Making of the Second Cold War*, 2nd edn, London 1986, ch. 8.

12. Jimmy Carter, *Keeping the Faith*, London 1982, pp. 148–9.

13. Chanda, pp. 185–7.

14. For the best account of the background to this dispute, cf. S. Samuel Marwan, *Contest for the South China Seas*, London 1982.

15. Selig S. Harrison, *China, Oil and Asia: Conflict Ahead?*, New York 1977, p. 194.

16. In King C. Chen, ed., *China and the Three Worlds*, London 1979, pp. 272–4.

17. For a more detailed discussion, see Stephen Fitzgerald, *China and the Overseas Chinese: A Study of Peking's Changing Policy 1949–70*, Cambridge 1972.

18. Hoang Nguyen, 'When the Hoa Became Peking's Political Cards Against Vietnam', in *Vietnam Courier* (ed.), *The Hoa in Vietnam, Dossier 2*, Hanoi 1978, p. 12.

19. Quoted by Charles Benoit, 'Vietnam's 'Boat People'', in David W.P. Elliott, ed., *The Third Indochina Conflict*, Boulder 1981, p. 144.

20. Cf. Pao-min Chang, 'The Sino-Vietnamese Dispute over the Ethnic Chinese', *China Quarterly*, no. 90, 1982, p. 197.

21. Benoit, p. 143.

22. *Vietnam Courier*, no. 78, November 1978.

23. Chanda, p. 234.

24. Benoit, p. 145.

25. On the involvement of the Vietnamese officials, cf. Barry Wain, *The Refused: The Agony of the Indochinese Refugees*, Hong Kong 1981, ch. 4.

26. Quoted by Frank Frost, 'Vietnam, ASEAN and the Refugee Crisis', *Southeast Asian Affairs 1979*, Singapore 1980, p. 361.

27. Chanda, pp. 187–91.

28. Ibid., pp. 257–8.

29. See ibid., ch. 9, for the fullest account of US–Vietnamese negotiations in 1978.

3

Laos: The Eclipse of 'Neutralist' Communism

The cessation of American aid to Laos in mid-1975 effectively ended the Lao sojourn within the western sphere of influence, while the complete Pathet Lao takeover in December of that year registered Laos' decisive shift into the 'socialist camp'. It is common wisdom among most journalists and many academics writing about Indochina that from that point on Laos became a virtual Vietnamese 'colony'. Arthur J. Dommen, author of a major study on Laos before the Communist takeover, calls the country 'a satellite of Vietnam' and the Vientiane government a 'puppet' of Hanoi.[1] Another specialist, Martin Stuart-Fox, has written of Laos: 'All major areas of decision-making from foreign policy to economic planning and military security are dependent on Vietnamese direction'.[2] Indeed many have asserted that Laos was Vietnam's prototype for the formation of the 'Indochina Federation' – composed of Vietnam, Laos and Cambodia. No one has put this view more forcefully than Dommen:

> The stationing of Vietnamese troops in Laos today is obviously aimed at defending the independence, sovereignty, territorial integrity and cultural construction not of Laos, but of a Greater Vietnam, envisioned by Ho Chi Minh's successors and supported by the Soviet bloc. This Greater Vietnam will make Laos far more a part of Vietnam than the Indochinese Federation Ho envisioned when his preoccupation was with the expulsion of the French. ... Vietnam has replaced France as the colonial power in Indochina.[3]

No one is denying that the relationship between Laos and Vietnam is an uneven one, a relationship in which Hanoi has more power and influence than Vientiane; the most cursory study of the political resources the two regimes can marshal quickly establishes that elementary fact. But many writers treat formal equality as of no significance, and blur all the crucial distinctions between outright annexation, federation, colonial rule, and the formation of alliances between sovereign states in their discussion of Lao–Vietnamese relations. In the passage just quoted, Dommen appears to imagine that the formation of an 'Indochina Federation' is the equivalent of annexation by a state he calls 'Greater Vietnam', and that this is what has happened in Indochina. Faced with such a flight of fancy, it is necessary to make a few elementary observations. In the first place, neither of the political entities to which Dommen refers actually exists – the Lao People's Democratic Republic (LPDR) is recognized by the United Nations, the United States, China and a host of other governments as a sovereign state with, among other things, the right to form alliances with other sovereign states if it pleases; and there are no institutions that can be considered part of an 'Indochina Federation' or 'Greater Vietnam'.

If we concentrate on the formal relationships – which are by no means unimportant, and all that international law, for example, can take into account[4] – the statements by Dommen and Stuart-Fox are demonstrably untrue. They are no more than careless rhetoric masquerading as political analysis. But if we put aside the muddled terms they use, the basic points that these authors appear to be making are twofold. The first is that, despite its formal equality, the government of Laos has in fact come under the informal control of the Vietnamese government. The second is that this control is exercised to the detriment of Laos. In other words, it is alleged that the relationship is of the type that some writers have termed 'neo-colonial'. It needs to be emphasized that the point at issue is not one of inequality, of Vietnamese influence in Laos – it is one of Vietnamese control and exploitation of Laos. The allegedly malevolent nature of Vietnamese power has to be demonstrated, not merely asserted or assumed.

Certainly, it cannot be disputed that the relationship between the two governments is a close one. It was the Lao prime minister and secretary general of the Lao People's Revolutionary Party (LPRP), Kaysone Phomvihane, who first spoke of the 'special relationship' between Vietnam and Laos in a speech to the 4th Congress of the Vietnamese Communist Party (VCP) in mid-1976:

In the history of world revolution, examples of the radiant spirit of proletarian internationalism are not lacking, but never has there been anywhere an alliance of militant solidarity so especially durable. Thirty years it has run, and yet it remains clear. This solidarity and durable alliance places high value on the spirit of independence and sovereignty as well as the values of each people. Each joins forces with the peoples of the other two countries to help in combat and carry off victory, accomplishing at the same time the noble historical mission before each of our nations and before the revolutionary movement of the world. The relations between Vietnam and Laos have become special relations of great purity, imprinted with an exemplary and rare fidelity, which has consolidated and developed more and more each day.

Dommen, no doubt, would see this speech as no more than a vassal paying homage to his master at court. Yet, as we shall see, Kaysone's speech was probably a rare example of highblown political rhetoric expressing real beliefs.

Most critiques of the Lao–Vietnamese 'special relationship' assume that there is a 'natural' antagonism between Lao nationalism and Vietnamese nationalism, and that the alliance between the two countries involves the subordination of the former to the latter. Much of this has been based on woolly assertions about 'historic antagonisms' between the two countries and ethnic differences, but no one has really argued this point of view at length, and like so much else it remains a background 'taken-for-granted' assumption.

In fact, there is little evidence for it. Laos is so ethnically fragmented that, to a large portion of the population, there is little to choose between lowland Lao and lowland Vietnamese rule. And, as we saw in chapter 1, mass nationalism came to Laos quite recently, largely as a result of the activities of the pro-Vietnamese Pathet Lao. The idea of 'historic antagonisms' between the Lao and Vietnamese nations has even less foundation than the corresponding claims about the Khmer and Vietnamese nations.

One of the few empirical studies to address itself to this question was a Rand Corporation study by Paul Langer and Joseph Zasloff in the 1960s. They concluded:

A widely held thesis holds that the Lao dislike the Vietnamese. Our research points to a more complex relationship. For one thing the typical lowland Lao rarely exhibits the acute, virulent nationalism and xenophobia so common in contemporary Asia and so often directed against the neighbouring people. Among the broader population, therefore, anti-Vietnamese feelings do not appear to be intense. It is true, however, that many members of the Lao elite fear what they perceive as Vietnamese aggressiveness, as well as organization and drive ... The feeling of inadequacy vis-à-vis the Vietnamese is particularly evident among those educated Lao who were once placed in positions subordinate to the Vietnamese by French colonial officers, whose administrative policies tended to discriminate against the Lao.[5]

The last sentences, of course, refer to the American-supported Royal Lao Government elite, not the Pathet Lao elite.

Our experience indicates that the ethnic antagonisms that do exist between the Lao and the Vietnamese are no more serious than those found between different groups in a country like Australia, or between the ethnic Lao and the various hill tribes, or indeed between the various tribal groups themselves. Such feelings only become politically significant in specific conjunctures, and then only if they are promoted by some organized political group, party or government which exploits them politically. The Lao right wing, for example, encouraged anti-Vietnamese sentiments; the Communists do not. If anything, a major theme of the Pathet Lao government is ethnic reconciliation.

What is extraordinary about the long relationship between the Vietnamese and Lao Communists is that it is hard to find a single instance where the two movements were at loggerheads with each other. From 1949 onwards the Pathet Lao leaders were supported militarily, politically and diplomatically by the Vietnamese at every turn: they were supported when they decided to enter the coalition government in 1958 and when it collapsed under right-wing pressure they found Vietnamese support waiting for them when they escaped back to the mountains. The Vietnamese supported them in the military actions and diplomacy surrounding the Geneva negotiations on forming a new coalition in Laos in 1962, and again during the Paris negotiations. Indeed, at critical times, such as in the late 1950s, it is certain that the Pathet Lao base areas only survived because of Vietnamese support.[6]

Of course, the Vietnamese had good national reasons for giving this support because the base area provinces of Sam Neua and Phong Saly were on its border, and when the Vietnam war started in earnest in the early 1960s the Ho Chi Minh trail, which wound its way down along the Lao–Vietnamese border, was a critical supply route for guerrillas in South Vietnam. Thus the zones liberated by the Pathet Lao acted as a buffer for the Vietnamese Communists. But the fact that the Pathet Lao has had Vietnamese support for such a long time does not make it a 'creature' of Hanoi.

The general absence of substantive conflicts naturally inclined the Lao Communists towards the Vietnamese version of Marxism. The traditional social structure of Laos, like that of Cambodia, had produced no substantial intelligentsia, as had the Confucian system in Vietnam, and the French had concentrated their educational resources for Indochina in Vietnam. This predisposed the Lao towards a degree of dependence on the Vietnamese Marxist canon, and therefore there never appears to have been any basic ideological clash between the two movements.

Thus the national interests of the Lao and the Vietnamese Communists have tended to converge historically rather than diverge, and it is for this reason above all that Kaysone could speak with such confidence of the 'radiant spirit of proletarian internationalism' binding the two countries. However, the glow would most certainly fade if their national interests did ever seriously diverge.

It was therefore predictable that the Vietnamese and Lao governments would cooperate closely after 1975. Two months after the founding of the LPDR Kaysone led a government and party delegation to Hanoi (on 5–11 February 1976), following which the two countries pledged to strengthen economic and cultural cooperation, and Vietnam offered to help Laos train economic, scientific and other technical experts. The treaty of friendship signed in July 1977 simply extended this by stressing a desire to increase economic and trade cooperation between the two countries. The pledges of mutual assistance were largely one-way: Vietnam offered Laos duty-free access to the Port of Da Nang and interest-free loans over the period 1978–80. In 1983 *Nhan Dan* gave further details of Vietnam's aid. It had pledged, from 1976 to 1985, 1.3 billion dong ($146.7 million) to cover the rebuilding of Sam Neua township and two smaller towns; the repair of 300 kilometres of roads; provision of 900 specialists; and the training of half of the 10,000 Lao students who go abroad. 'Almost half' of this aid, the paper said, would have to be reimbursed. This is not exactly standard neo-colonial practice.

The treaty also said that Laos and Vietnam would 'cooperate closely in increasing their capability of defending and protecting their independence, sovereignty and territorial integrity'. This undoubtedly served Vietnam's regional diplomatic objectives well. By this stage the dispute with Pol Pot was well under way, and at the same time Vietnam was coming under mounting pressure from China over the South China Sea. The treaty with Laos secured their one friendly border, blocking what Hanoi saw as a possibility of complete 'encirclement' by pro-Chinese forces.

However, it also needs to be recognized that the Lao government itself had a strong interest in military cooperation with Vietnam. The LPDR is a weak state, with a long and virtually indefensible border with Thailand. Relations between the governments in Bangkok and Vientiane, and the atmosphere along this border, were tense in 1977. The Vientiane government also faced harassment from several hundred right-wing guerrillas, mostly remnants of Vang Pao's former CIA 'secret army' operating in the mountains of central Laos and out of refugee camps in Thailand. An immediate result of the treaty was the launching, in late 1977, of a major offensive against this source of harassment, which appears to have been removed by early 1978.

The treaty legitimized the presence of Vietnamese troops who had been stationed in the country for many years. It was the presence of these troops that was regarded as the main proof of Vietnamese domination in Laos. The exact figures over the years have never been revealed, but they were substantial. According to a supposedly senior Lao government official, who defected to Thailand in 1979, Hanoi's troop strength in Laos was between 24,000 and 30,000 at the end of 1977, and was subsequently lifted to 50,000 as regional tensions grew. Most of these soldiers were based near the Lao–Chinese border.

A large number of the soldiers engaged in construction work throughout the country. In Xieng Khouang, where the link to Vietnam is being upgraded so that vital fuel supplies can be trucked into the province from Vietnam, we have seen them at work on road construction. These troops were unarmed, unlike an army of occupation. Throughout its long presence the Vietnamese army has shown sensitivity to the feelings of the local population. Indeed, over the many years of Vietnamese presence in Laos, there were remarkably few reports of harsh treatment of the local population. The Vietnamese army appears to have acted similarly in Cambodia, where its experience in Laos stood it in good stead.

The 1977 treaty also said that the two countries 'would build the Lao–Vietnamese border into a border of fraternal friendship', and later an agreement was signed delineating the border. There should have been few problems with this – the areas on both sides had long been under the control of political groups cooperating with each other, and both agreed that the border established by the French should be accepted. The French had taken the watershed of the Annamite mountain chain as the border, and both sides accepted this in principle. But the region has never been thoroughly surveyed, and some modern maps show the border cutting across the headwaters of certain rivers.[7] Since some of these flow to the Mekong (through Laos) and others to the Gulf of Tonkin (through Vietnam), adjustments according to the principle established by the French would be roughly mutually compensatory. The border has subsequently been delineated but the agreement remains unpublished.

Despite this, Hanoi was later to praise border relations with Laos as a 'model for good neighbourliness and friendship' – doubtless thinking of the problems it had encountered with China and Cambodia over these matters. Dommen, on the other hand, presents a typical western assessment:

> The text has never been published, but presumably it legalizes 'adjustments' in Vietnam's favour that the former royal government had been unwilling to concede. There are already reports that Vietnam is colonizing the disputed border areas in Xieng Khouang and Savannakhet provinces.[8]

Neither Dommen nor anyone else has ever presented any evidence to support these assertions.

The research we have carried out close to the Vietnamese border in Houa Phan province and interviews conducted with Hmong refugees who have lived along the border of Xieng Khouang province and Vietnam since 1977, show Dommen's assertions about colonization to be untrue. With regard to Savannakhet province, we gleaned an interesting early snippet of information about the border. A church minister from Savannakhet said that the number of Christians in the province had increased since the treaty because a village formerly on the Vietnamese side of the border which had Christians in it had since come under Lao jurisdiction. Thus the only detail we have of the border 'adjustments' made under the 1977 agreement indicates that they favour Laos. No doubt, however, adjustments elsewhere have been made in Vietnam's favour as a trade-off.

Even though the signing of the treaty was motivated on Vietnam's side by its deteriorating relations with China and Cambodia, this was still being kept under wraps by Hanoi in 1977 in the interests of 'international proletarian solidarity'. Thus a joint statement by Laos and Vietnam spoke of the need 'to strengthen their militant solidarity and relations of cooperation with the USSR and China', and the treaty called for 'militant solidarity, lasting cooperation with and mutual assistance to fraternal Cambodia'.

Laos's immediate concern was the extreme right-wing Thanin Kraivichien regime in Bangkok and its desire to break the Thai monopoly over its access to the sea. From its early days this had been a stated aim of the LPDR, and access through Cambodia had figured in its calculations. In December 1975 Phoumi Vongvichit, deputy prime minister and foreign minister, spoke of a plan to cooperate with the Vietnamese to build roads to the sea. Then he continued:

Apart from Vietnam, we may have passage to the sea through Cambodia. After building highways reaching Pakse and Cambodia, we may go as far as Kompong Som port in Cambodia. Prince Sihanouk has said that we can tell him where we want facilities and build them as we wish. If this is done we shall have many routes to the sea. We shall choose the route which permits us to pay less for the transport of goods. This will make it unnecessary for us to kowtow to anyone, as we did before ...

A government delegation to Phnom Penh, at the request of the Cambodian government, followed on 15–18 December. The delegation, led by Phoune Sipraseuth, held talks with Prime Minister Penn Nouth and other Khmer leaders in what was said to be 'an extremely friendly, cordial and warm atmosphere'. The main focus of the talks, however, seems to have been the continued US presence in Thailand and demands that Lao and Cambodian rightists be prohibited from establishing bases there. No doubt Sipraseuth discovered during his stay in Phnom Penh that neither Penn Nouth nor Prince Sihanouk had any say in the running of Democratic Kampuchea. Nothing ever came of the plans for Laos to use the outlet of Kompong Som.

There is no doubt that Hanoi was successful in creating the 'special relationship' it desired between itself and the LPDR. But it is misleading to view this as some kind of colonial relationship, between master and subject. Vientiane had good reasons of its own for fostering closer cooperation with Hanoi. A more fruitful approach is to focus on the geopolitical position in which the new Lao government found itself after 1975. We also need to consider the LPDR's relations with Thailand, China and Cambodia, as well as Vietnam, to get a balanced picture, as this is rarely done by other commentators.

As a small and weak state, Laos has frequently found that its destiny has been decided for it by the actions of more powerful states. Its strategic location in Southeast Asia did not allow it to retreat into isolation: Laos has the dubious distinction of sharing borders with all the major states of the region – China, Vietnam, Thailand, Burma and Cambodia. Involvement in their disputes was inescapable, though Laos itself had little to gain from other peoples' quarrels. Neutralism has always been a tempting option for Lao politicians, but rarely one they could afford.

Laos and Thailand

The fundamental importance of Thailand's power in relation to Laos is neglected by almost all contemporary commentators on Indochinese politics. Before 1975 the Bangkok government had exercised considerable influence among RLG politicians, had actively supported the RLG in the civil war by allowing US airstrikes to be flown against the Pathet Lao from Udon airbase in the northeast of Thailand, and when the cease-fire was announced in 1973 it had at least 20,000 Thai military 'volunteers' fighting in Laos against the Communists. The Communist victory, therefore, abruptly reduced Bangkok's influence in an area it had come to regard as its own. However, even though the Thai were pushed back to their side of the Mekong River they still held a powerful political weapon – the ability to blockade landlocked Laos.

Thailand provides Laos with its main outlet to the world market. Furthermore, Thailand itself has always been Laos's main trading partner. Over the period 1973–76, for example, 65 per cent of Lao exports were absorbed by Thailand, and goods from Thailand accounted for 98 per cent of Lao imports in 1973. On the other hand, Laos figures as a very minor partner in Thailand's overall trade. On top of this, a great deal of informal trade has always been conducted back and forth across the border, and because internal communications within Laos are so poor sections of the Lao economy are more closely integrated into the adjacent Thai economy than into the Lao economy.[9] The cumulative effect of this is that Bangkok possesses a great deal of economic power over Vientiane – greater than anything Vietnam has ever exercised or is likely to exercise for the foreseeable future.

Ironically perhaps, it was Bangkok's power of blockade that dictated the timing of the formation of the LPDR in December 1975. The Lao economy was already a shambles at the end of 1975 because of the instability caused by the drawn-out nature of the Communist takeover after the formation of the coalition government in April 1974. The cessation of US aid in mid-1975 had caused runaway inflation, so when the Thai closed their border with Laos on 18 November because of frontier clashes the economic impact on the Lao economy was immediate and crippling. For the population in the Mekong River cities and the former RLG zones it brought unprecedented austerity. The crisis forced the Lao Communists to call the National Congress together in early December, although they had not been expected to assert complete control until the elections already announced for April 1976. *Le Monde* commented on the hardening of Thailand's attitude, 'the prolonged closing of the frontier formed by the Mekong and the halt of deliveries of fuel and foodstuffs have no doubt driven the Laotian Communists to close their ranks and to provoke a political transformation which will allow them to deal rapidly with economic problems.'

Because of Thailand's actions during the civil war, the Lao Communists had good reason to be wary of Bangkok's intentions towards the new regime. However, from the beginning of 1976 moderates began to get the upper hand in Thai politics. The border was reopened at several points in January and in March the Thai authorities set a deadline of 20 July for the US Military Assistance Command Thailand to leave the country. In April the liberal leader of the Democratic Party, Seni Pramoj, took command of the coalition government in Bangkok, and indicated that he favoured a policy of detente with Communist Indochina. Improved relations with Laos quickly followed. The two governments signed a communiqué on 3 August which stated that relations between them would be based on the five principles of peaceful coexistence first enunciated at Geneva, and contained clauses covering a range of commercial and political agreements.

This *rapprochement* was strongly opposed by the right-wing Thai parties and the military, who overthrew the Pramoj government in October 1976, installing a government led by the reactionary judge Thanin Kraivichien. This dealt a bodyblow to Thai–Lao relations and over the following year border trading points between the two countries were restricted, while

mutual recriminations about border incidents were traded back and forth
between Vientiane and Bangkok.

The establishment of the Thanin regime in Bangkok coincided with
a rapidly deteriorating economic situation in Laos, which in 1977 reached
crisis proportions. A mild drought in 1976 became a severe one in
1977. A joint study by the Lao Agriculture Ministry and the United
Nations Development Programme in September 1977 estimated that
the harvest was down 40 per cent nation-wide compared with the previous
year, and an appalling 95 per cent in some provinces in the south.
Only large infusions of international food aid staved off famine. In
this situation the hostile policies of the Thanin regime were seen as
a direct attempt to bring the government in Vientiane to its knees.
The Thanin regime also provided a safe haven for right-wing Lao resistance groups which could make sabotage raids into Laos from base
areas in Thailand.

It should not have been surprising, therefore, to find the Pathet Lao
actively moving, in mid-1977, to solidify its ties with its long-time ally,
Hanoi. Already, at the end of 1975, Vietnam had acted swiftly to help
the Lao overcome the difficulties imposed by the first blockade when
it trucked vital supplies across the Annamite mountain chain from Da
Nang to Savannakhet. At this time the Soviets had also brought in vital
supplies by air. Both these countries immediately came to Vientiane's
aid again when it came under pressure from the Thanin regime. When
Laos and Vietnam signed their treaty of friendship and cooperation in
1977, an accompanying statement clearly identified Thailand's policies
as a motivating factor on the Lao side:

Since the October 1976 coup the Thai administration has pursued a hostile
policy towards Vietnam and Laos, resorted to the application of economic
pressure against Laos, oppressed and terrorized Vietnamese nationals and failed
to implement the joint communiqués signed between Vietnam and Thailand
on 6 August 1976, and the joint communiqué signed between Laos and Thailand
on 3 August 1976 ... The fact that the administrations of a number of ASEAN
member-countries are actively strengthening bilateral military alliances under
the anti-Communist label will lead to a danger of transforming ASEAN into
a de facto military alliance.

While this latter reference apparently alluded to joint Thai–Malaysian
operations against guerrillas in southern Thailand, Vietnam, and Laos
in particular, obviously felt that such actions could just as easily be turned
against them.

Cambodia and Laos

The geopolitical location of Laos meant that it inevitably stressed the need for Indochinese cooperation. We have already noted Vientiane's early expression of interest in access to Kompong Som port. As the conflict between Vietnam and Cambodia intensified, the Lao government attempted to act as mediator. Indeed the LPDR maintained an embassy in Phnom Penh right up to the fall of the capital to Vietnamese troops on 7 January 1979 – which earned it a spray of bullets from Pol Pot troops during their rapid departure from the capital.

Relations between Phnom Penh and Vientiane never degenerated into the acrimony that passed between Phnom Penh and Hanoi. The overriding reason for this was their shared border with Thailand. As the *chef du cabinet* of the Lao Foreign Ministry, Soubanh Srithirath, explained in early 1979: 'We could limit the very minor problems we had with Cambodia. Vietnam could not. The politics are different there. We have a border with Thailand. Vietnam does not.'

Another important general reason for the absence of Khmer–Lao antagonism was the fact that Cambodian nationalism was not formed in relation to the Lao, and vice versa. Both nationalisms were defined relative to their two powerful neighbours, Thailand and Vietnam. Not even in the deranged historical fantasies of Pol Pot did the ghost of the old Lao kingdom of Lane Xang loom menacingly on Cambodia's northern border (although Sihanouk had invoked it in moments of extreme exasperation). Lao–Cambodian relations from 1975 to late 1978 were relatively calm, though not untroubled. In one of the Pol Pot regime's saner diplomatic moves, Phnom Penh donated food aid to a desperate Laos in mid-1977. The political capital this won in Vientiane was dearly bought – many Khmer themselves were close to starvation at the time.

By late 1977 the border war between Cambodia and Vietnam was in full swing. A delegation headed by President Souphannavong and Foreign Minister Phoune Sipraseuth was dispatched to Phnom Penh over 17–21 December in a bid to avoid an open rupture between their Communist neighbours. On the day before the delegation arrived Phnom Penh radio had broadcast an account of Lao history which said that, like Cambodia, Laos had been a victim in the past of 'the expansionist ambitions of the Annam feudalists from the east and the Siam feudalists from the west'. The Lao, it said, had every reason to establish common cause with Cambodia against Thailand, but more particularly against Vietnam. Needless to say, the Lao delegation had little success in smoothing the Pol Pot regime's quarrel with Vietnam.

The differences between the two governments were obvious from Souphannavong's opening speech in Phnom Penh, when he spoke of the

Lao party continuing 'the splendid work of the Indochinese Communist Party, jointly with the Cambodian people and the Vietnamese people'. This favourable reference to the old Indochinese Communist Party (ICP) directly challenged the line of the Pol Pot leadership, which was currently attacking the Vietnamese for supposedly advocating an Indochina Federation. Souphannavong also went on to speak of the Lao–Vietnamese treaty of friendship, and the treaty on the delimitation of their frontiers, as good examples of how neighbours should conduct their international relations. This also was a position categorically rejected by the leaders of the Democratic Kampuchea government. There had also been reported clashes on the Lao–Khmer border, which both sides had denied at the time, but clearly Souphannavong had these in mind as well.

The only journalist who ever got near the Lao–Khmer border region was Nayan Chanda, who visited Pakse in November 1978. He reported that it was clear from his talks with local officials that the situation on the border had been deteriorating since the end of 1976. The Cambodian donation of 3,000 tonnes of rice in mid-1977 was the last time that Route 13 across the border had been used, after which the Khmer Rouge dug trenches across the road and laid mines. At the same time, strengthened Khmer Rouge border patrols began shooting at Lao fishermen on the river, and anyone else who strayed too close to the frontier.

In mid-1978 several Lao soldiers were killed and the Cambodian ambassador in Vientiane, Sam San, visited the border area and saw the bodies. He expressed regret over the deaths 'caused by mistake', but the incidents continued. Phoune Sipraseuth visited the border a number of times and instructed Lao soldiers not to return the fire so as not to aggravate the situation and thereby embroil Laos in a costly conflict. Chanda also reported:

> In conversation with local officials, it was revealed that in pursuance of their good-neighbour policy, the Lao authorities had sent back (at least until the end of 1976) a large number of refugees who had fled Cambodia. Asked when they decided to stop sending refugees back, one source said: 'When we realized that all the returned refugees had been executed. When we tried to send some refugees back they pleaded with us to kill them rather than send them back to Cambodia. Then we realized things over there were really bad'.[10]

Within a fortnight of the Lao delegation's departure from Phnom Penh in December 1977, Cambodia broke off diplomatic relations with Vietnam and made the dispute between the two Communist countries public. The Soviet Union and most Eastern European countries, including Albania, immediately condemned Phnom Penh. The LPDR, on the other hand, continued to chart a neutral course in the dispute. Claims by the Japanese press and Reuters that the Vietnamese had placed a division of troops on the northern Cambodian border in southern Laos were strongly denied by Vientiane on 17 January 1978: 'The Lao Party and government ... have always been persistent in pursuing their policy of solidarity with Vietnam and Cambodia ... there has never been any military operation carried out by Vietnamese forces through Lao territory.' A day later Prime Minister Kaysone sent identical letters to both the Vietnamese and Cambodian governments expressing his wish that they would 'make joint efforts to settle the disputes at an early date by holding negotiations on the basis of respect for each other's independence, sovereignty and territorial integrity'.

The belligerence of Phnom Penh made this 'neutralist' stance increasingly difficult to sustain. The Vietnamese peace proposals put forward on 5 February 1978 were welcomed in Vientiane, but their rejection in Phnom Penh ensured the final divergence between the two countries. By mid-year a joint statement by Kaysone and Souphannavong said 'we support Vietnam's stand for the settlement of differences' through negotiation, a course Cambodia still rejected.

Meanwhile the Lao were increasingly viewed as Vietnamese puppets by the Pol Pot regime. Elizabeth Becker relates:

> When I was in Pol Pot's Cambodia (in December 1978) officials there said Laos had been 'Vietnamized' and the Lao race threatened with extinction due to forced marriage with Vietnamese. This proved outlandish but worth mentioning because the Pol Pot regime believed it and acted accordingly.

She added: 'The Lao, in fact, have preserved their own culture much better than Cambodia did under Pol Pot.'[11]

China: The Unavoidable Enemy

One of the first foreign policy tasks of the LPDR in 1975 was to stake out a new form of neutralism in relation to the Sino-Soviet dispute. The task fell to Phoumi Vongvichit, who said in 1975:

> At present there are several countries which cannot get along with each other. However they can get along with us. This is because we have used correct diplomatic means ... My policy is to win more friends while decreasing the number of enemies ... as a friend, I hope that you two will be able to get along sooner or later. I side with neither you nor him ...

Such studied aloofness from the implications of this dispute was in the end no more possible for Laos than it was for Vietnam. As regional tensions mounted, Laos was inexorably drawn into the conflict.

Up to 1978 Vientiane's links with Beijing were cordial but distant. When the conflict between Vietnam and China came to the surface the Lao initially tried to keep their distance in much the same way as they had over the Vietnamese–Cambodian conflict. But as all the disputes became interlocked so the Lao eventually had to shift their position. The reluctance of a number of Lao leaders to accept a more partisan role in the gathering political storm can be seen in remarks made by Kaysone in March 1978 when he said that 'a number of individuals are influenced by psychological warfare tactics employed by the enemies' and by 'narrow-minded nationalism'. This revealed a persistent neutralist current in Lao politics, and possibly some resentment at what the Vietnamese had led them into. No doubt many Lao approached the impending conflict in Indochina with trepidation: after all, it was unlikely that they could have any decisive influence on the course or outcome of events; yet they would have to bear the consequences, whatever they might be.

As 1978 proceeded Vientiane's position on the politics of the region became tougher. In late June, Radio Vientiane broadcast a statement that 'the unity between the army and the people must be further strengthened, as well as the army's international unity with the Vietnamese army and people.' In the following month an editorial in *Sieng Pasason* marking the anniversary of the treaty with Vietnam said that the Lao government would 'stand by the side of the Vietnamese people' and was 'determined to smash all divisive schemes of the imperialists and international reactionary forces' (the latter term a Vietnamese code-phrase for China). At the same time Kaysone made a thinly veiled attack on China by saying that 'imperialists and international reactionaries have incited dissension among our people of various nationalities' and called for struggle against schemes 'trying to incite the nationalities to carry out prolonged resistance against our revolution'. Kaysone repeated the charge in August. Beijing reacted strongly, accusing Moscow and Hanoi of trying to 'poison relations between China and Laos'.

It was at this point, when the regional barometer was about to explode, that differences within the LPRP on the country's strategic options came briefly into public view. At a gathering of party functionaries to celebrate the thirty-third anniversary of Lao independence day, Souphannavong gave a speech which, while praising the Russian Revolution and celebrating the founding of the ICP, went on to say that 'imperialists and the international reactionary forces are attempting to sow divisions between Laos and other socialist countries, especially Vietnam'. But most significantly, he went on to add:

> More seriously still, recently they spread the rumour that Lao traitors in exile
> ... now have a new supporter, that in Great China, and that China would
> attack Vietnam and then Laos. This is very wicked and dangerous propaganda
> aimed at sowing bedevilment and anxiety among our people to make them
> lose confidence in the line and policies of our party and state, to sow division
> between the Lao people and the Chinese people and, finally, to sabotage our
> revolution.

This speech cannot be read (as some have) as an anti-Vietnamese statement, or as a pro-Chinese one; it is either a statement of the position
of Lao 'neutralist' Communism directed at the staunchly pro-Hanoi stance
of Kaysone, or a veiled attack on great-power pressure by China itself,
accusing it of spreading rumours of its support for anti-government
activity similar to those which had circulated in Hanoi and had recently
panicked the Hoa there to flee to China.

There had never been a solid pro-Beijing faction in the leadership of
the Pathet Lao. Deputy Premier Vongvichit had often been rumoured
to be pro-Chinese, in much the same way as Truong Chinh has been in
Vietnam. There is no real evidence for this (before 1975 Kaysone was
often depicted as pro-Chinese and Vongvichit as pro-Soviet). Again,
October 1978, Vongvichit said:

> As to the Vietnam–China and the Vietnam–Cambodia conflicts, we want them
> to end and that peace should prevail in Indochina and in Southeast Asia. We
> believe that the differences in views, the conflicts can be settled in a peaceful
> way. This is why we back the proposal of the Vietnamese comrades to settle
> conflicts through negotiations.

But both China and Cambodia had at this stage rejected such proposals.

The debate within the LPRP, however, is a long-standing one in Lao
politics – between a neutralist tendency and one arguing for a closer
alliance with powerful friends. For the right wing in the old RLG it
meant closer ties with Bangkok and Washington in opposition to Prince
Souvanna Phouma (at least until the early 1960s). For the Communists,
the options have been a form of neutralism or a close alliance with Hanoi.
In 1978 the Communist 'neutralists' were particularly worried about
adding to the country's problems through antagonizing their powerful
northern neighbour by identifying too closely with Vietnam. However,
the gathering regional power struggle cut the ground from under their
feet. They realized that Beijing, Phnom Penh and Hanoi would not brook
a policy of neutrality in the coming conflict. It was also clear to them
that it would be absurd to trade the Vietnamese and the Soviets as allies
for an alliance with China. Long-standing political ties with the Vietna-

mese, and Soviet aid and expertise, could not be balanced by the Chinese. Moreover, if Vietnam, by virtue of its size and proximity, posed a threat to Lao sovereignty, this was also the case many times over in the case of China.

Nevertheless, it is notable that the Lao government has maintained a relaxed attitude towards its ethnic Chinese community. In 1983, Chinese traders still dominated the free market in Vientiane. A Chinese school continued to operate. But the Maoist literature that had been available in Vientiane bookshops had disappeared by 1980. In the northern provinces, the government has made no serious attempt to bar border trade and other contacts with southern China. This approach is in notable contrast to that of Vietnam over such matters.

Overall, the march of events in Indochina offered the LPDR few options. The one it finally took was both logical and predictable – indeed, the only real surprise has been the relatively lenient treatment Laos received from the USA.

The Eclipse of Neutralist Communism

The Vietnamese invasion of Cambodia, or rather the political deadlock that made it inevitable, sealed the fate of Lao neutralist Communism. Immediately before the offensive the Thai supreme commander, General Serm Na Nakorn, claimed that most of the 40,000 Vietnamese troops stationed in Laos had been moved to the Lao–Cambodian border in preparation for an invasion. These forces were allegedly launched into Cambodia from staging areas in Laos, in a dramatic reversal of the Lao policy enunciated less than a year earlier of not allowing 'any country to use Lao territory to invade another country'. This propelled it irrevocably into the vortex of the conflict, and China could not be expected to overlook Vientiane's complicity in the invasion.

This, in turn, made the alliance with Hanoi vital to Lao security in 1978–79, for there was a possibility that China could strike at Vietnam through Laos. The Lao government was increasingly preoccupied with its northern border, for Thai pressure on Laos had eased considerably following the overthrow of Thanin on 20 October 1977. The new Thai government, headed by General Kriangsak Chomanan was committed to improving relations with all three Indochinese states. The economic blockade of Laos was lifted at the end of November, and an agreement for the resumption of flights by Thai International Airways was signed in early December. Around the same time, Kriangsak held a meeting with provincial governors in an attempt to harness them to the government's more conciliatory policy toward Laos and Cambodia. Right-wing

Lao and Cambodian refugee leaders were reportedly asked to leave the country.

Kriangsak and his followers were obviously aware that Bangkok's blockade simply deepened Lao dependence on Vietnam and its other socialist supporters. The signing of the treaty between Laos and Vietnam had clearly jolted the more astute politicians into realizing that Thanin's extreme anti-Communism was only isolating Thailand from the Indochinese countries.

During the Thanin period the Lao had little to retaliate with. One bargaining chip was restricting use of their airspace which, combined with a ban on overflights of Vietnam pending Bangkok's diplomatic recognition of the Hanoi government, was costing Thai International Airways dearly on its flights to Hong Kong. Not surprisingly, the airline lobbied Bangkok for a softer line on Indochina. Theoretically, the Lao could also have threatened to cut off hydro-electricity supplied from its Nam Ngum dam to northeastern Thailand. However, Laos could not afford the loss of revenue this would cause, and thus it was no real source of leverage.

The Vientiane government's only other bargaining chip was its provision of weapons and a base area for the Communist Party of Thailand (CPT). Both governments could play the game of promoting insurgencies. However, in 1977–78, Laos was supporting a still unified and potentially ascendant force, while the rightist Lao rebels backed by Bangkok, or at least its regional commanders, were fragmented and declining. Bangkok's fears over Lao support for the CPT were also fuelled by the consideration that the CPT was particularly strong in the northeast, a region characterized not only by poverty and agrarian discontent but also by a population that was predominantly ethnic Lao and by geographic proximity to Laos itself.

It was probably inevitable that Lao support, or otherwise, for the CPT would become an adjunct of its foreign policy. It was obvious that any substantial bargain struck between the Thai and Lao governments would involve the mutual cessation of active support for armed rebels in the other country's territory. Achieving such an agreement with the Lao was a central aim of Kriangsak's foreign policy, alongside his concern to stall the formation of an Indochinese bloc of states.

Accord was reached between the two governments in lengthy negotiations in 1978. The importance of this for Bangkok was underlined by the fact that a meeting to sign an agreement set for December was delayed only slightly by the Vietnamese invasion of Cambodia, while a shooting incident on the Mekong, which on other occasions would have closed the border, was ignored. In Vientiane on 6 January 1979 the prime ministers of Laos and Thailand issued a joint communiqué 'ushering in a new era in Lao–Thai relations of friendship, cooperation and peaceful coexistence'. The communiqué also included a Lao pledge to 'terminate all support previously given to the Communist Party of Thailand', whose ally, Pol Pot, was driven from his capital by Vietnamese troops the following day.

Forsaking the pro-Beijing CPT had been made all the easier for the Lao by Vietnam's growing tensions with China and Cambodia, and Pham Van Dong's renunciation of support for the Thai Communists during his mission to Bangkok in September 1978. The weakening of ties between Laos and China over 1978 also helped to rationalize the step. However, the Lao attitude to the CPT was primarily a direct product of bilateral negotiations between Vientiane and Bangkok, and their need for cordial relations.

According to CPT sources, the Lao and the Vietnamese had attempted since 1976 to try to reorientate their parties' strategy away from armed struggle. Unable to sway the CPT's leadership towards a strategy that would accommodate continued support from the Indochinese states, Lao and Vietnam finally disowned it. In the following year the fratricidal struggle in Indochina rebounded on the CPT, shattering its constituency into warring factions – some pro-Hanoi, some pro-Beijing and some independent. Since then the CPT has suffered a succession of military setbacks and mass defections, and its role in the regional power struggle, and in Thai politics as well, was over.

Conclusion

As we said at the beginning of this chapter, it is up to critics of the Lao–Vietnamese relationship to demonstrate the malevolence of Vietnamese influence. None has done so. The features usually identified as malevolent Vietnamese influence are in reality common to most Communist states to date – a one-party state, absence of liberal freedoms, collectivization, and so on. So, in a sense, the critique of Vietnamese influence is really a critique of Communism *per se*. Embedded in this critique are some weighty inferences that if the Lao Communists were truly Lao they would not be Communist; or if they are Lao and are implementing Communist policies then they must be doing it under duress or are somehow not really Lao. No doubt the latter explains the obsession of western commentators with the family relations of some Lao leaders which include a spouse or a parent of Vietnamese ethnicity. An unstated assumption is that these affinal or genetic connections explain the policies adopted. In other contexts such a racialist perspective has potentially serious consequences, as we shall see in the following chapter on Cambodia under Pol Pot. One did not even have to have a genetic connection there; one only had to be 'Vietnamese in one's mind' to invite extermination. A similar sort of racialism was sometimes expressed by the People's Republic of Kampuchea (PRK) when it implied that Pol Pot had Chinese ancestry; and the Vietnamese have also sometimes resorted to such racialist innuendo as have the Lao and the Thai. What is most disturbing is the ease with which western journalists and some academics have adopted the racialist categories of the various protagonists in the region. The idea that political ideologies of any kind are naturally homologous with particular nationalisms or with so-called 'national characters' – Vietnamese, Lao, Russian, American – strikes us as absurd and wholly unproven. Yet it is a pervasive assumption.

A related idea is that of national interest. Can the notion of national interest have any objective meaning independent of the state which rules the nation? Naturally there will always be different subjective perceptions about what is in the national interest, but that is something political parties argue about. The winner has the privilege of implementing a specific interpretation of the national interest, and it is this which is objective. Many writers fail to distinguish between the objective interests of, for example, the LPDR and their own subjective interpretations of what the Lao state's interests *should* be. All serious writers, including ourselves, agree that abstractly it is in the best interests of Laos to follow broadly neutral or non-aligned policies simply because of its lack of power and strategic location. Yet it has rarely been able to do this. Since 1975 its deviation from this 'ideal' state has usually been blamed on Vietnamese pressure and therefore Vietnam is shown to have damaged Lao national interest. States, however, do not exist in 'ideal' political vacuums and therefore objective national interest must be considered to be historically contingent. Brown and Zasloff are among the few writers who appear to recognize this when they write that the LPRP leaders regarded

the only plausible foreign policy orientation worth their consideration, neutralism, as fraught with grave dangers. A neutral Laos, they calculate, would be quickly severed into sharply contending spheres of interest; the Chinese in the north, the Vietnamese in the east, and the Thai along the Mekong valley.[12]

The examples given by various writers of how Lao national interests have suffered because of the alliance with Vietnam are: the enmity of China and the loss of its aid; aggravated relations with Thailand; and to a lesser degree strained relations with the USA. In a purely abstract sense this is all true. But, as this chapter has demonstrated, there were no realistic alternatives. Vientiane's alliance with Vietnam was motivated primarily by its relations with Thailand, whereas Hanoi's alliance with Laos was motivated primarily by its relations with China. Laos sought both diplomatic and military support from Vietnam in its disputes with Thailand, while the Vietnamese looked for diplomatic support from Laos in its dispute with China. It is in the very nature of alliances that allies support each other, especially in grave situations.

It is often implied, however, that this alliance has been imposed on Laos by Vietnam, but this can only be sustained by denying the significance of Thailand in Lao calculations – something most commentators have done. Leaving aside the neutralist scenario offered by Brown and Zasloff, few others have considered the implications of Laos breaking its alliance or 'special relationship' with Vietnam. Given that an alliance with Thailand was out of the question such a rupture with Vietnam would have required not only paranoid isolationism but an even more massive and probably bloody purge of the LPRP and Lao army than occurred in Cambodia under Pol Pot. Its magnitude would have been such that a 'Lao Pol Pot' probably would have had no alternative but to turn to China for military support at least. In this light, claims that China's foreign policy toward Laos was a benign support for neutralism looks far less convincing[13] and its consequences much more catastrophic than even Brown and Zasloff's scenario of partition.

What is especially peculiar about suggestions that the alliance was somehow imposed on Laos is that the commentators who either suggest this or openly assert it indicate that this alliance was an obvious and natural outcome of the long and close working relationship between the Lao and the Vietnamese Communists. Brown and Zasloff write:

> There have been no reliable indications that the LPRP leaders have been inclined to challenge the Vietnamese-directed policy line. Indeed, they have been so intimately intertwined with their senior partners since the outset of their revolutionary movement that they may not normally discern a Laotian national interest as distinct from the Vietnamese one.[14]

And Martin Stuart-Fox writes that 'Among old comrades, the need for a close and continuing "special relationship" between Laos and Vietnam is taken for granted.'[15] Yet simultaneously these authors wish to imply or openly assert that the Vietnamese are in 'control' of Laos and are somehow imposing unacceptable policies on it, a manoeuvre these authors usually accomplish by reference to an abstract concept of national interest. Stuart-Fox writes that Vietnam

> enjoys the power to exercise ultimate control over the political processes of the LPDR if and when it deems it necessary to do so. It is precisely this ultimate control which permits the relaxation of Vietnamese influence in Laos on a day-to-day basis, and leaves the Lao a degree of freedom of action in dealing with their own internal affairs.[16]

Until it is exercised, however, it is impossible to know whether Stuart-Fox's assertion of Vietnamese 'ultimate control' is in fact true. The empirical evolution of events in Laos, as we shall show later, suggests that it is not. Indeed, as these authors also partly recognize in more sober moments, Vietnam can live with a relatively non-aligned Laos.

Vientiane's foreign policy orientation after 1975 was not dictated by Hanoi, but by the conjunctural interaction of all the larger states surrounding Laos. Given the LPRP's long and close working relationship with the Vietnamese, it is not surprising that it should support them when the march of events finally forced a choice. Realistically, they had no other option. This, however, is not evidence of colonialism, 'neo' or otherwise. There is no evidence of Vietnamese economic exploitation of Laos – if anything the reverse situation applies. Laos is poor and has relied on Vietnam, the USSR and other Eastern bloc countries for aid and expertise to establish the most rudimentary aspects of a socialist economy. Indeed, Vietnam's influence in this area is limited because of its own poverty.

Arguments about colonialism or neo-colonialism do not help us understand the Lao situation in Indochina. There is no question that its alliance with Vietnam drew it into a quarrel it could do without – but then, in an abstract sense, Vietnam could equally have done without it. There is no question that Vietnam has been dominant in the alliance, but one cannot conceive of any alliance in which Laos would be the dominant partner. Disparities of power, however, do not add up to colonialism or political control. As we have seen, the alliance held mutual benefits for both parties.

Notes

1. Arthur J. Dommen, 'Laos: Vietnam's Satellite', *Current History*, December 1979, p. 201.

2. Martin Stuart-Fox, 'Laos: The Vietnamese Connection', in *Southeast Asian Affairs 1979*, Singapore 1980, p. 208. This is argued even more strenuously in a later monograph by the same author, *Vietnam in Laos: Hanoi's Model for Kampuchea*, Claremont 1987.

3. Dommen, p. 202. See also A.J. Dommen, *Laos: Keystone of Indochina*, Boulder 1985.

4. Cf., for example, Michael Akehurst, *A Modern Introduction to International Law*, London 1970, pp. 74–5. Oddly, two leading western political scientists apparently downgrade the importance of these formalities. MacAlister Brown and Joseph J. Zasloff, in their otherwise excellent *Apprentice Revolutionaries* (Stanford 1986) criticize Vietnam for maintaining the 'fiction of equality among the three Indochinese nations' (p. 241). But what else are the Vietnamese to do? Revert to pre-modern ideologies of tributary relationships between states? Modern international relations maintain the fiction of equality between states, and the United Nations is founded on it, yet no one believes that within that institution, for example, Fiji carries the same weight and influence as the United States or even Australia.

5. Paul F. Langer and Joseph J. Zasloff, *North Vietnam and the Pathet Lao: Partners in the Struggle for Laos.* Cambridge, Mass. 1970, p. 17. See also Joel M. Halpern and William S. Turley, eds, 'The Training of Vietnamese Communist Cadres in Laos', mimeo, 1977. The only serious sociological attempt to look at the Vietnamese in Laos in the post-1975 period, as far as we are aware, is Ng Shui Meng's short article 'The Vietnamese Community in Laos', *Sojourn*, vol. 1, no. 1, 1986.

6. By far and away the best account of this relationship is in Brown and Zasloff.

7. J.R.V. Prescott, D.F. Collier, and D.F. Prescott, *Frontiers of Southeast Asia*, Melbourne 1977.

8. Dommen, 'Laos: Vietnam's Satellite', p. 202.

9. Bunyaraks Ninsanda, *et al.*, *Thai–Laos Economic Relations: A New Perspective.* Bangkok 1977, p. 11.

10. *Far Eastern Economic Review*, 8 December 1978.

11. Elizabeth Becker, 'Laos: The Widening Indochina Conflict', *Indochina Issues*, no. 2, June 1979.

12. Brown and Zasloff, p. 244.

12. Stuart-Fox, *Vietnam in Laos*, p. 49; C.L. Chiou, 'China's Policy Towards Laos: Politics of Neutralization', in Martin Stuart-Fox, ed., *Contemporary Laos*, St Lucia 1982.

14. Brown and Zasloff, p. 240.

15. Stuart-Fox, *Vietnam in Laos*, p. 10.

16. Ibid., p. 20.

4

Cambodia: The Politics of Perfect Sovereignty

At first glance, it is not obvious why events in Cambodia should have taken such a contrasting path to those in Laos. Like the Pathet Lao, the Cambodian Communist movement originated as an outgrowth of the Viet Minh's struggle against French colonial rule in Indochina. As in Laos, the backwardness of the social and political milieu was reinforced by the relatively limited impact of capitalist imperialism on the outlying parts of French Indochina. The result was that in Cambodia the revolutionary movement remained weak and dependent on Vietnamese sponsorship for many years before developing its own momentum. As with the Pathet Lao, the Khmer Rouge was accused by its enemies of being a Vietnamese puppet. Both countries were strategically important to Vietnam, and the Vietnamese inevitably took a similar interest in the affairs of both Laos and Cambodia. One might, therefore, expect similar influences to produce similar outcomes in both countries.

As the reality of the conflict between Phnom Penh and Hanoi after 1975 became increasingly obvious, the view that the Khmer Rouge was a Vietnamese 'puppet' passed out of fashion. It was now discovered by some commentators that the Khmer Rouge consisted of Cambodian 'patriots' struggling against Vietnamese attempts to dominate Cambodia.

Early Disputes on the Vietnam–Cambodia Border

Elizabeth Becker blamed the outbreak of fighting on the Vietnam–Cambodia border following the Communist victories in 1975 on Hanoi's designs. She writes: 'Immediately there were volleys with the Vietnamese, who wanted to change the "bourgeois" boundaries and open negotiations over territory.'[1] A closer examination reveals that this claim is false. Clashes

81

on the Vietnam–Cambodia border were first reported in May–June 1975. The Vietnamese had agreed to withdraw from their Cambodian sanctuaries after the war ended in South Vietnam. Becker asserts that the fighting erupted because the Vietnamese were 'slow' to observe this agreement.[2] But the Vietnamese were not particularly slow in leaving. According to the Democratic Kampuchea (DK) regime's *Black Book on Vietnamese Aggression* the Vietnamese agreed to pull out in May–June, but the Cambodian side drove them out in April–May!

The Khmer Rouge closed the border with Vietnam at this time. They pursued and shot Cambodians trying to escape to Vietnam, as well as the departing Vietnamese. This led to incursions which bought them into conflict with Vietnamese troops stationed along the border.[3] In addition there was some confusion over where the border between Cambodia's Mondulkiri and Ratanakiri provinces and Vietnam actually ran on the ground. This is scarcely surprising in this remote area of rugged, jungle-clad mountains. But the poorly demarcated areas were not large. As Stephen Heder notes, the area in dispute was less than 100 square kilometres along the whole border.[4] There was no substantial territorial dispute on the land border.

There were also serious clashes over islands in the Gulf of Thailand in May 1975. Khmer Rouge forces based on Poulo Wai forcibly seized Phu Quoc and Tho Chu islands from the Vietnamese. Two weeks later Vietnamese forces recaptured these islands and pursued the Khmer Rouge back to Paulo Wai, and occupied it.

Such problems could still be settled by diplomatic means. In mid-1975 Pol Pot led a Cambodian delegation to Hanoi, and discussed the border issue with Le Duan. After he returned to Phnom Penh *Nhan Dan* announced that 'a complete identity of views' had been achieved. Pol Pot blamed the fighting on the geographic ignorance of local commanders. Le Duan agreed to return control of Paulo Wai to Cambodia. Border liaison committees were established to settle local disputes. They also agreed to a high-level meeting in June 1976 to work out a border treaty that would clear up any remaining problems.

But this meeting was never held. Preparatory talks in Phnom Penh in May 1976 broke down. The Khmer Rouge side rejected a Vietnamese proposal that anomalies on the land border could be eliminated by minor adjustments made on the basis of mutual consent. But when the Vietnamese presented their proposal concerning the maritime border, the Cambodians walked out altogether, and refused to rejoin the talks.

The French had paid little attention to the question of maritime borders, and subsequent governments in Indochina also had more pressing matters on their hands. In the 1960s a geological survey of the Gulf of Thailand found that large areas are potentially rich with oil. This helped focus attention on the ambiguities of maritime borders. The Cambodians claimed that the sea border between Vietnam and Cambodia was established by the 'Brevie line' laid down by the French in 1939 (see Map 2). This had not been intended to define a territorial boundary. Brevie had specified that 'only matters of administration and the police are considered here, the question of whose territory these islands are remains outstanding'. Nevertheless the Vietnamese had agreed in 1967 to use the Brevie line as the basis for establishing sovereignty over the offshore islands. But the maritime border, in the sense of a definition of territorial waters, was still unresolved. The Vietnamese did not want this to follow the Brevie line, because it made most of the coast of the Vietnamese island of Phu Quoc accessible only through Cambodian waters. They proposed that the border be drawn to give them easier access to Phu Quoc. In exchange, territorial waters further out to sea on the Vietnamese side of the Brevie line could be ceded to Cambodia in outlying areas. This would allow shipping easier access to the Cambodian port of Kompong Som.

The Khmer Rouge walked out in response to this proposal. In its statement of 31 December 1977, Pol Pot's government explained that the Vietnamese had 'rejected entirely' the maritime border to which it had agreed in the 1960s and introduced 'plans of annexation of a big part of the seas of Cambodia.' Becker's interpretation of these events is that Hanoi 'wasted no time in presenting the Cambodians with ... a difficult series of foreign confrontations'.[5] But the problem on the land border was not Vietnamese foot-dragging; nor was it Vietnamese actions which led to the fighting over the islands. In both instances, the immediate cause of problems was the trigger-happy approach of the Khmer Rouge. And it was the Cambodian side which rejected negotiations.

Furthermore, Vietnam was not the only country which found the Khmer Rouge regime a difficult neighbour. The opening of relations between Bangkok and the new authorities in Phnom Penh was also marred by clashes between Khmer Rouge and Thai forces in May–June 1975. Here, too, there was confusion over a poorly demarcated border and clashes resulting from Khmer Rouge attempts to seal the border and prevent the flight of refugees. For some reason, Becker does not interpret these events as Bangkok 'presenting the Cambodians with a difficult series of confrontations'. On the Thai as on the Vietnamese border, diplomacy smoothed over some of the initial problems created by the upheaval in Cambodia. Ieng Sary, the Cambodian foreign minister, visited Bangkok in October 1975 and signed a joint communiqué declaring mutual recognition of 'present frontiers' between the two countries, and respect for each other's 'independence, sovereignty and territorial integrity'.

The border between Laos and Cambodia is remote and short, and no problems were reported at the time. Later inquiries confirmed that it was peaceful until 1977 (see chapter 3).

If the early border problems between the new governments in Vietnam and Cambodia had been largely settled by the middle of 1976, why did war erupt between the two countries in 1977–78? Heder's answer is that these incidents brought the radically different perspectives of the two regimes into conflict. These problems came to a head at the May 1976 meeting and fuelled full-scale fighting in 1977. Both sides certainly had different approaches to the border problem. The Vietnamese adopted the position that the border established by the French should be accepted as an accomplished historical fact. Any adjustments made should be minor, and on the basis of mutual consent. They saw the territories ruled by the pre-colonial states as irrelevant, both legally and morally, to contemporary negotiations. But the DK regime took the view that the existing border was unfair to Cambodia, and that the Vietnamese should conduct themselves accordingly. Heder explains:

> The Cambodians approached the question as the sole aggrieved party, and expected a certain recompense for their historical losses and their willingness to cease contesting them. They offered not negotiations in the regular sense, but unilateral resolutions of outstanding problems that provided such recompense in a minor way. They demanded that the Vietnamese either accept or reject their proposals and not try to tinker with them.[6]

The Khmer Rouge saw 'Kampuchea Krom' – the Mekong Delta and the area around Saigon – as 'lost territories' to which Cambodia still had a moral claim. No doubt it occurred to the Vietnamese that to concede Cambodia's moral right to 'lost territories' that included Vietnam's most productive rice-bowl would be to pave the way for legal claims. These demands exhausted what Heder terms Vietnam's 'apparent flexibility' on the border issue. Even so, it should be noted, it was the Cambodians and not the Vietnamese who walked out.

The basis of the Khmer Rouge position was the fact that the Vietnamese had won the lower Mekong through war against the old Khmer Empire. Such 'historical' arguments have a strong appeal to nationalist passions, but next to no recognition in international law. If accepted, these arguments would also allow the Cambodians to advance similar claims against the Thai, the Lao, and even the Burmese, as well as the Vietnamese. Innumerable counter-claims could be advanced in the names of empires or city-states (most of them as defunct as the Angkor Empire) which suffered military defeats at the hands of the Khmer at some point in the past. It is obvious that 'historical' arguments of this sort open up a Pandora's box of revanchist claims and counter-claims. This is especially the case in the former colonial empires, where boundaries were decided by the military and diplomatic rivalries of faraway powers. Colonial boundaries often cut arbitrarily across local geographical and political realities. But they were mapped and recognized in treaties, which gave them a much sharper definition than the often ill-defined possessions of pre-colonial rulers.

Thus the rule generally accepted among Afro-Asian and Latin American countries is, 'as you possess, so you shall continue to possess'. Vietnam's position followed this principle; the Khmer Rouge position did not. It was not the Vietnamese who were unhappy with the 'bourgeois' border between the two countries, as Becker suggests, but the Khmer Rouge. And their point of reference was neither 'proletarian internationalism' or 'bourgeois' national sovereignty – it was the regional dominance of a 'feudal' empire.

Heder argues that with neither side willing to back down these border disagreements escalated steadily into full-scale war. Once war broke out between Vietnam and Cambodia, the DK side cited the border negotiations as proof of Hanoi's aggressive intent. But all this showed was that Vietnam did not accept Cambodia's revanchist stance. It did not show that Hanoi had any territorial claims on Cambodia.

Nor was there steadily intensifying conflict on the border itself. Heder speculates that, following the collapse of the May 1976 talks, both sides became 'more and more impatient with the deadlock' which 'probably' created mounting tension. But he himself reports that border incidents in the second half of 1976 were 'apparently infrequent and small-scale'. They were readily dealt with by the border liaison committees.[7] The fallacy in Heder's argument is the assumption that disagreements between governments must lead to war, that 'peaceful coexistence' is an impossibility. But the fact is that many border disputes remain dormant in many parts of the world because the governments concerned do not think it worthwhile pressing the issue. By mid-1976 the DK regime had established working relationships along all its borders, with Vietnam as well as with Laos and Thailand. Far from being the 'spark' that ignited a wider dispute, the tensions arising out of the instability of 1975 had been resolved.

But then, early in 1977, the situation suddenly deteriorated along all of Cambodia's borders, especially the border with Vietnam. It was this which set in motion the events which led to the Vietnamese invasion of 1978. What was it that overturned in 1977 the apparent stability that had been achieved in 1976? Why was it decided that it was now worthwhile trying to resolve the border disagreements by force?

The 'Indochina Federation'

The answer of the DK leadership was that Hanoi was determined to annex Cambodia into an 'Indochina Federation'. In June 1978 Ieng Sary asserted that the Vietnam–Cambodia conflict was not a 'normal border dispute'. It could not be resolved by diplomatic means because its roots lay

> in the fact that Vietnam has the intention of swallowing Cambodia, subverting and aggressing against it, attempting to engineer a *coup d'état*, to force it to join an Indochina Federation under its domination so that Vietnam can annex Cambodia within a set period of time and take a step towards fulfilling its ambitions in Southeast Asia.

The most detailed and authoritative version of the Khmer Rouge accusations was the *Black Paper* of September 1978, which purports to document Vietnamese designs on Cambodia from the fifteenth century to the present. The matters covered range from territorial annexation in dynastic wars to the 'sordid use' of Vietnamese girls. The historical exegesis concludes that the Vietnamese 'have always sought by all means to take possession of Cambodia's territory'.

A whole chapter is devoted to the question of the 'Indochina Federation'. All that is offered by way of documentation of Vietnamese Communist expansionist ambition is the name of the Indochinese Communist Party (ICP) in the 1930s. If the Vietnamese had no designs on Cambodia, the *Black Paper* asks, why didn't they call their party the Vietnamese Communist Party? In fact, that is just what they did! The name was subsequently changed in response to criticism from Moscow.[8] Far from reflecting Vietnamese designs on Laos and Cambodia, it reflected the Communist International's idealistic vision of socialist revolution sweeping away all divisions based on race and nationality.

Vietnam's repeated involvement in Cambodian affairs since the 1940s has flowed from geographical and strategic concerns which were far more compelling than the Comintern slogans dredged up from the 1930s by the *Black Paper*. The French drew forces from throughout Indochina for their war with the Viet Minh. In both Laos and Cambodia they tried to nurture anti-Vietnamese sentiment and mobilize native recruits for their army. In response, the Viet Minh leaders threw their weight behind anti-French forces in Laos and Cambodia.

The lesson they drew was spelt out by General Vo Nguyen Giap in 1950:

> Indochina is a single strategic battlefield, and we have the mission of helping the movement to liberate all of Indochina. This is because, militarily, Indochina

is one bloc, one unit, in both the invasion and defence plans of the enemy. For this reason, and especially because of the strategic terrain, we cannot consider Vietnam to be independent so long as Cambodia and Laos are under imperialist domination, just as we cannot consider Cambodia and Laos to be independent so long as Vietnam is under imperialist rule.

The colonialists used Cambodia to attack Vietnam. Laos and Cambodia have become the secure rear areas of the enemy and simultaneously their most vulnerable area in the whole Indochina theatre. Therefore, we need to open the Laos–Cambodia battlefield resolutely and energetically.[9]

Realization of the strategic importance of Cambodia and Laos did not lead the Vietnamese to promote the idea of an Indochina Federation. On the contrary, they dissolved the ICP, and encouraged separate national movements. But they did expect that the 'fraternal' national liberation movement in Cambodia would – like their Lao brethren – cooperate with the Vietnamese against their common enemies.

These lessons were reinforced when the Americans replaced the French as the main enemy. In due course the Second Indochina War also engulfed Cambodia and Laos as well as Vietnam, and the outcome was a new round of cooperation between the three national liberation movements. The First Indochina War had ended with anti-Communist regimes in power in Vientiane and Phnom Penh, with little interest in cooperation with Hanoi. The Second Indochina War, by contrast, brought Hanoi's wartime allies to power.

The Vietnamese maintained that the basic framework for the post-war relations between the three governments was laid down in the statement of the Summit Conference of the Peoples of Indochina in 1970. This recognized 'the independence, sovereignty, unity and territorial integrity' of the three Indochinese nations, and specifically pledged respect for 'the territorial integrity of Cambodia within her existing borders'. Relations between them would conform to the 'five principles of peaceful coexistence'. But the statement also put a strong emphasis on long-term cooperation:

The parties affirm their determination to preserve and develop the fraternal friendship and the good neighbour relations between the two countries, with a view to mutual support in the struggle against the common enemy and to lasting future cooperation in the building of each country according to its own way.

Prince Sihanouk, who headed the Cambodian delegation, said the keynote of the conference was a celebration of the alliance between Vietnamese, Lao and Cambodians:

Some 'experts' in the West like to write about the things which divide our three peoples, and dwell on 'traditional hostilities'. But we like to think more and more about the factors that units us. Today, above all, it is the fact that we are victims of American aggression. ... We are three weak nations against a giant. Unless we stand together, we fall singly. It is 'unite and win' against 'divide and rule'. ... This was the central idea of the Summit Conference of the Peoples of Indochina. ... We agreed that while each component would retain its separate entity, we would combine our efforts until final victory. For the first time the Indochina put together by the French would become a living reality. For that, at least, we owe our thanks to Richard Nixon.[10]

The Vietnamese elaborated the idea of wartime cooperation into the notion of a post-war 'special relationship' between Vietnam, Cambodia and Laos. 'We insist on a special relationship', a Vietnamese official explained in 1978, 'because there is not another example in history of such a relationship where the two people shared each grain of rice, every bullet, suffering and victory'.[11] This involved more than Communist sentimentality based on past struggles. The Vietnamese were also hoping for expanded economic relations, and cooperation in security matters.

All this was unacceptable to the men and women now in power in Phnom Penh. They despised and feared their wartime allies. Sihanouk later wrote of his own 'trusting and affectionate friendship with Pham Van Dong and Vo Nguyen Giap' during the war. But even then, he observed, the Khmer Rouge leaders spoke of 'the Yuon's [the Vietnamese] hypocrisy' and the 'need ... to beware of North Vietnam's desire for hegemony after our foreseeable joint victory over the Yankee aggressors and the traitor Lon Nol'.[12] After the war, they saw cooperation as a vehicle for Vietnamese domination, and peaceful coexistence as a betrayal of the Cambodian national cause.

Cambodian Communism and the Vietnamese

What had led the Cambodian Communists to view their allies and ideological brethren in Vietnam as the main enemy? Partly, it was a matter of the political culture within which the Khmer Rouge leaders had been raised. Khmer Rouge fears that Cambodia would be engulfed by a re-united Vietnam, their insistence that they be acknowledged as the aggrieved party in current border negotiations because of the territorial losses of the Angkor Empire centuries before – all this was taken over directly from the backward-looking royalist nationalism forged by Sihanouk in the 1950s, with its vision of Vietnam as the 'historic enemy'.

Specific factors reinforced this anti-Vietnamese perspective among Sihanouk's Communist opponents. As with Laos, we have seen that much of the early impetus in creating a Communist movement in Cambodia came from the Viet Minh. However, in Laos relations between the Pathet Lao and the Vietnamese remained friendly. Despite its weaknesses the Pathet Lao was a force to be reckoned with in a country characterized by a 'feudal' fragmentation of political power. Hanoi was never seriously tempted to sacrifice its interests to curry favour with the Royal Lao Government. The story was different in Cambodia.

The first generation of Khmer leftists were those who linked up with the Viet Minh during the war against the French. But the Communist movement remained weaker in Cambodia. At the time of the Geneva Conference, there were only about 2,000 members of the Khmer People's Revolutionary Party (KPRP). About half of these were forced to 'regroup' in Hanoi, and Sihanouk did not allow them to return. The handful of remaining pro-Communist activists in Cambodia formed a political party, the Pracheachon, but it never succeeded in becoming more than just another clique in Phnom Penh. In the late 1950s, the secretary of the party, Hieu Seng, secretly betrayed his followers to Sihanouk's police. The party's ranks were further decimated, and the survivors were left with a visceral fear of betrayal and treachery within their own ranks.

As Sihanouk destroyed his enemies and consolidated his power Hanoi and Beijing both cultivated his government. As Becker comments: 'North Vietnam and China were more concerned with keeping Sihanouk a friend than supporting a Cambodian communist challenge to his rule.'[13] The Vietnamese urged Khmer leftists to support Sihanouk's 'progressive' government, and turned a blind eye to his suppression of the Cambodian Communists. As a new Communist leadership took shape in Cambodia in the wake of the Hieu Seng débâcle, it blamed the party's misfortunes on Vietnamese 'treachery' as well as betrayals in its own ranks.

The new party leaders were drawn from a group of former student radicals, most of whom attended the elite Sisowath school in Phnom Penh and went on to university studies in Paris during the First Indochina War. Ieng Sary was the most active of the student radicals, and he played an important role in bringing Saloth Sar (later known as Pol Pot), a technical school student, into the Sisowath radical circle.

Unlike the original leaders of the People's Revolutionary Party of Kampuchea (PRPK), the student radicals had little contact with the Viet Minh. (Ironically, in view of later events, the only one to get any such experience was the first returnee from Paris – Pol Pot.) Indeed, many seem to have absorbed the anti-Vietnamese prejudices promoted by official French and Sihanouk political culture. They were all strongly nationalistic, but beyond that their ideas diverged widely, ranging from moderate social-democratic reformism to Maoist-orientated Communism. Some, such as Khieu Samphan, joined Sihanouk's Sangkum Party, and even served in his government. Others, such as Pol Pot, joined the PRPK and its 'front' organization, the Pracheachon. In the small world of 'progressive' Phnom Penh politics, they all knew each other and worked together to varying degrees. It is, in most cases, impossible to work out when particular individuals became members of the outlawed Communist Party. The PRPK changed its name to Communist Party of Kampuchea (CPK) in 1960, and Pol Pot became secretary general following the mysterious disappearance of his predecessor, Tou Samouth, in 1962.[14]

Whereas the leadership of the Pathet Lao remained in the hands of men and women for whom Vietnamese Communism had been a formative influence, in Cambodia the leadership of the CPK was taken over by young radicals on whom the influence of the Vietnamese was at best marginal, and who were coming to view the moderate line pushed by the Vietnamese as a betrayal of the revolutionary cause. Pol Pot and his colleagues were also becoming disenchanted with working in 'progressive' politics in Phnom Penh, inevitably centred around Sihanouk. The alternative was to abandon the capital for rural areas. In 1963 he and his supporters left Phnom Penh to mobilize the peasants against Sihanouk's government. They were able to reactivate some the survivors of the struggles of the 1940s and 1950s. But they won little support among the peasants of the central rice-growing plains and the Mekong valley. They apparently had more success among the minority peoples of Cambodia's mountainous northeastern periphery. The hill-tribe people of these mountains were resentful of the intrusion of the lowland state into their world, and were more easily incited to rebellion than lowland peasants.

Even so it was not until 1968 that Pol Pot's group felt strong enough to pronounce that the 'armed struggle' had been launched. Even so, it remained a guerrilla movement in its earliest possible stage – small and poorly armed bands whose main activity was raiding isolated police stations and small guard posts in attempts to acquire weapons. The peasant revolt at Samlaut, in western Cambodia, in 1967, and the government's harsh reaction, has led some to argue that the CPK was capitalizing on agrarian unrest and emerging as a major threat to the Sihanouk regime. This is not persuasive. The Samlaut revolt was based on localized grievances and it failed to spread for that reason, despite attempts by CPK cadres to organize other uprisings. Behind this lay the fundamental fact that exploitative relationships that have sparked off peasant rebellions elsewhere had not developed extensively in the Cambodian countryside.[15]

Resentment at the atrocities with which the Phnom Penh government had suppressed the revolt turned the Samlaut area into a redoubt for anti-Sihanouk forces. The CPK tried to seize the initiative, but with little success, and many of its sympathizers fell victim to government repression. On the eve of Sihanouk's overthrow, it still had only a few thousand men under arms (Pol Pot himself said 4,000), and perhaps 800 party members.[16]

Sihanouk feared that the Vietnamese were behind the activities of the Cambodian Communists. Pol Pot's efforts to foment 'armed struggle' in Cambodia thus immediately jeopardized Hanoi's good relations with the Sihanouk government. But, according to Pol Pot's *Black Book*, the Vietnamese had consistently opposed his 'line'. They argued that Cambodia was not ripe for a peasant revolution, and accused him of being 'ultra-leftist and adventurist'. As the war in South Vietnam escalated, the Ho Chi Minh trail became increasingly important to the Vietnamese Communists. They relied more and more on Sihanouk's willingness to look the other way, and their disagreements with Pol Pot's group intensified.

Pol Pot personally led a CPK delegation to Hanoi in late 1965 to thrash out his differences with the Vietnamese party leaders. These discussions went very badly. Pol Pot wanted firm Vietnamese backing for his revolution but, as the *Black Book* relates, the Vietnamese 'dragged on the discussions' and made a 'stand-up attack' on Pol Pot's position, after which he went to Beijing. It was at this point that Pol Pot discerned the 'true nature' of the Vietnamese.[17] Relations between the CPK leaders and Vietnam deteriorated once more after the events of 1967–68. Pol Pot went to Hanoi for another bout of acrimonious and unsuccessful talks in 1969. Again, he adjourned to Beijing afterwards. He was there when Lon Nol overthrew Sihanouk in March 1970.

Tensions between the Vietnamese and the Pol Pot group continued through the war of 1970–75, though they were now allies. These tensions became particularly acute from 1973. The Vietnamese succeeded in negotiating the Paris agreements with the Americans, bringing about a ceasefire in South Vietnam (temporary) and in Laos (permanent). The Americans also pressed for a ceasefire in Cambodia. According to the *Black Book*, throughout late 1972 and early 1973 the Vietnamese urged Pol Pot to negotiate. He refused, accused Hanoi of collaborating with the Americans, and claimed the proposed negotiations with Lon Nol were part of a Vietnamese plot to 'swallow' Cambodia. This argument threw the Vietnamese into a 'towering rage'.[18] In 1973 the Americans signed agreements covering Vietnam and Laos, and then launched a bombing campaign that dropped more than 250,000 tonnes of bombs on Cambodia in six months before Congress, to Kissinger's fury, halted it. Pol Pot blamed the devastation on the 'selfish egoism' of the Vietnamese. Sihanouk wrote that when he returned to Cambodia in 1975, he was impressed by the 'bitterness and even hatred' the Khmer Rouge leaders bore towards Hanoi over this 'sellout'.[19] Pol Pot's refusal to do a deal with Kissinger in 1973, which presumably would have led to the formation of a coalition government (as in Laos), precipitated immense destruction and prolonged the fighting in Cambodia for another two years. Pleas by the Lon Nol government in 1974 for unconditional negotiations were summarily rejected by the Khmer Rouge leaders. Even the announcement that the Lon Nolist side was laying down its arms was cut short on 17 April 1975 by a Khmer Rouge declaration: 'We are not coming here for negotiations; we are entering the capital by force of arms.'

Post-1975 attitudes towards Vietnam were undoubtedly heavily influenced by these historical factors – by the dominance of Sihanouk's traditionalistic, backward-looking nationalism, absorbed even by the revolutionaries who had set out to overthrow him; by the long-standing quarrels between the Cambodian and Vietnamese Communists; and by Pol Pot's outright rejection of negotiations as a way of settling disputes. But the peculiarities of the regime Pol Pot set up in Cambodia after April 1975 played a central role in the dispute.

The Purges in Cambodia, 1975–78

The Khmer Rouge came to power as a result of the social disintegration and political collapse that occurred when Sihanouk was overthrown and the country was abruptly propelled into the vortex of the Indochina war, rather than as a deep-seated movement of social protest and political change. By 1975 the CPK had 14,000 members and an army of 58,000.[20] Their ranks had grown enormously in a mere five years, but the Khmer Rouge had very few people through which to rule a nation of 7 million people, especially civilian cadres. About 3 per cent of the Vietnamese population and 1 per cent of the Lao population are party members. Had the CPK recruited as successfully as the Vietnamese Communist Party, its membership would have been more than 200,000. Had it done as well as the Lao People's Revolutionary Party, it would still have had 70,000 members, rather than a mere 14,000.

And it was not just a matter of numbers. Apart from the original core of high-ranking leaders, the Khmer Rouge won few urban recruits. Many of its middle-ranking cadres were veteran fighters from rural areas, and the rank-and-file were often teenage peasant soldiers. Very few possessed the administrative and political skills needed to run a modern state. This shortage was much more acute than in Vietnam, where the educated middle class was larger (if still small by western standards), and yielded many more recruits to the revolutionary cause than in Cambodia.

For six years before the overthrow of Sihanouk, Pol Pot had operated among Cambodia's most primitive peoples. Here he found his first truly reliable cadres, 'very faithful to Cambodia's revolution' and 'much feared' by enemies, as the *Black Paper* revealingly put it. By contrast, the lowland sections of the CPK were not to be trusted, for 'some elements' among them had been 'duped and corrupted' by the Vietnamese. Bitter experience had already made the Pol Pot group profoundly suspicious, and after the Hieu Seng affair, who could know who was a traitor? And then the upheaval of 1970 threw them into an unexpected alliance with the despised Sihanoukists and Vietnamese, and drew new recruits by the thousands into their ranks. The Pol Pot group exploited to the hilt the opportunities this situation presented, but they did not change their basic outlook. More supporters meant more people who might betray the cause. As the CPK grew, the regional party secretaries emerged as powerful figures, ruling quasi-independent fiefdoms and running their own army.

The 'centre's' response was to try to impose highly centralized top-down controls, and an obsessive secrecy. This went far beyond the preoccupation with discipline and secrecy normal in revolutionary organizations. One Khmer Rouge recruit later described the situation as follows:

> Contacts between the upper levels and the lower levels were like contacts between heaven and earth. . . . A comrade only knew about himself and himself alone. There was no question of knowing anything about matters of the situation in which one found oneself.[21]

At the same time the party's 'security branch', working under the direction of the highest leaders, set about eliminating those regarded as untrustworthy. This was not a matter of open arrests of known opponents of the party 'centre'. Those who were suspected simply disappeared, before they had a chance to do any damage.

Thus, even while the Khmer Rouge leaders themselves were collaborating with Sihanouk and the Vietnamese, they were quietly eliminating followers they regarded as pro-Sihanouk and pro-Vietnamese. As the Pol Pot group won ascendancy over the National United Front of Kampuchea (NUFK) policy in the Khmer Rouge zones increasingly reflected their ideas. These were a hodge-podge of ideas borrowed from non-Communist Cambodian nationalism and from the Chinese, and moulded by the Khmer Rouge's own wartime experiences – courageous, selfless leadership would win the loyalty of the masses, and arouse their enthusiasm; the old exploiting classes would be suppressed, and collectivization would replace the 'individualism' of peasants with firm discipline; fired by mass enthusiasm and strong leadership, these leaders believed, there was little that a disciplined people could not achieve.

Through such an approach the Khmer Rouge had vanquished its wartime enemies. Now these tried and tested methods would be applied to the problems of peace. Borrowing from Mao, and going one better, it would launch a 'Super Great Leap Forward' which would transform Cambodia from a poor, backward country to a modern agricultural one in five to ten years, and into an industrial one in fifteen to twenty years. This would all be done on the basis of 'self-reliance', and building up Cambodia's traditional strength, agriculture. It would rely on labour, not capital or machinery to do this. The nation would be cut off from the corrupting outside world, just as the 'exemplary' Khmer Rouge zones had been cut off from the Vietnamese and from the rest of Cambodia during the war.

Once they had taken control of their own destiny once more, and needed nothing from foreigners, no one would ever again be able to tell the Cambodian people what to do. This would not be tolerated even from 'friends' like the Chinese and North Koreans. As for the 'traditional enemies' lurking on Cambodia's borders, if they misbehaved a strong Cambodia would at last be in a position to teach them a firm lesson. It followed that, despite the coming of peace, the expansion and modernization of their military forces to match those of the Vietnamese and the Thai was a top priority for the Khmer Rouge.

With the collapse of the Lon Nol regime in 1975, the Khmer Rouge faced a daunting problem – some 3 million town-dwellers and refugees suddenly fell under their control. The Khmer Rouge apparat was already over-strained in the countryside. It had no chance of maintaining control – at least not the sort of control it thought necessary – in the towns. Indeed, it could not even organize food supplies for them (the Khmer Rouge did not have the logistics to supply its own army during the siege of Phnom Penh, and had relied on US food aid sold to it by corrupt Lon Nol officials). The towns were the strongholds of the 'oppressors', where even the common people were deeply infected with 'individualism'. But Pol Pot knew what to do. A hastily called NUFK Congress in February 1975 endorsed his proposal for the evacuation of the urbanites to rural areas.[22] There Khmer Rouge control was already firmly established, and there the urbanites could be 're-educated' in the virtues of collectivism and hard work.

Pol Pot explained his policies at his first 'press conference' (an interview with Yugoslav journalists) in 1978:

'We are building socialism without a model,' smiled the head of the Communist Party and Premier of Democratic Kampuchea, Pol Pot. 'We do not wish to copy anyone; we shall use the experience gained in the course of the liberation struggle. There are no schools, faculties or universities in the traditional sense, although they did exist in our country prior to liberation, because we wish to do away with all vestiges of the past. There is no money, no commerce, as the state takes care of provisioning all its citizens. We did not have money or commerce in the liberated territory either. The cities have been resettled, because this is the way things had to be. Some three million town dwellers and peasants were trying to find refuge in the cities from the depredations of war. We could not provide enough food for them, and there were imperialist plans to organize guerrilla movements and a counter-revolution in the populated cities. ... We evacuated the cities; we resettled the inhabitants in the rural areas where the basic living conditions could be provided for this segment of the population of new Cambodia. The countryside should be the focus of attention for our revolution, and the people will decide the fate of the cities.'[23]

The urban population was thus driven out into the countryside. Within a few weeks, however, it was decided that it was best to concentrate these new workers in the northwest, one of Cambodia's traditional rice-bowls. Hundreds of thousands of people were marched across the country, and the population of the northwest was doubled. At the same time, a purge was launched against those who had been involved in the army, police and public service of the Lon Nol regime. The severity with which these 'counter-revolutionary' elements were suppressed varied widely. In some parts, the severity of the repression was such that refugees fleeing the country were convinced that the government's objective was the complete extermination of the old upper and middle classes.

In the now almost empty capital, Pol Pot's group set about planning Cambodia's 'Super Great Leap Forward'. Ignoring the bombed-out and abandoned farmlands that surrounded them, they took estimates of Cambodia's arable land from pre-war textbooks. They took it for granted that, with no machinery or fertilizer, yields could be raised to three tonnes per hectare in a few years (it had been done in pre-war days). But in how many areas would they be able to achieve six tonnes? And how could they best utilize the resulting surpluses to achieve rapid economic development and rising living standards?[24]

In the countryside cadres drove half-starved people, working with little more than their bare hands, to plant crops and dig canals. Achieving the targets assigned by the 'centre' necessitated the imposition of a system of harsh discipline on the entire population. The violation, or neglect, of instructions was frequently punished by executions. So were manifestations of 'individualism'. Malnourished people were prevented from gathering food for themselves, and disease was soon rife. In the evenings, the cadres called weary people together for 'political education' and lectured them on the evils of individualism. Many probably had little more idea than their audience what this meant. But they did know what the price of failure would be.

The ascendancy of the Pol Pot group was by no means secure in April 1975. The government was still not even exclusively Khmer Rouge. Officially, it was still the Royal Government of National Unity of Cambodia. Sihanouk remained head of state, and Penn Nouth remained prime minister. Within the CPK leadership, there was open disagreement from figures within the leadership such as Hou Yuon. Furthermore, the party 'centre's' control over the regional apparatus was still limited. At first, things went Pol Pot's way. Hou Yuon disappeared in September 1975, presumably murdered by Pol Pot's 'security' forces. A new constitution was approved by another 'Special National Congress' allegedly held a fortnight after the evacuation of Phnom Penh, although the constitution was not proclaimed until 5 January 1976. Elections were held in March. On 4 April Sihanouk resigned, and the Royal Government was formally dissolved. Its place was taken by a DK government, with Khieu Samphan taking Sihanouk's place as head of state. Pol Pot, who had previously held no government position, now assumed the post of prime minister. Ieng Sary continued in the post of foreign minister.

The DK regime lacked most of the characteristic features of modern govenments. The impression one gets is that the government was little more than a temporary encampment of guerrilla leaders in the city they had conquered. The formal executive of the government functioned only intermittently. Government ministers were expected to fulfil their duties on a part-time basis and they devoted most of their energies to work in the rice-fields, and no bureaucracy was established to implement policy (apart from Pol Pot's secret police). As Richard Dudman put it, DK 'never really rose above the shadowy, underground insurgency it had been before it overthrew the previous ... government'.[25]

In mid-1976 news that things were not working out as planned finally filtered through to the CPK 'centre'. Pol Pot then dispatched Ieng Thirith (his sister-in-law, and Ieng Sary's wife) to investigate charges that there were shortcomings in health, food and housing conditions in the north-west. Thirith toured the region, and concluded that conditions were indeed bad.[26] This episode is instructive for two reasons. In the first place, the fact that the 'centre' was so out of touch with what was happening was indicative of the failings of the DK machinery of government. In the second place, Thirith's response was typical of the Pol Pot group. It apparently did not occur to her that the goals of the 'Super Great Leap Forward' might be unattainable. Instead, she decided that traitors in the northwest must be sabotaging its implementation.

The 'centre' feared that disillusion with their leadership was now spreading in the ranks of DK. Becker asserts that there was 'little reason for this', for regional and district cadres had faithfully followed the centre's orders to this point.[27] However, pressure for change was mounting. At about this time officials in the northwest sent a petition to Phnom Penh calling for 'the party to have mercy on the people' and adopt a 'democratic system'. Such a position must have had significant support within the central leadership. Pol Pot resigned the prime ministership in September 'for health reasons'. Becker reports that shootouts between rival Khmer Rouge groups took place in Phnom Penh at this time. Ieng Sary later described these events as a 'coup'. If so, it was at best partially successful. Pol Pot retained the party secretaryship, and Nuon Chea, a loyal supporter, took over the prime ministership. These events were followed by the first arrest of a top CPK leader, Keo Meas, not to mention the despatch of troops to carry out purges in the northwest. Pol Pot was made prime minister again in October,[28] but he made no official public appearance for almost another year.

Unlike Becker, Pol Pot certainly believed that there was widespread disillusion with his leadership. In late 1976, he showered the party with 'consciousness documents' defending his policies. One of these, from December 1976, has survived and has been translated. It makes absorbing but depressing reading. The party had the correct line, Pol Pot claimed. But in 'three-quarters of the country' it had failed to meet the people's need for food. This was because people failed to grasp the revolutionary line with sufficient firmness. These failures, in turn, were caused by a 'sickness' in the party, due to the presence of 'ugly microbes'. For ten years 'treacherous secret elements' had been 'entering the party continuously'. 'From every direction', he said, 'traitors continue their activities. ... They are waiting. they operate under every kind of appearance: hot, cold, open, secret, tender, vicious, and so on.' These people were aiming at removing Pol Pot's group from power and overturning his political line:

A group of traitors has hidden and buried itself in our flesh and blood. They have big plans. They would destroy our leadership; they would dissolve the Kampuchean revolution. They would take Kampuchea and make it dependent on foreign countries.[29]

Pol Pot believed that the way to overcome 'contradictions' like this was to go on the offensive against the enemy. Those who openly opposed his policies (as Hou Yuon had) were, of course, easy to deal with. It was more difficult to identify those who had not yet revealed their treachery in either word or deed. Pol Pot recommended the 'method of life-histories'. Over the next few months government offices in Phnom Penh were swept by arrests carried out by security forces loyal to Pol Pot. Confessions extracted by torture at the notorious Toul Sleng interrogation centre in Phnom Penh soon revealed how fruitful the 'method of life-histories' could be.

As she refuses to believe that there was serious disillusion with Pol Pot, Becker can see only 'madness', 'the spell and romance of violent revolution' in what was happening.[30] And it is true that, as always, much of what people confessed under torture was false and absurd. But much else shows that Pol Pot's fears that the CPK was by this time riddled with 'microbes' waiting for their chance were not misplaced. One of them was Hu Nim, Pol Pot's minister for information. He confessed he had become disenchanted with the 'Super Great Leap Forward' before the end of 1975. Trips to the countryside had convinced him that foreign aid, capital and technology were needed to build a 'system of plenty' in Cambodia. He discussed these ideas cautiously with like-minded people in private, but said nothing in public. He also confessed to being one of the party members 'who were heavily prone to private property, and who had middle-class, feudalist, and capitalist stands' who were 'greatly disturbed' by Pol Pot's 'consciousness documents' of late 1976. It is impossible to say how many such members there were.

One of Hu Nim's colleagues came out in open opposition to the Pol Pot line. But Hu Nim failed to support him. He remained silent for a compelling, if less than honourable, reason: 'I then conformed to the collective position – if I had not done so I would have had my face smashed in along with Prom Sam Ar.'[31] The fact that he had never once lifted his little finger against Pol Pot was not enough to save Hu Nim from a worse fate than his friend. Prom Sam Ar committed suicide before the 'method of life-histories' could be applied to him. Hu Nim was 'crushed to bits' in Toul Sleng prison in May 1977, after weeks of torture.

The purge at the 'centre' quickly spread out into a massive assault on the regionally based structures of the party–government apparatus. These involved renewed killings of those in the general population suspected of sympathizing with 'the enemy' – a term that now referred to the old local Communists as well as to the surviving remnants of the Lon Nol regime. Pol Pot himself played a large role in these events. In his capacity as general secretary of the party, he undertook an extensive tour of the country, personally investigating the loyalty and competence of many local cadres.[32] The purges were carried out by his lieutenants Son Sen and Nuon Chea, and by Khaing Gech Iev (better known as 'Brother Duch') who ran the secret police and personally supervised proceedings at Toul Sleng. Another key ally in this struggle was Ta Mok, the party secretary for the southwest.

The purges continued throughout 1977 and 1978, with some areas undergoing the ordeal twice in less than twelve months, the beneficiaries of one purge being wiped out in the next. The climax came in mid-1978, when Pol Pot finally moved in force against the eastern region. So Phim, the party secretary for this region, refused to implement many of the 'centre's' more outrageous demands after 1975. For a time, Phim got away with this. He was a tough leader with an independent power-base and an army than commanded respect from the 'centre'. But in 1977–78, he resisted Pol Pot's demands for a wholesale purge of 'traitors' in the eastern region. In May 1978 troops commanded by Son Sen and Ta Mok launched a full-scale military attack, and overran the eastern region. So Phim committed suicide, and his followers fled to the jungle. Some escaped to Vietnam.[33]

The eastern region, one of Cambodia's most productive rice-bowls, then became the scene of unrivalled brutality and devastation. Captured cadres of soldiers were killed on the spot; whole villages deemed unfaithful were massacred; and tens of thousands of people (perhaps hundreds of thousands) were forcibly deported to other regions, many only to be executed *en masse* when they reached their destinations. Most of the mass graves unearthed since the fall of the Pol Pot regime appear to date from this period.

It is unlikely that the human cost of Pol Pot's regime will ever be known accurately. The Heng Samrin government and the Vietnamese have charged that 3 million people out of a total of 7 million perished. For their part, the Khmer Rouge leaders have admitted excesses but insist that the figures were much lower. In February 1981 Khieu Samphan told us: 'Our estimate is that we committed excesses harming the lives of 3,000 people.' The DK leadership subsequently also said that 20,000 people had died as a result of food shortages in 1975. Such figures, of course come from parties to the dispute. Most observers would probably accept Amnesty International's estimate that between 1 million and 2 million people perished, mostly of malnutrition and disease. Amnesty put the number of executions by Khmer Rouge forces at 200,000 in 1975–77, and a further 100,000 in 1978.[34]

Under these circumstances, the Pol Pot group finally emerged as the unchallenged master of the country in 1978. The central government consisted of Pol Pot, Ieng Sary, Son Sen and their wives – CPK leftists who had followed Pol Pot's line from the early 1960s onwards – and a handful of others. Pol Pot, Nuon Chea and Ta Mok controlled the party apparatus. Khieu Samphan, who had taken over from Sihanouk as head of state in 1976, stayed on, the only one of the old Sangkum leftists who had joined with Pol Pot in the late 1960s to survive the purges. Apart from Pol Pot's faction, the entire leadership of the 1970–75 revolution had been swept away – of the seventeen Communists holding posts in the central government in 1975–76 there were only seven known survivors; and except for Pol Pot and Ta Mok, none of the 1975 party regional secretaries survived.[35]

Pol Pot himself finally resurfaced publicly in September 1977. The Chinese had long been pressing the Cambodians to proclaim the existence of the CPK (the identity of the ruling party in 'Democratic Kampuchea' had officially been a secret!). Pol Pot did so, and proclaimed himself as its leader in a marathon speech of five hours' duration, largely devoted to a tendentious and self-glorifying history of the party. The next day Phnom Penh radio announced that he was to make a state visit to Beijing.

The need to be strong in order to put Cambodia's 'traditional enemies' in their place was a primary justification for the 'Super Great Leap Forward'. In August 1976 Pol Pot explained that Cambodia had to move ahead at maximum speed because the 'contemptible people to the east and the contemptible people to the west' would always attack and torment Cambodia, and take its territory, while the country remained weak. Only if Cambodia was strong could it abandon a 'defensive position' and 'strike back' at its enemies.[36] In his December 1976 'consciousness paper' Pol Pot thought the main challenge was internal. But he spoke as if Cambodia was already at war, and it was only the strength of DK which was deterring Vietnamese attacks.[37]

Following the victory of April 1975, the Khmer Rouge leaders had expanded their army rapidly, with Chinese assistance. They also boasted of their military prowess, which had allegedly enabled them to defeat the USA singlehandedly. Sihanouk later related:

In September 1975, the first time I returned to 'liberated' Cambodia at the invitation of the Khmer Rouge leaders, I was surprised to hear Khieu Samphan, Son Sen, and Co. tell me, all smiles and looking perfectly pleased, that their soldiers were 'unhappy' with the Party because it would not give them the green light to recapture 'Kampuchea Krom' – that is, Lower Cambodia (South Vietnam) – as well as the border districts along the Thai frontier that had once belonged to Cambodia (Aranya, Surin, etc.). Son Sen, Vice Minister in Charge of National Defence, claimed his glorious 'revolutionary army of Cambodia' felt it could make quick work of General Giap's army, not to mention Kukrit Pramoj and Kriangsak Chomanan's much less imposing Thai army.[38]

Son Sen also informed Sihanouk that the 'Vietnamese threat' was like a cancer eating away at Cambodia's body, and that the survival of the Khmer people depended on its 'total eradication'. The Khmer Rouge leaders explained to Sihanouk that this would be accomplished with a 'three-part surgical operation':

1. Categorically refusing Vietnamese citizens, whoever they might be, the right to live in Cambodia. The Khmer Rouge efforts in this direction were the physical elimination of a large number of Vietnamese residents 'suspected of being agents or spies for the Vietminh or Vietcong' and the forced repatriation of all other Vietnamese residents. . . .

2. Giving all Cambodian men and women the order to work twice, ten times as hard as the Vietnamese people, in order, Khieu Samphan told me, to make

Cambodia much stronger from every point of view (military, economic, ideological). According to the Khmer Rouge leaders, this frantic work they were making their people do would turn Cambodia into an 'impregnable fortress'. . . .

3. 'Accepting' a large-scale engagement with Vietnam: to what end? The problem of Vietnamese sanctuaries had to be fought out; they must be eliminated. A 'more just' delineation of the border between Cambodia and Vietnam was also necessary. Finally, the threat of Soviet-Vietnamese expansionism had to be met head on. Without Democratic Kampuchea to stop it, it would end up spreading through the rest of Southeast Asia and even further.

In their official pronouncements, the DK leaders were much more circumspect. But refugees did remember lower-level cadres, including one as high as Ta Mok, talking of the need to take 'Kampuchea Krom' back from the Vietnamese.[39] The CPK leaders may thus have been under pressure from the wild men in their own ranks, as well as the moderates. As you cannot purge everybody simultaneously, the price of moving against the latter may well have been to give people like Mok their head on the Vietnam border, as well as internally.

Pol Pot believed that his external and internal enemies were working together against him. The core logic of his purges was that there is no such thing as honest disagreement, only treachery. Since the success of the 'Super Great Leap Forward' was essential to defend the country against its enemies, anyone who questioned it was *ipso facto* serving enemy interests. As suspected malcontents were purged, Duch toiled away at the 'method of life-histories' in Tuol Sleng to uncover the fiendish plots by the CIA, the KGB, and above all the Vietnamese, which were fomenting such disillusionment.

It seems clear, however, that the growing disagreement with Pol Pot's line was based on revulsion at its consequences rather than subversion by the Vietnamese or other outsiders. Certainly all the leading victims of the purges of 1976–78 had collaborated to a greater or lesser degree with Pol Pot and his version of 'patriotism' before this. The *Black Paper* offered no evidence of Vietnamese penetration other than a few insubstantial references to 'confessions'. This was presumably a reference to documents from Tuol Sleng, and Pol Pot was probably wise not to publish them. They revealed much about him, nothing about the Vietnamese.

As its support disintegrated, the CPK 'centre' also hoped that a major confrontation with Vietnam would rally all 'patriotic' Cambodians, even those who had suffered grievously at their hands, to their cause. Pol Pot had seen both Sihanouk and Lon Nol play this particular card, and now followed suit. Sihanouk relates that Pol Pot and Ieng Sary sought

to provoke Vietnam, despite their fears of reprisals. Sihanouk wrote of
Khieu Samphan:

> He unabashedly told me that 'to unite our compatriots through the Party,
> to bring our workers up to their highest level of productivity, and to make
> the yotheas' (soldiers') ardor and valor in combat even greater, the best thing
> we could do was incite them to hate the Yuons [Vietnamese] more and more
> everyday.'

Khieu Samphan added: 'Our *bang phaaun* [literally, older and younger
brothers and sisters] are willing to make any sacrifices the minute we
wave the "Hate Vietnam" flag in front of them.'[40] Thus the crisis that
shook the DK regime to its foundations in 1976 impelled Pol Pot's group
towards a suicidal confrontation with 'the contemptible people' to the
east and west of Cambodia.

Tension on the Thai Border, 1977

Before dealing directly with the eruption of fighting on the Vietnam–
Cambodia border, it is instructive to recall that it coincided with a rash
of incidents along Cambodia's borders with both Laos and Thailand.
This had nothing to do with Vietnam, and much to do with DK policies.
We saw in chapter 3 that the situation on the Lao border first became
tense at the end of 1976 and deteriorated thereafter. The situation on
the Thai border was much more serious. On 28 January 1977, Khmer
Rouge soldiers clashed with Thai troops at the village of Ban Noi Parai,
to the north of the frontier town of Aranyapratet. Both sides apparently
called for reinforcements, and thirty Thai and an unknown number of
Khmer were killed in the ensuing fighting.

The Bangkok government did its best to publicize the incident, charging
that a Cambodian invasion of Thai territory had taken place. Reporters
were taken to see the shattered, abandoned houses and the mangled
bodies, and generally accepted the Thai government's account. But Phnom
Penh asserted that the villages involved were on Cambodian territory,
and that what had happened there was an 'internal affair' which was
nobody else's business: 'The measures taken by the Government of
Democratic Kampuchea in its own territory are answerable to the absolute
sovereignty of Democratic Kampuchea.' It charged that the villages had
been bases for right-wing Khmer Serei ('Free Khmer') guerrillas whose
activities were being encouraged by the Thai military dictatorship.

It is not an easy business to establish the rights and wrongs of this incident.[41] The Thai–Cambodian border has not been properly demarcated to the north of Aranyapratet, and it runs through a flat, largely featureless landscape. Ban Noi Parai was apparently a recent settlement, and is not to be found on maps of the area, so on whose territory it was located is genuinely uncertain. The border zone was a centre of smuggling and insurgent activity despite vigorous Khmer Rouge efforts to suppress both.

Relations between the local Khmer Rouge and Thai authorities had already taken a turn for the worse before the shooting at Ban Noi Parai. It may well be that the military coup in Bangkok in October 1976 meant that Thai army and police on the border were given a freer hand, but the immediate catalyst was a Cambodian offensive against Khmer Serei encampments in the mountains to the south of Aranyapratet. The Khmer Serei fled into Thailand, and there were several violent clashes between the Khmer Rouge soldiers pursuing them and Thai border police.

Both sides responded by reinforcing their forces all along the border, and the undemarcated zone to the north of Aranyapratet immediately became an area of tension. When the Thai–Cambodian border liaison committees met in December, both sides blamed each other and the Cambodian side bitterly accused the Thai of actively supporting Khmer Serei activity on the border. Ban Noi Parai soon emerged as the focus of these quarrels, and the meeting broke up with the disagreement unresolved. Whoever was responsible for the violence at Ban Noi Parai three weeks later, it seems likely that it was a deliberate provocation.

There can be little doubt that this incident marked the adoption of a more aggressive stance on the part of the Cambodians. They ignored Thai calls for further meetings of the border liaison committee, and answered Thai calls for demarcation of the border with demands that the Thai abandon their support for the Khmer Serei groups. Reports of Khmer Rouge attacks on Thai villages and clashes with Thai border police and soldiers became almost a daily occurrence over the next few months, not just in the poorly demarcated sector around Ban Noi Parai, but all along Cambodia's western border. In August the Thai prime minister accused the Cambodians of about 400 incursions since the start of the year, and said that Thailand would have no choice but to go to war unless the Cambodians desisted.

Such were the first fruits of Pol Pot's attempt to deal with the 'contemptible people to the west' from a position of strength. But after August, the number of incidents on the Thai border fell off, and by January 1978 a Thai military spokesman was able to declare that the border 'has been quiet of late'. Phnom Penh's attention, one surmises, was increasingly absorbed by the crisis unfolding on Cambodia's eastern border.

The Vietnam–Cambodia Border War, 1977–78

The clash over Ban Noi Parai illustrates how readily minor clashes of
obscure origin can escalate into full-scale confrontations when both sides
are intransigent. Heder argues that this is what happened on the Vietnam–
Cambodia border. After the collapse of the May 1976 talks, both sides
became 'more and more impatient with the deadlock', and there were
'probably' mounting border tensions as a result. Such tensions ultimately
flowed from the contrasting ideologies of the two regimes, and, it is
implied, Pol Pot was no more responsible for what happened than the
Vietnamese.

This is plausible, but it does not fit the facts. The second half of 1976
was a period of calm on the border. Heder himself reports that actual
incidents were 'apparently infrequent and small-scale'.[42] They were readily
handled by the border liaison committees established for that purpose.
Tensions really erupted after Pol Pot's group triumphed in the Cambodian
inner-party struggle. It was no coincidence that trouble erupted at the
same time on all of Cambodia's borders, and it was not the result of
a Vietnamese–Lao–Thai conspiracy. It was the result of applying Pol
Pot's methods of 'resolving contradictions' to Cambodia's foreign relations.

In the first three weeks of January 1977 Cambodian forces launched
armed attacks on civilian settlements in six out of Vietnam's seven border
provinces. The worst attacks were in the provinces of Kien Giang and
An Giang, which run from the Mekong River to the coast. They are
also opposite Cambodia's southwest region, run by Ta Mok. In May
the capital of An Giang province, Chau Doc, and the coastal town of
Ha Tien (population 30,000) were bombarded by Cambodian artillery.
Vietnamese boat people arriving in other countries from this region had
at the time reported heavy fighting and widespread Khmer Rouge atrocities. Later, Khmer refugees from the border area also confirmed that
the Cambodian side had attacked Vietnam. Nor did the Pol Pot regime
deny the charges.

Heder admits that the Cambodian side was responsible for initiating
hostilities in 1977. As he puts it, the Pol Pot regime decided to 'increase
the pressure' on Vietnam by sending troops to 'demonstrate a Cambodian
presence' in the Vietnamese-held areas to which the Cambodian side had
laid claim. When the Vietnamese responded to this 'intensified patrolling'
by reinforcing their border defences, the Cambodian side 'began to initiate
military activities' on the border in April 1977. By this stage, he says,
they were no longer concerned with disputed areas, but were trying to
'demonstrate that the Cambodians had a capability to strike at Vietnamese
territory'. All this Heder sees as part of a 'negotiating strategy':

The Cambodians probably saw themselves attempting to break the deadlock by suggesting that they were willing to make it costly ... for the Vietnamese to rely upon their superior military strength to maintain the status quo. ... [These] Cambodian military initiatives were part of a negotiation strategy. The Cambodians were not making any new territorial claims nor were they trying to permanently occupy any of the targets of their attacks. Rather, they still believed themselves to be responding in kind to what they saw as long standing de facto Vietnamese aggression against Cambodian territory.[43]

This is probably how the DK regime did see the situation. But this analysis (which Heder does not criticize) was as dangerously detached from reality as the drive for the three-tonne harvest yield inside Cambodia.

According to this topsy-turvy logic, armed attacks on undisputed Vietnamese territory to enforce a demand for the unilateral right to adjust the border at Vietnam's expense were 'defensive' in character. Military actions, including the slaughter of civilians, are just a peacetime 'negotiating tactic' – even though it was the DK side which was refusing to negotiate. For, as Heder has already explained, the Khmer Rouge leaders understood 'negotiations' to be the unconditional acceptance of their demands by the other side. And if the Vietnamese resist unconditional demands, and defend their territory and citizens against armed attack, they are guilty of 'aggression'.

This is convoluted, apologetic nonsense. Vickery is surely right to call a spade a spade:

Whatever Cambodian sensitivities may have been, a unilateral claim to an exclusive privilege to readjust a border agreed to with another country can have no validity in international law, and military actions taken to enforce such claims are hostilities pure and simple. ... [The] initial Cambodian attacks in 'disputed zones', as Heder describes them, and even more the further attacks in areas clearly Vietnamese were ... violations [of international law], and they justified, in traditional practice, a military response.[44]

Through his determination to put the 'contemptible people to the east' in their place, Pol Pot was leading his regime down an exceedingly dangerous path.

The Vietnamese responded to these attacks by building up their border defences, but they apparently did not launch any counter-attacks in the first half of 1977. The Vietnamese responded passively to early Cambodian attacks, in the hope that restraint would make a negotiated settlement easier. On 7 June they sent a conciliatory letter to Phnom Penh, proposing that a high-level meeting should be held to resolve the border problem as soon as possible. The Pol Pot government rejected this proposal on 18 June. With the failure of this diplomatic initiative, the Vietnamese began moving towards the military option. In July General Giap made a heavily publicized inspection tour of the border regions. This was a clear warning to the Cambodian side to desist. But on 24 September, shortly after Pol Pot's re-emergence from obscurity and just before his triumphant visit to Beijing, Khmer Rouge forces launched an attack into Vietnam's Tay Ninh province and slaughtered hundreds of civilians.

Hanoi retaliated with force. According to Nayan Chanda, a week after the Cambodian attack, Vietnamese forces quickly thrust deep into Svay Rieng province, and then withdrew. The Khmer Rouge units who came after them in hot pursuit were drawn into an ambush on Vietnamese soil, and suffered heavy casualties. Fighting continued on the border into December, when Vietnamese forces again struck deep into Cambodia. They withdrew in early January 1978. Hoang Tung, the editor of *Nhan Dan*, told Chanda that the Vietnamese purpose was 'first to chase them from our territory and then deal a heavy blow to their divisions, to make them realize that we are not as passive as they have assumed and to tell them that they have to choose the other solution – negotiations.'[45]

These actions did not jolt the Khmer Rouge leaders into a more restrained stance. Instead, Phnom Penh chose to escalate the dispute. On 31 December 1977 it broke off diplomatic relations with Hanoi and finally made the whole dispute public by launching a barrage of propaganda against Vietnam. Nor did the Khmer Rouge leaders respond favourably when Vietnam withdrew its forces in January. They vaingloriously saw this as proof that the Vietnamese were weak and cowardly, and in retreat. In its statement of 31 December the Cambodian government declared its willingness to engage in negotiations over the border conflict 'in a spirit of friendship'. But when the Vietnamese responded with a call for the two sides to 'meet as early as possible, at whatever level, so as to solve together the border issue between the two countries in a spirit of brotherly friendship' the Cambodians refused. A statement by the DK Ministry of Information on 3 January 1978 declared that the Vietnamese would have to 'first create an atmosphere of friendship and mutual confidence' before the DK government would consent to negotiate with them.

Following the withdrawal of their troops in January, the Vietnamese again offered to negotiate. On 5 February 1978 Deputy Foreign Minister Nguyen Co Thach proposed an immediate end to all hostilities on the border, a withdrawal of the armed forces of both sides to five kilometres from the border, and a conference to draw up a treaty 'on the basis of respect for each other's territorial sovereignty within the existing border' and reach agreement on 'an appropriate form of international guarantee and supervision'. The Cambodian side refused to discuss these proposals on the grounds that they had not been transmitted to Phnom Penh via official channels (the Vietnamese embassy there having been closed). The Vietnamese then sent a letter describing these proposals to Ieng Sary via the Lao ambassador to Phnom Penh, but Sary refused to accept the note. Pol Pot himself finally went on Phnom Penh Radio on 12 April to give the Cambodian response. He reiterated DK's refusal to negotiate, and proclaimed Cambodia's 'right' to 'demand the revision of border documents and changes in the demarcation of land and sea borders', and 'the resettlement of the "Kampuchea Krom" issue'.

Over the following months the diplomatic deadlock continued. In June 1978 the Cambodian Foreign Ministry justified the Cambodian refusal to negotiate by declaring that the Vietnamese proposals were aimed at 'misleading world opinion' and that the proposal to withdraw Cambodian troops five kilometres from the border 'automatically lets Vietnam annex a belt of Cambodia's territory five kilometres wide'. Meanwhile, the military conflict intensified, a development for which the Cambodian side openly claimed responsibility. On 10 May Phnom Penh Radio stated that after the 'victory' over the Vietnamese in January 'we did not let the Vietnamese initiate further attacks against us, but kept on launching attacks against them'. It is clear that the main responsibility for the conflict lay with the regime in Phnom Penh. The early clashes on the land border had been resolved, and practical measures for dealing with any future ones had been adopted. There were disagreements over the maritime border, but when the crisis came these played no significant role. It was the Cambodian side that initiated the fighting in 1977, escalated it, and then blocked any negotiated solution.

Elizabeth Becker writes: 'While it is clear that Cambodia started the border war with Vietnam, it is less obvious why Vietnam interpreted that challenge as an invitation to invade and occupy Cambodia.'[46] She speculates that they may been impelled by an ancestral drive to secure control over the Mekong valley. Needless to say, she does not produce a jot of evidence in support of this. But no such woolly speculation is needed to explain Vietnam's reaction. In two years, the Khmer Rouge destroyed twenty-five townships and ninety-six villages, and rendered 257,000 Vietnamese people homeless. One hundred thousand hectares of farmland had to be abandoned because of the fighting. No government can tolerate such destruction for long without striking back.

The Road to Invasion

The Vietnam Communist Party's Central Committee was in a grim mood when it met after DK rejected the ceasefire proposals of 5 February 1978. Since the Pol Pot faction had blocked every attempt at a peaceful settlement, it seemed obvious that there would be no peace until Pol Pot was removed. A military invasion was one possibility, but the Central Committee opted for the alternative of throwing its full weight behind the anti-Pol Pot forces within the CPK and backing them with Vietnamese military force if it proved necessary.

The first public signs of the shift in Vietnamese policy towards Cambodia appeared in early April. In addition to denunciations of the Pol Pot clique and its murderous policies, Hanoi Radio now began issuing open calls for the Cambodian people to overthrow the regime. Then General Hoang Cham, who had commanded the Vietnamese forces fighting in Cambodia in 1970–72, was put in charge of the Vietnamese troops in the border region. Hanoi also encouraged the organization of an anti-Pol Pot resistance movement among the large Cambodian refugee population in Vietnam (more than 150,000 people). When Nayan Chanda spoke to Cambodian refugees at a camp in Tay Ninh province, Khmer Communists were busy organizing a resistance movement. Many of the people he spoke to were eager to return to Cambodia to overthrow the Phnom Penh regime, and 2,000 people had already been recruited at this particular camp. Not all were Communists. One man Chanda spoke to said that, while he was not a Communist himself, he accepted that this movement would establish another Communist government in Phnom Penh – at least, he said, 'it will be a Communist government with justice, not barbaric like the present one'.[47]

The Vietnamese also tried to establish contact with the anti-Pol Pot forces controlling Cambodia's eastern region. The *Black Paper* alleges that the Vietnamese began plotting with So Phim only in February 1978. However Pol Pot struck in force against the eastern region before anything came of these contacts, if indeed they did occur. The survivors of So Phim's forces who made it across the border to Vietnam were led by his deputy military commander, Heng Samrin. The elimination of the eastern region Communists ended the possibility of Pol Pot's overthrow by an internal upheaval, and after that the conflict headed for a straightforward military denouement. Through the rest of the rainy season both sides reinforced their troops along the border. By the end of October 1978 General Cham had 100,000 troops under his command. Cambodian anti-Pol Pot forces, operating mainly as small guerrilla units, numbered somewhere between 10,000 and 20,000. Facing them were 60,000 Khmer Rouge troops, two-thirds of all Pol Pot's forces.

Meanwhile, a frantic race for diplomatic support went on. China was Pol Pot's main backer, and the Vietnamese increasingly looked on Pol Pot as a tool of Beijing. Hanoi moved to protect itself from Chinese retaliation by committing Vietnam more firmly to the Soviet bloc – joining the Council for Mutual Economic Assistance (Comecon) in July and signing a 25-year treaty of friendship with Moscow in November. Both sides set about wooing ASEAN countries in earnest. Pham Van Dong made a tour, offering treaties of friendship to anyone who was interested. Ieng Sary patched up relations with Thailand (they had been strained by some over-enthusiastic Khmer Rouge forays into Thailand in April and May 1978), established trade relations with Singapore, and visited the Philippines and Japan. Chinese Vice-Premier Deng Xiaoping did the rounds in November, trying to counter Dong's tour.

On 3 December 1978 Hanoi Radio announced that a Kampuchean National United Front for National Salvation (KNUFNS) had been established 'somewhere in the liberated area' of Cambodia, with Heng Samrin as president. It issued a programme calling for the overthrow of 'the reactionary Pol Pot–Ieng Sary clique' and the establishment of a regime 'tending towards genuine socialism'. Phnom Penh responded six days later, branding KNUFNS as 'a Vietnamese political organization with a Khmer name' and a tool of 'the Soviet expansionists'.

The Vietnamese finally launched their military onslaught against the Pol Pot regime on Christmas Day 1978 with twelve divisions (about 120,000 troops). The attack was directed by the Vietnamese army chief of staff, General Van Tien Dung, who had been in charge of the final Communist offensive in South Vietnam in 1975. They faced a DK army expanded to 100,000 with hastily drafted youths. Becker, who visited Cambodia at this time, commented: 'The new army of Democratic Kampuchea resembled Lon Nol's old forces in its sloppy training and its air of hysteria more than it did the Khmer Rouge who had won the 1970–75 war.'[48] The Khmer Rouge concentrated half its forces in Svay Rieng and Kompong Cham provinces in expectation of a Vietnamese offensive along Highway 1, the most direct route from Ho Chi Minh City (Saigon) to Phnom Penh. But Dung opened the campaign with flanking attacks. In the north troops under the command of General Hoang Cham struck from Ban Me Thuot and Pleiku towards Kratie and Stung Treng. They ran into relatively light resistance, and the provincial capitals fell on 30 December and 3 January. Forces commanded by General Le Duc Anh attacked along roads leading to Kompong Cham in the centre, and Takeo in the south. General Anh pounded the Khmer Rouge main forces around Highway 1 with fierce artillery and air attacks for a week before committing troops in the Parrot's Beak salient. There were two days of heavy fighting before the Khmer Rouge defence line collapsed.

By 4 January, most of Cambodia east of the Mekong was in the hands of the Vietnamese. That, according to Chanda, had been Vietnam's initial objective. It created a security buffer protecting Vietnam's borders from attack by Pol Pot's forces, and delivered territory and population into the control of KNUFNS which it would organize for the next stage of the struggle. But the speed and completeness with which the Khmer Rouge military and political apparatus fell apart in the face of the Vietnamese offensive tempted Hanoi to go for broke. It launched a three-pronged drive to capture Phnom Penh.[49]

In the Cambodian capital, Pol Pot was still insisting that all was well. On 5 January Phnom Penh Radio declared: 'News of the victories of our revolutionary troops ... has been received every day and makes our people happy and satisfied. It also makes us trust and be confident in our heroic struggle. We are confident we must win.' Two days later Pol Pot fled Phnom Penh, and the Vietnamese entered the city unopposed. Ieng Thirith later told Becker that the Khmer Rouge packed only a few clothes, because they thought they would be back soon.[50] It seems that the delusions remained intact almost to the end.

Having captured Phnom Penh, the Vietnamese struck out into western Cambodia. By now the Khmer Rouge forces were falling apart everywhere. Three weeks after the attack began the Vietnamese were in control of all the main towns and communications in Cambodia. They began moving out along the sideroads to mop up the remaining Khmer Rouge forces. In many places, they found that villagers had already driven out or disarmed Khmer Rouge cadres and fighters.[51]

By the end of January 1979 Pol Pot's forces were regrouping, and starting to strike back. But nowhere did they regain the initiative. In March and April the Vietnamese launched a series of sweeps to clear Khmer Rouge forces from the rice-growing plains of western Cambodia, forcing them to retreat into the mountains of southwestern Cambodia or to the Thai border. On 10 April they captured a heavily defended underground complex at Ta Sanh, which the Khmer Rouge leadership had been using as a headquarters – they were forced to leave it so quickly that the Vietnamese captured Ieng Sary's passport, along with many documents.

At one point Pol Pot's forces escaped only by retreating into Thailand. Western journalists watched as between 50,000 and 80,000 people trekked for fifty kilometres along roads well on the Thai side of the border before re-entering Cambodia. There were thousands of tough young soldiers herding along a captive workforce of sullen and malnourished villagers at gunpoint – 'a walking concentration camp' was how one of the observers later described this weary procession. The military situation stabilized in May and June 1979, as the monsoon rains set in. The Vietnamese were in control of the main populated parts of the country, the eastern border region, and the central and western rice-growing plains, but security was still poor in the outlying districts. The Pol Pot forces controlled areas in the largely uninhabited mountains of the southwest, and along the Thai border. The only significant town still in their hands was Pailin.

From these bases they could still range through much of the western part of the country and through the southern mountains, and they could launch occasional raids on the highways between Phnom Penh and Battambang, and between Phnom Penh and Kompong Som. There were also units loyal to Pol Pot operating in Kompong Thom and Ratanikiri provinces, in the centre and east of the country, but they preferred to lie low for the time being. On the whole, it was clear that Khmer Rouge control of the people of Cambodia had been broken.

Pol Pot's army had been severely mauled. Western intelligence sources estimated that its numbers had fallen to 35,000 by mid-1979; in six months' fighting it had lost two-thirds of its number. Nevertheless, it remained a functioning military force, and the DK leadership was intact on the Thai border. Within a few weeks it had regrouped and was trying to rally support inside and outside Cambodia for a struggle against the new, Vietnamese-sponsored government in Phnom Penh.

Notes

1. Elizabeth Becker, *When the War Was Over*, New York 1986, p. 181. No sources are given for this assertion, despite the use of inverted commas suggesting a direct quotation.

2. Ibid., p. 207.

3. Barry Wain, *The Refused: The Agony of the Indochina Refugees*, Hong Kong 1981, pp. 50–51.

4. Stephen R. Heder, 'The Kampuchean–Vietnamese Conflict', in David W.P. Elliott, ed., *The Third Indochina Conflict*, Boulder 1981, p. 28.

5. Becker, p. 207.

6. Heder, p. 25.

7. Heder, pp. 31–2.

8. William J. Duiker, *The Communist Road to Power in Vietnam*, Boulder 1981, p. 143.

9. Quoted by William S. Turley, 'Vietnam/Indochina: Hanoi's Challenge to Regional Order', in Young W. Kihl and Lawrence E. Grinter, eds, *Asian-Pacific Security: Challenges and Responses*, Boulder 1986, pp. 183–4.

10. Norodom Sihanouk, *My War with the CIA: Cambodia's Struggle for Survival*, Harmondsworth 1973, pp. 182, 185.

11. Quoted by Nayan Chanda, *Brother Enemy*, San Diego 1986, p. 122.

12. Norodom Sihanouk, *War and Hope: The Case for Cambodia*, London 1980, pp. 16–17.

13. Becker, p. 115. It is thus hard to understand why Becker elsewhere (pp. 104, 109) asserts that the Vietnamese encouraged a new, aggressively anti-Sihanouk leadership at this time. She does not document this claim.

14. Ben Kiernan, *How Pol Pot Came to Power*, London 1985, pp. 197–8, 241 (fn. 135), suggests that he may have been murdered by Pol Pot's group. The evidence for this is very flimsy. We are inclined to suspect Sihanouk's police, but in the absence of any solid evidence the only reasonable verdict is an open one.

15. The most detailed examination of these events is in Ben Kiernan, 'The Samlaut Rebellion 1967–68', in Ben Kiernan and Chanthou Boua, *Peasants and Politics in Kampuchea 1942–81*, London 1981. See also Kiernan, *How Pol Pot Came to Power*, pp. 249–58, and W.E. Willmott, 'Analytical Errors of the Kampuchean Communist Party', *Pacific Affairs*, vol. 54, 1980.

16. Kiernan, *How Pol Pot Came to Power*, p. 284.

17. *Black Book on Vietnamese Aggression*, p. 22.
18. Ibid., p. 69.
19. Sihanouk, *War and Hope*, p. 21.
20. Becker, p. 179, quoting an unpublished paper by Tim Carney.
21. Hem Samin, quoted by Becker, p. 150.
22. William Shawcross, *Sideshow*, London 1979, p. 373; Ben Kiernan, 'Wild Chickens, Farm Chickens and Cormorants: Kampuchea's Eastern Zone under Pol Pot', in David P. Chandler and Ben Kiernan, eds, *Revolution and its Aftermath in Kampuchea*, New Haven 1983.
23. Slavko Stanic, 'Kampuchea – Socialism without a Model', *Socialist Theory and Practice* (Belgrade), October 1978, p. 67.
24. Cf. 'The Party's Four-Year Plan to Build Socialism in All Fields, 1977–1980', in David P. Chandler, Ben Kiernan and Chanthou Boua, eds, *Pol Pot Plans the Future: Confidential Leadership Documents from Democratic Kampuchea, 1976–1977*, New Haven 1988.
25. Richard Dudman, 'Cambodia – A Land in Turmoil', *St Louis Post–Dispatch*, 15 January 1979.
26. Becker, pp. 246–7.
27. Ibid., p. 273.
28. Michael Vickery, *Cambodia 1975–1982*, Sydney 1984, p.148.
29. 'Report of Activities of the Party Centre According to the General Political Tasks of 1976', in Chandler, Kiernan and Boua, pp. 184–6, 189.
30. Becker, pp. 281, 288.
31. 'Planning the Past: the Forced Confession of Hu Nim', in Chandler, Kiernan and Boua, p. 313.
32. Gareth Porter, 'Vietnamese Policy and the Indochina Crisis', in D. Elliott, ed., *The Third Indochina Conflict*, Boulder 1981.
33. Cf. Kiernan, 'Wild Chickens', and Vickery, pp. 131–8, 172. Becker, p. 193, challenges the view that there was a rift between Pol Pot and So Phim. She argues that Phim was a ruthless man who did not hesitate to shoot those who opposed him, ran a 'fierce' and disciplined army, and 'was as close to the inner circle as any zone secretary'. This is no doubt true, but it merely underscores Pol Pot's for reasons thinking carefully before moving against him. Becker herself notes that So Phim was able to 'adopt an independent stance on a number of issues', including allowing peasants to 'keep large shares of their harvest'.
34. Amnesty International, *Kampuchea: Political Imprisonment and Torture*, London 1986, pp. 16–17. These estimates are given as background in a study of developments since 1979, and no explanation of the figures is provided. Vickery (pp. 184–8) argues that total deaths due to the regime were more likely to have been closer to 740,000 than 1–2 million. Since Vickery's estimate of the numbers executed (between 200,000 and 300,000) is close to Amnesty's, the disagreement is about the prevalence of lethal diseases, not the lethality of the DK regime.
35. Cf. Kiernan, 'Pol Pot and the Kampuchean Communist Movement'; Vickery, pp. 144–9.
36. 'Preliminary Explanation before Reading the Plan, by the Party Secretary', in Chandler, Kiernan, and Boua, pp. 126–7.
37. 'Report of Activities of the Party Centre', pp. 190–91.
38. Sihanouk, *War and Hope*, p. 38.
39. Ben Kiernan, 'New Light on the Origins of the Vietnam–Kampuchea Conflict', *Bulletin of Concerned Asian Scholars*, vol. 12, no. 4, October–December 1980; Vickery, pp. 190–94.
40. Sihanouk, *War and Hope*, pp. 45–6.
41. The most thorough attempt is by Larry Palmer, 'Thailand's Kampuchea Border Incidents', *News from Kampuchea* (Sydney), vol. 1 no. 4, October 1977.
42. Heder, pp. 31–2.
43. Ibid., p. 32.
44. Vickery, p. 196.
45. Chanda, *Brother Enemy*, p. 206.
46. Becker, p. 336.
47. Nayan Chanda, *Far Eastern Economic Review*, 21 April 1978.

48. Becker, p. 326.
49. Chanda, *Brother Enemy*, pp. 345–6.
50. Becker, p. 438.
51. Nayan Chanda, *Far Eastern Economic Review*, 4 April 1980.

5

China: The Pedagogy of Power

The Chinese government responded to the Vietnamese invasion of Cambodia in the most violent terms. It accused Hanoi of 'militarism, wild aggression and expansion' and promised to do its 'utmost' to help the deposed Khmer Rouge regime 'in every way'. During his visit to the United States in January 1979 Deng Xiaoping made his famous remarks on the need to teach Vietnam 'some necessary lessons'. On his way back to Beijing, he said in Tokyo that Vietnam must be 'punished severely'.

Deng's exercise in pedagogy began at dawn on 17 February, when approximately 100,000 Chinese People's Liberation Army (PLA) troops poured across the 1,300-kilometre border, backed by tanks and artillery. The attack quickly became bogged down, and their numbers had to be boosted to 200,000 before it was resumed. The immediate military objective of the Chinese was the capture of the capitals of Vietnam's six provinces bordering on China, four of which had fallen to them by 23 February. The decisive battle of the campaign then took shape around the town of Lang Son – situated in a natural pass through the mountains separating China and Vietnam (this strategically located town has been the site of many historic battles). The Chinese attacked on 27 February and, after bitter fighting in the surrounding hills, managed to push their way into Lang Son itself on the evening of 2 March. The battle was still proceeding in the town three days later, when Beijing announced that it was withdrawing its forces. However, it was not until 16 March that the withdrawal was complete, largely because the Chinese troops methodically demolished all major Vietnamese fortifications and many buildings before pulling out.

The cost of the month-long war was immense. The Chinese admitted suffering 20,000 casualties themselves, but claimed to have inflicted 50,000 on the Vietnamese; for their part, the Vietnamese claimed that 20,000

Chinese had been killed and that the total of Chinese casualties was more than 60,000. During America's Vietnam war these northernmost provinces had been largely insulated from US bombardment because of their proximity to the Chinese border, but this same geographic fact had now exposed them to widespread devastation. Lang Son still lay in ruins when we visited it a year after the invasion. Most of the main buildings had been reduced to heaps of rubble, and much of the housing had been utterly wrecked. Some homes had been rehabilitated, but most of the town's 30,000 inhabitants still lived in primitive shanties similar to those in refugee settlements elsewhere in the region. According to the Vietnamese, the Chinese had demolished four provincial capitals (Lang Son, Cao Bang, Lao Cai and Cam Duong) and 320 villages. Two hundred and fifty thousand people were rendered homeless: forty-one state farms and agricultural stations, as well as factories, mines, hospitals and schools were destroyed; 58,000 hectares of rice-fields had to be abandoned; and vast areas of forest had been burnt out.

Beijing duly announced its satisfaction with the punishment it had inflicted on Vietnam. However, in an interview with Oriana Fallachi in the Milan *Corriere della Sera* in August 1980, Deng Xiaoping admitted that the operation 'was not very successful'. It was true that the Chinese had achieved most of their immediate military objectives inside Vietnam, but the price had been distressingly high. Only in the battle of Lang Son had the Vietnamese committed one of their main force divisions (the crack 308th Division, transferred from Hanoi's defence perimeter). For the rest, 200,000 main-force PLA troops had been contained by half that number of Vietnamese regional troops and local militia – an outcome that seemed to expose China's military weakness rather than show off its strength.

The Chinese clearly underestimated the capabilities of Vietnam's defence forces, which were well entrenched in a rugged terrain that they knew intimately. The PLA's equipment was generally out of date. The Chinese weaponry was mostly of late 1950s or early 1960s vintage, whereas the Vietnamese fought with modern weapons supplied by the Soviets or captured from the Americans. Vietnam's air superiority meant that the Chinese infantry had to attack without the protection of air cover. Chinese logistics proved inadequate – their supply trucks moved slowly on the twisting mountain roads, and they were not able to keep their troops fully supplied with ammunition. Chinese tactics also proved unsatisfactory. As in the Korean war, the PLA relied on 'human wave' assaults, which enabled well-entrenched and well-equipped defence forces to inflict devastating casualties, especially in rugged terrain that slowed the advance of the infantry. In the battle for Lang Son, the Chinese also used cavalry, which suffered heavy casualties in the face of modern, rapid-fire weaponry.

The Chinese relied on bugle calls to coordinate their units, and Vietnamese snipers were able to throw them into confusion by picking off the buglers. Some reports suggested that the Chinese expected to be welcomed as 'liberators' by the local population, but this did not happen.

It is not surprising that the war sparked off a lengthy debate in Chinese military circles over the validity of Mao's 'people's war' tactics under modern conditions and on the need to modernize China's fighting equipment. It was also followed by the most extensive shake-up among PLA leaders for years, but this appears to have been more closely related to factional struggles in the Chinese Communist Party than to the outcome of the war as such.

Even more important than the PLA's poor battlefield performance was the failure of the invasion to achieve its political objectives. Beijing's ostensible aim was simply to secure a 'peaceful border' with Vietnam. It claimed that Chinese troops had been forced to launch a 'self-defensive counter-attack' to safeguard China's territorial integrity in the face of incessant Vietnamese provocations. As Han Nialong, leader of the Chinese delegation to the subsequent Sino-Vietnamese negotiations, put it: 'Their bullying became simply intolerable.'

However, the conflict was a political one rather than a boundary dispute. Although it is true that certain points were not accurately delineated, on the whole this was one of the best-defined borders in the region.[1] Both sides agreed that there had been no significant problems before 1974, but from that point on incidents on the border had multiplied as relations between Hanoi and Beijing deteriorated. The situation was especially tense in the second half of 1978, each side accusing the other of deliberate provocations.

The issues at stake became clear when negotiations on the problem opened in Hanoi in April 1979. The Vietnamese side put forward a three-point proposal to deal with the border problem itself: an end to hostilities and a demilitarization of the border; restoration of normal transport and communications; a settlement of any territorial problems on the basis of 'respect for the border line' established in the Sino-French agreements of 1887 and 1895. The Chinese side refused to consider this proposition and put forward an eight-point proposal of their own. They rejected a demilitarization of the border and demanded that territorial problems be settled 'on the basis of Sino-French conventions' rather than on the basis of the actual border line that resulted from these agreements. They also demanded Vietnamese recognition of the Paracel and Spratly Islands as an inalienable part of China's territory.

The Chinese also demanded an end to the persecution of Chinese 'nationals' in Vietnam and the restoration of 'friendly relations' between the two governments. Their second point read:

Neither side should seek hegemony in Indochina, Southeast Asia, or any other part of the world, and is opposed to efforts by any other country or group of countries to establish such hegemony. Neither side shall station troops in other countries and those already stationed abroad must be withdrawn to their own country. Neither side shall join any military blocs directed against the other, provide military bases, or use the territory and bases of other countries to threaten, subvert or commit armed aggression against the other side or against any other countries.[2]

In short, the Chinese served notice that there would be no end to the conflict on the Sino-Vietnamese land border unless the Vietnamese were willing to surrender sovereignty over their South China Sea possessions, withdraw from Cambodia, and end their alliance with Moscow. In a subsequent round of talks (on 5 July) the Chinese brushed aside discussion of the border itself and demanded that negotiations 'proceed from the crux of the matter – opposition to hegemonism', accusing Vietnam of setting up an Indochina Federation embracing Laos and Cambodia in coordination with the alleged Soviet 'drive for world hegemony'.

The border negotiations were thus stalemated from the beginning. The Chinese tried to coerce Hanoi with threats of another attack – Deng Xiaoping declared on 29 May that China 'reserved the right' to teach Vietnam another lesson if it continued its 'provocations' – but the Vietnamese refused to budge. The talks became simply a propaganda forum, and were abandoned in 1980.

The official Chinese explanation for its invasion as a defensive response to Vietnamese 'bullying' on the Sino-Vietnam border is almost everywhere recognized as a trumped-up excuse, and indeed is hardly mentioned in most western commentaries on the conflict. In reality, the Chinese invasion was a reaction to Hanoi's overthrow of Beijing's allies in Cambodia, and to its continued links with the Soviet Union. The war was not forced on the Chinese by circumstances; the Beijing leadership had consciously opted for military aggression as an instrument of policy. China's objectives in attacking Vietnam were generally believed to be twofold: first, to demonstrate to Hanoi that China was a major power whose wishes could not be defied; and second, to take the heat off Pol Pot's forces by compelling the Vietnamese to withdraw troops from Cambodia to defend their own northern border.

In both regards, it was not successful. The Vietnamese remained defiant, having dealt with the Chinese invasion without withdrawing any troops from Cambodia, where they proclaimed that the situation was 'irreversible'. Hanoi maintained its relationship with China's antagonist, the Soviet Union, and proceeded to strengthen its 'special relationships' with Vientiane and the new regime in Phnom Penh. All this served to intensify further Bejiing's outrage at the 'ingratitude' of the Vietnamese. The stage had been set for an enduring conflict between two supposedly 'fraternal' Communist governments.

There are some ironic parallels between the Sino-Vietnamese conflict and the Vietnam–Cambodia conflict. Vietnam had sought a 'special relationship' with Cambodia, and China was in effect demanding a 'special relationship' with Vietnam and the other Indochinese countries. Hanoi reacted so vigorously to Pol Pot's actions in part because it perceived a 'Chinese threat' to Vietnam behind them, and China in turn perceived a 'Soviet threat' behind Vietnamese actions. Vietnam had justified military intervention in Cambodia in December 1978 on the grounds of legitimate self-defence, and it is no doubt more than a coincidence that China justified its own invasion of Vietnam on identical grounds.

The political relationships involved can be conceived of as a hierarchy of power with the Soviet Union (and beyond that, the United States) at one end and the Democratic Kampuchea (DK) regime and Laos at the other end. The two countries in the middle of the hierarchy, China and Vietnam, each sought to maximize their own freedom of manoeuvre by resisting the power above them and pressuring the ones below them into an alliance. The Lao government was willing to align with Vietnam, but the factional struggle inside the Communist Party of Kampuchea (CPK) obliged Pol Pot to turn against it. Thus the government with the most naive pretensions to absolute sovereignty found itself with the least room for manoeuvre. It availed itself of the option of countering Vietnam's pressure by seeking Chinese protection, and in turn Vietnam sought Soviet protection against China, and China sought American protection against the Soviet Union.

But when it came to the crunch, Vietnam was willing to forgo its 'special relationship' with Cambodia when the Pol Pot government rejected it in 1975–76. By contrast, China has shown no signs of forgoing its demands on Indochina and has demonstrated its willingness to initiate full-scale war to achieve its goals. The parallels between the Vietnam–Cambodia war and the Sino-Vietnamese war break down at another level, too – the middle power, Vietnam, found itself under attack from both a weaker country, Cambodia, and a stronger country, China. If he had respected symmetry, Pol Pot would have tried to create a 'special relationship' with Laos but his military adventurism led him instead to attack Vietnam. Finally, whereas Vietnam's December 1978 invasion of Cambodia was aimed at the elimination of Pol Pot's regime, and was largely successful, China's February 1979 invasion of Vietnam had a more limited objective even though the troop numbers were larger, and it proved unsuccessful.

'Great Han Chauvinism'

The Chinese response to Vietnam's intervention in Cambodia was a dramatic demonstration of the desire of the Beijing government to reassert China's status as the pre-eminent power in the East Asian region. There has been a curious lack of recognition of this desire on the part of many western commentators. In the 1950s and 1960s it was commonly assumed that because the new government was Communist it was not really 'Chinese', and was best understood as a puppet of the Soviet Union. It was depicted as militant and expansionist, but in the service of foreign masters. The nationalist aspect of Chinese Communism became widely appreciated only after the Sino-Soviet split made it blindingly obvious. More sympathetic interpretations of Chinese foreign policy came into favour in the 1970s, but these tended to give too much credence to China's self-image as the leading opponent of 'big-power hegemonism'. The nationalism of the Chinese leadership had been recognized, but not the possibility that this might lead to an assertion of Chinese power at the expense of other nations.

The Chinese had constantly depicted themselves as the leading opponents of the power politics practised by the Soviet Union and the United States. 'All nations, big or small, should be equal; big nations should not bully the small, and strong nations should not bully the weak' proclaimed the Chinese side in the Shanghai communiqué of 1972. 'China will never be a super-power, and it opposes hegemony and power politics of any kind.'[3] This left many ill prepared for a situation where China would proclaim its own 'right' to intervene militarily in smaller countries which displeased it in order to teach them a 'lesson'.

Hanoi offered its explanation of Chinese power politics in a White Paper issued by the Vietnamese Foreign Ministry in October 1979. This argued that the Chinese rulers had revived traditional 'Great Han chauvinism', believing that the retreat of western imperialism would allow China to resume its old position as the dominant power throughout Southeast Asia. The leaders of the People's Republic of China, the Vietnamese declared, had for a long time 'dreamt of conquering' Southeast Asia, 'a traditional target for Chinese expansionism throughout the centuries'. They linked China's war with Vietnam to its border disputes with India, the Soviet Union and Mongolia, and argued:

> The Chinese leaders have appeared in their true colours as big-nation chauvinists and bourgeois nationalists! The Chinese rulers' present policy towards Vietnam, although well camouflaged, remains the same as that pursued by the rulers of the 'Celestial Empire' during the past millenniums – a policy aimed at annexing Vietnam, subduing the Vietnamese people and turning Vietnam into a satellite of China.[4]

The Vietnamese White Paper reviewed Chinese policy since the Geneva Conference of 1954 in the light of this assessment, arguing that it had been two-faced. The Chinese had appeared to support the Vietnamese revolution, but all the while had been conniving with its enemies. Their real objective was to keep Vietnam divided, weak, and dependent on China. An independent, unified Vietnam, Hanoi argued, would be 'a major obstacle to the Chinese leaders' global strategy, [and] first of all, to their expansionist policy towards Southeast Asia'. The Chinese, needless to say, hastened to deny this. They quoted past statements of praise for China from Le Duan and other Vietnamese leaders, and then took their current views as proof of grave 'degeneration' in Hanoi's ruling elite.[5]

The Vietnamese Communists had thus come to agree with the analysis of some western China specialists, such as C.P. Fitzgerald, who had maintained that despite the Communist takeover 'the Chinese view of the world has not fundamentally changed'.[6] Maoism had updated, but not basically altered, the traditional Sinocentric view of China as the sole upholder of civilization and virtue, and lawgiver to the barbarians that surrounded it. There is some force in this argument, but it is misleading to view the foreign policy of the modern Chinese state as simply a continuation of traditional policies, as if these remained unaffected by changing practical circumstances.

As the powerful 'civilized' centre of a 'barbarian' universe, the Celestial Empire had been able to command deference from the smaller and less powerful states surrounding it. This deference was institutionalized in the tributary system and, until the coming of the French, the courts in Hue, Phnom Penh and most of the Lao principalities all paid tribute to the imperial court in Beijing. The attitudes this fostered among Chinese rulers is exemplified by the message the Emperor Ch'ien Lung (Qianlong) sent to George III in response to British requests for diplomatic representation in Beijing and trading rights in China:

Swaying the wide world, I have but one aim in view, namely, to maintain a perfect governance and to fulfil the duties of the state. ... Our dynasty's majestic virtue has penetrated unto every country under heaven, and kings of all nations have offered their costly tribute by land and sea ... It behoves you, O King, to respect my sentiments and to display even greater devotion in future, so that, by perpetual submission to our Throne, you may secure peace and prosperity for your country hereafter.[7]

While the tributary states were left to run their own internal affairs, the Chinese government saw itself as the arbiter of disputes between them, with the right to punish the recalcitrant. As for the idea of leaving them to establish independent economic and political relations with outside powers, as Qianlong explained to George III, this would be 'quite impossible'.

In the case of Vietnam, a modern historian has described the traditional tributary relationship in these terms:

> the relationship was not between two equal states. There was no doubt in anybody's mind that China was the superior and the tributary state the inferior. The Vietnamese kings clearly realized that they had to acknowledge China's suzerainty and becomes tributaries in order to avoid active intervention by China in their internal affairs. ... China felt that she could not govern this area directly; at the same time, however, she wished to avoid trouble in frontier regions. ... Tributary status was granted by China not to a country but to a ruler. This status could be granted only after the foreign ruler had manifested his acknowledgement of China's superiority. ... The investiture of a tributary ruler was apparently viewed by the Chinese emperor as similar to the appointment of an official within the empire. Hence investiture could be withdrawn if the ruler failed in his duty. ... In such a case the tributary king could be punished just like any other high official of the empire.[8]

This is the system which, according to Hanoi, the Chinese leaders wish to restore today.

In keeping with this, it has been suggested that all the Vietnamese leaders really have to do to restore peaceful relations with China is to 'pay tribute', to pay lip-service to Chinese supremacy while pursuing their own independent line. On this reading, the Chinese leaders are preoccupied with 'saving face' and maintaining ancient traditions. It assumes that they will be satisfied with the formalities rather than the realities of power.

We are not convinced. The traditional Chinese imperial order rested on the isolation of East Asia from the other great state systems of world history. When the maritime expansion of the European powers broke into this closed universe, the supremacy of the Chinese empire came to an end. The tributary states were stripped away and in due course the central power of the empire itself collapsed. Chinese territory fell increasingly under the sway of European imperialism. Modern Chinese nationalism developed out of this trauma. When a centralized state was re-established by the Communist revolution of the 1940s, its rulers confronted a radically different international environment, one of competing territorial nation-states. Although some of the old attitudes towards the 'barbarians' persisted, basically, the modern Chinese nationalists (including the Communists) 'were quite willing to exchange the Chinese world order for a strong Chinese nation'.[9]

The Communists have explicitly rejected the notion of hierarchy central to the old Confucian system and affirm, as we have seen, the modern concepts of state and sovereignty and equality. But while there is no real evidence that they wish to rebuild the old tributary relations, there is little doubt that the old attitudes linger on in a more diffuse expectation of regional affirmation of their leading role. Only against this background can the fury of the Chinese leaders over the 'ingratitude' of the Vietnamese Communists, who, having driven the Americans out, refused to subordinate themselves towards China, be understood.

But arguments that explain present Chinese policy solely in terms of 'Great Han chauvinism' are unsatisfactory. They bestow a life of its own on the 'Chinese political tradition' and fail to identify the institutions and forces that would sustain this tradition in a radically changed context. The tributary state system is, for the present generation of Chinese, even more a matter of ancient history than the binding of women's feet. If attitudes derived from it have persisted, it is because they have been kept alive by present-day forces. Looking at the question from this angle, we can see that the analysts in Hanoi have got the answer the wrong way around. The Chinese are not practising power politics today because they are prisoners of their imperial past: rather, the ideology of 'Great Han chauvinism' has persisted because the Chinese have been practising power politics in modern times.

We argued in chapter 1 that the Communist revolutions in Asia are best understood as the radical wing of a much broader anti-imperialist revolt. Like their bourgeois and monarchist counterparts, they are engaged in the effort to modernize a traditional society and forge a modern nation-state. Nationalist ideology serves to mobilize popular support for this endeavour. Having thrown off foreign rule and created a sovereign state, each nation state seeks to advance its interests and defend its security as best it can in an anarchic world of competing nation-states. And all the democratic and egalitarian rhetoric in the world cannot disguise the fact that some states are more powerful than others. Their strength makes some capable of advancing their interests more forcefully than weaker states, and therefore more valuable as allies. In this situation the 'proletarian internationalist' succumbs to the logic of power politics as readily as the 'bourgeois nationalist'.

In this regard both the Vietnamese and the Chinese Communists are alike. Nationalism was a driving force in both revolutions and, having won state power, in a short space of time both had demonstrated their willingness to use it against other nations in defence of what they saw as their own national interests. But there is still an important difference between them. Quite apart from its Sinocentric, imperial tradition, the very fact of China's vast size (its population was estimated at 985 million in 1981) prompts its rulers to have realistic ambitions of global power despite the country's poverty. Vietnam, by contrast, can never aspire to be more than a regional power. Thus Communist China is a modern nation-state, a great power, whose relations with Vietnam, and Southeast Asia generally, have been in large part shaped by its relations with other great powers; whereas those of imperial China had been shaped largely by the isolation of the Chinese 'world-system' from the pressure of powerful rivals.

It is to a consideration of modern China's relations with the other great powers that we now turn. Essentially, the story is one of the rise of China as a great power in the context of Soviet–American antagonism. Since the outlines of this story are obscured by so much confusion, and wishful thinking, by both the Left and the Right, it is necessary to describe them in some detail.

China in the Modern World: The Emergence of a Great Power

The Chinese Communists saw their revolution as a triumph of Chinese national self-assertion after a period of humiliating foreign domination. In September 1949 Mao declared: 'Our nation will never again be an insulted nation. We have stood up . . . Let the domestic and foreign reactionaries tremble before us.' But, in fact, in its early years the People's Republic of China remained a weak state. It had been through a period of economic chaos and ruinous war, and its new rulers were obliged, in another of Mao's famous phrases, to 'lean to one side, the side of the Soviet Union' in international affairs.

When China was aligned with the Soviet Union, western commentators depicted it as a militantly expansionist power – blithely ignoring the realities of Chinese weakness at that time. Since then this picture has been drastically revised in the light of the Sino-Soviet split and the Sino-American *rapprochement*. China is now commonly depicted in much more sympathetic terms, as essentially playing a passive role. Thus the Sino-Soviet split is seen as the result of Soviet 'bullying', and China's turn to the West as a defensive reaction to Soviet expansionism.

Such an interpretation accords with common Cold War prejudices, but it obscures the reality of China's growing assertiveness as an independent power in world politics. It was the Chinese side that initiated the Sino-Soviet split, and, in the wake of the Sino-American *rapprochement*, China finally emerged as a great power with an active policy of expanding its influence in Southeast Asia.

Tensions were evident at the time of the formation of the Sino-Soviet alliance (though they were largely ignored by contemporary western commentators). Stalin was still smarting from his failure to intimidate Tito in Yugoslavia, and suspected that Mao's nationalism would make him a 'second Tito'. Mao, for his part, resented Stalin's high-handedness towards China. But these tensions were overridden by the threat to a weak China by the USA's aggressively anti-Communist stance in Asia. Whatever their private reservations about their Soviet ally, the Chinese Communist leaders were aware that it provided them with urgently needed military protection and diplomatic support, as well as the aid, trade and investment funds needed for economic development. It is now ironic that when they were accused by the Americans of reducing China to colonial status by entering an alliance with the Soviet Union, the Chinese Communist press responded with indignant articles refuting charges of 'red imperialism' against the USSR.

By the mid-1950s the bargaining position of the Chinese leaders had improved dramatically. Their successful economic reconstruction within China had been widely praised. Chinese troops had performed well in Korea and in 1953 the Americans reluctantly accepted a ceasefire that allowed the survival of China's (and Russia's) ally, North Korea. In Vietnam, American-backed French forces were finally defeated by the Viet Minh in 1954. Through their roles at the Geneva Conference on Indochina and Korea in 1954 and the Bandung Conference of Afro-Asian countries in 1955, the Chinese leaders believed they had won recognition as a great power in their own right. A *People's Daily* editorial on Geneva declared:

> For the first time as one of the Big Powers, the People's Republic joined the other major powers in negotiations on vital international problems and made a contribution of its own that won the acclaim of wide sections of world opinion. The international status of the People's Republic of China as one of the big world powers has gained universal recognition. Its international prestige has been greatly enhanced. The Chinese people take the greatest joy and pride in the efforts and achievements of their delegation at Geneva.[10]

In addition, the easing of the extreme Cold War tensions of the early 1950s gave China more room for manoeuvre.

The result was the adoption of a more assertive approach by China, which immediately produced growing strains in the Sino-Soviet alliance. The Chinese moved increasingly away from the Soviet model of socialism. Mao's collectivization drive of 1955 and the 'Great Leap Forward' are usually assessed in terms of domestic politics, but they had an important international dimension – the aim was to demonstrate China's ability to surpass the Soviets in the building of socialism. But China's economic backwardness meant that stress had to be placed on doctrinal purity and moral virtue. The cult of Chairman Mao intensified and in 1958 the *People's Daily* hailed him as the greatest living Marxist-Leninist theoretician. This implicit rejection of the Soviet leadership's claim to doctrinal authority for the whole Communist bloc was made explicit in the early 1960s, when the Chinese launched a series of increasingly open polemics against Soviet 'revisionism'.

To read the major documents of this period is to gain the impression that the split was overwhelmingly a matter of esoteric ideological disputes, but the split itself has endured well beyond the fall of Maoism in China. In fact the quarrel over ideology was in reality a struggle over the legitimate source of authority for the international Communist movement. The polemics of the early 1960s on the general line of the international Communist movement signalled that China and the USSR had become open rivals for leadership of the Communist bloc and for influence among the newly emerging nations. China was laying claim to the position of great power of the Communist bloc; and since the Soviets were unwilling to accept this claim, almost every international event of the period became the occasion for bitter polemical exchanges.

When Khrushchev first put forward his doctrine of 'peaceful coexistence' between the Communist and the capitalist powers in the mid-1950s, it was endorsed by the Chinese. But by the late 1950s they were becoming increasingly vocal in their criticism of Soviet 'capitulation' to imperialism. Partly, this was a response to the unwillingness of the Soviets to give the Chinese the full support they demanded in a series of crises that erupted on China's borders – the Quemoy–Formosa crisis (1958), apparently initiated by Beijing in an attempt to press Moscow into a stronger commitment to Chinese unification in the face of continued American support for Chiang Kai-shek; the rebellion in Tibet (1959); and the ensuing tension with India that resulted in the Sino-Indian border war (1962).

For their part, the Soviets became increasingly exasperated with the Chinese challenge. They first entered the ideological argument by carefully marshalling quotes from Lenin in support of 'peaceful coexistence'. But within a couple of years Khrushchev was furiously castigating 'lunatics and maniacs' and 'pseudo-revolutionary windbags'. A series of Soviet actions added more fuel to the flames. In 1959, shortly before his visit to the USA, Khrushchev repudiated secret Soviet promises to help China build up an independent nuclear capability (years later, when they revealed this, the Chinese said it was 'Khrushchev's gift to the Americans'). Then, in 1960, he withdrew all Soviet technicians from China, claiming they were being mistreated. Coming just at the time of the economic crisis that followed Mao's 'Great Leap Forward', this was a blow to Chinese plans for development that would be remembered and resented for decades. The Chinese responded by raging at the 'arrogant and dictatorial' attitudes of the Soviets.

But it was the emerging triangular relationship between Beijing, Moscow and Washington that lay at the heart of Chinese tirades against Soviet aspirations for 'peaceful coexistence'. The intensifying quarrel with Moscow, occurring at a time when Chinese relations with Washington were still bitterly antagonistic, left Beijing dangerously isolated. Any sign of 'collusion' between the Soviets and the Americans was denounced as a 'betrayal' of the cause of Communism. When the USA and the USSR signed a Partial Test Ban Treaty in July 1963, the Chinese denounced it violently and a commentator in *Red Flag* charged that a 'Holy Alliance' had been formed comparable with the anti-revolutionary alliance forged by Metternich after the Napoleonic Wars, and predicted a similarly unhappy end for it.

For all the rhetorical overkill, Chinese fears of 'collusion' and a 'secret deal' between the USA and the USSR to contain Chinese influence were not unfounded. The Laos crisis of 1961 was the first occasion on which China appeared as an independent third power, and both Moscow and Washington actively tried to limit Beijing's influence – even to the extent of signing a secret accord, the 'Pushkin Pact', on the matter.[11]

By the mid-1960s it was clear that China's bid to take over the mantle of leadership of the Communist bloc from the Soviet Union had failed dismally. Almost all the ruling Communist parties had sided with Moscow, apart from some (most notably North Vietnam and North Korea) who tried to remain neutral and balance the two Communist great powers against each other. Only Albania – once Stalin's favourite example of total insignificance in international politics – had wholeheartedly endorsed the Maoist version of Communism. But China's ardent revolutionism was more attractive to those Communist parties still struggling to win power. Most of the Southeast Asian parties sided with China, but elsewhere they gained the support of only the New Zealand party and small breakaway sects. Attempts to win over the leaders of Afro-Asian nations, struggling to consolidate new and fragile states, to Mao's ideas also met with little success. China's first bid for great power status in its own right had proved premature, leaving China more isolated than ever.

In this context the Americans massively escalated the Vietnam war in 1965, simply ignoring Chinese outrage over the matter. Beijing was again faced with large-scale American military intervention in an area vital to its security, as it had been in Korea a decade earlier. Then the Chinese had intervened themselves, but now they were no longer protected by the Russian military umbrella. The majority of Chinese Communist Party leaders around Liu Shao-ch'i and Deng Xiaoping believed that

America's action had made it imperative for China to close ranks with the Soviet Union once more. But Mao had by this stage gone right out on the limb of 'anti-revisionism' and his personal prestige would have suffered if this course had been adopted. Instead, he called for the strengthening of China's 'self-reliance' and an intensified campaign against the Soviets.

Defeated inside the party, Mao and his ally, Defence Minister Lin Biao, launched a campaign of 'mass criticism' against their opponents, which snowballed into the Great Proletarian Cultural Revolution of 1966–68. This destroyed Mao's opponents, but it left the party in ruins and the country in chaos. By 1969 the army under Lin Biao had managed to restore order and was basically running the country, while Mao sought to create a ruling party more to his liking than the pre-Cultural Revolution party had been. This brought him closer once more to moderates such as Zhou Enlai, under whose patronage Deng Xiaoping and other veteran administrators were cautiously rehabilitated – to the great annoyance of the radicals who had suddenly risen to power during the Cultural Revolution.

Mao's 'personality cult' was exploited to the hilt in the struggle for power during the Cultural Revolution. His thought was proclaimed to the whole world as the supreme wisdom of the modern age. But beneath this veneer of extravagant universalistic rhetoric, the country had plunged into a self-absorbed isolationism reminiscent of the old Chinese empire. Even according to a sympathetic writer, China in this period disdained the international diplomatic community and largely abandoned state-to-state relations with the outside world. Only the bearers of tribute to Mao's thought were welcome in Beijing.

While it was primarily an internal upheaval, the Cultural Revolution was partly triggered off by foreign policy problems, and in turn had devastating effects on China's foreign policy. China's relations with the outside world had already reached a low point in 1965. Now, according to Mao, China had to gird itself for a final, apocalyptic confrontation with its enemies. In March 1966 Mao told a visiting delegation from Japan that a war between China and America was 'inevitable' within two years, and that the Soviets would then invade as well. China's foreign policy became increasingly xenophobic, its shrill anti-westernism matched only by the ferocity of its denunciations of the Soviet bloc.

Indeed, Sino-Soviet relations had sunk lower than low. In 1966 the Chinese foreign minister, Ch'en Yi, charged that the Soviets were thieves who had stolen 1.5 million square kilometres of Chinese territory, and Red Guards poured into the border province of Singkiang to organize two-million-strong demonstrations demanding the return of 'lost territories'. Early in 1967 there were violent mass demonstrations outside the

Soviet Embassy in Beijing, and Chinese students in Moscow fought with the Soviet police.

Mao had been pressing for a renegotiation of the Sino-Soviet border since 1963, but following Ch'en Yi's statement, tensions mounted as both sides built up their forces on the border, climaxing in the fighting on the Ussuri River in March 1969. The details remain obscure, although most western writers believe that the fighting was initiated by the Chinese and that the Soviets retaliated in force. The Chinese linked the border clashes to the occupation of Czechoslovakia by Warsaw Pact forces the preceding August as another manifestation of Soviet 'social imperialism', but some commentators believed that Mao and Lin Biao provoked the incident to rally support in China. In any case, the rhetoric of the Sino-Soviet confrontation now reached the point where both sides were hinting at the use of nuclear weapons. At this point, the Chinese were obliged to beat a diplomatic retreat. Having boasted in March that 'the anti-Chinese scum will end badly', they were by October reassuring Moscow that there was 'no reason whatsoever' for a border war and promising the restoration of state-to-state relations. Shortly afterwards, negotiations on the border, suspended by the Chinese in 1964, were reopened (though they made no progress in settling the dispute).[12]

The Soviet Union had secured its border with China, but only by outright coercion and at the cost of publicly humiliating and further alienating the Chinese regime. The Chinese leaders were willing to bow to superior force if necessary, but this made any subsequent reconciliation between the Soviets and even the anti-Maoist factions in Beijing unlikely. Still, the fact that Mao's 'anti-revisionist' line had pushed China to the brink of nuclear war must have led to a renewed appreciation in Beijing of the value of great and powerful allies. It drove home the point that by 1969 the attempts by the Chinese Communists to secure recognition as a great power had achieved very little; in the aftermath of the Cultural Revolution, the Beijing regime was more isolated and vulnerable than at any time since 1949. At this point, Mao's eyes turned to the USA.[13] This led to a falling out between Mao and Lin Biao, who died violently in 1971 as a consequence.[14]

In the meantime, there had been some hard thinking about China going on in Washington. The USA had at first responded to the Sino-Soviet split by denying its reality, and then by favouring the more 'moderate' side, that is, Moscow. But the fact that Beijing had responded to American provocation by stepping up its attacks on Moscow awakened American strategists to the possibility that it could use the 'extremists' in Beijing against the Soviets. However, any immediate prospect of Sino-American detente was soon overwhelmed by the tidal waves of the Cultural Revolution, and in 1968 Washington still had no more communications with

Beijing than Moscow did. President Johnson began publicly hinting at his desire for improved relations with China, as did presidential candidate Richard Nixon. Shortly after Nixon's election to the presidency in November 1968, the Chinese proposed renewing talks over an agreement on peaceful coexistence and the Americans responded favourably. Despite some setbacks – notably as a result of Chinese apprehension when American and South Vietnamese forces invaded Cambodia in May 1970 – relations between the two countries steadily improved. This process culminated in Nixon's dramatic visit to Beijing in February 1972.

By this stage the Chinese government had also taken the initiative in restoring the diplomatic links with the outside world that had been broken during the Cultural Revolution. Coupled with the obvious signs of a Sino-American *rapprochement*, this led to the United Nations General Assembly finally voting to recognize the Beijing rather than the Taipei government as the representative of China. By the end of the decade, the People's Republic had normal diplomatic relations with most countries around the world. Ironically, once it entered the public arena, Sino-American efforts at *rapprochement* became bogged down, mainly as a result of the unwillingness of either side to be seen to compromise over Taiwan. When relations were finally normalized in December 1978, their willingness to bury their differences over this issue emphasized the extent to which it was a result of the convergence of their global perspectives in opposition to the Soviet Union. At the start of the 1970s, China had been deeply suspicious of Soviet–American 'collusion', anxious to upset the *detente* between the two superpowers. By the end of the decade, Beijing and Washington were competing with displays of public hostility towards Moscow; the precondition for the strengthening of Sino-American relations had turned out to be the breakdown of Soviet–American detente, which plunged the world into the New Cold War in the late 1970s.

China's foreign relations had been revolutionized in the early 1970s. In barely three years, it had gone from a 'revolutionary' contempt for normal state-to-state relations under Lin Biao to acceptance of a permanent seat on the five-member UN Security Council, a position signifying formal international recognition of the People's Republic's status as a great power. After this breakthrough, China's foreign policy problems ceased to be those of an emergent revolutionary state. They became those of defining, consolidating and strengthening China's position as a great power in a world of competing powers. This inevitably meant redefining China's relations, not only with the other great powers, but also with the smaller states of the East Asian region.

The task of providing an authoritative statement of the principles of Chinese foreign policy in the wake of this diplomatic revolution fell to Deng Xiaoping, now rehabilitated after his fall from grace during the

Cultural Revolution. His exposition of Chairman Mao's 'Theory of the Three Worlds' at the UN in April 1974 marked the demise of any lingering expectation that China might revert to a 'two-worlds' (capitalism versus communism) view of international politics. According to Deng:

> all the political forces in the world have undergone drastic division and realignment through prolonged trials of strength and struggle. A large number of Asian, African, and Latin American countries have achieved independence one after another, and they are playing an ever greater role in international affairs. As a result of the emergence of social-imperialism, the socialist camp which existed for a time after World War II is no longer in existence. Owing to the law of uneven and combined development of capitalism, the Western imperialist bloc, too, is disintegrating. Judging from the changes in international relations, the world today actually consists of three parts, or three worlds, that are both interconnected and in contradiction to one another. The United States and the Soviet Union make up the First World. The developing countries in Asia, Africa, Latin America and other regions make up the Third World. The developed countries between the two make up the Second World.[15]

Since the 'socialist camp' is no longer in existence 'and the imperialist camp is disintegrating' as well, China was officially freed from any residual ideological basis for distinguishing between the two 'superpowers'. Deng's speech marked the complete triumph of *realpolitik* in China's foreign policy. Indeed, while Deng had formally bracketed the Soviet Union with the United States, the Chinese believed that their main future rival for influence in the Far East would be the Soviet Union. Hence Deng argued that the USA was 'in decline' and that the USSR was the most dangerous of the two superpowers because it was still in an 'expansionist' phase. Despite the Communist ideology shared by the two powers, opposition to Soviet 'social imperialism' became the cornerstone of Chinese foreign policy for the next seven years.

Sino-Soviet Rivalry in the 1970s

China's move to the West has often been seen in terms of the threat posed to China by the growing role of the Soviet Union in East Asian affairs. Most western commentators see this as an extension of Soviet power beyond its legitimate sphere of interest and as symptomatic of Moscow's expansionism. But a glance at the map is enough to establish a point of cardinal importance that is often forgotten – the USSR covers 22.3 million square kilometres, and sprawls across all of northern Asia as well as half of northern Europe. Seventy-five per cent of the territory and 29 per cent of the population of the Soviet Union are Asian. Even if the European sections are left out of consideration, the Soviet Union is one of the largest and most populous of Asian states. Given this, as Geoffrey Jukes has noted, what needs to be explained is not current Soviet interest in Asian affairs so much as the lack of interest in them in the Stalin era.[16]

The first concern of Soviet Far Eastern policy in the 1970s was to make its territorial boundaries – so long as to be almost indefensible – safe and secure. Here the Chinese border was a major headache: 7,500 kilometres long, it separated a large, thinly populated region with valuable natural resources from a hostile power that had traditionally dominated the area. Second, the Soviet Union had sought to promote the development of its Asian territories. Particularly in order to develop Siberia and the port of Vladivostok, it has sought a partnership with Japan. But Japan's eyes have been on the potential of the Chinese market, and the Sino-Japanese *rapprochement* that followed the Sino-American *rapprochement* minimized Soviet influence in North Asia.

In the 1970s the Soviet Union also tried to take advantage of the climate of detente to expand its diplomatic presence, its aid to and trade in Southeast Asia. However, the results of what was often described as Moscow's 'offensive' in Southeast Asia were modest. The Soviets did succeed in opening diplomatic relations with all countries in the region. But the development of commercial relations remained extremely limited, and only in Indonesia were there any Soviet aid projects of any significance. Even so, Jakarta continued to look primarily to the USA, Western Europe and Japan for aid. Compared to that of their American and Chinese competitors, Soviet influence remained minimal. Far from forming part of a much broader pattern of expanding Soviet penetration of the Far East, Indochina was Moscow's solitary success in the region.

In the military sphere, there have been two main aspects of the Soviet Union's 'thrust' into the Far East. The first has been the military build-up on the Sino-Soviet border, especially since the fighting on the Ussuri River in 1969. The Soviets were estimated to have 400,000 troops stationed on the border, with 1.5 million Chinese troops deployed against them. The second has been the development of its Pacific naval fleet, based in Vladivostok. Both its naval rivalry with the USA and the expansion of its mercantile shipping have given the Soviet Union an important strategic interest in maintaining its freedom of navigation in Southeast Asian waters, and in access to ports and naval facilities in the region. By trying to match US naval forces in the Pacific, the Soviets built their navy up beyond that of regional powers such as China and Japan. This created considerable apprehension, and increasing Soviet military power proved politically counter-productive.

Concern about the Soviet 'thrust' into Asia has diverted attention from the more rapid growth of Chinese influence in Southeast Asia in the 1970s. Beijing's initial breakthrough was the normalization of relations with Burma in 1971, but the turning point was the opening of formal diplomatic relations with Malaysia in 1974 and with the Philippines and Thailand in 1975. Beijing downplayed its support for local Communist insurgencies and formally renounced its previous claims to be the protector of the overseas Chinese communities to reassure those still suspicious of its aims. Both official and unofficial leadership consultations were used to build up friendly relations with non-Communist governments. Only Singapore and Indonesia continued to withhold formal recognition, but here, too, informal contacts multiplied rapidly. Trade relations also expanded rapidly, the value of China's trade with ASEAN countries rising to US$2.4 billion, or over 6 per cent of ready market for their exports in Southeast Asia. 'Chinese influence has spread rapidly in the region,' one writer sums up, 'especially among the non-Communist states, which in the past had strongly feared PRC intentions.' The cultivation of relations with Southeast Asia has been 'one of the major success stories in Chinese foreign policy in the 1970s'.[17]

The thrust of China's policies in Southeast Asia in the 1970s was directed towards the exclusion of Soviet influence from the region. Clauses pledging joint opposition to 'hegemonism' (the Chinese code-word for the Soviets) were included in the Zhou–Nixon Shanghai communiqué of 1972, and in the communiqués normalizing relations with Southeast Asian countries. After the normalization of Sino-Thai relations, the Chinese depicted this as a link in a Chinese-sponsored 'anti-hegemony front' designed to 'guarantee' Southeast Asia from 'intensified Soviet expansion'. The other side of this attempt to weld Southeast Asia into a Chinese-led anti-Soviet bloc has been the encouragement of a continued American military presence in the region to give it some teeth. Whereas Beijing had once proclaimed itself the most militant opponent of 'US imperialism', the Chinese now began to talk of the USA as 'an Asian and Pacific nation' with a 'deserved and responsible role' in Southeast Asia.[18]

The Beijing leadership was thus able to view the fruits of its policies in Southeast Asia with considerable satisfaction. In broad terms, it had been successful in ensuring that Chinese rather than Soviet influence had expanded in Southeast Asia as the American presence waned after its defeat in Indochina. These were matters on which, for all their other disagreements, all the main factions in the Chinese leadership could agree. Hence the deaths of Zhou and Mao (1976), the fall of Jiang Qing (Madame Mao) and the 'Gang of Four' (1976), the rise and fall of Hua Guofeng (1976–81), and the rise of Deng Xiaoping (1977 onwards) had surprisingly little impact on the directions of Chinese policy. Indeed, it may be that the preoccupation of the Chinese leaders with the internal power struggle contributed to the general rigidity of China's foreign policy in this period.

Putting the Squeeze on Vietnam

From Beijing's point of view, a major ground for dissatisfaction was Vietnam itself. The Beijing government had aided the Communists in Vietnam, and fully expected that China rather than the Soviet Union would be the main great-power beneficiary of their victory. Chinese pressure on Hanoi intensified, but the Vietnamese tried to maximize their independence from Beijing by continuing to balance Chinese and Soviet influence, and by seeking an opening to the West. Especially in the light of the resounding successes of Beijing's anti-Soviet policies elsewhere in the region, the Chinese leaders saw this attempt by Hanoi to continue its balancing act between Moscow and Beijing as a display of 'ingratitude' that it was no longer necessary to tolerate. The strains in Sino-Vietnamese relations multiplied rapidly as Beijing's pressure on Hanoi mounted.

In the polemical exchanges following the Sino-Vietnamese war of 1979, the Chinese were content to date these tensions to 1974, but there is little doubt that they went back much earlier. They explained it in terms of the growing ingratitude of Le Duan and his colleagues, who had allowed their victory over the Saigon regime to go to their heads. The Chinese polemics do not mention Beijing's mounting pressure on Hanoi but they do make it clear that China expected that its wartime aid to Vietnam would be paid back, in deference to China's strategic objectives in the region, by the exclusion of Soviet influence.

The Vietnamese White Paper of October 1979 depicts the Chinese as consistently obstructing the Vietnamese revolution from the Geneva Conference onwards. Hanoi alleged that the Chinese were really in collusion with the French at Geneva, and that they pressured the Vietnamese into accepting a compromise solution that left Vietnam and Laos partitioned and gave no regroupment areas at all to the Khmer Issaraks, at a time when the situation on the battlefield placed total victory within grasp. When the USA subsequently intervened to shore up the anti-Communist regime in Saigon (and, one should add, Vientiane), China did its best to restrain the Communist side. China gave a 'green light' to the ensuing American escalation by making it clear that China would not respond militarily to the American actions; it actively sought to prevent a united response by the Communist bloc, and then tried to avert a negotiated settlement of the conflict. All this, the White Paper argued, was done with the intention of keeping Vietnam weak and divided in order to facilitate Chinese expansion in Southeast Asia.

If this was mildly hysterical, the Chinese reply was singularly unconvincing. They preferred to dwell on the volume of Chinese aid to Hanoi and the harmonious relations of the 1949–54 period (matters on which the Vietnamese White Paper said as little as possible), and they tried to get over the main points of the Vietnamese indictment by bluff and bluster. On the assessment of China's role at Geneva, for example, they responded by pointing out that the positions of the Communist countries had been 'closely coordinated', without giving any more details. Because of the Vietnamese, the Soviets and the Chinese were 'unanimous' in the face they presented to the outside world. Hoang Van Hoan maintains that the claims by 'Le Duan and company' of behind-the-scenes conflict must be 'very foolish': 'Were the delegations of Vietnam and the Soviet Union mere puppets to be manipulated by China during the Geneva Conference?'[19] In fact, western analyses of the power play at Geneva confirm the Vietnamese claims.[20] Chinese interests were satisfied by a Communist state in northern Vietnam and Pathet Lao control of Phong Saly province in Laos. Beyond that, the Chinese sought a compromise with the West (hoping that in this way it could keep a hostile USA out of Indochina), whereas the Viet Minh looked forward to the complete liberation of Indochina following its military victory over the French at Dien Bien Phu; and far from having been unanimous in their actions, Zhou Enlai acted on several occasions to undercut Pham Van Dong.[21]

It is also true that in the 1960s, despite the militant rhetoric, Beijing did its best to avoid entanglement in a direct military confrontation with the USA over Vietnam. Before 1965 China had supported a negotiated settlement, and had no obvious objections to a separate state of South Vietnam. With the American escalation of the war in that year, Beijing abandoned hopes of a peaceful settlement. It sent as much aid as it could to North Vietnam's war effort but it refused to join with Moscow in a united opposition to the Americans, and did its best to obstruct the USA–North Vietnam negotiations encouraged by Moscow. It also urged on Hanoi a low-risk, long-haul strategy of protracted war, rather than any attempt to achieve a decisive victory. In their reply to Hanoi's White Paper the Chinese avoided any specific discussion of these matters.

Chinese policy towards Vietnam in this period seems to have been governed mainly by national security considerations, and by the triangular relations between Beijing, Moscow and Washington. On the one hand, it wanted to see the hostile American forces 'encircling' China defeated; on the other hand, it tried to prevent any direct involvement or any action by the Vietnamese that might provoke American retaliation against China itself. Finally, it also sought to avert any 'collusion' between Moscow and Washington. There is little doubt that these basic policies (not to mention the excesses of the Cultural Revolution) led to serious strains in the Beijing–Hanoi relationship just as the diverging interests of the Vietnamese and Cambodian Communists led to tension in their relationships.

But Hanoi's polemicists are surely stretching things too far when they describe Beijing's policies as 'giving the green light' to American aggression in a Machiavellian attempt to keep Vietnam divided. There seems no reason to doubt that, before the Sino-American *rapprochement* of the early 1970s, the Chinese saw US activities in Vietnam as a threat to China itself. They were able to cite the volume of their aid to North Vietnam during the war ($20 billion, according to Beijing) as evidence of genuine opposition to the US intervention. Nor is Hanoi able to produce any evidence of the master plan guiding Chinese policy towards Vietnam after 1954, apart from a string of boastful (but vague) quotes from Chinese leaders.[22] Although it is not as crude and simplistic, Hanoi's White Paper shares a fatal flaw with Pol Pot's *Black Paper* – since it is unwilling to acknowledge that 'fraternal' Communist regimes may have divergent national interests, it is obliged to explain the conflicts that arise from these divergences in terms of Manichaean conspiracies.

Serious Sino-Vietnamese tensions thus existed throughout the late 1950s and the 1960s. But China's *rapprochement* with the USA in the early 1970s fundamentally recast Beijing's policies, leading it to adopt a much more assertive stance towards Hanoi. In the first place, the American move towards China was clearly intended to increase the pressure on Hanoi. In the 1972 Shanghai communiqué the American side promised that its forces would be progressively withdrawn from Taiwan 'as the tension in the area diminishes'. In this 'artfully crafted' statement, as Kissinger's biographers put it, 'the Americans implied that if China wanted to accelerate the US pullout from Taiwan, it had only to pressure Hanoi into a compromise settlement.'[23]

Second, once it was clear that the USA was on the way out in Indochina, China's main rival for influence became the Soviet Union. And after the 'ceasefire' in South Vietnam and Laos, the reliance of local Communist forces on weaponry provided by Moscow lessened, which opened the way for renewed Chinese influence in the region. Secret Chinese internal briefings known as the 'Kunming Documents' show that the Beijing leaders were preparing for a major contest with the Soviet Union for influence in Southeast Asia following the Paris peace agreement of 1973:

The Vietnam armistice is ... in our interests. ... After the Korean Armistice, the game on the Southeast Asian chessboard became unplayable. The game has now been revived by the Vietnam Armistice. Once the United States departed, its running dogs in Asia became very uneasy. The rulers of countries like Thailand, Singapore, and the Philippines, realizing that the United States could not hang on, all wanted to enter into relationships with us ... In the past, Soviet revisionism intervened in Southeast Asia under the pretext of supporting Vietnam. Now that the Vietnam war has stopped, we can, by working harder, more effectively strike at Soviet revisionism.[24]

As Robert Ross argues, China's interests were best served by the situation in Indochina in 1973–75. US forces had been withdrawn. Vietnam was still divided, and Hanoi could not afford to alienate Beijing. This limited Soviet influence,[25] and Beijing did not hesitate to respond to Thieu's provocations in the Paracels by forcefully asserting its claims in the South China Sea. But then the Saigon regime suddenly disintegrated in early 1975, and a reunited Vietnam emerged which was, from China's point of view, far too willing to deal with the Soviets. The same applied, with only minor qualifications, to Laos. Only Pol Pot's regime had no dealings with the Soviets, and it was on it that the Chinese bestowed their favours after 1975.

Hanoi had previously tried to balance the demands of its two major patrons, but as Beijing intensified its pressure after 1973 this became increasingly difficult. Hanoi responded by moving closer to Moscow, both a wealthier and a less exacting supporter, and by seeking an opening to the West that failed to materialize. By 1976 Chinese pressure had become open, with Mao declaring that the Vietnamese had not fought for forty years only to let the Soviets take the country over, but the death of Mao in September 1976 precipitated a bitter factional struggle in Beijing that gave Hanoi respite for several months.

After the purging of the 'Gang of Four' there was a brief improvement in Sino-Vietnamese relations. For a time, China's new leaders tried to woo Hanoi away from Moscow, rather than to force it. But Beijing could not compete with Moscow's offers of economic largess, and Hanoi clung doggedly to its Soviet connection. As the 'soft' approach failed to yield the desired results, China swung back to the 'hard' approach in May 1977.[26] It began to apply the screws over the South China Seas, and over the Hoa in Vietnam. The situation on the Sino-Vietnamese border began to deteriorate seriously. But the most explosive development was Beijing's decision openly to back Pol Pot's border war against Vietnam.

The importance of Cambodia in Beijing's foreign policy was not new. China had enjoyed good relations with Sihanouk's government since the Geneva Conference. Beijing's main objective at this time was to avert a US military presence, and Sihanouk's neutralist regime satisfied this aim. From 1956 Beijing provided him with substantial economic aid and, according to one expert, gave his government a 'guarantee' of security against the Vietnamese.[27] They gave little if any practical support to the Communist Party of Kampuchea (CPK), disagreeing like the Vietnamese with Pol Pot's strategy of overthrowing Sihanouk. But when Sihanouk was toppled by the right wing in 1970, it was Zhou Enlai who persuaded him to join forces with the Khmer Rouge. Both Sihanouk and the CPK distrusted the Vietnamese Communists, with whom they now became allied, and Moscow's prompt recognition of the Lon Nol regime in Phnom Penh may have unwittingly helped push both of them into the Chinese camp. In 1972 China served warning that it was opposed to a situation in which Indochina was dominated by any one country (that is, Vietnam).[28]

The ties between China and the Khmer Rouge were strengthened after April 1975. Chinese planes were reported flying into Cambodia immediately after the Khmer Rouge victory, and for some months provided the country's only link with the outside world. Indeed, China was the only country with which the new regime in Phnom Penh developed close relations. Within months, Beijing was providing substantial military aid, underwriting the expansion of the Khmer Rouge army that took place with the coming of peace. In August 1975 Khieu Samphan visited Beijing and signed an agreement on economic cooperation, under which China agreed to provide Cambodia with $200 million of aid over five to six years. On the same occasion he also signed a joint communiqué condemning Soviet 'hegemony'.

In the light of these commitments, it was inevitable that the Chinese would become embroiled in Pol Pot's border war with Vietnam. It is hard to agree with Steve Heder that China's stance in the Vietnam–Cambodia dispute was one of neutrality.[29] China had established what Heder describes accurately enough as 'an anti-Soviet alliance' with the Khmer Rouge regime. But it was actively trying to pressure Vietnam into following suit, not simply seeking to prevent a 'deterioration' of its relationship with Hanoi, as Heder maintains. While Vietnam retained its Soviet connections, the Chinese were bound to oppose its attempts to develop a 'special relationship' with Phnom Penh. Indeed, encouraging Pol Pot was a useful way for China to step up the pressure on Vietnam.

In any case the Chinese 'balancing act' ended with the escalation of the Vietnam–Cambodia dispute in 1977. When Pol Pot celebrated his victory in the inner-party struggle with a visit to Beijing in October, he was given an exceptionally warm welcome. Hua Guofeng, temporarily the top man in Beijing politics, personally presided over his reception, which was attended by nine other members of the Chinese Politburo. This came just after large-scale border attacks by Khmer Rouge forces, and Pol Pot treated his hosts to a diatribe against the Vietnamese.[30] China cut all military cooperation with Vietnam on 31 December, the day Cambodia broke off diplomatic relations with Hanoi. China dropped the pretence of neutrality after the Vietnamese offensive in December 1977 and blamed the Vietnam–Cambodia border war on Vietnamese 'aggression'.

In January 1978 Zhou Enlai's widow, Deng Yingchao, visited Phnom Penh and signed an agreement stepping up military aid to Cambodia. Fresh shipments of ammunition and weapons arrived the following month. These included 130-millimetre artillery, promptly deployed to bombard Vietnam. In March Chinese engineers arrived to rebuild the Kompong Som–Phnom Penh railway line. When this task had been completed they remained in place, apparently to signal to Hanoi that any action against Phnom Penh would involve the Chinese.

All of this was still part of what one American expert describes as a Chinese policy of 'restraint' towards Vietnam. This ended in May 1978, when the Chinese 'began a series of . . . moves which appeared designed to exert much stronger pressure on Vietnam'.[31] When Vietnam, determined that Pol Pot had to go, moved to protect itself by joining Comecon, Beijing's *People's Daily* responded by accusing Vietnam of annexationist ambitions, repeated Pol Pot's 'Indochina Federation' charges and accused Vietnam of being an 'Asian Cuba'. The Chinese stepped up their military aid to the Cambodian regime, ended all aid to Vietnam, and closed the Sino-Vietnamese border. Following this the number of armed clashes on the border rose rapidly.

From this sequence of events the Vietnamese Communists concluded that the sinister hand of Beijing lay behind their troubles with Cambodia. Echoing arguments that were advanced to us in Hanoi, Wilfred Burchett has written:

> Why was a negotiated solution to problems between two neighbouring states, headed by supposedly comradely Communist Parties, impossible? It is now clear that by 1977 Peking was running Khmer Rouge affairs. . . . Whereas Vietnam had stubbornly refused to be placed in China's pocket, Pol Pot had jumped into it himself. China has been charged on many occasions with being interested in fighting the United States to the last Vietnamese and was certainly no less averse to fighting Vietnam to the last Cambodian.[32]

With this assessment we must disagree. For better or worse, it seems clear to us that Pol Pot's group had its own home-grown reasons for provoking a feud with Hanoi. While Beijing sought to exploit this situation to its own advantage, it was no more in control of Pol Pot than Hanoi was.

When Vietnam joined Comecon, Pol Pot's defence minister, Son Sen, was promptly dispatched to Beijing to drum up more support, but the results must have been deeply disappointing to him. Since Pol Pot's visit, the power struggle in Beijing had gone against the friends of the Khmer Rouge regime, and Sen had to deal not with Hua Guofeng, but with

Deng Xiaoping – who doubtless had not forgotten that he had been personally denounced over Phnom Penh Radio as an 'anti-socialist and counter-revolutionary' in 1976. Deng apparently tried to push Pol Pot's regime onto the path of moderation. It is said that he bluntly told Son Sen that while China would do its utmost to prevent a collapse of the Phnom Penh regime, all the Chinese aid in the world would be of no avail if Pol Pot continued on his current political course.[33]

Deng was as strongly committed as anybody in Beijing to the notion of using the Phnom Penh regime as an instrument against Soviet–Vietnamese 'hegemonism' in Southeast Asia, but he is said to have argued that if Cambodia continued its violent provocations on the Vietnam border on the scale it was then doing, it would make a Vietnamese invasion inevitable. The outcome would be Vietnamese domination of all Indochina, rather than Deng's own personal preference, a pro-Chinese Cambodia slowly 'bleeding' Vietnam.

Son Sen thus returned from Beijing with the sorry task of trying to talk Pol Pot into moderation just at the time when he was taking his final vengeance on the 'pro-Vietnamese traitors' of Cambodia's eastern region. Pol Pot allowed Sihanouk to make a few cosmetic public statements in support of the Democratic Kampuchea (DK) regime, but beyond that appears to have been unresponsive to Deng's pressure. In early September another of Pol Pot's cohorts, Nuon Chea, visited Beijing, apparently unsuccessfully seeking a commitment of Chinese troops to Cambodia. Instead, Deng urged the Khmer Rouge to start preparing for a drawn-out guerrilla campaign against the Vietnamese occupation forces. The Chinese began shipping supplies of arms, canned food and radio equipment into Cambodia, for use in such a struggle. Son Sen took charge of preparing bases in the mountains and shifting stocks of rice and other supplies up into them.

When the Vietnamese signed their friendship treaty with the Soviet Union in November 1978, the Chinese promptly sent a delegation to Phnom Penh to reassure the Khmer Rouge leaders of Beijing's support. Pol Pot went on Phnom Penh Radio to praise what he described as Beijing's 'unconditional support' for Cambodia's struggle against Vietnam. But the reality was much less reassuring. Deng Xiaoping had dispatched Wang Dong Xing, one of his political enemies (whom he would finally sack in February 1980) to Phnom Penh, while he himself did the rounds of the ASEAN capitals to counter Pham Van Dong's earlier tour.

By this stage, Deng had apparently written off the Pol Pot regime. In Bangkok he predicted that Vietnam would invade and that Cambodia would be completely overrun. His objective was not to keep Pol Pot in Phnom Penh, but to persuade the ASEAN countries to join with China in supporting an armed insurgency in Cambodia against a Vietnamese-backed regime in Phnom Penh. He also said that China's direct response to the impending Vietnamese invasion would have to be restrained because of Vietnam's close relationship with the Soviet Union, though he added that he would not rule out 'a punitive raid by China in the same way as it attacked Indian forces in 1962'.[34]

At this stage the Chinese leaders were still divided over what course to take. When Vietnam countered Chinese pressure by opting for a close alliance with Moscow in June, some, such as Hua Guofeng, apparently believed that China should immediately take drastic measures. But Deng Xiaoping emphasized the need for caution because of the danger of Soviet retaliation if China took any military measures against Vietnam.[35] In this delicately poised situation, American support for China tipped the balance in favour of war.

While relations between China and Vietnam deteriorated, rapid progress was made in the normalization of relations between Beijing and Washington. The two processes were interconnected, because it was the desire to strengthen their anti-Soviet policies that induced both sides to compromise over the Taiwan issue, and the anti-Soviet hardliners in Washington encouraged China to take a tough line against Vietnam. During the visit of May 1978, which finally opened the way to full normalization of Sino-American relations, Brzezinski proclaimed that the USA shared China's 'resolve to resist the efforts of any nation which seeks to establish global or regional hegemony' – 'regional hegemonists' being Beijing's code-word for Vietnam. China's turn to display a tough policy towards Vietnam came only four days later. The USA had already blocked Vietnam's first post-war endeavours to open to the West, and in the second half of 1978 it continued to reject Hanoi's increasingly desperate attempts at reconciliation.

When Vietnam signed its military treaty with the Soviet Union in November, the USA responded by announcing that it no longer opposed military sales to Beijing, and in early December it came down unequivocally against Hanoi in the Vietnam–Cambodia border dispute. When the Chinese pointedly welcomed these moves as helping to limit the influence of Moscow's 'surrogate', Washington did not object. The agreement to normalize relations between Washington and Beijing, announced on 15 December, duly emphasized the commitment of both sides to opposition to 'international hegemony' (the Soviet Union), and there were no US objections when Hua Guofeng added that the agreement would also be useful against 'regional hegemonism'. Ten days later Vietnam invaded Cambodia, toppling Pol Pot's regime with a speed that dismayed even those (such as Deng) who had been most sceptical of DK's military capabilities.

The Chinese began military preparations for their invasion of Vietnam in mid-January, assured that US support would protect them against possible Soviet retaliation. But Deng was evidently not fully satisfied until after his visit to the USA at the end of the month. In private, Deng informed the American president of the planned invasion; publicly he spoke of the need to 'teach Vietnam a lesson'. Carter says that he privately advised Deng against the invasion.[36] Publicly, while they did not endorse Deng's statements on the need to 'teach Vietnam a lesson', the Americans did not object. But they did not publicly warn China against invading, or threaten any form of diplomatic retaliation if it did. They waited until Deng had left the country before declaring that these views were not necessarily the USA's as well as China's. Deng appears to have taken this as tacit support. The final decision to go ahead with the invasion was reportedly made the day after his return to Beijing.

According to Victor Zorza, a well-informed observer, the main motivation for American policy at this juncture was to strengthen Deng's faction in the unfolding power struggle in Beijing. A fortnight before the Chinese invasion, he reported:

> Senior White House officials have ... said that one reason why President Carter had decided to move rapidly towards normalization was his wish to show support for Deng. This is one reason why Carter made the concessions on Taiwan that exposed him to the charge that he was abandoning a long-time ally. If there had been no understanding on Taiwan and no normalization with the United States, then Deng would have been unlikely to prevail against Hua.[37]

The Americans had been alarmed by hints of a thaw in Sino-Soviet relations, and by reports that Hua favoured a partial withdrawal of troops from the Sino-Soviet border as a conciliatory gesture to Moscow before striking at Vietnam. Deng, by contrast, was especially anxious to secure American support because he wanted to maintain an antagonistic posture on the Sino-Soviet border as well as to punish Vietnam.

The USA thus indulged China's invasion of Vietnam while condemning Vietnam's invasion of Cambodia in the strongest terms. The Carter administration did not even slow up the process of diplomatic normalization of relations with China as a sign of displeasure, while in the case of Vietnam it rejected normalization altogether.

The Sino-Vietnamese war was the culmination of steadily mounting Chinese pressure on Vietnam following the Sino-American *rapprochement* of the early 1970s. This opened the way for a rapid expansion of Chinese influence in Southeast Asia, to which Vietnam proved the most resistant. China went to war with Vietnam because Hanoi had overthrown Pol Pot's regime in Cambodia. This was in no way a threat to China's national security (as Pol Pot's attacks were to Vietnam's security), but it did damage

China's new-found prestige as a great power in the Southeast Asian region. Not only had the Vietnamese persistently defied Chinese pressure to break with Moscow, but they had also overthrown a regime to whose protection China had committed itself. In the face of this, the fact that Deng's moderate faction, at least, regarded Pol Pot's regime as suicidally destructive was beside the point. Vietnam's actions were intolerable in the eyes of Beijing; Hanoi had to be punished, and China's rapidly growing ties with the USA provided insurance against Soviet retaliation. In the West, these conflicts were perceived through the prism of Soviet–American Cold War antagonisms: while Vietnam was condemned and ostracized for invading Pol Pot's Cambodia, China's retaliatory invasion of Vietnam was viewed with considerable indulgence.

China's invasion of Vietnam was thus a classic exercise in power politics. Deng's announcement that China had the 'right' to teach Vietnam 'lessons' whenever it wanted was an assertion that Vietnam fell into a Chinese sphere of interest. It was an effective practical rebuttal of benign interpretations of Chinese foreign policy based on its democratic rhetoric.[38]

But China's attempt to coerce Vietnam into submission failed. On the battlefields of northern Vietnam in 1979, it was China's military weakness rather than its irresistible strength that was displayed. Vietnamese military forces in Cambodia had soon reduced Pol Pot's forces to an isolated guerrilla force. As a pro-Vietnamese government was installed in Phnom Penh official Chinese influence in Laos was eliminated. Hanoi remained obstinately defiant and reaffirmed its position over the South China Sea. Chinese policy towards Indochina had in 1975–79 proven counter-productive. From a position of considerable influence in 1975, Beijing's policies resulted in its influence shrinking to next to nothing, and by 1980 it was faced with the prospect of a bloc of solidly pro-Soviet states in Indochina – the very outcome it had been trying to avoid. The stage was set for a new struggle with Vietnam and its Soviet patron, on considerably less advantageous terms for China.

Notes

1. Cf. J.R.V. Prescott, J.H. Collier, D.F. Prescott, *Frontiers of Southeast Asia*, Melbourne 1977, p. 60.

2. *Peking Review*, 4 May 1979.

3. In King C. Chen, ed., *China and the Three Worlds: A Foreign Policy Reader*, London 1979, p. 128.

4. Ministry of Foreign Affairs, Socialist Republic of Vietnam. *The Truth about Vietnam–China Relations over the Last Thirty Years*, Hanoi 1979, p. 12.

5. Cf. the three articles by *People's Daily* and Xinhua (the official Chinese news agency) commentators in *Peking Review*, 30 November–7 December 1979. The last of these was accompanied by a lengthy article by VCP veteran Hoang Van Hoan, who defected to China in the wake of the Sino-Vietnamese war. Hoan concludes that the crisis occurred because 'Le Duan is not honest and decent'.

6. C.P. Fitzgerald, *The Chinese View of their Place in the World*, London 1964, pp. 71–2.

7. In Franz Schurmann and Orville Schell, eds, *Imperial China*, vol. 1, New York 1967, pp. 107–8.

8. Truong Buu Lam, 'Intervention versus Tribute in Sino-Vietnamese Relations, 1788–90', in John K. Fairbank, ed., *The Chinese World Order: Traditional China's Foreign Relations*, Cambridge, Mass. 1968, pp. 178–9. This volume is the standard modern work on this subject.

9. Benjamin I. Schwartz, 'The Chinese Perception of World Order, Past and Present' in Fairbank, p. 285.

10. Quoted by Michael B. Yahuda, *China's Role in World Affairs*, London 1978, p. 67.

11. Gerald Segal, 'China and the Great Power Triangle', *China Quarterly*, no. 83, 1980, pp. 492–3.

12. For the best account of the Sino-Soviet dispute to this point, see O. Edmund Clubb, *China and Russia: The 'Great Game'*, New York 1971.

13. It was not the first time. Like the Vietnamese after their victory, the Chinese Communists in the 1940s had actively sought a *rapprochement* with the USA. On 13 March 1945 Mao told John Service, a political officer in the American embassy in China: 'China's great post-war need is economic development. She lacks the capitalistic foundation necessary to carry this out alone. Her own standards of living are so low that they cannot be depressed any further to provide the needed capital. America and China complement each other economically; they will not compete. China does not have the requirements of a heavy industry of major size. She cannot hope to meet the United States in its highly specialized manufactures. She also needs to build up light industries to supply her own market and raise the living standards of her own people. Eventually she can supply these goods to other countries in the Far East. To help pay for this foreign trade and investment, she has raw materials and agricultural products. America is not only the most suitable country to assist in the economic development of China, she is also the only country fully able to participate' (Joseph W. Esherwick, ed., *Lost Chance in China: The World War II Despatches of John S. Service*, New York 1975, p. 373). It was even proposed that Mao and Zhou Enlai travel to Washington to explain the Chinese Communist Party's position to Roosevelt, but this idea was scotched by the US ambassador in China at this time, the anti-Communist Patrick J. Hurley. One can only speculate on the course that Asian history might have taken if there had been a positive American response to these overtures, but as it was American hostility pushed the Chinese in the direction of the Soviet Union.

14. The official version, presented at the trial of the 'Gang of Four' in Beijing in November 1980–January 1981, was that Lin died in a plane crash in Mongolia, attempting to flee the country after a failed attempt at assassinating Mao and staging a coup. In 1983 an account was published by a pseudonymous Chinese author, claiming that Mao organized the assassination of Lin before the plot reached maturity, and that the story of Lin's death in Mongolia was concocted to protect Mao's reputation: see Yao Ming Le, *The Conspiracy and Death of Lin Biao*, London 1983.

15. In Chen, p. 86.

16. Geoffrey Jukes, *The Soviet Union in Asia*, Sydney 1973, p. 2.

17. Robert G. Sutter, *Chinese Foreign Policy after the Cultural Revolution 1966–77*, Boulder 1978, p. 113.

18. Quoted in ibid., pp. 55, 118–19.

19. *Peking Review*, 7 December 1979.

20. Cf. G.D. Loescher, 'The Sino-Vietnamese War in Recent Historical Perspective', *Survey*, vol. 24, 1979, for a good treatment of the linkages between the Geneva Conference and the events of the late 1970s.

21. In its discussion of the Geneva Conference Hanoi weakened its own case by tactfully refraining from mentioning that the Soviet Union had supported China's position – although this point has doubtless been filed away for future reference and may yet appear in a white paper on Soviet–Vietnamese relations. The agreement between its two great-power patrons left the Viet Minh with a choice between accepting the compromise pushed by

Zhou and total diplomatic isolation. It is therefore ironic that the Cambodian Communists, supported by China, should accuse the Vietnamese of betraying them at Geneva.

22. However, some confirmation for Hanoi's analysis is given in a book by a former member of the Pakistani cabinet, Golam W. Chowdry. Chowdry played an instrumental role in developing the secret contacts between Washington and Beijing in 1969–71, and went to Columbia University when he was forced to leave Pakistan in 1971. According to Chowdry, Beijing's hostility towards Hanoi went back to well before the 1970s, and was one of the reasons for the Sino-American detente: 'Chinese Vice-Foreign Minister Han Nialong told me in July 1979 that China could foresee Hanoi's regional ambitions, or hegemonic aspirations in Southeast Asia, as early as the 1950s, yet neither Mao nor Zhou could publicly support the US cause in 1972. Just as the United States had to reaffirm its commitments for the defence of the Republic of China [Taiwan], so the Chinese leaders had to restate their position on the Vietnamese war in the Shanghai Communiqué' (*China in World Affairs: The Foreign Policy of the PRC since 1970*, Boulder 1982, p. 74). Frankly, we think that on this occasion Han was feeding him a line, hoping to have a favourable influence on the American position over Taiwan.

23. Marvin Kalb and Bernard Kalb, *Kissinger*, New York 1975, p. 318.

24. In Chen, pp. 149–50.

25. Robert S. Ross, *The Indochina Tangle: China's Vietnam Policy 1975–1979*, New York 1988, pp. 27–8.

26. Ibid., p. 128.

27. Roger M. Smith, *Cambodia's Foreign Policy*, Ithaca 1965, pp. 117–18.

28. Yahuda, p. 263.

29. Stephen R. Heder, 'The Cambodian–Vietnamese Conflict', in David W.P. Elliott, ed., *The Third Indochina Conflict*, Boulder 1981, pp. 43–4.

30. Ross, p. 158, argues that this shows Pol Pot was being 'defensive' in the face of Chinese pressure to moderate this stance. It is difficult to see the logic of this.

31. Robert G. Sutter, 'China's Strategy toward Vietnam and its Implications for the United States' in Elliot, *The Third Indochina Conflict*, pp. 175–6.

32. Wilfred Burchett, *The Vietnam–China–Cambodia Triangle*, London 1981, p. 149.

33. Nayan Chanda, *Far Eastern Economic Review*, 8 September 1978. However, Ross, pp. 192–3, rates Son Sen's visit to Beijing a success.

34. Chanda, *Far Eastern Economic Review*, 24 November 1978.

35. Sutter, 'China's Strategy', pp. 181–2. Cf. Ross, pp. 230–33.

35. Jimmy Carter, *Keeping the Faith*, London 1982, pp. 206–9.

37. Victor Zorza, *Guardian Weekly*, 4 February 1979.

38. In a book published shortly before the war, one expert had written: 'the Chinese have not sought to act as a conventional great power, demanding exclusive spheres of influence on its periphery. Nor has China sought to dominate the lesser countries on its border.' Even at the time it was written, this blissfully ignored many facts. Chinese policy towards Indochina he summed up in these terms: 'China's relations with the countries of Indochina ... continued to follow a strictly correct policy of total commitment and support. All these countries were independent of China and there were no attempts to cajole or dragoon them into following the Chinese line' (Yahuda, pp. 264, 262). Any commentary on this should be superfluous now, except to note that it is appropriate that the author took as proof of China's reluctance to engage in power politics its 'readiness to negotiate' over the South China Sea.

6

Indochina:
Federation or Alliance?

In the early months of 1979 the Vietnamese had succeeded both in over-throwing Pol Pot's regime in Cambodia and in rebuffing China's military response. The immediate crisis had been resolved in their favour, but they now faced a long struggle to consolidate their gains. The Hanoi government found itself more isolated politically than it had ever been, with its economy disrupted, and facing a long-term threat to its security from China. It had to scrap its plans for economic development and put a war-weary people in a state of military preparedness once more. It had to seek out reliable allies to support its defiance of Chinese power. Above all, it had to create a stable and sympathetic government out of the shambles in Cambodia after Pol Pot.

Vietnam under Siege

The contrast between the hopes of the Vietnamese Communist Party (VCP) of 1976 and the economic realities of 1979 could hardly have been more stark. Vietnam's national income was growing at 12 per cent per annum in 1976. By 1979 the growth rate had fallen to zero.[1] Above all, rice production stagnated at a level of 10 million tonnes, while the population continued to grow at 2.6 per cent per annum. The growth of exports (principally of agricultural products) anticipated by the planners failed to materialize, while foreign debt rose rapidly. The optimism of 1976 was shattered. To Huu, a deputy premier, told Wilfred Burchett: 'We will be poor and we will be hungry until the end of this century.'[2]

Vietnam's post-war economic strategy had been completely wrecked by the unfolding of the unanticipated conflict with the Khmer Rouge regime and China, as well as by the failure to make the expected break-

147

through to the West after 1975. The measures taken by the Hanoi regime in 1977–78 in response to this crisis (the crackdown on trade and the collectivization drive in the south) had added to the economic disruption, particularly in the agricultural sector. Then, in 1978, the economy was put back on a war footing – by 1980 about 14 per cent of gross national product was being channelled to the military.

The 1976 plan had been dependent on outside financial assistance, and left Vietnam vulnerable to outside pressures. China cut off all its aid in 1978. Japan and many western countries followed suit after the Vietnamese toppled the Pol Pot regime. Since then Washington has also been going out of its way to obstruct any aid from international organizations flowing to Vietnam.

The economic pressure on Vietnam was evident to visitors in the early 1980s in the empty shops, the low rations, and shortages of goods of almost every kind. Doctors reported a rise in malnutrition-linked diseases, especially among children. The pressure was also reflected in the continuing exodus from the country, and in the changed ethnic composition of the refugees. Whereas in 1978–79 most had been ethnic Chinese and many from a bourgeois background, from 1980 the great majority were ethnic Vietnamese and many were from humble backgrounds. Most were fleeing, not from political oppression, but from biting poverty. A US analyst commented in 1985: 'What started out between 1975 and 1981 as a genuine refugee flow has slowly shifted to a migratory flow now composed of some refugees, a growing number of family reunification cases, and an ever larger economic migrant component.'[3]

The leadership in Hanoi responded to the crisis by rethinking its economic strategy. The process began with the 6th Plenum of the VCP Central Committee in September 1979, which retreated from the hardline approach adopted in 1978. It announced a policy aimed at reducing the barriers to the private circulation of goods and encouraging private production for the market, as well as running state enterprises more efficiently. The brakes were applied to the collectivization movement in the south. A contract system was introduced allowing individuals, families or cooperatives to rent land and implements belonging to collective farms, and allowing farmers to sell surplus produce on the private market.

The results were soon evident. In the towns, thousands of small workshops and street stalls sprang up, and people talked of the economy exploding. State enterprises also appear to have increased their output sharply. Even more important, agricultural production rose, and exports picked up. The decline in national income was reversed, and it was growing at 5–6 per cent per annum in the early 1980s.[4] These positive results encouraged further experiments in liberalization, in which officials in the south played a leading role. Others warned of the revival of capitalism, and struggled to reassert central control.

The VCP's 5th Congress, held in 1982, was described by foreign commentators as the 'Congress of Self-Criticism'. The Political Report, read by Le Duan, declared the Second Five Year Plan of 1976 a failure:

> The results of the implementation of the economic plans in the years 1976–80 have not reduced the serious imbalances in our national economy. ... There are shortages of food, fabrics, and other essential consumer goods. Great shortages exist in the supply of energy and materials, in communication and transport. Many enterprises operate below capacity. There are still great disparities between budget revenues and expenditures, commodities and money, imports and exports. ... Prices are unstable. There are still large numbers of people who are unemployed. The livelihood of the working people, especially workers, state employees and peasants, is fraught with difficulties.[5]

The main economic goal was to stabilize, and eventually to improve, the country's standard of living. Vietnam's Third Five Year Plan, which the Congress endorsed, was considerably less ambitious than the Second Five Year Plan of 1976. Instead of 15 per cent, it aimed at an economic growth rate of 5 per cent per annum.

But Le Duan was ambiguous about how this would be achieved. While calling for all-round self-criticism he praised both the 'correct general and economic policies' of the 4th Congress in 1976 and the 1979 reforms, which helped 'create a new drive and new progress in production'.[6] These ambiguities reflected unresolved differences within the Vietnamese leadership. The Congress had been delayed for several months as the party leaders attempted unsuccessfully to settle these, and the Political Report adopted at the Congress was a compromise.

After the Congress, Vietnam's economic crisis slowly eased. Over the period 1982–85 the economy grew at about 7 per cent per annum. Agricultural production increased, and the 1985 harvest was 18.2 million tonnes. Per capita food production had risen from 266 kilos in 1980 to 304 kilos in 1985. Exports grew at around 15 per cent per annum, while imports grew at about 7 per cent. In 1981 payment on Vietnam's foreign debt ate up 86 per cent of the country's export earnings; by 1985 the figure was down to 45 per cent. Even so, the country still had a long way to go. The increase in the food supply did no more than provide a bare subsistence minimum. Exports were still only half the level of imports. The country had to suspend loan repayments to the IMF in 1981, and in January 1985 the IMF declared that it would no longer provide Vietnam with new credits.

Shortages of raw materials, spare parts and power meant that many factories operated at only 40–50 per cent of capacity. Government officials put unemployment at 2.5 million (some western estimates put the figure as high as 4 million). And the increase in population went still unchecked. A confidential IMF report drawn up in 1984 highlighted continuing weaknesses in enterprise management:

> Although a major part of investment has been directed towards centrally managed enterprises, the performance of these enterprises has been disappointing and has contributed to shortages of both investment and consumer goods. In addition, labour productivity and the quality of output remained low in most sectors of the economy.

Generalized shortages and a large government deficit fuelled inflationary pressures, and too often enterprises responded to the relaxation of central controls by putting up their prices, rather than by increasing production. Inflation was believed to be running at about 50 per cent in 1984–85.

The party leadership continued to be divided over economic policy in the early 1980s. The compromise at the 5th Congress was a fragile one. One of the most outspoken of the southern reformers, Nguyen Van Linh, was sacked from the Politburo at the Congress itself. Later in 1982, northern officials launched an attack on the Ho Chi Minh City party leadership, accusing it of ideological deficiencies and of ignoring directives from Hanoi. An editorial in the party journal in 1983 warned that, due to the laxity of the leadership, the VCP was in danger of losing the struggle against capitalism in the south. The hardliners wanted to step up the campaign of 'socialist transformation' launched in 1978.

But the policies of 1978 had helped plunge Vietnam into chaos, and the reforms of the early 1980s were delivering positive results. Thus the political balance inside the party gradually shifted in favour of the reformers. By the end of 1983 the northern leaders were referring favourably to the successes of the new economic policies in the south. Less was heard of the need for 'socialist transformation'. In early 1985 a Vietnam News Agency commentary, praising Ho Chi Minh City for achieving an annual growth of gross product of 13 per cent, even emphasized the contributions of the southern capitalist class, with its 'high proficiency in business operations'.[7] By this time Hanoi was feeling the need for such skills. At the Central Committee Plenum in July 1984, the leadership had decided that the 'central task' was increasing production, and that the main obstacles to this were 'bureaucratism and the old mode of management'. The meeting issued a communiqué declaring that it was necessary to step up reform 'to broaden the initiative and the innovative spirit of the production and business units'. Yet little was done. Visitors spoke of a sense of drift in Hanoi in 1984–85. David Jenkins commented that the country was still in the hands of the 'Dien Bien Phu generation' of revolutionaries – 'not very well educated, not very innovative, not able to bring about change'. He added that 'though younger cadres, educated in the Soviet Union or elsewhere, may know the country is missing out, they are not really in a position at this point to do anything about it'.[8]

In the 1980s the VCP was also facing the problem of a leadership succession. This has often proved to be a destabilizing business in Communist political systems, especially where there are divisions over policy issues. William Duiker has written that the Congress 'failed to deal effectively with the problem of succession'.[9] This is not really true. To ensure continuity and stability, the party leaders wanted the succession to take place by instalments. On the eve of the 5th Congress *Nhan Dan* declared that the need was to 'rejuvenate the Politburo ... gradually and slowly'.[10]

The 5th Congress did launch the party into a leadership transition. Six out of the seventeen members of the 1976 Politburo stood down, and were replaced by seven new members. Most of those who stood down did so because of their advanced age. But some, most notably Nguyen Van Linh, had fallen victim to the in-fighting over economic policy. The most senior leadership remained unchanged. Le Duan was re-elected general secretary, although he was now aged and his health was failing. Truong Chinh and Pham Van Dong also stayed on. The period of drift in Hanoi politics ended with the Central Committee Plenum of June 1985. This marked the triumph of the reformers. The meeting reappointed Nguyen Van Linh to the Politburo and adopted what Radio Hanoi described as 'a drastic and far-reaching reorientation in our party's positions and policies'.

In the foreign policy proclaimed at the 5th Congress in 1982, there were few echoes of the 1976 attempt to balance China and the Soviet Union. The Political Report did refer to Vietnam's 'good neighbourly policy' but it dwelt mainly on the nation's 'historic mission': 'to face and defeat Chinese big-nation expansionism and hegemonism'. The Chinese were 'truculent, cruel and perfidious', but Vietnam's alliance with the Soviet Union guaranteed eventual victory. The Soviet bloc was 'increasingly stepping up its action as the crucial factor determining the trends of human society, a powerful force for peace, and a reliable prop for the revolutionary struggle of people throughout the world'.[11] The keystone of Vietnamese foreign policy was thus 'solidarity and all-round cooperation' with the Soviet Union.

The Soviets tided Hanoi over the 1979 crisis by sharply increasing their economic aid. Douglas Pike estimates that Soviet economic aid to Vietnam jumped to US$3 billion in 1980. As the worst of the crisis passed, this was cut back to $1.5 billion a year. But this was still roughly twice the level of Soviet assistance in the mid-1970s.[12] As other trade outlets dried up, Vietnam's trade with the Soviet bloc expanded rapidly. In the early 1980s, it provided two-thirds of the beleaguered country's imports.

Hanoi's Third Five Year Plan depended heavily on Soviet largess. It incorporated $5 billion worth of Soviet funding, including three electricity generation schemes and forty industrial projects. In return the Vietnamese agreed to expand exports of agricultural and textile products to the Soviet Union and Eastern Europe. Moscow and Hanoi also signed agreements on scientific and technical cooperation, including oil and gas exploration.

By 1985 some 60,000 Vietnamese 'guest workers' were employed in the Soviet Union and Eastern Europe. In contrast to Vietnam, these countries were experiencing shortages of labour. About a third of the wages of the 'guest workers' went to paying off Vietnam's foreign debt. But they still earned substantially more than they would have at home, and had access to consumer goods unavailable in Vietnam. They picked up valuable work skills, and had the prospect of a better job when they returned home. Western critics accused Hanoi of 'exporting slave labour', but in Vietnam workers were willing to pay large bribes to get an overseas job.

Soviet–Vietnamese military cooperation also expanded rapidly. In the early 1980s, according to Pike's estimates, Soviet military aid ran at around $1 billion a year – substantially higher than during Vietnam's American war. This enabled Hanoi to 'harden' its defences considerably along its northern border, and strengthened its hand in Cambodia as well. In return, Hanoi granted the Soviets access to the deep-water harbour facilities built by the Americans at Cam Ranh Bay. Mid-way between Vladivostok and the Indian Ocean, this was of considerable strategic value to Soviet naval forces in the Far East. The USSR had been seeking access to Cam Ranh Bay since 1975 but Hanoi, clearly aware of the hostility this would invite from Beijing, had refused. The first visit by Soviet ships to Cam Ranh took place in March 1979, a matter of weeks after the Chinese invasion made such considerations redundant.

Soviet use of the facilities at Cam Ranh grew slowly but steadily. In 1979 there were only two dilapidated piers at Cam Ranh. By 1985 the Soviets had added five floating piers, a floating dock, and a fuel storage tank. Soviet submarines and warships were using these facilities regularly. The US-built airfield was also brought back into operation, and a squadron of Soviet planes was stationed there. In addition, the Soviets had established a radio communications centre at Cam Ranh, which presumably enabled them to gather signals intelligence from southern China and Southeast Asia. The Americans insisted that this amounted to a permanent, fully operational military base. The Vietnamese and the Soviets say that it is not a military base, but a point of supply and replenishment for Soviet forces; sovereignty over Cam Ranh remains in Vietnamese hands. Pike comments: 'In terms of technical military usage, this is correct.

The more important point, however, is that the usage to which the USSR is permitted to put these facilities meets all of its strategic requirements in the Southeast Asia region.'[13]

It was often claimed that the great attraction of Cam Ranh to the Soviets was that it enabled them to threaten one of the most travelled shipping routes in the world – that between the Middle East and Japan. But the most thorough assessment by a US military analyst concluded, despite much Cold War rhetoric, that the Soviet presence at Cam Ranh 'is unlikely to have a specific, aggressive regional intent, since that would be quite out of character for a power that, at least until now, has revealed itself as ... cautious and non-confrontational'.[14] Cam Ranh is useful to the Soviets in more mundane ways. It enables them to make air reconnaissance missions in the South China Seas, and probably to eavesdrop on both American and Chinese military communications. By providing repair and refuelling facilities for the Soviet navy, it has extended the operating time of vessels on missions far from Vladivostok. This has given the Soviets the capability of a greater presence in the Indian Ocean. But the facilities at Cam Ranh are hardly comparable to those at Clark Air Base and Subic Bay in the Philippines.

Whatever one's assessment of the threat capacity of the Soviets in Cam Ranh Bay, their presence there does underscore one point. China and the USA have been able to hurt Vietnam badly through continued economic pressure, but they had not bled it into submission. Indeed, by 1985 it was clear that the result was the exact opposite of what they had hoped. Rather than breaking off its relationship with Moscow, a defiant Hanoi had reinforced that relationship. Vietnam was recovering from the crisis of the late 1970s and early 1980s. While Soviet support for Vietnam remained firm, the chances of economic pressures forcing Hanoi to abandon what it saw as vital strategic interests in Cambodia were increasingly remote.

'A Land of Skulls, Gore and Stench'

After the Vietnamese toppled Pol Pot's regime in 1979, outsiders had access to abundant evidence of the appalling brutalities that had taken place under his rule. A Polish journalist who visited Prey Veng in February 1979 described the discovery of thousands of putrefying corpses left behind by the fleeing Khmer Rouge. Survivors of the massacre told him that 22,000 people had been killed in the town market and their bodies thrown into the town sewers; the slaughter was brought to a halt only by the Vietnamese invasion. 'Have you heard of liquid bodies?' he later asked a journalist in Bangkok. 'What we saw were the remains, which were just liquefied flesh with millions of maggots and worms.' Western journalists were soon allowed in, and confirmed this picture. The Cambodia Pol Pot left behind was described in March by AAP reporter Harish Charandola as 'a land of skulls, gore and stench'. Taken to Prey Veng, he found the stink 'unbearable'. It was not just that the town sewers were choked with rotting corpses; in the surrounding countryside, 'shallow, unmarked graves are everywhere. Bones are everywhere just below the surface.'

In the wake of the Vietnamese invasion the bonds of coercion that had held the Khmer Rouge economic system together were broken. No longer compelled to stay where they were, millions of people who had been relocated took to the road once more, returning to their old homes, or searching for family members from whom they had been separated under Pol Pot. Much of the year's main harvest stood abandoned in the fields, and was consumed by pests or trampled by wild animals and abandoned water buffaloes. Rather than work on the harvest, in many areas villagers broke into Khmer Rouge collective storehouses and feasted – often consuming seed rice as well as milled rice. In many villages livestock was also recklessly killed and eaten. Thus, for a few weeks after the invasion, many ate well, even very well – but then, as stockpiles of food were exhausted, the consequences of the widespread failure to gather the year's main rice harvest began to bite.

In February 1979 the new authorities in Phnom Penh (the People's Republic of Kampuchea, PRK) warned that 'the quantity of rice available for the people is negligible'.[15] By July they were warning of an impending famine in Cambodia and calling for urgent international aid. American officials attacked this statement as 'alarmist'; UN and Red Cross officials went to investigate the situation, and were appalled by what they found. Hunger and malnutrition were widespread; much of the population was anaemic and malarial, while intestinal diseases (gastro-enteritis and dysentery), parasites (such as hookworm) and tuberculosis were endemic; there had been outbreaks of anthrax and bubonic plague; and medical facilities were to all practical purposes non-existent (the few there had been having been smashed by the Khmer Rouge before the Vietnamese takeover). Still more ominous, very little of the following season's crop had been planted. Vast numbers of people were still roaming the countryside rather than settling down to productive activity, and there were few tools and livestock. Barely 40 per cent of the fields in Cambodia were under any cultivation at all, while in the fertile lower Mekong provinces the figure was under 10 per cent.

The officials remarked that Pol Pot's attempt to 'turn the clock back' had turned a once fertile land into a 'desert' and warned that 2.5 million people could starve to death in the following few months unless something was done quickly. In September the British journalist John Pilger took a television crew to Cambodia to make a documentary on the state of the country. On his return he wrote: 'During twenty years as a journalist, most of them spent in transit at wars and places of contrived upheaval, I have not seen anything to compare with what I saw in Cambodia.'[16] The images of starvation and suffering Pilger presented to television audiences may have been overdrawn. But they did much to alert the western public to a disaster that was indisputably real.

Pilger was much criticized for being simplistic and sensationalist. William Shawcross later objected to him calling Pol Pot an 'Asian Hitler'. This was supposedly an attempt to conceal the Communist lineage of his crimes. But Pilger had also compared Pol Pot's rule to Stalin's terror and Mao's Cultural Revolution. And Shawcross had no objections to those who compared the Vietnamese with the Nazis.[17] Such pettifogging criticism was indicative of the extent to which the Cambodian question became embroiled in Cold War rivalries.

The dispute soon came to a head in the United Nations. Previously, the Pol Pot regime had repeatedly spurned any suggestion of taking the Vietnam–Cambodia dispute to the UN. But on 1 January 1979 Ieng Sary, as Democratic Kampuchea (DK) foreign minister, called on the UN Security Council to convene an emergency session to condemn Vietnam. His call was promptly supported by China and the USA. Before the meeting could open, Pol Pot and Ieng Sary were forced to flee Phnom Penh. Heng Samrin declared that the DK government had 'ceased to exist' and that the PRK was the sole legitimate representative of the Cambodian people. But Pol Pot had dispatched Sihanouk to the UN as the DK representative, and it agreed to continue recognizing the DK regime. Sihanouk condemned the Vietnamese invasion as 'naked aggression from one country against another without any justification'. He was followed by the Chinese delegate who demanded the UN take 'effective action' to force the Vietnamese to withdraw. After an acrimonious debate a majority of the Security Council opted to vote for the withdrawal of foreign forces from Cambodia, but avoided committing UN forces to the conflict. Even this was promptly vetoed by the USSR. With China and the USA lobbying on his behalf, Pol Pot did better in UN forums than he did in Cambodia itself. In September 1979 the UN General Assembly reaffirmed recognition of the DK regime by 71 votes to 35, with 34 abstentions. Not one western country voted against the Pol Pot regime, although Austria, France, Spain and the Scandinavian countries did abstain.

It was against this political background that the effort to aid the stricken people of Cambodia got under way in 1979. Moscow had no difficulty coming to the assistance of the latest recruit to the Soviet camp. By

December, about 1,500 tonnes of food from Soviet-bloc countries was being unloaded daily at Kompong Som port; in addition, medical supplies were being delivered by air, and Soviet-bloc technicians were flown in to help rehabilitate the country's shattered transport system. Soviet-bloc aid played a key role in opening the docks at Kompong Som and on the Mekong River at Phnom Penh, and in restoring the road and rail links between Phnom Penh and Battambang in the west.

It was a different story for Washington. Although US officials in Bangkok pointed to the gravity of the situation, their superiors in Washington were initially opposed to any western effort to aid Cambodia at all. The USA had launched a campaign to persuade the western countries to 'punish' Vietnam by cutting off aid. In this context, a major aid project to Cambodia amounted to breaking the siege. Officials in Washington at first refused to send any aid to Phnom Penh, and tried to discount reports from Thailand that food shortages in Cambodia were reaching crisis proportions. In June 1979 Washington agreed to send aid to Cambodia, but proposed sending it only to operations on the Thai border. Then it was argued that the requirements of 'neutrality' made aid to the 1–2 per cent of the population under Khmer Rouge control an essential precondition for giving aid to the rest. One US official explained: 'The only way we can help in Cambodia is by giving aid for both sides. If we can't find a way to help the people on Pol Pot's side it's unlikely that we'll be in a position to do anything even indirectly for those under Heng Samrin.'[18] On 2 July 1979 US Secretary of State Cyrus Vance called for direct famine relief for Cambodia. But President Carter let three months elapse before he announced that the USA itself would make any contribution to this effort. Aid shipments from Oxfam, a British agency not dependent on the US government, began in August. Before the American commitment in October, shipments of western aid to Phnom Penh were paltry compared to the flow of Soviet-bloc aid. By 12 October, when an Oxfam shipment of 1,500 tonnes arrived, western aid to the stricken country had totalled only 200 tonnes.

The basic reason for this was that the Red Cross and Unicef, the main international relief agencies, found themselves caught in the political crossfire between Washington and Phnom Penh, and their negotiations with the PRK government became bogged down as a consequence. While Washington was withholding its funds and insisting that aid to both sides was essential, the Heng Samrin government was bitterly opposed to international humanitarian aid being channelled to Pol Pot's forces. It claimed to be the sovereign government and insisted that all aid be sent via Phnom Penh. But beggars cannot be choosers, and in September 1979 the PRK needed western aid more than it needed to deny supplies to the Khmer Rouge. On 26 September, Phnom Penh granted approval to the Red

Cross and Unicef for large-scale relief operations in Cambodia. The Americans had won the tug-of-war: aid would flow to the insurgents, as well as to the PRK-controlled areas. On 24 October 1979, just five days after Prime Minister Kriangsak of Thailand had announced an 'open door' policy towards refugees from Cambodia, President Carter announced a $69 million aid programme to Cambodia to prevent a 'tragedy of almost genocidal proportions'. At a conference at the UN headquarters in New York on 5 November, aid totalling $20 million was pledged.

Western aid began to flow into Cambodia in increasing quantities, and by the start of December it was arriving at the rate of 1,000 tonnes a day. In fact, due to the still broken-down state of their transport system, the Cambodians were unable to distribute all the aid that now arrived. On 17 December the PRK foreign minister, Hun Sen, said that the bulk of western aid was being stockpiled in warehouses, and pointed out that until a recent delivery of 600 lorries from the Soviet-bloc countries, the government had only forty trucks to shift all the aid that was delivered. As the warehouses in Kompong Som and Phnom Penh were largely filled within a month, deliveries of western aid were cut from 30,000 tonnes a month to a more manageable level of 13,000 tonnes a month at the end of December.

Even before this the Americans had repeatedly attacked the PRK over aid distribution. In October, before the USA itself had agreed to give one cent in aid, the US government condemned the PRK authorities, the Vietnamese and the Soviets for failing to bring 'any discernible influence to bear to alleviate the situation'. The Vietnamese were accused of diverting what aid the West had sent from Cambodia to Vietnam itself. In November, President Carter accused the PRK of 'genocide', and reportedly cried in anguish: 'Is there no pity?' Leader-writers and editorialists took their cue. The resultant wave of self-righteous denunciations of Vietnam and Phnom Penh probably reached its zenith in the comment of Emmett Tyrell Jr, in the *Washington Post* on 24 December 1979: 'The lesson of Cambodia is the lesson of the Nazi concentration camps and the Gulag. Some people are immune to Western decency.' The fact that aid officials and journalists in Cambodia denied these reports was ignored by the zealots of 'Western decency'. The Hong Kong bureau chief of ABC News wrote:

It is commonly acknowledged that Cambodia's food distribution is slow and inefficient. But no competent observer, aid official or journalist who has visited Cambodia for longer than a week has concluded that the bottlenecks are the result of conscious Vietnamese or Cambodian policy. Instead, they say the delays are caused by a complex bureaucracy, inexperienced and inefficient administrators, lack of transport, and primitive communications.[19]

Investigating aid officials concluded that some aid was pilfered, but that it amounted to less than 1 per cent, much less than the amount lost to rats. In the end, even the US ambassador to Thailand admitted that there was no evidence that the Vietnamese or the Phnom Penh authorities were blocking the distribution of aid.

When we visited Cambodia early in 1980 we found the country in much better shape than we had expected. Supplies were obviously short, but there was rice, fish and fruit in local markets. Inadequate nutrition was widespread, but we saw no signs of outright starvation in the areas we visited. Children with bloated stomachs could still be seen, but there were none of the pitiful 'walking skeletons' that had attracted so much media attention a few months earlier. Many people told us that they had gone hungry in the second half of 1979, and that there had been some deaths from starvation. Conditions had been worst in the western provinces, where military insecurity was the greatest. For a few crucial months, large numbers of people had survived mainly by foraging, and it was thus the natural richness of the countryside rather than international aid that had saved them. Pressure on food supplies inside Cambodia had also been eased by the departure of about a million people from the worst areas to the Thai border.

Conditions had improved rapidly from November 1979, partly because of the flow of international relief. But the government had concentrated on feeding administrators and urban workers. By early 1980 distribution points had been established on the main highways, but only a limited amount of aid had reached the rural population, and none at all in the more remote areas. The situation had improved mainly because the year's main rice crop was gathered in November–December. The peasants were allowed to keep what they produced. But it was a meagre harvest, estimated at only 300,000 tonnes.

In order to break out of the vicious circle of famine conditions and poor harvests into which Cambodia appeared to be locked at this point, Phnom Penh and the aid agencies decided to take a major gamble. Though large quantities of food aid would still be needed, especially in the second half of the year, they would take advantage of the breathing space provided by the harvest to bring in seed rice and agricultural implements. Over the rest of the dry season they also made major efforts to improve the efficiency of transport and distribution of aid.

Pointing to the inefficiencies of distributing aid to rural areas via Phnom Penh (particularly in western Cambodia) the agencies adopted a US proposal that seed rice be handed out on the Thai border. The PRK protested bitterly, but allowed the scheme to go ahead. Politically, the result of the 'land-bridge' scheme was temporarily to attract large numbers of farmers into the orbit of the anti-Phnom Penh groups on the border, and to sour relations between the PRK and the aid agencies. Economically, the result was that in 1980 seed rice was distributed both via Phnom Penh and the border in substantial quantities, and the harvest turned out to be more than twice that of the previous year.

As the food crisis inside Cambodia eased, the political dimension of the aid operation came increasingly to the fore. Agencies operating inside the country were criticized for becoming involved in agricultural rehabilitation programmes, as well as providing emergency relief. This, it was argued, represented 'political' rather than 'humanitarian' aid. By helping put the national economy back on its feet, it inevitably helped the PRK consolidate control. By 1983, a few western agencies were still operating in Phnom Penh. But almost all donors had earmarked their aid for the Thai border.

Shawcross tried to assess 'the quality of mercy' – the effectiveness of aid to Cambodia from 1979 to 1983. He found little to be pleased with: 'A lot of the aid delivered ... helped millions of ordinary Cambodians. ... But overall its results were not a cause for rejoicing.'[20] He catalogued bureaucratic inefficiency and bungling, and the sometimes prickly relations between the Phnom Penh government and western aid agencies. By this time western agencies had spent a total of over $600 million on Cambodian relief. Roughly half went to the Thai border, and half to the interior of Cambodia. According to Shawcross's calculations, this meant that an average of $1,124 per head was spent on refugees inside Thailand, $439 a head on those who came to the border, and $48 a head on those who stayed inside Cambodia.[21] Such a lopsided pattern of spending clearly served to draw people out of Cambodia to the border, from PRK-controlled territory into the orbit of the anti-PRK groups.

Many 'ordinary Cambodians' were doubtless pleased to receive help, such as it was, from any quarter during the crisis. That, however, was not enough to satisfy Shawcross. Behind the pose of high moral purpose, his primary concern was political. He condemned the fact that humanitarian aid 'made viable' both the PRK government in Phnom Penh and the Khmer Rouge on the Thai border. The inability of western aid to eliminate the two rival Communist groups was a failure of 'political imagination'. Shawcross rebuked the PRK leaders for suspecting hostile political intent behind western humanitarian aid. His own attitude shows clearly how accurate their suspicions were, and his figures show how severely Cold War politics strained the quality of mercy in Cambodia. Overall, the Soviet bloc sent less aid than the West. But it refused to have anything to do with the Thai border operations, and sent all its aid direct to Phnom Penh. Shawcross is correct to criticize the Soviet bloc for sending what was to hand, rather than what was needed most. Much Soviet food aid was red corn which, Cambodian peasants complained, they did not know how to cook. But this was an emergency, and the inability of Soviet agriculture to provide what is needed even under normal circumstances is notorious.

Once the worst shortages were over, Soviet-bloc aid concentrated on economic reconstruction rather than emergency relief. In 1982 Moscow agreed to provide road-building equipment, fertilizer, and other inputs to boost agricultural production. By 1984, the Soviet Union had provided non-military aid worth $450 million to the PRK. By that time aid from the West had virtually ceased.

In 1975 the DK leaders had sought salvation for a small, war-shattered country in 'self-reliance'. In 1979 the leaders of the PRK pursued the opposite strategy, actively seeking international assistance. By 1982 the emergency was past, but acute political problems remained. The PRK had been established by force of Vietnamese arms, and was supported largely by Soviet-bloc aid. Western countries preferred to channel their aid to areas in the hands of guerrillas seeking to destabilize, and ultimately overthrow, the pro-Vietnamese government in Phnom Penh.

Consolidating the PRK

By 1980 the number of Vietnamese troops in Cambodia had risen to 200,000 but Cambodia did not look like a country under military occupation. It was common enough to see individual soldiers or small groups of them wandering around unarmed, sitting by the side of the road chatting with Khmer peasants, or bargaining in town markets like anybody else. Nobody seemed to take any particular notice of them. The Vietnamese soldiers built their own barracks, grew vegetables for themselves, and concentrated on their garrison duties, interfering as little as possible in the activities of the Khmer population.

The Vietnamese concentrated their own efforts on the military objective of securing the country against Pol Pot's forces. Behind the shield they provided, their Cambodian allies set about creating a new government structure. The PRK administration was built up slowly, from the top down and from the centre outwards, which means that at the village level there was a period of anarchy between the overthrow of the Khmer Rouge and the establishment of local authorities integrated with the central government. In the eastern and central regions this phase lasted for only a few weeks, but in the west of the country it was not until May or June 1979 that the new administration was able to consolidate its control, and it remained fragile for some time after that.

The resources with which the PRK was built up were pitifully few. Pol Pot's terror had decimated the ranks of Cambodia's initially small class of educated and professionally skilled people, and many of those that survived took advantage of the chaos that followed the Vietnamese invasion to flee the country. But it was not just a shortage of suitable people – almost everything was lacking. Even in February 1980, when there was a clearly functioning administration, it had to do without almost all the usual paraphernalia of modern bureaucracy. There were pens and paper, but they were not easy to come by. There were no telephones, and hardly any typewriters.

Vietnam's critics charged that Hanoi's aim was the annexation of Cambodia, and that the new regime was a mere façade for direct rule from Hanoi. Thai intelligence duly produced defectors from the PRK who confirmed this. The most prominent was Dy Lamthol, who had worked as personal secretary to the foreign minister, Hun Sen, and who defected in 1982. According to Lamthol, the VCP had established a special office, designated B-68, to oversee relations with Cambodia. He knew nothing of its operations, but he interpreted cables and telegrams arriving from Hanoi as 'instructions' and 'directives'. Asked if the Cambodians ever initiated policies, he replied: 'No, everything comes from the Vietnamese.'[22] It is probable that Lamthol was embellishing his story to please his interrogators. But there is no doubt that immediately after it was established the PRK opened close relations with Hanoi. In February 1979 Pham Van Dong led a Vietnamese delegation to Phnom Phenh to sign a 25-year treaty of 'peace, friendship and cooperation' between the two countries. The two governments agreed to 'assist each other in all fields on the basis of respect for independence, non-interference in internal affairs, and equality'. The PRK was presented as a sovereign state allied to Vietnam, rather than a subordinate state. Hanoi and Phnom Penh proclaimed the aim of strengthening 'the traditional friendship between the Cambodian, Lao and Vietnamese people'.

In 1981 the PRK shed its provisional character. Elections were held for local government positions in March. In May, a constitution was proclaimed. Elections were held for a National Assembly, which became the formal seat of governmental power. As the PRK consolidated itself, it took on the familiar contours of the Communist party-state. In the elections of May 1981, only candidates supporting the programme of the government-sponsored 'Salvation Front' were allowed to stand. The state administration was closely intertwined with that of the ruling party, especially at the local level. The Vietnamese had encouraged the formation of a new Communist party to assume the 'leading role' in the government, but it took some time before an effectively functioning organization emerged. The People's Revolutionary Party of Kampuchea (PRPK) was formed in 1979 with a only few hundred members.[23] It held what it billed as its 3rd Congress on 5 January, shortly before Pol Pot's regime fell (asserting its continuity with pre-Pol Pot Communism, the party regarded the congresses of the Khmer People's Revolutionary Party in 1951 and 1960 as its 1st and 2nd Congresses). The existence of the party was well known, at least to the politically informed. But it was not until after the 1981 elections that the PRPK went fully public, when it held its 4th Congress.

Twelve of the twenty-one members of the PRPK Central Committee unveiled at this time were veterans of the independence struggle of the early 1950s, forced into exile in 1954. Most had returned to Cambodia in 1970, and had broken with the Pol Pot clique by 1975. The most prominent among them was Pen Sovan, who was elected general secretary. Another six were former eastern region DK cadres who fled to Vietnam in the face of Pol Pot's repression in 1977–78. These included the PRK's president, Heng Samrin, and its foreign minister, Hun Sen. Two more had backgrounds elsewhere in the DK regime, and one had no revolutionary background.[24]

In the early 1980s, most western commentators asserted that the PRK was run by faithful yes-men, Cambodians who had lived in Vietnam since 1954 – that is to say, veterans of the struggles of the 1950s driven into exile by Sihanouk. Pen Sovan was depicted as Hanoi's man in Phnom Penh, and the strong-man of the regime. These commentators were therefore confounded when Pen Sovan resigned in December 1981, and Heng Samrin took over his party and government posts. Pen Sovan was later reported to be living under house arrest in Hanoi.[25]

It was promptly argued that he was really anti-Vietnamese, and had been booted out by the real yes-men for this reason. But no evidence was produced to support this claim. In fact, Pen Sovan's demise was the most dramatic episode in the political decline of the returnees. They provided half the PRPK leadership in 1979, but they held only two of the eleven positions on the Politburo that emerged from the 5th Congress in October 1985. The most prominent was Say Phouthang, who became head of the newly-established Party Inspectorate.

The political demise of the veterans meant an increase in the other main group in the government in 1979, former DK cadres who fled Pol Pot's purges in 1975–78. They accounted for ten members of the new Central Committee and five in the new Politburo. One of them, Heng Samrin, was re-elected general secretary. Another, Hun Sen, became prime minister following the death of returnee Chan Si from heart disease in December 1984. A further eight members of the Central Committee and two members of the Politburo were former Khmer Rouge who had broken with Pol Pot's group before 1975.

However the most striking change in the composition of the Central Committee was the emergence of younger figures who had no revolutionary background. They accounted for most of the new members added to the Central Committee, although only two had reached the Politburo. What is surprising is not that there so few of them at the top, but that any had made it at all in only six years.[26]

Under these circumstances, the anti-PRK propaganda line changed. Now it was alleged that they were 'loyal Khmer Rouge leaders' who had participated willingly in the mass murders of 1975–78. The major effort to indict them was made by Elizabeth Becker, and she came up with nothing. The PRK is a coalition of those, Communist and non-Communist, willing to cooperate with the Vietnamese to oppose the return to power of the Khmer Rouge. Much effort went into building the PRPK party organization. The result was a slow but steady expansion from a very small base. The PRPK membership went from perhaps a hundred in 1979 to 800 in 1980, and then to 7,500 by the time of the 5th Congress. But the leadership was not satisfied with this result. Heng Samrin's Political Report complained that the PRPK organizational structure was 'still thin and weak', especially at the district and grassroots levels. Over the next twelve months party membership rose to 10,000.[27]

From its inception the PRK was under armed attack from foreign-backed insurgents, and it could not expect to be protected by the Vietnamese for ever. In 1980 it began building up its army and security forces, under Vietnamese guidance. By the mid-1980s the PRK armed forces had been built up to a strength of about 30,000 troops. These regulars were supplemented by local, part-time militia. The introduction of conscription in 1985 foreshadowed further expansion. But western military analysts were derisory about the PRK armed forces' capabilities.[28]

Little is known of the development of the PRK's internal security forces. But in 1983 they launched a major crackdown against 'counter-revolutionary' elements in the capital and in the northwestern provinces. As a result, according to a report by Amnesty International, based on sources on the Thai–Cambodian border, there were 'several thousand political prisoners' in Cambodia by the middle of the decade. Most, but not all, were advocates of 'armed opposition to the authorities'.[29] Amnesty's sources indicated that even though the PRK authorities had given 'strict instructions to avoid the use of torture', these were often ignored.[30] If true, this is certainly deplorable. But it is scarcely surprising in a country with 7 million people, and a government combating an insurgency. It did not justify the propaganda claim that the PRK authorities were creating a system as repressive as that of the Khmer Rouge – 'a society which is comprehensively totalitarian, and in which torture, corruption, arbitrary arrest and imprisonment, political oppression, and cruel and degrading punishments are routine'.[31] But the fear that this would happen was enough to spark an exodus of several thousand Cambodians to the Thai border in 1983–84. It is not known whether this was what led to the dropping of the minister of the interior (responsible for the security forces), Khang Sarin, from the PRPK Politburo at the 4th Congress.

In December 1978 the Kampuchean National United Front for National Salvation (KNUFNS) programme had promised to replace the Pol Pot economic system with one based on 'genuine socialism'. This was to be based on a combination of state planning and free markets, and to allow prosperity and progress for the people. As the PRK consolidated itself, it appointed managers to restore production in the country's few industrial plants. Peasants were encouraged to form solidarity units (*krom samaki*). The right of free movement was restored, and private trade was legalized. The towns were settled, and Phnom Penh's population soon returned to pre-war levels of around 600,000. In 1981 a new official currency (the riel) was issued.

Along with the inflow of foreign aid, this helped bring about a rapid economic recovery. This cannot be charted in any detail because of the lack of any statistics for national income or product in Cambodia. But the country enjoyed a 'baby boom' in the early 1980s that lifted the population, on the UN Food and Agriculture Organization's estimates, from around 6 million in 1979–80 to 7.38 million in 1984–85. Over the same period, rice-paddy production had risen from 538,000 tonnes to 2 million tonnes. This brought the country almost – but not quite – to the brink of self-sufficiency in food.[32]

As domestic production increased and foreign aid was wound down, the PRK imposed various taxes to finance its activities. Like jails and the draft, taxes are never popular. In 1984 David Chandler suggested that 'support for the People's Republic may be fading somewhat as the regime begins to govern the country (after several years of presiding over it) by collecting taxes, putting criminals in jail, conscripting soldiers, and so on.'[33] To Chandler, this showed that the Vietnamese were 'tightening their grip'. In fact, what it showed was that the PRK was – in his own words – 'increasingly governing the country'.

Most anti-Vietnamese analysts assumed that Hanoi could never allow a strong government in Cambodia. Pao Min Chang wrote: 'a completely independent Kampuchea from Hanoi's viewpoint is all but synonymous with a hostile neighbour.'[34] But the Vietnamese actually saw it very differently. A weak and vulnerable Cambodia could be exploited by hostile powers (such as China), and would be a chronic threat to their own security. The solution they wanted was a Cambodia which was both strong and friendly. This was a contradiction in terms to both the Cambodian Right and to the Pol Potists, but not to Hanoi or the PRK leaders.

Anti-PRK propagandists tried to show both the servility of the 'quisling' regime in Phnom Penh and the malign intentions of Hanoi by claiming that the Vietnamese were annexing Cambodian territory and destroying Cambodian culture, and that the country was being taken over by Vietnamese settlers. But none of these claims withstand examination.

The 1979 treaty of friendship declared that Vietnam and the PRK would negotiate a border treaty 'on the basis of the present border line'. This was finally signed on 27 December 1985.[35] Anti-Vietnamese sources promptly claimed that the border had been moved thirty-five kilometres at Cambodia's expense. Sihanouk said 'the border between Cambodia and Vietnam seems to be somewhat modified. ... The offshore islands of Kep and Ream are now occupied by Vietnam and there are changes in the Cambodia–Vietnam [land] border.' He rejected the border treaty signed by the PRK, and declared that the border of 'independent Cambodia' is the 'former border'.[36] Sihanouk was correct in saying that there were some modifications to the land border. But these were of a very minor character. The 'new' border follows all the main landmarks of the old one; the chief difference is a tendency to define the border in more detail. The French had the typically colonial habit of, when faced with inhospitable terrain, simply drawing a straight line on the map between two familiar points. The 1985 treaty defines these sections of the border, using both map coordinates and natural features. It would take a detailed, specialist study to ascertain whether this involved any net gain or loss to either side. As far as the maritime border was concerned, the 1985 treaty provided only a statement of intention. Work on a treaty was to commence soon. If, as Sihanouk claimed, the Vietnamese had occupied Cambodian islands (and he provided no evidence), this was in no way legalized by the December 1985 treaty. The conclusion to be drawn is simple. Vietnam made no significant changes to the border, because it did not have territorial ambitions in Cambodia. As we documented in chapter 4, that was never what the Vietnam–DK war was about, contrary to Chang's claims.

Anti-PRK propagandists have also claimed that Hanoi has embarked on a programme of 'Vietnamization' and the destruction of Khmer culture. Much of this is blatant propaganda. Chang asserts that the Vietnamese set about destroying Cambodia as a functioning society – purging ethnic Chinese, starving, gassing and killing Khmer, and replacing those who perished with a vast influx of Vietnamese settlers. But he did not bother to document any of this – apparently assuming that Pol Pot could never tell a lie.[37] The Khmer Rouge claimed that Hanoi's aim is to exterminate the entire Khmer race. One of its representatives declared in 1986 that since 1979 the Vietnamese had put 'millions' of Cambodians to death with poison.[38]

Marie-Alexandrine Martin has provided the most serious attempt to document 'Vietnamization'. She argues that the Vietnamese have pursued a policy which she calls 'ethnocide' – while not claiming that they have been carrying out a programme of mass-murder, she does claim that they have sought to obliterate Cambodian culture, and to swamp the Khmer race with Vietnamese settlers.[39] The fight against the Vietnamese is thus nothing less than a fight for the survival of Cambodian national identity. Martin is highly selective in the evidence she uses. She quotes from unidentified sources on the border, and ignores all observers inside Cambodia. Even so, her own evidence disproves her conclusion.

She shows that the education system, which collapsed under the Khmer Rouge, was revived under the PRK. Vickery reported that 1.7 million children were being given primary schooling in the mid-1980s. Contrary to some claims, instruction was not in Vietnamese but in Khmer. But Martin objects that the PRK has used the schools to propagate its own political 'line' – teaching children that the Khmer Rouge were mass murderers, and that the Vietnamese are 'friends'. She complains that anti-Vietnamese and anti-Communist ideas cannot be taught openly under the PRK. She also shows that the PRK has attempted to revive traditional Khmer music, dance and fine arts, and has allowed a limited restoration of Buddhism. With Soviet assistance, it has established a television station in Phnom Penh. But again she is angered by the fact that the PRK has used this to get pro-government messages across to the mass of the population.

In short, Martin shows that the PRK has sought to identify itself with national traditions and culture, and to manipulate mass education and religion to encourage popular identification with the new state. She brands these practices, followed by every new state in Southeast Asia except for Pol Pot's, as 'Vietnamization' because she (and, presumably, her informants on the Thai border) dislikes their political content. She assumes that 'true' Cambodian nationalism must be anti-Communist and anti-Vietnamese.

The last component of the alleged 'Vietnamization' process was a flood of Vietnamese settlers into Cambodia. They were said to have taken the best land and houses, and treated Cambodians as second-class citizens in their own land. Martin also waxes indignant that racially mixed marriages, while not common, 'are occurring all over the country' under the PRK (a claim that seems to reveal more about the racial attitudes of her informants than about developments inside Cambodia). In fact, intermarriage has been common for generations, especially in the towns. Various figures were given for the number of settlers alleged to have arrived since 1979. Hun Sen said in 1983 that some 60,000 survivors from Cambodia's pre-war ethnic Vietnamese community of half a million had returned to the country. In 1984, US officials claimed the figure was around 300,000, while anti-PRK Cambodians on the Thai border claimed it was 600,000.

Martin claims the figure was 800,000 by 1986. Vietnamese/PRK policy, she says, was to 'eliminate the Khmer population from the main cities'. Already half the population of Phnom Penh was Vietnamese, and the Cambodian capital was 'destined to become a Vietnamese city', 'the new Ho Chi Minh City'. Such an influx, Sihanouk proclaimed in 1985, would mean that by 1990 'Cambodia will be depopulated of Khmers but infiltrated by millions of Vietnamese masquerading as Khmers.' American writers Doan Van Toai and David Chanoff were also impressed. Population movement on this scale, they wrote, 'is an impressive step toward de facto annexation and the eventual absorption of the Khmer people. This may well be Hanoi's long-term solution to the Indochina impasse.'[40]

Visitors to Phnom Penh in the mid-1980s attested that some settlement of ethnic Vietnamese had occurred, but not on the scale claimed by anti-PRK propagandists. Most were to be found in the same places and occupations as in pre-war years – fishermen, shopkeepers and café proprietors, hairdressers and prostitutes. But they were fewer in number than in pre-war days. Many were members of families that had lived in Phnom Penh before 1970. A few were indeed new settlers, with no previous connections with Cambodia. In looking around private businesses in Phnom Penh, it was notable that the Chinese Khmer had also made a major comeback. Westerners who went to rural areas found a similar pattern. A journalist who visited Kompong Chhnang found entire villages made up of predominantly ethnic Vietnamese. But these people were returnees who had lived there before 1970, or members of their families.[41] Visitors to Prey Veng and Svay Rieng provinces, adjacent to the Vietnam border and allegedly swamped with Vietnamese settlers, found fewer Vietnamese than in pre-war days.[42]

Martin says the PRK officially adopted the policy of 'Vietnamization' in 1982. This appears to be a garbled reference to a policy adopted in September 1983. The PRK permitted ethnic Vietnamese who were Cambodian citizens to return to their homes. They were allowed to bring their families with them. The PRK granted them (and members of other ethnic groups) the same rights of citizenship as Khmer. It did not, as Martin claims, legalize free movement of Vietnamese settlers into Cambodia. Some of those in Phnom Penh in the mid-1980s had entered the country illegally. The authorities periodically rounded such people up and deported them back to Vietnam; many, however, soon found their way back to Phnom Penh.

Fears of 'Vietnamization' are widely held by Cambodians. But their basis does not lie in Vietnamese policy in Cambodia in the 1980s. Vietnamese policy has aimed at building up a sovereign but allied government in Phnom Penh, not at the destruction of the society or polity of Cambodia. These had largely been destroyed already by 1979, and the task confronting the new authorities was to rebuild them. The basis of these fears is twofold. First, the official propaganda of three successive regimes told Cambodians that this is what they should expect from the 'traditional enemy'. Second, significant numbers of Cambodians objected to the political line of the PRK. Rightly or wrongly, they were unwilling to accept even the mild version of socialism practised by the PRK.

'Standing Shoulder to Shoulder'

While the Lao People's Democratic Republic (LPDR) was not a key participant in the Cambodian conflict, as an ally of Vietnam's it was soon drawn into confrontation with the Chinese and the Thai. This only served to strengthen its ties with Vietnam and the Soviet bloc.

The LPDR was the second government to recognize the Heng Samrin regime. Prince Souphannavong headed a delegation to Phnom Penh in March 1979 and signed a five-year agreement with the Heng Samrin government providing for economic, cultural and technical cooperation between the two states. Though there was no military clause in the formal agreement, the presence of the military commander for southern Laos in the delegation implied the possibility of informal military cooperation. A joint communiqué by Vietnam, Laos and Cambodia welcomed the overthrow of the 'dictatorial and fascist regime of the Pol Pot–Ieng Sary clique' and declared:

> it is entirely legitimate for the peoples of Cambodia, Laos and Vietnam to build their solidarity by standing shoulder to shoulder and giving one another mutual support and assistance in defending their countries against aggression and interference by the imperialists and Beijing reactionaries.

Thus the three Indochinese countries had come together into a politico-military bloc under Vietnamese leadership to resist Chinese pressure. Pol Pot's radio station denounced the Lao government as a 'puppet' of the Vietnamese the day after the LPDR delegation left Phnom Penh. Beijing began to criticize Laos openly: 'Vietnam', announced the *People's Daily* 'has placed Laos under tight control with its 50,000 troops and thousands of advisers.' But it was the Chinese invasion of Vietnam in February that swung the remaining neutralists in Vientiane into the pro-Vietnamese camp. When the strike into Vietnam failed, Chinese troops were reported massing on the Sino-Lao border, and it looked as if they were preparing for a thrust through northern Laos. This possibility even drew the former neutralist prime minister, Souvanna Phouma, who was still resident in Vientiane, into the fray with a public expression of fear that the Chinese might invade Laos in order to strike into Vietnam via Dien Bien Phu.

The Chinese military build-up on the Lao border was first reported in *Pravda* on 2 March, then by the Vietnamese on 4 March, and the Lao on 6 March. The Chinese seized on this as proving that Laos was a puppet of Moscow. Western intelligence sources said that there was no Chinese build-up on the Lao border beyond that connected with the invasion of Vietnam. Whether the Soviet report was true, or a piece of 'disinformation' published to panic the Lao into the Vietnamese camp is impossible to tell (at least for those like us who regard unverifiable intelligence reports from both Moscow and Washington as untrustworthy). Certainly, the government in Vientiane was in no immediate position to verify or disprove it, and with full-scale war in northern Vietnam and in Cambodia it was an alarmingly plausible scenario.

But it did not happen, and further reflection reveals that the Chinese had good reason to desist. The Chinese army had got into trouble in northern Vietnam, and it was not obvious that it would necessarily make the situation any better by embroiling itself in a wider war. Western opinion had been willing to view China's attack on Vietnam indulgently, given Vietnam's preceding attack on Cambodia. But an invasion of Laos, which had clearly done little to provoke the Chinese, would surely have been greeted differently. Furthermore, it would do irreparable damage to China's relations with the ASEAN countries. The Thai have even less interest in seeing Chinese soldiers staring at them across the Mekong than they do in seeing Vietnamese soldiers on their border.

Unease in Vientiane over the influence of the Chinese in northern Laos had been evident since early 1978. The mountainous terrain of the country meant that northern provinces such as Phong Saly formed part of a natural economic region with southern China, with relatively few linkages with the Vientiane lowlands. For eighteen years the Chinese had been aiding the integration of these areas into the Lao national economy by using People's Liberation Army troops to construct an extensive road network through the mountains of northern Laos. By 1978, this network ran from the provincial city of Mong La in China's Yunnan province to Dien Bien Phu, near the Lao–Vietnamese border, and almost to Luang Prabang in the centre of northern Laos. In the changing political circumstances of the time, this could only take on an increasingly sinister aspect. This road network would give the Chinese military tremendous mobility, which is one of the main reasons why the Vietnamese were so concerned about the political allegiance and military security of their neighbour.

The LPDR asked most of the 18,000 Chinese troops in Laos to leave in 1978, after a major section of the road was completed, and the day after it received reports of Chinese war preparations on the border. Vientiane then asked the rest to leave 'for their own security'. A week later, the LPDR charged that the Chinese troops had been making military preparations by digging trenches, and accused China of making armed incursions into Lao territory, and of supporting anti-government rebels.

By mid-1979 the Chinese embassy in Vientiane had to divest itself of military personnel and limit its staff to twelve – it was placed on a par with the US mission in Laos. From this time onwards the propaganda war between Laos and China became increasingly maledictory. Sino-Lao relations continued to deteriorate. Growing Sino-Thai collaboration over Cambodia began to appear ominous from the perspective of Vientiane, flanked as it is by both countries. Serious armed clashes were reported on the Sino-Lao border in 1981, and on 16 September Beijing Radio proclaimed that Vietnam had colonized Laos and turned it into a base for its anti-China operations, but that the Lao people were resisting vigorously:

> At present the flames of anti-Vietnam guerrilla warfare of the Lao people are blazing up, and they are attacking the aggressors everywhere. Laos, like Cambodia, has become a heavy burden for the Vietnamese aggressors. This burden will certainly drag them to defeat in the end.

In the face of Chinese pressure the LPRP showed remarkable cohesion. While there were stories of some weeding out of pro-Chinese elements in the middle levels of the bureaucracy and the party, the top leadership remained united.[43]

Yet the rhetorical exchanges between Beijing and Vientiane were not marked by the bitterness of those between Beijing and Hanoi. From Beijing's point of view, Laos had to be punished for siding with the Vietnamese. But Beijing had no real quarrel with Vientiane itself, and saw no threat to its security from Laos. In the mid-1980s China had three divisions stationed on the Lao border, backed up by regional forces. They vented Beijing's displeasure by constant minor trespassing operations.[44] Thus, after the rapid deterioration in the early 1980s, Sino-Lao relations were simply put on hold until things changed elsewhere. Rather than an independent factor, Sino-Lao relations were an index of Chinese policy towards the region.

An 'Un-Lao' Laos

Vientiane found its relations with Thailand a bigger headache than those with China. For some eighteen months after the Vietnamese invasion of Cambodia, the Kriangsak government tried to retain some Thai influence in Vientiane. But the polarization of regional politics made this increasingly difficult. As Vientiane aligned itself more closely with Hanoi, relations with Bangkok became increasingly tense. The fall of Kriangsak in February 1980 added to the strain. Under Prime Minister Prem Tinsula-nond and Foreign Minister Siddhi Savetsila, the Thai increasingly saw the hand of the Vietnamese behind all Lao actions.

A shooting incident on the Mekong in June 1980, of the sort that had been habitually ignored under Kriangsak, was seen by Bangkok as linked to a Vietnamese incursion on the Thai–Cambodian border. The Thai thus decided to restrict cross-border trade in an attempt to bring the errant Lao to heel. Beside limiting border-trading points to two, in December 1981 the Thai banned all export of 273 'strategic goods' to Laos. These ranged from bicycles and canned food, items which are at least arguably of some military significance, to sanitary napkins. The aim was, as one of the main Thai dailies put it at the time, 'to make Laos realize that it is more dependent on Thailand than on Vietnam. Although it is under the political influence of Vietnam, it cannot obtain economic relief from that country.'

But the 'special relationship' with Vietnam broke the Thai monopoly over Lao access to the outside world, and goods destined for Laos were unloaded at Da Nang. Work upgrading Route 9, linking Da Nang and Savannakhet, was turning this into an all-weather road. 'Thailand closes the border anytime it wants', complained Soulivong Phatsihideth, general secretary of the Lao Foreign Ministry. 'The significance of this road is our independence. When Route 9 is finished ... the Thai can close the border or open it whenever they like.'

The Lao thus proved unresponsive to Thai whip-cracking. Bangkok ideologues responded by recalling happier times when the 'gentle Lao' had always been deferential. 'The Thai have always found the Lao willing to compromise, but in the past few weeks they have found their stand to be very un-Lao', a diplomat in Bangkok explained in 1980. 'They say that they have felt that it was no longer Lao but Vietnamese who were coming to talk to them.'

With Vientiane unyielding, the principal result of Thai trade restrictions was further to sour relations between the two countries. For the next few years Thai–Lao relations fluctuated between acrimonious exchanges following border incidents and fitful attempts at improving relations. Little came of the latter, for the Prem government saw easing the pressure on Laos as a concession to Vietnam. Faced with such blatant Thai political manipulation of trade between the two countries it is little wonder that we find Phoumi Vongvichit still stressing in mid-1985 the LPDR's 'special emphasis on building a highway to the sea through the SRV and, in the future, through the PRK'.

Thai pressures in fact pushed the Lao to strengthen their relationship with Vietnam, which further fuelled Thai distaste for the LPDR. Thai–Lao relations reached their low-point in 1984, with serious armed clashes occurring in the 'three-villages dispute'. At the beginning of that year Thai troops began building a strategic road into a former stronghold of the Communist Party of Thailand along the border of Pitsanalok (Thailand) and Sayaboury (Laos) provinces. By March they had reached three remote villages which, according to the Thai, were six kilometres from the border on their side. But the Lao maintained that these villages were on the Lao side, that their inhabitants were Lao citizens, and that the Thai army was intruding illegally into Lao territory. A three-month war of words followed. Then, in June, skirmishes between the two armies led the Thai forcibly to occupy the three villages.

Negotiations failed to settle the dispute. The Lao produced French maps showing the disputed villages on the Lao side of the border, and pointed out that these maps were the basis of the 1904 and 1907 Franco-Siamese border agreements. The Thai side produced US maps drawn up in the 1960s, showing the villages in Thai territory. These, they said, were more up to date, and more accurate. Maybe so, responded the Lao side, but they have no legal standing. Unfortunately for the Thai, the American cartographers had explicitly stated that their maps could not be used to demarcate borders. To justify their reliance on the US maps, the Thai now had to ignore the Franco-Siamese treaties. These were, they argued, 'unequal treaties' which had been imposed by force, and were unjust. As a matter of historical fact, this was true. As a moral claim, it was dubious – the French had negotiated the border with the Thai from a position of strength; but they had never bothered to consult the Lao at all. But all this was irrelevant as a point of law: the fact was that the Thai had signed a treaty recognizing their border using the French maps.

Lao acceptance of the Thai position would have had far-reaching consequences. In early 1985, the Thai themselves announced that there were at least seventy sections of the border that needed to be redefined. The Thai argument in fact cast the whole border into doubt. It was a recipe for continuous disputation and conflict. At the same time, they insisted that demarcation of the border was merely a technical matter which could be handled easily at a local level. The Lao side should thus accept it without negotiations. Vientiane's response was to insist that Bangkok accept the primacy of the early French maps in any attempt to demarcate disputed areas. Despite the political–legal quagmire it opened up, the three-villages dispute itself quickly faded from the headlines.[45] As a conciliatory gesture the Thai withdrew their troops from the disputed area in October 1984, shortly before the issue was taken to the UN. With the conflict on the ground defused, the Thai side proclaimed the dispute over. But as far as the Lao were concerned, nothing had been settled. Worse, there was now no agreement between the two governments on the border between the two countries. Every point was potentially a flash-point, and the border question could be revived any time Bangkok wished to bring additional pressure to bear on Vientiane.

Both sides soon presented their cases to the world in the now obligatory format of White Papers. Vientiane reasserted the legal primacy of Franco-Siamese treaties, and recalled Thai depredations against Laos. Lao defer-ence, so fondly recalled in Bangkok, was remembered differently in Vien-tiane – it had been enforced by military expeditions which, among other things, had sacked the city in the eighteenth and nineteenth centuries. In a more contemporary vein, the Lao recalled the Thai seizure of Saya-boury province in World War II, raised the spectre of 'pan-Thai' expan-sionism, and accused Bangkok of colluding with Beijing against the countries of Indochina.[46]

In its White Paper, the Bangkok government had little to say on legal technicalities. In the political climate of 1984, it could hardly admit that the maps its soldiers used had no legal standing. Not only would this be an embarrassing loss of face, it would only encourage the LPDR to persist in its 'un-Lao' ways. Worse, it might be seen as appeasing 'Vietna-mese Communist expansionism'. The Thai preferred to dwell on the alleged racial and cultural affinities between the Thai and Lao peoples, and to speculate on why 'the two peoples were unable to unite into one single kingdom'. In Bangkok's view, the answer was Vietnamese interfer-ence in Laos. It claimed Laos had passed under the control of the Vietna-mese and that, unless rectified, this would mean that 'the Lao people as a race ... [would] in the end completely disappear'.[47]

It is evident that for Bangkok settlement of the border dispute itself was a secondary issue. The primary Thai concern was to exclude Vietna-mese influence from Laos, and bring Vientiane into its own orbit. As the stronger state, Thailand had a vested interest in nurturing ambiguity on the border; it could use it to bring pressure to bear on Laos whenever it chose. This strategic objective was cloaked in a traditional–familistic rhetoric which presented Laos as the 'little brother' which should always submit to 'big brother' Thailand.

Two other aspects of this instructive if obscure episode are worthy of note. First, the Thai government adopted towards Laos precisely the same attitude as Hanoi's enemies accuse the Vietnamese of adopting to-wards Cambodia. Much of the Thai case against the Vietnamese may be a classic case of psychological projection. (At an academic seminar in Bangkok, a senior official dismissed criticisms of the factual accuracy of his interpretation of Vietnamese actions in Cambodia by saying, 'Well, if I were in their position, that's what I'd do.') Second, in repudiating borders defined by 'unequal treaties' the Thai position echoed the stance Pol Pot took on the Vietnam–Cambodia border, and the stance Mao took on the Sino-Soviet border.

Foreign commentators as well as the Lao and the Thai appealed to the common 'racial' and religious bonds between the two peoples, but most foreigners were unprepared for the ferocity of the polemics which broke out between the two countries, particularly on the Lao side. The strident Lao response was not a the result of a hidden Vietnamese hand. It was partly a product of it being the weaker party in the dispute, but one rejecting the deference demanded by the 'elder brother' in Bangkok. Lao nationalism defines itself primarily in relationship to Thailand, and only secondarily in relation to Vietnam. The Thai failed to understand that for as long as Thailand confronted Laos, militarily or using economic coercion, Vientiane would rely heavily on its alliance with Vietnam to protect itself. Their logic was similar to that of the anti-Vietnamese Cambodian nationalists who ended up in alliance with Bangkok against Hanoi – although at no point in its dealings with the Thai did the LPDR embrace a revanchism parallel to that embraced by the Pol Pot regime.

The Lao also sought wider support, with some success. Having previously contented itself with working via Hanoi, the Soviet Union in 1981 decided to establish a direct relationship with Vientiane. The Soviets promised substantial economic and technical assistance for the Lao Five Year Plan (1981–85), and Brezhnev himself awarded Prime Minister Kaysone the Order of Lenin. Some commentators saw this as a sign of Soviet–Vietnamese rivalry for influence in Indochina. At the Congress of the LPRP in April 1982, Kaysone explained Vientiane's relations with Moscow and Hanoi in these terms: 'In foreign policy, we advocate relying decidedly on the Soviet Union and the other fraternal countries, strengthening the special militant alliance of our people with the Vietnamese and Cambodian peoples.' Lao officials explained that this meant 'a regional security alliance with Vietnam within the framework of strategic reliance on Moscow for material support'.[48] This division of labour is a practical one – Moscow is hardly in a position to send troops to Laos, while Vietnam is hardly qualified to advise the Lao on economic planning and technological matters. Soviet influence has grown steadily in Vientiane. The rise of Gorbachev strengthened a pattern of economic thought which had already been gaining ground in the LPRP. Kaysone met Gorbachev in Moscow in August 1985 and the Soviets pledged support for Lao foreign policy initiatives, in particular Lao attempts to improve relations with both Thailand and China.

In view of US policies towards Hanoi and Phnom Penh, Washington has pursued a surprisingly lenient policy towards Vientiane. It continued to recognize the LPDR, although the relationship was plagued by the same problems about property and its missing servicemen (MIAs) as were given as grounds for not opening relations with Hanoi. In October 1981,

US Assistant Secretary of State for Asia and the Pacific John Holdridge declared:

> Laos does retain at least some degree of autonomy and many officials there appear to welcome closer relations with the West. . . . We maintain our embassy in Vientiane to contribute to this effort and to offer some small counterbalance to the Soviet–Vietnamese influence.

The basic US approach was to keep a foothold in Indochina via Vientiane while venting its displeasure against Hanoi and Phnom Penh. In 1983 joint US–Lao teams began investigating crash-sites for the remains of American MIAs, and the following year the US government supplied some food aid on a humanitarian basis to Laos. In 1985 Laos was removed from the USA's list of enemy states, thus opening the possibility of direct US development aid.

The US stance had a major impact on the attitude of many western nations towards Laos. Whereas Hanoi and Phnom Penh were ostracized, most countries maintained amiable relations with Vientiane. Governments which cut off all aid projects in Vietnam in 1979 continued to fund them in Laos. The UK closed its embassy there, but this was a matter of Thatcherite cost-cutting rather than a political protest. UK interests in Laos were so small that it found it more convenient to let them be represented through the Australian Embassy.

The conflict over Cambodia certainly inconvenienced Laos. But regional polarization reinforced rather than weakened Vientiane's basic political orientation. The smallest state in the region, Laos remained hostage to forces beyond its control. It would benefit from a change in the political climate, but there was little that could be done to bring this about. Vientiane's policy was essentially to wait for things to get better, and to guard its borders. If there is one thing of which the Lao have much experience, it is waiting for things to get better.

The 'Indochina Federation' Revisited

By the mid-1980s Vietnam appeared to be succeeding in its basic strategy for resisting Chinese pressure. It had created a viable ally in Cambodia and consolidated its close relationship with Laos. This regional alliance was underpinned by substantial support from the USSR, and this Soviet commitment placed a further restraint on Chinese actions against the Indochinese states.

The emergence of an Indochina political bloc was driven home to the rest of the world in February 1980 when the foreign ministers of Vietnam, Laos and Cambodia met in Saigon. While the foreign policies of the

LPDR and the PRK had been closely aligned with those of the SRV, and the governments had been bound together by 'treaties of friendship', they now issued a joint communiqué stressing 'the identity of their views on international problems'. There was, they declared, no room in Cambodia for Pol Pot's group or for 'other reactionaries including Sihanouk' who were working to subvert the PRK government. China was described as the most dangerous enemy of the Indochinese people, and while China, the USA and 'other reactionary forces' maintained their hostility towards the Indochinese states, the presence of Vietnamese troops in Laos and Cambodia was 'very necessary' for their defence.

Trade and other economic ties between Vietnam, Cambodia and Laos all expanded. Provinces in Laos and Cambodia were 'twinned' with provinces in Vietnam to nurture cooperation and cultural exchanges. A committee was established to coordinate action on the UN's International Mekong Committee (IMC), a body established to facilitate international cooperation in the development of the Mekong basin. This gave Cambodia an indirect voice on the IMC (as the UN recognized the DK government, the IMC was obliged to give the Cambodian seat to Pol Pot's representative; but the Khmer Rouge's sole interest in this body was preventing the PRK taking up the seat).

Hostile critics charged that this 'special relationship' amounted to the complete subjugation of Laos and Cambodia to Vietnam. Many saw this as a vindication of Pol Pot's allegations of Vietnamese designs for an 'Indochina Federation'. King C. Chen has written that the 'development of the special relationship system has demonstrated that Indochina is running virtually under federalism without the name of federation'. Chen asserted that this 'federation' is administered by Vietnamese officials ('advisers') who 'are present in the two countries down to the village level'.[49] Anyone who has been in villages in Cambodia or Laos knows that these assertions are false. However, such arguments betray not only practical ignorance but also conceptual confusion. These authors accuse Vietnam of establishing a federation when they mean a unitary state, and when they are referring in fact to an alliance. These terms need to be clarified.

Most of the world's governments are unitary states. They may have been formed by conquest, or by voluntary union. They may be small or large, centralized or decentralized. But the central power is sovereign. If local authorities exist, their powers are delegated to them by the central state, and may be withdrawn by the central power. The United Kingdom of Great Britain and Northern Ireland is an example of a unitary state. So is the People's Republic of China. When a federation is formed, several states join in a new state, to which they delegate specific powers – in particular the power to conduct foreign affairs. Only the federal government is recognized as a state in international law. But in a federation, in contrast to a unitary state, the member governments retain full rights of internal sovereignty, except for those specific powers transferred to the central government. The United States of America is one example, the Commonwealth of Australia another.[50] An alliance is an agreement between sovereign states, but it does not involve the formation of a new state. No matter how close the relationship may be, its members remain in charge of the conduct of their own foreign affairs. They are regarded as independent states in international law, and any institution created by that alliance (the Supreme Command of NATO, for example) is not recognized as a state. In theory, alliances are freely entered into and may be terminated when the interests of member states no longer coincide. In practice, however, they are often dominated by the most powerful state.

In the case of Indochina we are clearly dealing with an alliance, as the Vietnamese maintain. No federal state has been formed. Diplomatically, Vietnam and Laos are recognized by China, the USA and other countries as sovereign states, responsible for the conduct of their own foreign affairs – including the right to form alliances. The main objective of Indochinese diplomacy has been to gain the same recognition for the PRK. One of the more balanced early appraisals of the relationship was offered by journalist Richard Nations, commenting on the treaties signed between Vietnam, Cambodia and Laos in 1979:

> they provide the sturdy legs of a simple diplomatic structure dominating Indochina with its apex in Hanoi. The technical accords between Vientiane and Phnom Penh now furnish a cross-beam – a necessary, if not a load-bearing part of the whole structure ... The treaties and accords which have been wrapped around the backbone of the Vietnamese troops in Indochina over the past few years in no way subordinate national sovereignty to a federation, at least from a legal point of view. With the structure of these agreements, Hanoi hardly needs such a federation.[51]

A later scholarly consideration of the 'Indochinese Federation Idea' by MacAlister Brown confirms this view. He writes: 'The existing cooperative/consultative/advisory arrangements worked out under Vietnamese leadership among the three states are close to optimal in terms of costs and benefits for Vietnam.' It would, he argues, be counter-productive for Hanoi to push for a federation.[52] Vietnam, like Laos, is part of a modern state system which is based on the not insignificant 'fiction' that all states are equal. That these formally equal states need to enter into alliance systems, on the other hand, is a practical recognition of disparities of power between states. It is the changing constellation of power between states which is the stuff of international politics regionally and globally.

Notes

1. Tetsusaburo Kimura, *The Vietnamese Economy, 1975–86*, Toyko 1989, p. 11.
2. Quoted by Nayan Chanda, 'Vietnam's Economy: Bad but Not Worse', *Indochina Issues*, no. 41, October 1983, p. 5.
3. Jerry M. Tinkler, 'US Refugee Policy: Coping with Migration', *Indochina Issues*, no. 55, March 1985, p. 1.
4. Kimura, op cit.
5. Vietnamese Communist Party (VCP), *5th National Congress: Political Report*, Hanoi 1982, pp. 23–4.
6. Ibid., pp. 25, 18.
7. Nguyen Nguoc Tu, Vietnam News Agency, 22 April 1985.
8. David Jenkins, *Far Eastern Economic Review*, 8 November 1984.
9. William J. Duiker, *Vietnam Since the Fall of Saigon*, revised edn, Athens, Ohio 1985, p. 68.
10. Quoted by Carlyle A. Thayer, 'The Regularization of Politics: Continuity and Change in the Party Central Committee, 1951–1986', in David G. Marr and Christine P. White, eds, *Postwar Vietnam: Dilemmas in Socialist Development*, New York 1988, p. 189.
11. VCP, pp. 14, 16, 128.
12. Cf. the table in Douglas Pike, *Vietnam and the Soviet Union: Anatomy of an Alliance*, Boulder 1987, p. 139. Pike says his figures are drawn from a wide variety of sources, but he does not explain how they were derived.
13. Ibid., p.181. Buszynski likewise observes: 'The Soviet Union has not yet acquired a base in Cam Ranh Bay. ... The Soviet reliance on floating docks and limited installations demonstrates a reluctance to make a permanent commitment and an avoidance of major investments which shows that the Soviet build-up at Cam Ranh Bay has been restricted and controlled' (Leszek Buszynski, *Soviet Foreign Policy and Southeast Asia*, London 1986, pp. 205–6).
14. Alvin H. Bernstein, 'The Soviets in Cam Ranh Bay', *Quadrant* (Sydney), July–August 1986, p. 54. Dion W. Johnson reaches similar conclusions: 'The Soviets are committed to exploiting opportunities, yet are conditioned to doing so with acute regard to risk. ... Moscow is not likely to launch a sudden military venture in East Asia. ... [For the USA] Cam Ranh is a small but unavoidable problem' (*Bear Tracks in Indochina: An Analysis of Soviet Presence*, Maxwell 1987, pp. 78, 92).
15. Memorandum on Agricultural Problems, Provisional Revolutionary Council, Phnom Penh, 22 February 1979 (*Keesing's Contemporary Archives*, 25 May 1979, p. 29620). William Shawcross is thus wrong in asserting that 'Hanoi and Phnom Penh maintained through early 1979 that little was amiss with food supplies inside Cambodia' (*The Quality of Mercy*, London 1984, p. 99).
16. John Pilger, 'Letting a Nation Die', in John Pilger and Anthony Barnett, *Aftermath: The Struggle of Cambodia and Vietnam*, London 1982, p. 63.
17. Shawcross, pp. 138–9, 93–4.
18. Quoted by Elizabeth Becker, *Far Eastern Economic Review*, 20 July 1979; see also her articles in the *Guardian Weekly*, 2 December 1979 and 24 February 1980 (both reprinted from the *Washington Post*). Two editions of *Indochina Issues* also deal with the aid question: Murray Hiebert and Linda Gibson Hiebert, 'Famine in Kampuchea: Politics of a Tragedy', no. 4, December 1979, and Linda Gibson Hiebert, 'Kampuchea: Breaking the Cycle', no. 5, April 1980.
19. Jim Laurie, *Far Eastern Economic Review*, 18 January 1980.
20. Shawcross, p. 414.
21. Ibid., pp. 391–3.
22. John McBeth, *Far Eastern Economic Review*, 15 October 1982.
23. In *Brother Enemy: The War after the War*, San Diego 1986, Nayan Chanda gives the membership as 200 at one point (p. 371) and 800 at another (p. 373).
24. Michael Vickery, *Kampuchea: Politics, Economics and Society*, London 1986, pp. 73–5.
25. Paul Quinn-Judge, *Far Eastern Economic Review*, 31 October 1985.

26. Cf. Vickery, pp. 79–84, for further details on the PRPK leadership in 1985.

27. Nick Cumming-Bruce, *Far Eastern Economic Review*, 25 December 1986. Cf. Vickery, pp.78–9, 83.

28. Cf. Timothy Carney, 'The Heng Samrin Armed Forces and the Military Balance in Cambodia', in David A. Ablin and Marlowe Hood, eds, *The Cambodian Agony*, New York 1987. This paper was originally written for a conference in 1982, but appears to have been updated to 1983–84.

29. Amnesty International, *Kampuchea: Political Imprisonment and Torture*, London 1987, pp. 22–3, 51–4. One could debate whether Amnesty's evidence supported the claim of 'several thousand' political prisoners. Its figures indicated a total of about 1,200 prisoners in Cambodian jails. It assumed that all were there for political reasons. These figures were incomplete, but they did cover all the main jails.

30. Ibid., p. 35.

31. Greg Sheridan, *Australian*, 2 June 1987.

32. FAO figures quoted by Eva Mysliwiec, *Punishing the Poor: The International Isolation of Kampuchea*, London 1988, p. 25.

33. David P. Chandler, 'Kampuchea: End Game or Stalemate?', *Current History*, December 1984, p. 417.

34. Pao Min Chang, *Kampuchea Between Vietnam and China*, Singapore 1985. p. 159.

35. Cf. *Nhan Dan*, 6 March 1986, for the text.

36. Voice of the Khmer, 6 September 1986.

37. Chang, pp. 105–6.

38. Ngo Hac Team, quoted in the *Bangkok Post*, 17 September 1986. Western observers dismiss such claims.

39. Marie-Alexandrine Martin, 'Vietnamised Cambodia: A Silent Ethnocide', *Indochina Report* (Singapore), no. 7, July–September 1986.

40. Quoted by Michael Richardson, *Age*, 27 September 1984.

41. John Spragens, Jr, *Far Eastern Economic Review*, 31 May 1984.

42. Vickery, pp.166–7; Ben Kiernan, 'Kampuchea Revisited', *Inside Asia*, November–December 1986.

43. MacAlister Brown and Joseph J. Zasloff, *Apprentice Revolutionaries*, Stanford 1986, p. 152.

44. *Far Eastern Economic Review*, 26 April 1984.

45. But see Grant Evans, 'A quarrel over maps', *Inside Asia*, February–March 1986, and Joseph J. Zasloff, 'The Three Village Dispute between Laos and Thailand', *UFSI Reports*, no. 23, 1985. For an example of western incomprehension of the issues, see Arthur J. Dommen, 'Laos in 1984: the Year of the Thai Border', *Asian Survey*, vol. 25, 1985.

46. Ministry of Foreign Affairs of the Lao People's Democratic Republic, *The Truth About Thai–Lao Relations*, September 1984. For a more nuanced statement of the Lao position, see Pheuiphanh Ngaosyvathn, 'Thai–Lao Relations: A Lao View', *Asian Survey*, vol. 25, 1985. See also KPL Newsagency, *Facts and Data on Lao–Thai Relations in the Past Ten Years (1975–1985)*, 1985.

47. Thai Ministry of Foreign Affairs, *The Evolution of Thai–Lao Relations*, Bangkok 1984, p. 33. See also Sarasin Virapol, 'Reflections on Thai–Lao Relations', *Asian Survey*, vol. 25, 1985.

48. Nayan Chanda, *Far Eastern Economic Review*, 28 May 1982.

49. King C. Chen, *China's War with Vietnam, 1979*, Stanford 1987, pp. 161, 158.

50. For a summary of the relevant issues, see, for example, Michael Akehurst, *A Modern Introduction to International Law*, 3rd edn, London 1977, pp. 73–5.

51. Richard Nations, *Far Eastern Economic Review*, 6 April 1979.

52. MacAlister Brown, 'The Indochinese Federation Idea: Learning from History', in Joseph J. Zasloff, ed., *Postwar Indochina: Old Enemies and New Allies*, Foreign Service Institute, US Department of State, Washington, DC 1988, p. 99.

7

ASEAN:
The Dominoes Push Back

The non-Communist country most immediately affected by developments in Indochina was Thailand. The Thai government had played a central role in the USA's struggle to 'contain' Communism in Asia – when SEATO was formed in 1954, its headquarters had been established in Bangkok. After the fall of Indochina to Communism, and the visible retreat of American military power in the region, many of Thailand's political and military leaders believed that they faced a serious danger of invasion from Vietnam, and that support from Laos and Cambodia for the Communist-led insurgents operating in the north and northeast of Thailand would make it almost impossible for the government to defeat the insurgents.[1] The smiles from Hanoi after 1975 were welcome, but the fear and the mistrust remained. The fall of Pol Pot's regime to Vietnamese troops in 1979 only intensified these feelings. The belief that Thailand would be the next 'domino' to fall was shared by many on the Left as well.[2]

For twenty years after the coup led by Sarit Thanarat in 1951 the Thai military leaders had relied on the 'threat' of Communism to attract unconditional support from the USA and to justify the suppression of their domestic opponents. The Cold War served them well, and they had welcomed the intensification of the USA's involvement in Indochina with enthusiasm. But when the USA began seriously searching for a way out of Vietnam, from 1968 on, the Thai were, in John Girling's words, 'left stranded with a militant anti-communist commitment, but deprived of the means to fulfil it'.[3]

They responded by moderating their reliance on the Americans; as early as 1969, Bangkok announced the scaling down of the American military presence in Thailand, and began cautiously seeking a dialogue with Beijing. However, the aim was a policy of equidistance from all the great powers rather than subservience to another one. The Thai policy that crystallized as the war in Indochina reached its conclusion was well summed up in a speech by the Thai foreign minister in January 1974. The Thai government would, he said, continue to have friendly relations with the USA but would correct 'the overemphasis on military co-operation'. Thai policy aimed at achieving a 'balance' between all the powers with interests in the region; in this context, not only did he predict developing relations with China, he also described the Soviet Union as being in a 'strong position' to contribute to the stability of Southeast Asia.

Like Vietnam, Thailand was seeking to balance Moscow and Beijing against each other – though Bangkok's aim was to bring as much restraining influence as possible to bear on a reunited Vietnam. Hanoi proved receptive to this policy, which was in keeping with the general relaxing of tensions in the detente of the early 1970s. But Thai policy was to fall victim to the escalation of the Vietnam–Cambodia and Vietnam–China conflicts, especially as these coincided with the breakdown of *detente* and the shift towards the New Cold War.

Even before this happened, however, the policy of 'balance' proved unacceptable to influential right-wing elements in the army. To them, Thailand was accepting the loss of its influence in Vientiane, Saigon and in Phnom Penh without demur. This 'capitulation to Communism' they linked to their loss of influence after the establishment of a civilian government in Bangkok in 1973, and the 'disorder' of the democratic politics it ushered in. In October 1976 the Thai military staged a coup which it claimed saved the country from an impending Communist takeover. The government it installed, headed by Thanin Kraivichien, adopted a militantly anti-Communist stance with the intention of reviving the American alliance. But Washington was anxious not to jeopardize the emerging Sino-American detente, and quickly made it clear that it had no intention of being drawn into a military commitment to Thailand. In this context, Thanin's opposition to improving relations with China and the Indochinese countries was driving Thailand into dangerous isolation. Disillusioned, the military overthrew Thanin in another coup in October 1977.

His successor, General Kriangsak Chomanan, reverted to a more pragmatic approach. Accepting the retraction of American power, he looked to Communist China as a great power that would help maintain stability in Southeast Asia and moved to improve relations with Indochina. In this regard, Kriangsak was discomfited by the belligerence of the Khmer Rouge regime towards Thailand. Even more important, when he visited Beijing in March–April 1978, he found that Deng Xiaoping's main objective was to push Thailand into a regional alliance with Pol Pot against the Vietnamese. Kriangsak's acceptance of a 'constructive relationship' with China at this critical juncture no doubt excited the worst suspicions in Hanoi.

Another thread of Thai foreign policy in the 1970s was the attempt to weld the non-Communist countries of the region into an effective counter-balance to Vietnam. This was achieved in 1979, in response to the crisis over Cambodia and the 'boat people'. The emergence of ASEAN as a regional anti-Communist bloc matched the emergence of the Communist Indochina bloc, although this aspect of the situation attracted relatively little comment.

ASEAN: An Anti-Communist Bloc

Originally formed in Bangkok in 1967, ASEAN brought together the Philippines, Thailand, Malaysia, Singapore and Indonesia, but for several years conflicts and rivalries between member states ensured that it was of little practical significance. When ASEAN was formed, Singapore had only recently broken away from the Malaysian Federation. Malaysia had also faced the armed challenge of Indonesia's *konfrontasi* policy until the coup against Sukarno in 1965, and a territorial claim by the Philippines on the eastern Malaysian state of Sabah, which was finally abandoned only in October 1982. Both Thailand and the Philippines were members of SEATO, while Malaysia, Singapore and Indonesia leant more towards neutralist policies.

The US débâcle in Vietnam strengthened neutralist tendencies in ASEAN. As early as 1971, a Malaysian proposal for a 'zone of peace, freedom and neutrality' was given general endorsement, although nothing was done to eliminate the American military presence. In 1974–75 the ASEAN countries began to open up diplomatic relations with China and North Vietnam, and recognized the new governments in South Vietnam, Cambodia and Laos. SEATO was phased out, and the American bases in Thailand (though not those in the Philippines) were closed down.

Fears that a weak and divided non-Communist Southeast Asia would be threatened by a vigorous and united Indochina spurred the ASEAN countries to bury their differences after 1975. But after 1975 the ASEAN countries experienced an economic boom while Indochina was gripped by economic and political crisis. Singapore's foreign minister, Sinnathamby Rajaratnam, commented in 1978:

The dominoes have not fallen. It seems to be working the other way ... instead of the consolidation of the Communist wave that was foreseen after their victory, we see the disintegration of Communist solidarity. ASEAN is consolidating instead of disintegrating.

This situation, so favourable to the ASEAN countries, came to an end when the Vietnamese toppled Pol Pot's regime. The speed and effectiveness of Vietnam's military intervention was in itself alarming to non-Communist Southeast Asia, which knew that it did not possess such military capability. Moreover, the main consequence of the intervention was to create the unified Communist Indochina bloc that the ASEAN countries had feared would emerge in 1975. It is not surprising, therefore, that they deplored 'the armed intervention threatening the independence, sovereignty and territorial integrity of Cambodia', affirming 'the right of the Cambodian people to decide their own future without outside interference or influence from outside powers', and calling for the 'immediate withdrawal of all foreign troops from Cambodian territory'.

Despite the display of unanimity on this occasion, there were serious differences between ASEAN members over the Cambodia issue. Thailand was in the uncomfortable position of a 'front-line state'. While anxiety about Vietnam's intentions was naturally strongest in Thailand, Singapore also pushed a strong anti-Vietnamese line. But Malaysia and Indonesia were inclined towards a more accommodating position.

These divergences were in part a reflection of differing attitudes towards China. The old fears of the southward expansion of Chinese Communism had been allayed by Beijing's courting of the ASEAN countries in the 1970s, but they were not extinct. China's insistence on maintaining relations with 'fraternal' Communist parties leading insurgencies was one source of friction in its relations with the ASEAN governments. Another was its influence in the overseas Chinese communities in these countries. Distrust over these matters was particularly sharp in Malaysia and Indonesia, which were inclined to sympathize with the idea of an independent Vietnam as a barrier to Chinese influence. By contrast, in both Singapore and Thailand, the local Chinese business community exerted a strong influence on the government in favour of friendly relations with Beijing. Bangkok's attitude was further influenced by the consideration that Thailand had traditionally competed with Vietnam for influence in Laos and Cambodia.

Over the next few months the situation on the Thai–Cambodian border became increasingly tense. Disorder, fighting and food shortages in western Cambodia resulted in a stream of refugees fleeing into Thailand. As this exodus of 'land people' coincided with the flood of 'boat people' from Vietnam, they were part of a refugee problem for the ASEAN countries of alarming dimensions. At the same time, Pol Pot's forces were retreating to the Thai border with the Vietnamese hot on their tails and it was feared that the fighting between them would spill over into Thailand. The Thai government rather inconsistently proclaimed its neutrality towards the conflict inside Cambodia while condemning the Vietnamese and supporting Pol Pot's Democratic Kampuchea (DK) government as the legitimate government of the country.

When the foreign ministers of the ASEAN countries conferred over the refugee crisis at Bali in June 1979, the meeting was dominated by the anti-Vietnamese hardliners. The most outspoken was once again Singapore's Rajaratnam, who said that Vietnam had 'declared war' on ASEAN and was 'carrying out a policy of genocide'. 'Today it is the Chinese–Vietnamese. The Cambodians have already been added to the list of those who are going to die ... Why not Thailand tomorrow, and Malaysia, Singapore and others who stand in the way of Vietnam's dreams?' He warned his fellow ASEAN members against any policy of accommodation with Hanoi, arguing that Vietnam could not be treated as 'an essentially peace-loving neighbour'.

The final communiqué adopted at Bali condemned the Vietnamese and called for 'international support' for Cambodia's 'right of self-determination', equating this with the DK regime. No military pact was drawn up at Bali, but the communiqué made it clear enough that if Thailand came under attack, the others would go to its aid. Following this conference, the American Secretary of State, Cyrus Vance, pledged that the USA would come to the assistance of any ASEAN country attacked by an outsider.

Military cooperation among the ASEAN states accelerated after Bali. This was underpinned by a sharp increase in military spending, supported by military aid from the USA. The reasons why ASEAN evolved in the direction of a military alliance were well understood by western commentators, and there were none of the half-baked theories that were characteristic of discussions of the Indochina bloc. No attempts were made to characterize ASEAN as a 'federation', or to depict it as an instrument of the 'colonialism' of one of the dominant member states, or of the USA. Partly, of course, this is a reflection of the fact that no single country could dominate ASEAN to the same extent as Vietnam could dominate an Indochina alliance. But western observers had no difficulty perceiving a Vietnamese threat to Thailand, and understanding ASEAN's response as a defensive reaction.

The same commentators were usually unable to perceive that the Indochina bloc was also defensive in character. They saw a Vietnamese threat to Thailand in the invasion of Cambodia but were incapable of seeing the Chinese threat to Indochina, despite China's invasion of Vietnam. But despite these parallels ASEAN and the Indochinese countries were fundamentally at cross purposes over Cambodia: for ASEAN the prime concern was ending the perceived threat to Thailand by bringing about a Vietnamese withdrawal from Cambodia, while China was a secondary issue; for Indochina, however, the Chinese threat was the primary concern, and the Vietnamese presence in Cambodia was secondary.

Negotiations between the ASEAN and the Indochinese countries never got off the ground. In 1980 the Vietnamese stated repeatedly that they would not negotiate on the future of Cambodia over the head of the government in Phnom Penh, but the ASEAN countries would not be party to any negotiations that included the 'puppet' Heng Samrin administration. The Vietnamese also made it clear that their troops would remain in Cambodia as long as the 'Chinese threat' to the Indochinese states remained. They offered to withdraw *some* of their troops in exchange for Thailand denying sanctuary and supplies to the Khmer Rouge, but would not accept a *complete* withdrawal while China's stance remained hostile. But ASEAN insisted on a complete withdrawal. Hanoi tried to mollify Bangkok's fears of Vietnamese 'expansionism' by offering Thailand a non-aggression pact. But in Thai eyes, such a pact had little meaning in the light of Vietnamese actions in Cambodia, and Bangkok rejected the offer. Vietnam proposed a demilitarization of the Thai–Cambodian border, which Thailand rejected because this would implicate it as a party to the dispute in Cambodia. It countered with a proposal for a demilitarized zone between the warring factions inside Cambodia, which the Vietnamese rejected because it meant a *de facto* partitioning of Cambodia.

Over this issue the ASEAN countries found themselves in an alliance with the USA and, rather more uneasily, with China. They followed their diplomatic victory over the seating of Pol Pot at the United Nations by calling for an international conference on Cambodia under UN auspices. They proposed a total withdrawal of Vietnamese troops, the establishment of a UN peacekeeping force to maintain law and order in Cambodia after the departure of the Vietnamese, and UN-sponsored elections to create a new government.

The UN conference proposed by ASEAN went ahead in July 1981. Vietnam and Laos refused to participate while Pol Pot's regime was still accepted as officially representing the Cambodian people. Without the participation of the Indochinese countries, a conference on Cambodia was, as one diplomat put it, like clapping with one hand. The Americans preferred to force a confrontation which, they hoped, would enable them to 'crack' the will of the Hanoi leadership, even if it took five to ten years.[4]

The Indochinese countries blamed tension in the region on China's policies of expansionism and hegemonism, and argued that 'the basic factor for restoring peace and stability in Southeast Asia at present is that China must terminate its hostile policy towards the three Indochinese countries and its policy of interfering with other countries in this area'. The three governments declared their readiness

to sign bilateral treaties of peaceful coexistence with the People's Republic of China on the basis of the principles of absolute respect for each country's independence, sovereignty and territorial integrity, non-aggression, non-intervention in each other's internal affairs; equality; mutual benefit; good neighbourly relations and the settlement of all bilateral disputes through peaceful means.

This was dismissed by the Chinese. They would negotiate such treaties only if Vietnam withdrew its troops from Cambodia.

In relation to the ASEAN countries, the Indochinese side advocated an ongoing 'dialogue' between ASEAN and Indochina. It advanced a proposal for a regional conference involving the ASEAN and Indochinese countries, and perhaps Burma, to discuss 'the problems concerning them'. After these countries had concluded a treaty on peace and stability in Southeast Asia, the statement called for an enlarged international conference to recognize and guarantee this treaty. This differed from the ASEAN proposal principally in that it called on the countries of the region to work out their own negotiated solution to the Cambodian problem without the involvement of outside powers, which would then be presented to the great powers (China, in particular) as a *fait accompli* for their endorsement. The Indochinese statement also emphasized that the People's Republic of Kampuchea (PRK) should be taken as 'the sole genuine and legal representative of the Cambodian people'.

The diplomatic impasse continued from 1979 until 1987. Essentially, neither side was willing to make a real compromise and each was waiting for the other side to break. Deng Xiaoping frankly explained the Chinese approach to the Japanese Prime Minister in December 1979: 'It is in that way they [Vietnam] will suffer more and will not be able to extend their hand to Thailand, Malaysia and Singapore.'[5]

With a negotiated settlement seemingly impossible both sides concentrated on shifting the balance of political and military force in their favour. Vietnam concentrated on consolidating the Heng Samrin government, strengthening its 'special relationship' with Laos and Cambodia, and building up its defences on the Sino-Vietnamese border. Thailand, backed by ASEAN, tried to step up the pressure on Hanoi by manipulating the refugee crisis and covertly supporting the anti-Vietnamese insurgents operating on the Thai–Cambodian border.

The Vietnamese Invasion and International Law

Vietnam's military intervention in Cambodia was condemned by ASEAN, China and the West for basically strategic reasons, but the grounds given officially were legal ones. The Vietnamese were accused, not of shifting the regional balance of power against Thailand and ASEAN by their actions, but of flagrantly breaching international law. As a corollary of this, the ASEAN countries have maintained that, while they deplored the crimes perpetrated by the Pol Pot regime, they were obliged to recognize DK rather than the PRK as the legitimate government of Cambodia. To do otherwise was tantamount to 'legalizing aggression'.

The basis for the position adopted by ASEAN is Article 2(4) of the UN Charter, which reads: 'All members shall refrain in their international relations from the threat or use of force against the territorial integrity or political independence of any state, or in any other manner inconsistent with the purposes of the United Nations.' The UN Security Council is empowered to determine whether 'threats to the peace', 'breaches of the peace' or 'acts of aggression' have occurred, and to take action to maintain international peace and security, including the use of international military forces if necessary. However, the drafters of the Charter were aware that countries subjected to armed aggression could hardly be expected to wait for the UN Security Council to decide what it would do before taking effective action in their own defence. Article 51 of the UN Charter therefore provides that:

> Nothing in the present Charter shall impair the inherent right of individual or collective self-defence if an armed attack occurs against a member of the United Nations, until the Security Council has taken the measures necessary to maintain international peace and security. Measures taken by members in the exercise of this right of self-defence shall be immediately reported to the Security Council and shall not in any way affect the authority and responsibility of the Security Council under the present Charter to take at any time such action as it deems necessary to maintain international peace and security.

In fact almost all the armed conflicts since World War II have been resolved without effective involvement by the Security Council, and the deployment of UN peacekeeping forces has proven successful only where it has had the consent of all parties to the dispute. Furthermore, while fighting is in progress, the countries involved have rarely 'immediately reported' their actions to the Security Council.

Quite clearly, Vietnam has used military force against the 'territorial integrity and the political independence' of Pol Pot's regime – indeed, it tried to wipe it out of existence entirely. On this point, ASEAN rests its case. But Article 2(4) must be read in conjunction with Article 51. The UN Charter does not automatically condemn all recourse to military force by states, but rather makes the distinction between aggressive and defensive operations fundamentally important. Unfortunately, in the heat of battle this distinction is often difficult to apply. But for the legal argument, the question of which side *initiated* 'armed attacks' on the other side is central. The 'right of self-defence' exists only in response to armed attacks that have already occurred, and the Charter makes no general provision for what has been termed 'anticipatory self-defence'. Furthermore, the force used in self-defence must be proportionate to the scale of the attack; trivial border incidents cannot be used as a pretext for launching an all-out war. Finally, the right of self-defence does not extend to armed reprisals. As Akehurst puts it: 'if terrorists enter one state from another, the first state may use force to arrest or expel the terrorists, but, having done so, it is not entitled to retaliate by attacking the other state.'[6]

These are the criteria by which Hanoi's actions in its conflict with the Pol Pot regime should be judged under international law. From the evidence presented in chapter 4, it is clear that the Khmer Rouge initiated the conflict in 1977. The case against Vietnam thus rests on the argument that its response was disproportionate to the attacks to which it was subjected, and the invasion of December 1978 cannot be justified in terms of the 'right of self-defence'.

The distinction between acts of 'self-defence' and 'armed reprisals' applies to armed clashes between countries that are basically at peace with one another. But once the threshold has been crossed into a state of 'warlike operations' or a 'state of war' the prohibition no longer holds. Relations between Cambodia and Vietnam in 1977–78 were clearly 'warlike operations'. The legal consequences of this are summed up by D.W. Greig as follows:

> Prior to the Charter it was by no means clear how far a war undertaken in self-defence could justify action directed against the territorial integrity and political independence of the aggressor. The view of the states which defeated Germany and Japan in the Second World War was that they were entitled to occupy the territory of the enemy states and to take over the administration of those territories in order to establish democratic government and institutions on a firm foundation. It is believed that this principle, that an aggressor is not entitled to claim the benefit of what is now contained in Article 2(4) of the Charter, is also accepted by the Charter ... Article 2(4) is no barrier to action against an aggressor which has mounted an armed attack against any state ... A state which has reasonable grounds for believing that its existence is threatened, is entitled to protect itself even to the extent of launching an attack into the territory of the state from which the threat emanates. A state's 'territorial integrity' does not extend so far as to enable it to prepare, free from all interference, an invasion against a neighbouring state... Territorial integrity does not denote inviolability if what a state is preparing is a breach of the peace or act of aggression.[7]

In short, if it is accepted that a state of war or 'warlike operations' existed between Vietnam and DK; that the DK government was the aggressor; and that the government of Vietnam had 'reasonable grounds' for believing that this stage of affairs constituted a grave threat to it; then Vietnam was justified in eliminating the threat by invading and occupying Cambodia – just as the Allies were justified in invading and occupying Germany and Japan in 1945.

Greig continues:

> However, territorial integrity and political independence would obviously be applicable to prevent a state, initially acting in self-defence to meet a threat from another state, from annexing, whether in whole or part, the territory of that other state ... A *threat* of an attack will never justify the threatened state from taking over the government of the alleged 'aggressor' in order to oblige it to 'mend its ways'. It will seldom, if ever, justify the seizing of territory belonging to the 'aggressor'.

Thus there would be no justification for annexing territory from Cambodia or for placing it permanently under a Vietnamese administration; the invaders would be expected to hand over power to a new Cambodian government, administering the country within its existing borders. And this, of course, is precisely what the Vietnamese did by installing Heng Samrin's PRK administration.

The ASEAN case against the Vietnamese invasion of Cambodia on legal grounds is thus weak. In any case, the ASEAN states' response to China's invasion of Vietnam showed that in practice they are willing to accept military intervention – when it coincides with their interests. Even so, ASEAN won the propaganda battle over the Cambodia issue. It was helped by the fact that the Vietnamese initially tried to deny that they were involved in the Cambodian fighting, depicting it as a 'popular uprising', and then claiming its troops had been 'invited' by the PRK government. This transparent dishonesty only brought discredit on Hanoi.

The issue of the legality of Vietnam's intervention in Cambodia is closely linked to the question of whether the PRK should be granted international recognition. ASEAN argued that it had to continue recognizing the Khmer Rouge regime, because to recognize the PRK would be tantamount to 'legalizing aggression'. Recognition of a new government, such as the PRK, means a willingness to accept it as a legitimate member of the international community. In principle, most countries base recognition on effective control of territory and population, not on approval of a government's policies. This approach was classically stated by the British ambassador to the USA, Sir Roger Matkins, in 1954:

> If a government is in effective control of the country in question; if it seems to have a reasonable expectation of permanence; if it can act for a majority of the country's inhabitants; if it is able (though possibly not willing) to carry

out its international obligations; if, in short, it can give a convincing answer to the question, 'Who's in charge here?' then we shall recognize that government.

However, the USA has followed a different approach. In 1931 US Secretary of State Henry L. Stimson argued that the Japanese puppet state of Manchuko in Manchuria should not be recognized because it had been created by an illegal act of aggression, and urged that the League of Nations (the predecessor to the UN) should adopt this as a general principle. The argument that to recognize the PRK is to legitimize Vietnamese aggression appears to be an appeal to the Stimson doctrine. But the Stimson doctrine broke down the first time it came to the test – over Mussolini's conquest of Abyssinia in 1936. As diplomatic postures have to bow to political realities sooner or later, the main effect of trying to apply the Stimson doctrine has been to defer recognition, not to prevent it. Inevitably, it is applied in an arbitrary and politically selective fashion. While this moralist's approach to the question of diplomatic recognition has therefore been generally abandoned in favour of the realist approach spelt out by Matkins, the USA still holds to the view that granting recognition involves giving a stamp of political approval to a regime.

In the case of Cambodia, by the end of 1979 the answer to the question 'Who's in charge here?' was clear. The PRK government was in control of most of the country, and was consolidating its position. The DK 'government' controlled only enclaves in remote parts of the country. At the very least, by the usual criteria of control of territory and population there was no case for continuing to recognize the DK regime. It had become a legal fiction.

The inconsistencies of the ASEAN countries' position on Cambodia were thrown into relief by their attitude towards events in Africa at the same time. In 1978 Idi Amin's loathsome regime in Uganda was overthrown by a Tanzanian military intervention, after Amin had invaded Tanzania. Although the parallels with the Vietnam–Cambodia situation are quite close, there was no controversy over international recognition of the regime the Tanzanians installed in Kampala, although it proved to be much less stable than the PRK. The ASEAN countries, along with the rest of the world, did not hesitate in accepting the Tanzanian intervention as legitimate and in recognizing the new regime. There was no hypocritical attempt to maintain that Amin still had to be recognized as the country's legal ruler even by those who abhorred his crimes.

The USA found itself in a particularly anomalous position over Cambodia. It had refused to recognize DK in the first place. Then, after the regime had been toppled, the USA voted for the DK delegation as the country's legal representative in the UN. American officials argued that to support DK in the UN in no way involved recognition or support for the DK regime itself. Unlike the USA, the British government had granted full recognition to DK, on the grounds of its control of the territory and population of Cambodia. After the Vietnamese invasion these grounds were no longer valid, and recognition of DK was withdrawn in December 1979. After much hesitation, the Australian government followed suit in February 1981.

However, neither the UK nor Australia was willing to grant recognition to the government that did control the population and territory of Cambodia. They both hastened to reassure China and the ASEAN countries that they would refuse to recognize the PRK, on the grounds that it was dependent for its control on the Vietnamese. No such considerations had been involved, for example, in recognizing the new regime in Kampala, although its dependence on the Tanzanians was evident. The hope of these governments was that a viable alternative to both Heng Samrin and Pol Pot would emerge, that a non-Communist contender for power in Cambodia could be found.

The reasons for the refusal to recognize the new government in Phnom Penh had more to do with power politics than legal arguments: Vietnam was aligned with the USSR and had overthrown a pro-Chinese regime in Cambodia while the West hoped to cultivate China as an ally against the Soviet Union. Given this, the rights and wrongs of the Vietnamese intervention itself were immaterial. Uganda was an entirely different matter, not because of any point of law, but because the interests of the great powers were not involved.

A decade after the downfall of Pol Pot little had changed with respect to Cambodia's status in international law. The only detailed study dealing with this has underscored many of the points outlined here. Gary Klintworth has argued that, from the standpoint of international law, Vietnam's intervention was a 'reasonable and legitimate act of self-defence'. He adds that it met 'virtually all the criteria' for humanitarian intervention as well.[8] He does not address the issue of whether, from a legal viewpoint, a 'state of war' existed between Vietnam and the DK regime in 1977–78, and what the implications of that are.

The supporters of the ASEAN case have made no attempt to rebut these arguments. The reality is that they have had no need to do so; however weak their argument, they have had the numbers. Every year since 1979 the UN has voted to seat the Khmer Rouge as the legitimate representative of the Cambodian people (by 122 to 19 votes in 1988). If the Khmer Rouge had the support among the Cambodian people they enjoy on the floor of the UN General Assembly they would have routed the Vietnamese long ago.

A decade on, the chief question-mark that hangs over the legality of

Vietnam's intervention is its duration. As Klintworth notes, military interventions that were accepted as legitimate on defensive and humanitarian grounds by most countries (India and East Pakistan/Bangladesh; Tanzania in Uganda) were relatively short. This may be putting the cart before the horse, however. India and Tanzania were able to withdraw quickly precisely because their intervention was accepted as legitimate.

In the case of Cambodia, Vietnamese intervention was prolonged because foreign support soon revived the danger of a Khmer Rouge comeback. Had the world accepted the government in Phnom Penh as they had accepted those in Dacca and Kampala, Vietnamese troops would in all probability have been out of Cambodia much earlier. Instead, ASEAN, China and the USA opted to manipulate the refugee crisis that followed the collapse of the Pol Pot regime to fuel another decade of war in Cambodia.

Thailand's Refugee Crisis

During 1979–80 there was a massive influx of Cambodian refugees into Thailand. The exodus was a product of several factors – the economic collapse inside Cambodia, Vietnamese military campaigns against the Khmer Rouge base areas near the Thai border, and the policies pursued by the Bangkok government and the international relief agencies themselves. The refugee crisis placed Thailand under heavy strain, but it also provided it with a major lever of influence in the political struggle over Cambodia.

The movement of refugees into Thailand began in 1975, with the Khmer Rouge takeover, but it remained at a relatively low level until 1979. Over this period, a total of 34,000 Cambodian refugees had entered Thailand, 19,000 of whom had been resettled in other countries, leaving a residual 15,000. Contrary to a widespread impression, the Vietnamese invasion did not trigger a large-scale flight across the border. By mid-April 1979, only a further 5,000 refugees had entered Thailand. These were mostly survivors from the Phnom Penh middle class, former Lon Nolists, and others who had strong political objections to living under any Communist government.

The situation altered dramatically in April 1979 when the Vietnamese attacked Khmer Rouge strongholds near the Thai border. Tens of thousands of people, including several thousand Khmer Rouge soldiers, streamed into Thailand. The Thai allowed them to enter – officially, only if they laid down their arms – but denied the Vietnamese/Heng Samrin forces any right of pursuit into Thai territory. The government in Phnom Penh responded by angrily charging that Thailand was providing sanctuary for the Khmer Rouge. There was much speculation in the western press that the Vietnamese would pursue their enemies across the border even if this brought them into armed conflict with the Thai.

Many of the Cambodians who entered Thailand at this time returned more or less immediately to Cambodia, but large numbers sought more permanent refuge. By the end of May 1979 there were 80,000 to 90,000 Cambodians on Thai soil. The Thai government refused to grant refugee status to most of the Cambodians entering the country. The convention adopted by the UN in 1951 defines a refugee as a person who leaves the country of his or her origin 'owing to a well-founded fear of persecution for reasons of race, religion, nationality, membership of a particular social group or political opinion'. It has been accepted as a general principle that people in this situation should be given sanctuary, and should not be forcibly returned to their country. But the Thai would only accept as 'refugees' those who were able to provide firm guarantees that they would be resettled in a third country – and as a rule this was something that only a lucky minority of upper- or middle-class background could do. While most commentators still continued to refer to the rest as 'refugees', they were officially classified by the Thai government as 'illegal entrants'. The implication of this was that the Thai had the right to repatriate them to Cambodia when the situation 'normalized'.

The Thai government was still not reconciled to the presence of so many Cambodian refugees on its soil, and by June 1979 only 11,000 had been accepted for resettlement. The government decided to deal with the rest by forcibly repatriating them. On 8 June they trucked 42,000 to the frontier of the northern Cambodian province of Preah Vihear, and forced them across the border. There was an international outcry at this action. The government responded by arguing that the refugees were a burden that a poor country like Thailand could not be expected to bear, but on 18 June it announced its decision to postpone further forcible repatriations. Distressed by the plight of the Cambodian refugees, to which the action of the Thai government had attracted a blaze of publicity, governments and international organizations promised to provide greater humanitarian aid – without looking too closely at how it was being handled in Thailand.

In the second half of 1979 the situation on the border deteriorated alarmingly. By September refugees from Khmer Rouge zones were pouring into Thailand. 'These people tell us that as they walk through the forests towards Thailand, they see bodies lying everywhere,' said one relief official from Mai Rut camp. With their food stocks exhausted, the Khmer Rouge forces were being starved out by the Vietnamese, who had cut off all their access to food-producing areas in Cambodia. This attempted siege by the Vietnamese was the context in which the distribution of humanitarian aid along the Thai–Cambodian border began. In June 1979, the Thai allowed the Catholic Relief Service to distribute food on the border, and over the next few months most of the other agencies followed suit. They maintained that they gave aid to civilians only, but they admitted that they had no control over the situation. Inevitably, a significant amount of the aid went to Pol Pot's soldiers.

The stream of refugees into Thailand turned into a flood again in October 1979. With the rains easing, the Vietnamese launched a series of heavy attacks on Khmer Rouge positions around Phnom Malai. Pol Pot's troops had little choice but to retreat right to the Thai border, and even here they continued to come under artillery and mortar attack. The Thai government agreed to give them asylum on condition that they laid down their arms, and some 80,000 people crossed the border. Many others camped around the food distribution points hastily established by the Thai army, and here reporters watched Khmer Rouge porters hauling off sacks of rice provided by the UN's World Food Programme, by Unicef, by the Red Cross and the Australian government; while in the hospital tents the sick and wounded Pol Pot soldiers were treated by western doctors.

Reporters visiting the border were now able to get a first-hand glimpse of conditions in the Khmer Rouge zones. Michael Richardson crossed the border into one encampment in the Phnom Malai sector and described conditions there in these terms:

> Much of it is forest. To penetrate this gloomy world ... is to take a long walk through hell. We followed a track that winds for several kilometres past towering limestone mountains. ... On either side, far into the malaria-infested forest, people were huddled in groups under crude shelters of plastic, matting, branches and grass. The air was acrid with smoke from countless small fires as women crouched over pots cooking rice, corn, dried fish and green papaya. The vast majority of these jungle hermits are women and children with just a sprinkling of old folk. Some appear to be reasonably well-fed and healthy. But many, stricken with malnutrition, malaria or beriberi, were lying on beds of leaves or straw mats. Apart from this listlessness, the thing I remember most clearly was not the sound of subdued voices or wood being chopped, but of children wailing and people coughing.[9]

AP reporter Denis Gray visited another Khmer Rouge encampment, where he found similar conditions. Most people refused to talk to him, and those that did explained everything in terms of *angkar* ('the organiza-tion', that is, the Communist Party of Kampuchea). He concluded that 'even while the ultra-revolutionary movement may be preparing for its last stand, it makes no concessions to those under its control. The savagery and iron discipline remain.'

By 27 October some 30,000 starving and sick people had been deposited in a hastily established 'holding centre' at Sa Kaeo, sixty kilometres back from the border. Initially, this was nothing more than a fenced-in enclosure of sixty acres of badly drained paddy. People were transferred there from the border so hastily that no housing or sewerage had been established, and before supplies of food and medicine had been organized. About half the people had dysentery, and three-quarters of them had malaria. To cap it all, shortly after the camp was established it rained again, and the camp was flooded. With the help of volunteer workers, the aid agencies worked frantically to dig latrines, to set up tents and huts, and to organize food, water and medical services. Conditions at Sa Kaeo in the first few weeks were horrific, and the death rate was more than thirty-five per day.

By January 1980 conditions in the camp had improved greatly, and the death rate had fallen to only one or two a day. Perhaps half the camp population were Pol Pot supporters – the others having been a captive labour force – and about 7,000 were soldiers. Theoretically, they had laid down their weapons before they entered Thailand, but in Sa Kaeo they were equipped with machetes for building huts – 'tools not weapons' according to the Thai camp commander, and none of the hundred Thai soldiers responsible for maintaining order in the camp felt like investigating things too closely.

The camp leader, appointed by the Thai shortly after the camp opened, stalked around with a squad of half a dozen bodyguards, shouting orders to the refugees through a megaphone provided by the Thai. He was Colonel Phak Lim. He had organized the purges in the northwest region (Battambang and Pursat provinces) for Pol Pot in 1978, and thereafter held the post of security chief for the region. In Sa Kaeo, he had those who disobeyed *angkar* beaten, staked out on hot tin roofs in the sun, or buried up to their necks in the ground. Nor were western officials who displeased him exempt: one had to be transferred from the camp after a death threat.

The Vietnamese military offensive in western Cambodia in October 1979 brought them right to the Thai border at many points, and led to renewed tension between Vietnam and Thailand. As they attacked Khmer Rouge forces straddling the border, Vietnamese shells sometimes landed on Thai soil, and from time to time Vietnamese and Thai patrols exchanged shots. On 16 October the Thai government called on the UN secretary general to send observers to the border, and warned that Thailand might retaliate against flagrant violations of its territory by warring factions in Cambodia. Three days later, Nguyen Co Thach flew to Bangkok and assured the Thai government that the Vietnamese forces would not enter Thailand, but the Thai prime minister dismissed this as 'pure diplomatic deception to divide us and ASEAN'. Thach responded by making it clear that the Vietnamese assurances would be dependent on Thailand halting aid to Khmer Rouge forces.

It was widely expected that the Vietnamese would try and deal a knock-out blow to the Khmer Rouge in the 1979–80 dry season. But given the rugged terrain and the fact that they were straddling the Thai border, this would not be easy. There was speculation that Vietnam would launch a massive strike into eastern Thailand, to cut around behind the mountains and completely encircle Pol Pot's army. In October 1979, Deng Xiaoping pledged that China would come to Thailand's assistance if it was attacked by Vietnam. But the expected Vietnamese offensive never materialized. From Hanoi's point of view, there was no need for a thrust into Thailand. Their aim was to keep the Khmer Rouge bottled up in the mountains and to concentrate on building up the PRK into a viable government.

On 19 October 1979 the Thai government announced a decision that transformed the border situation. Kriangsak declared an 'open door' policy towards all displaced people from Indochina who sought asylum in Thailand. This immediately opened the way to a major international effort to aid them. On 1 November Kriangsak made a formal request to the UNHCR to provide care and maintenance for up to 300,000 Cambodians in Thailand, at a total cost of US$59.7 million. Two days later, the UNHCR agreed to the proposal, and at a UN conference in New York on 5 November £46 million was pledged to this project. As a result of the new policy a huge new holding centre was opened at Khao-I-Dang, twelve kilometres to the north of Aranyapratet.

When the international agencies began distributing food aid to those in need at points along the border not controlled by the Khmer Rouge conditions were deteriorating in the interior of Cambodia, and there was a large-scale movement of people to these sections of the border. Though they recounted stories of hardship, suffering, and sometimes famine conditions in PRK zones, they were in better physical condition than those who came across from the Khmer Rouge zones. It was the 'walking skeletons' who staggered out of Pol Pot's mountain strongholds who created the images of famine in Cambodia for the western media. With the encouragement of American 'genocide' claims, this image was inaccurately applied to the masses of refugees from the PRK zones.

By December 1979 there were perhaps between half a million and a million Khmer – nobody knew the precise number – encamped along the border in the flat country to the north of Aranyapratet. Sprawling shanty towns sprang up across miles of what had once been paddyfields and thin forest, and the whole area became a crowded shambles of dusty straw huts, primitive trading stalls, flies and faeces. Local Thai farmers watched helplessly as the refugees scavenged their fields for food and building materials, turning them into a barren waste and destroying their meagre livelihoods. Most of the refugees here looked in good health. Signs of malnutrition were rare, but sores and eye infections were common – an indication of a dangerously unsanitary environment. Health workers thought that the lack of sanitation was the major problem.

All these people were themselves unproductive, and mainly dependent on aid from the international agencies operating along the border. Like the peasants on whose land many of them were squatting, their only potential source of livelihood was trade. And so the refugee settlements became huge trading centres. One of the chief items of trade was the aid delivered to the border camps. This was supposed to be distributed to the refugees as rations, but much of it was commandeered for trading purposes by armed groups. In early 1980 a Red Cross official said that this happened to up to 80 per cent of the food the Red Cross delivered at the border, and the picture was much the same for the other agencies. 'We've had problems in many parts of the world trying to help people in need, but I have never seen anything like what is happening right now on that border' commented another official.

Private enterprise was quick to respond to the opportunities this situation presented. Thousands of Thai traders streamed to the Cambodian border, carrying goods for sale – fruit and vegetables, medicines, bicycle parts, tape cassette players, clothes, cartons of cigarettes, crates of beer bottles. The trade was immensely profitable, for the price mark-up between nearby Thai towns and the border camps was four- or fivefold. Aranyapratet was temporarily transformed from a sleepy provincial market town into a hectic boomtown whose streets were jammed with stalls selling everything conceivable.

From the other side of the border, thousands of Khmer traders arrived in the encampments every day, on foot or on bicycles, bringing gold and jewellery, or whatever valuable trinkets they could find in Cambodia. The border settlements became the centre of a huge network of trade stretching right across Communist Indochina, and at every step the prices were marked up. At its peak, in August 1980, the volume of the border trade was said to be 30–60 million Thai baht ($1.5–3 million) per day. By 1981, Thai goods were not only abundant in Phnom Penh but also readily available in the streets of Saigon, and even in Hanoi. Technically, this 'black marketeering' was illegal, but the authorities in Phnom Penh and Vietnam seem to have largely turned a blind eye to it.

As the money pledged to border-relief began to dry up in early 1980, the Thai became worried that they would be left saddled with an intolerable financial burden. But they rejected any idea of negotiations with the government in Phnom Penh, and tried to organize unilateral repatriations of refugees to insurgent-controlled territory in western Cambodia.

The exercise began in March with the repatriation of refugees from Khao-I-Dang to the border village of Mak Mun, then under the control of right-wing Cambodian guerrillas. Next, refugees were trucked back to the border from Sa Kaeo, including Colonel Lim and the camp's Khmer Rouge top brass. There was no response from the Vietnamese.

In May the Thai government began to talk publicly about large-scale refugee repatriations to a 'safe zone' in western Cambodia under UN supervision. Although the UN supervision was not yet organized, the Thai announced that the repatriations would commence, beginning with the refugees at Sa Kaeo. Singapore's Rajaratnam praised the Thai decision, and exhorted the Cambodians to 'go back and fight'. Then Phnom Penh Radio denounced Thailand's 'vile manoeuvre', and warned it 'not to play with fire'. The repatriation began in June. At Khao-I-Dang there were few volunteers. The great majority came from Sa Kaeo, where the process of 'volunteering' was overseen by Khmer Rouge cadres. As the first bunch of returnees left the camp, a UN official remarked to John Pilger: 'they're ready to fight ... we're sending back a whole division of the bastards. This is like a declaration of war.'[10] Early on the morning of 23 June 1980 the Vietnamese retaliated. They occupied Mak Mun and the nearby settlement of Nong Chan. Then they crossed the border and occupied three Thai villages. They warned the inhabitants to leave, and set up ambushes for Thai troops on the roads approaching the border. This led to two days of skirmishes between Vietnamese and Thai forces in which, according to the Thai, twenty-two Thai and seventy-five Vietnamese soldiers were killed. The Vietnamese then sealed off a fifty-kilometre stretch of the border to the north of Aranyapratet for a month, bringing a halt to border-relief operations and shutting down the black market.

The UNHCR had been unhappy with the Thai project in the first place, but after Vietnam's show of strength it called a halt to the exercise. 'We agree with the Thai government that we are not going to send refugees into a war zone', a senior UNHCR official announced diplomatically. 'The repatriation is off until further notice.'

More than a quarter of a million people have remained trapped in a legal and political limbo for a decade. After the first couple of years, few had a chance of being accepted for resettlement in the West. As 'illegal entrants', the Thai said the Cambodians would eventually be repatriated. But they refused to send them back to live under the pro-Vietnamese government in Phnom Penh – out of concern for their human rights, claimed one Thai official in 1987. In the meantime, they were trapped in 'temporary' camps in a war-zone, prevented from escaping by armed guards, and sustained by 'humanitarian' relief and voluntary aid agencies – a network of camps which Vickery dubbed the 'VOLAG Archipelago'.

These camps became the principal bases and recruitment pools for anti-Vietnamese resistance groups. Until a Vietnamese offensive in 1984–85, not even nominal attempts were made to separate the military and civilian components of the camp populations. Denied normal means of livelihood, people lived on rations, by petty trading and – for a lucky few – on remittances from relatives abroad. A large proportion of the camp populations were women and children. The boys grew up to become soldiers; the girls to have babies. Life, one inmate remarked despairingly in 1987, was 'worse than under Pol Pot'. The people, he explained, were well fed, clothed and housed – certainly better than they would have been fending for themselves inside Cambodia. But they were like prisoners – they had no security, no freedom, and no future. 'We knew that Pol Pot just could not last,' he said, and waved his arm around a vast camp that housed 130,000 people. 'But this – this could go on for ever.'

Notes

1. For the reaction in Bangkok to the Communist victories, see M. Ladd Thomas, 'The Perceived Impact of Communist Indochina on Thailand's Security', in Clark D. Neher, ed., *Modern Thai Politics: From Village to Nation*, 2nd edn, Cambridge, Mass. 1979, pp. 398–402. For recent general accounts of Thai foreign policy, see John L.S. Girling, *Thailand: Society and Politics*, Ithaca and London 1981, ch. 6, and Leszek Buszynski, 'Thailand: Erosion of Balanced Foreign Policy', *Asian Survey*, vol. 22, 1982.

2. See, for example, Malcolm Caldwell, 'Thailand and Imperialist Strategy in the 1980s', *Journal of Contemporary Asia*, vol. 8, 1978.

3. Girling, p. 239.

4. Quoted by Nayan Chanda, *Far Eastern Economic Review*, 21 December 1979.

5. Ibid.

6. Michael Akehurst, *A Modern Introduction to International Law*, London 1970, pp. 317–18.

7. D.W. Greig, *International Law*, 2nd edn, London 1976, pp. 849–95.

8. Gary Klintworth, *Vietnam's Intervention in Cambodia in International Law*, Canberra 1989, pp. 109–12.

9. Michael Richardson, *Age*, Melbourne, 22 October 1979.

10. 'Only the Allies are New', in John Pilger and Anthony Barnett, *Aftermath: The Struggle of Vietnam and Cambodia*, London 1982, p. 95.

Coalition of Lost Causes

Cambodia became the focus of a confrontation between Vietnam, intent on keeping the People's Republic of Kampuchea (PRK) government in place, and the ASEAN countries, which sought to overthrow it. Overarching this conflict was China's determination, backed by the USA, to exploit the situation in order to 'bleed' Vietnam. The key to the strategies of both ASEAN and China was the growth of the military capabilities of the anti-Vietnamese resistance forces on the Thai–Cambodian border. Non-Communist groups also operated here, but the Khmer Rouge was undoubtedly the most effective.

Rebirth of the Khmer Rouge

Pol Pot's forces were in a desperate state in the closing months of 1979. Vietnamese attacks had captured or destroyed most of their base camps, and their people had been reduced to a nomadic forest existence. Starvation and disease were rapidly reducing their numbers, and their organizations were disintegrating. The army had fallen to a total strength of about 20,000, but half of them were isolated and dispersed, totally cut off from the main force. Some units of the latter were breaking up into roaming bands of armed predators. The party leaders were still blaming all the setbacks they had suffered on 'traitors among the ranks of the party, the army and the people'.[1]

It was foreign support that relieved the pressure on Pol Pot's forces. With the commencement of large-scale food distribution across the Thai–Cambodian border in October 1979, the Khmer Rouge was assured of a regular supply of food. Economic rehabilitation had major political consequences. The distribution of food in Khmer Rouge zones was controlled by Communist Party of Kampuchea (CPK) cadres, and they used their powers of patronage to rebuild the party organization. Although aid across the border undoubtedly saved thousands of lives, one of its major consequences was the political revitalization of the Pol Pot forces.

Needless to say, this was also true of the military aid the Khmer Rouge forces received from China. This began flowing through Thailand in January 1979, as soon as Phnom Penh fell. Although Thailand officially maintained that it was neutral in the conflict, the Thai military took responsibility for transferring the Chinese supplies to the border.

The Khmer Rouge now embarked on an attempt to rally wider support. Ieng Sary conceded in June 1979 that Democratic Kampuchea (DK) had been responsible for some 'excesses' in the past, but promised a 'gentle and liberal' regime if the Khmer Rouge were restored to power. 'We are willing to forget the past', he announced, 'and I hope that others too will forget the past.'

In September 1979 the Khmer Rouge launched a new 'Patriotic and Democratic Front', whose programme promised free elections, freedom to form political parties, freedom of speech, of the press, and of religion. The economy, it promised, would be based on individual or family productive activity, and the rights of private property would be guaranteed.

In the new situation, it announced, 'our present task is no longer to make the socialist revolution and to build socialism. Our present task is not an ideological one, it is a struggle for the defence of the territory and race of our beloved Cambodia.' At the Khmer Rouge camp of Phnom Thmei (Nong Pru to the Thai) Khieu Samphan assured western visitors that the Khmer Rouge were patriots and democrats. In January 1981 he told us that nationalism rather than socialism had always been the driving force of the Cambodian revolution:

No more socialism. No more socialist revolution. ... Our ideal is the survival of Cambodia. As for Communism, we saw it as the way to lead Cambodia to independence and survival – a means only, not the ideal. Now, through the flesh and blood of people, we have been given the experience to know we cannot follow this path.

In December 1979 Pol Pot stood down as prime minister of DK, to be replaced by Khieu Samphan. Thereafter Pol Pot was not seen in public again. But he remained commander-in-chief of the armed forces and general secretary of the CPK, and was still believed to be the undisputed leader of the Khmer Rouge movement. In 1981 the Khmer Rouge leaders announced the dissolution of the CPK, but within a few years were speaking of their organization as the 'Party of Democratic Kampuchea'.

These moves, along with improved living conditions in the border camps made possible by international aid, did much to restore morale among Khmer Rouge supporters. But with the power-structure and leadership essentially unchanged, many remained uneasy. One Khmer Rouge supporter told Steve Heder:

> The cadres who were responsible for the ultra-left line and the killings still grasp all power. Now suddenly they've changed 100 per cent. ... But these guys do just what they want according to their subjective analysis of the situation. They could change back just as suddenly. Furthermore, no-one can question them about what went wrong before. They don't accept any criticism or admit that they were wrong. They blame everything on others. How can you trust them? They say everything depends on the concrete situation, but they're the ones who decide what the concrete situation is and sometimes even create the concrete situation, like after '75, when they screwed everything up. It could be like that again. Nobody could stop them.[2]

As conditions in its base camps stabilized and its political organization was rebuilt, the Khmer Rouge was able to renew the military struggle. Over the first half of 1980, the Khmer Rouge leaders made a determined effort to rebuild their armed forces. By mid-year they claimed to have 60,000 soldiers under arms. Analysts in Bangkok thought that the real figure was more likely to be somewhere between 25,000 and 30,000, but in any case this represented a substantial advance from their position in late 1979.

In early 1980 the Khmer Rouge attempted to go on the offensive again. It succeeded in retaking base camps in the Phnom Malai area from the Vietnamese, and holding them until the onset of the rainy season. This turned Cambodia's primitive backroads into quagmires, forcing the Vietnamese to break off their attacks. The Khmer Rouge forces responded by launching a 'monsoon offensive'. Away from the border they could only operate as small guerrilla bands, making night raids on bridges and isolated army outposts, ambushing cars and trains, and planting landmines and booby-traps.

This was still enough to convince some observers that the military initiative had passed from the Vietnamese to the Khmer Rouge. Cambodia was becoming 'Vietnam's Vietnam'. The real significance of the Khmer Rouge's 1980 offensive was very different. The Khmer Rouge found it was lacking the essential condition for waging successful guerrilla war, the support of the people. The brutality of its rule after 1975 had alienated not just the urban minority, but most of the rural population as well.

Except in some of the remotest and most isolated areas, in every village the Khmer Rouge entered, it found most of the people actively opposed to it; worse, they were willing to cooperate with the PRK authorities

against the Khmer Rouge. As a result, Steve Heder concluded after inter-
viewing soldiers involved in these operations, 'most of the populated
countryside was off limits to the Democratic Kampuchea fighters and
agents.' Henry Kamm summed up the situation in the wake of the Khmer
Rouge's 'monsoon offensive':

> Vietnamese occupation troops control all of Cambodia – the towns and villages,
> as well as the roads, railways and waterways that link them. ... The Pol Pot
> forces control only enclaves in formerly uninhabited areas. ... They control
> no roads and own no vehicles. Their leaders cross into Thailand to travel from
> one enclave to another.[3]

As soon as the rains cleared and the ground hardened Vietnamese
forces renewed their attacks on the Khmer Rouge border camps, and
guerrilla activity dropped off. But at the end of the 1981 dry season the
Vietnamese pulled back from their more remote outposts, where they
had experienced difficulties keeping supply-lines open during the previous
rainy season. The Khmer Rouge claimed this as a great victory, and
stepped up its guerrilla activities inside Cambodia. Ieng Sary predicted
that it would be ready to liberate provincial towns by 1982, but this
was not to be.

The war settled into a seasonal rhythm reminiscent of the First and
Second Indochina Wars. Big-unit forces, backed by tanks and artillery,
commanded the battlefield during the dry season. Guerrilla forces became
more active during the rainy season. But in this conflict, the insurgents
lacked the mobility enjoyed by successful guerrillas. The Khmer Rouge
forces were unable to expand their control beyond a belt of land about
25 kilometres wide along the Thai border, and here they took a heavy
bashing each dry season. Unless they could break out of their political
isolation, the Khmer Rouge forces would be slowly ground down by
the Vietnamese.

For the first couple of years after the Vietnamese toppled Pol Pot,
the ASEAN countries, China and the USA had all based their policies
on the assumption that the nationalism and fighting ability of the Khmer
Rouge made it a potent force against the Vietnamese. The Chinese were
content to stick with the Khmer Rouge. 'I do not understand why some
people want to remove Pol Pot', Deng Xiaoping said in 1984. 'It is true
that he made some mistakes in the past, but now he is leading the fight
against the Vietnamese aggressors.'[4] However, the ASEAN countries were
always embarrassed by their *de facto* alliance with Pol Pot. As the born-
again Khmer Rouge proved to be of limited effectiveness, their attention
turned to the non-Communist groups that had emerged on the Thai–
Cambodian border.

Re-emergence of the Cambodian Right

Banditry and smuggling had long been common along the Thai–Cambodian border, and right-wing Khmer Serei ('Free Khmer') guerrillas had operated here in the 1960s. In the 1970s the Khmer Serei had joined forces with the Lon Nol regime. After 1975 many of the surviving remnants of these groups had returned to smuggling and sporadic guerrilla activity on the Thai border. They were given a new lease of life by the influx of politically minded, anti-Communist refugees after the overthrow of the Pol Pot regime. The strongest and best organized of these groups in the early 1980s was the Khmer People's National Liberation Front (KPNLF). It had been formed in Paris in March 1979, but its existence was not proclaimed until October, after it had managed to bring several other anti-Communist splinter groups under its wing.

Its leader was Son Sann, a frail, bespectacled man in his seventies. Of mixed Khmer–Vietnamese ancestry, Sann studied in Paris in the 1930s, and served in the French Indochina administration. Under Sihanouk he had founded the Cambodian National Bank in 1955 and served as prime minister in the rightist government of 1967–68. When Sihanouk was overthrown in 1970 Sann went into exile in Paris, where he tried successfully to create a 'third force' opposed to both the Lon Nol regime and the National United Front of Kampuchea.

Most of the groundwork for the emergence of the KPNLF was done on the Thai–Cambodian border by Dien Del. Vietnamese by birth, Del had moved to Cambodia in his teens and served as a divisional commander in the Lon Nol army. Sann appointed him commander-in-chief of the KPNLF's military forces, and he was highly regarded by the Thai military, who gave their backing to the KPNLF in Khmer Serei faction fights. The KPNLF was opposed to Pol Pot and to Sihanouk, as well as to the Vietnamese and Heng Samrin. But in 1980 it could muster only about 2,000 troops.

The KPNLF's most serious rival on the border was the Movement of National Liberation of Cambodia ('Moulinaka'), formed in August 1979 by Kong Sileah, a former Lon Nol naval lieutenant. He maintained that the anti-Vietnamese struggle could rally wide support only if it were led by Prince Sihanouk and if the non-Communist groups were willing to collaborate with the Khmer Rouge. In 1980 Kong Sileah had less than 1,000 men under arms.

But most groups on the border in the early 1980s were more interested in the black market than in politics. Wan Sarin, a former Lon Nol soldier who had turned to banditry and teak smuggling in the Pol Pot period (after a short spell as a Buddhist monk), had established control of the settlement at Mak Mun. The influx of refugees brought some 200,000 people into the small area his forces controlled. Now calling himself Vong Atichvong, he announced the formation of a Khmer National Liberation Movement, with himself as commander-in-chief of its armed forces, and adopted the titles of 'marshal' and 'prime minister'. He was joined by André Okthol, who had spent the 1970s in France as a political science student but now attracted a following by calling himself Prince Norodom Soriavong and claiming to be a cousin of Sihanouk's. Wearing a neat safari suit, dark glasses and the wispy beginnings of a Zapata-style moustache, he held 'press conferences' at which he called on the West to provide him with the $800 million needed to liberate Cambodia from the Communists. A religious fanatic, he wore Buddhist amulets to ward off evil spirits and bullets, captivated the most despairing of the refugees with his mystic incantations, and terrified the rest with his violent outbursts of temper. Reporters nicknamed him the 'Mad Prince'. To the north, the encampment at Nong Samet was controlled by an uneasy coalition of former Lon Nolists led by In Sakhan and a group of defectors from the nearby Khmer Rouge settlement at Phnom Chat led by Mitr Don.

From late 1979 to early 1981 the struggle among these groups for control of the people and trade along the border repeatedly flared up into violence, aggravated by the occasional intervention of the Thai, the Vietnamese and the Khmer Rouge. Wan Sarin's group at Mak Mun was smashed; he himself fled to Thailand, where he was reportedly murdered. The 'Mad Prince' disappeared without trace. At Nong Samet, Mitr Don drove In Sakhan's followers out of the camp. In February 1981 Don himself was ambushed and killed after falling out with Dien Del. Kong Sileah resisted KPNLF control, but he died of cerebral malaria in August 1980. His followers quickly reached an understanding with Dien Del. The outcome was that by early 1981 most of the border to the north of Aranyapratet was controlled by the KPNLF, or at least by camp warlords who gave their allegiance to the KPNLF.

In 1982 Dien Del was replaced by a joint military command, consisting of Sak Sutsakhan, Thang Reng, Hing Kamthorn, and Chea Chutt. The first two were leading Lon Nolists, who had been persuaded to rejoin the struggle a few months earlier – Sutsakhan had been the last commander of the Republican Army in 1975, Reng the commander of a 'Special Forces' brigade. Kamthorn was a leading political figure in the KPNLF, one of Sann's lieutenants, while Chutt was the commander at Nong Chan. The meteoric rise of Sutsakhan and Reng indicates the substantial continuity of the KPNLF forces on the Thai border with the defeated Lon Nol regime.

The emergence of the KPNLF as the dominant force on the border restored some stability to rightist politics after 1981. This aroused great hopes among western commentators. To Becker, for example, Son Sann seemed 'like the leader Graham Greene's "Quiet American" died searching for'.[5] But in fact he can be taken as a symbol of the weakness of the Cambodian Right: an elderly banker was unlikely to be a successful leader of a guerrilla war.

The KPNLF brought together several groups descended from the Lon Nol regime under the leadership of a politician opposed to that regime. It inherited all the weaknesses of the Khmer Republic in exaggerated form – factionalism and disorganization, paralysing corruption, and lack of a positive political programme. This largely frustrated the efforts of those talented and committed people it did attract. Despite this the KPNLF won the support of much of the dispossessed middle class, in the non-Khmer Rouge border camps and in the growing Cambodian diaspora. By 1983 it had managed to build an army numbering around 9,000, but (as with the Khmer Republic before it) the peasantry inside Cambodia remained indifferent to its political appeals.

In the early 1980s the KPNLF overshadowed the Sihanouk supporters on the border. Sihanouk had acted as DK's representative at the UN in January 1979, and Moulinaka argued for an alliance between the non-Communist groups and the Khmer Rouge. Whatever the diplomatic merits of this line, it failed to arouse much enthusiasm among those who had lived through the Pol Pot years.

In 1979–80 Sihanouk concentrated on presenting himself as a suitable figure for a diplomatic compromise. He distanced himself from the Khmer Rouge, while continuing to denounce the Vietnamese and the PRK. The Thai would not allow him to visit his supporters on the Thai–Cambodian border. But the powers involved in the Cambodian conflict rejected any compromise solution at that time. By the end of 1980 a frustrated Sihanouk had concluded that his only chance of having any say in his country's future was to field an army of his own. Moulinaka and several other groups rallied to him, and provided the basis for the Armeé Nationale Sihanoukiste (ANS) and the Front Uni National pour un Cambodge Indépendant, Neutre, Pacifique et Cooperatif (FUNCINPEC). Sihanouk's western admirers, who thought of him as a 'charismatic figure' expected large numbers to rally to his cause. But in 1981 the ANS numbered only a few hundred.

Sihanouk's decision to throw himself into armed struggle was motivated only partly by the failure of his diplomatic strategy. A feudal king at heart, he could not think of himself merely as a politician thrown out of office ten years before. He was the 'father' of his people; whatever the vagaries of Cambodian politics, he could not repudiate his obligation to look after them (which meant, in practice, his obligation to regain power for himself).

These motives were compounded by personal pique. He announced that he resented critics 'from coffee shops in Paris, Montreal and Los Angeles' who accused him of doing nothing to save Cambodia from the Vietnamese and the Communists:

> since I could no longer live in peace and tranquillity, even here in Pyongyang, because these letters and telegrams arrive from them insulting me, calling me a pro-Vietnamese traitor and a selfish do-nothing, I said 'All right, I launch myself into war.' ... The Blue Khmers, carried away by their anti-Vietnamese phobia, refuse to see reality. They have lost all notions of the Cambodian people's misery. They don't realise that the people now have a much better life than under the Khmer Rouge, and they absolutely don't want the return of the Khmer Rouge. The whole policy is totally unrealistic. To go to war in Cambodia now is madness. But I have to participate in this madness because otherwise I will be called a traitor.[6]

Despite his international support, the political and military weaknesses of his forces ensured that Sihanouk's course of action would be dictated by others.

The Formation of a Coalition Government

While ASEAN hopes came to focus on the non-Communist Cambodians, the Chinese stuck by the Khmer Rouge. It seemed logical to both that both groups should join forces in opposition to the Vietnamese and the PRK. But they disagreed over who should enjoy the dominant position. China believed that a coalition with the non-Communist groups would enhance the popular appeal of the Khmer Rouge. But they did not think that the non-Communist groups had the strength to erode the PRK/Vietnamese position. They argued that nothing should be done to weaken its leadership and army. ASEAN argued that the clout of the Khmer Rouge side should be used to restore the non-Communists to power.

The Khmer Rouge made it clear that it would welcome a coalition as a way of gaining respectability and widening its recruitment base. But it showed no interest in the idea of others riding to power on its back. And a coalition with Pol Pot's forces had little appeal to the non-Communists. In November 1980 Sihanouk wrote:

> According to certain Westerners, the Khmer Rouge wolves are perfectly capable of transforming themselves into lambs. Such wishful thinking is dangerous, above all for the Cambodian people still in Cambodia. These people are hoping that the free world can find some means of saving them other than by supporting the infernal regime of Pol Pot, Ieng Sary and Khieu Samphan.[7]

But when Zhao Ziyang finally gave China's imprimatur to a united resistance at a press conference in Bangkok three months later, Sihanouk announced his willingness to cooperate with the Khmer Rouge. He met with Khieu Samphan on 10 March 1981 in Pyongyang, but their talks foundered when Sihanouk demanded the disarming of the Khmer Rouge. In April Sihanouk conferred with the Chinese foreign minister, Huang Hua, and called for Beijing to arm his forces. Hua said China would provide weapons for his followers only if he resolved his differences with the Khmer Rouge. Then he met the US chargé d'affaires in Beijing, J. Stapleton Roy, and asked him if the USA was willing to provide the arms he needed. But Roy also insisted he join forces with the Khmer Rouge. 'After that', he told Sihanouk, 'it will be easier for friendly countries to help you.'

Son Sann initially denounced Sihanouk for his willingness to deal with the Khmer Rouge. But he soon found himself compelled to follow the same course. To secure arms for his followers, he would have to join with the Khmer Rouge. He reluctantly agreed to this, but demanded that the entire Pol Pot leadership stand down first. 'We can't accept a coalition with them', one of his aides explained. 'They would murder us in our sleep.'

After nine months of tense negotiations the Coalition Government of Kampuchea (CGDK) was born in Kuala Lumpur on 22 June 1982. Sihanouk, Son Sann and Khieu Samphan signed an agreement written by the Thai Foreign Ministry, and gave each other ceremonial cheek-to-cheek embraces. Sihanouk and Sann later described their decision to join with the Khmer Rouge as 'agonizing', but they said that 'we have no other choice' since the issue was 'the survival of Cambodia'. Reminded of his statement that the Khmer Rouge wolves could not be converted into lambs, Sihanouk observed: 'I am a lamb. Son Sann is a lamb. We have to choose between being eaten by Khmer or being eaten by Vietnamese. As Khmer, we prefer to be eaten by Khmer, because we are nationalists.'

It was claimed that a united resistance would transform the political and military situation in Cambodia. In April 1981 Son Sann had declared that a united resistance would drive the Vietnamese out within four years. There was always a curious air of unreality about such claims, although the CGDK's sponsors did their best to overlook it.

The coalition bought together the most disparate elements – monarchists, anti-monarchist bourgeois republicans, and ultra-left Communists – together under the common banner of nationalism. Given the accumulated suspicions and hatreds produced by a decade of incredibly brutal civil war and revolution, it was surprising that even the façade of a coalition was created. This was a measure of the inability of the non-Communist groups to resist foreign pressures and set their own political agenda.

On the ground, however, the coalition did not exist. The first outsider to visit what were proclaimed as the capitals of the new government was Japanese journalist Isao Oglso, who wrote in the *Manchini Daily News* that the coalition existed only on paper. One of Sihanouk's aides told him: 'There isn't any such thing as an anti-Vietnamese coalition government. We are acting independently. The only thing we have for the Polpotians is antipathy and hatred.'

Each group was driven to seek out allies not because of any convergence of objectives, but because of its own weakness. The Khmer Rouge needed the international respectability that a coalition with Son Sann and Siha-nouk could provide, while Son Sann and Sihanouk needed the Khmer Rouge's military clout on the ground. Following the formation of the CGDK, all the resistance groups were rewarded with new flows of money and arms. Each tried to take advantage of the new situation.

By the start of 1984 the KPNLF had built its army up to a strength of 12,000 troops. But the KPNLF concentrated on making its head-quarters at Ampil a showcase for international visitors. A journalist later wrote:

From crude beginnings, the camp was progressively transformed into what ... Son Sann has described as a 'model city' – complete with everything from neatly laid-out dirt streets, schools, even day-care centres, to a military head-quarters and an officer-training school. It was not the sort of spectacle normally associated with a guerrilla force. ... [The KPNLF] has never held out any real hope of ousting the Vietnamese from the country by force of arms. ... Ampil ... represented a symbol of their political legitimacy on Cambodian soil.[8]

The only KPNLF military commander who was reportedly serious about building an effective guerrilla force was Prum Vit, the commander at Sok Sanh, in the Cardamon Mountains.

Few outsiders ever got into Sok Sanh. Two Italian journalists who visited the camp in late 1984 described it in romantic-heroic terms – heroic soldiers, noble commanders, dastardly enemies. But the details of their description revealed a decidedly unromantic situation. Sok Sanh was a network of bunkers and trenches 'on top of a foggy, jungle-covered moun-tain with an unhealthy climate and high rainfall'. It was linked to Thailand by a muddy track which was impassable for most of the year. Soldiers with 'at most a hammock and waterproof sheet to take shelter from the rain' huddled amid wrecked huts and blackened trees. Eighty per cent of them had malaria. The Vietnamese had twice driven the KPNLF out of Sok Sanh. Each time they had strewn the whole area with mines before withdrawing. Retaking the camp thus took a heavier toll on the KPNLF forces than the initial Vietnamese attacks. Even our Italian romantics noticed the consequences: 'The number of mutilated people hobbling around on crutches . . . is one of the most striking things about Sok Sanh.'9

Despite the admiration of western journalists for the KPNLF, Sihanouk soon proved the most effective in marshalling international support. Once he consented to head the CGDK he was given a friendly reception in Thailand, by the king and by Prime Minister Prem Tinsulanond. They allowed Sihanouk to visit Khao-I-Dang camp (previously a KPNLF stronghold), where he was allowed to persuade thousands of people to transfer to the newly established Sihanoukist camp of O-Smach in Thailand's Surin province. This enabled him to build his forces up to around 5,000 troops.

The non-Communist groups had always been criticized for avoiding combat with the Vietnamese. Once the CGDK was formed and supplies started flowing, it came under pressure to demonstrate it was effective. From late 1982 the non-Communist groups stepped up their military activities inside Cambodia, mostly in the northwest, close to the Thai border. But on occasion they were capable of penetrating more deeply into Cambodia. The Khmer Rouge let Sihanouk and Son Sann plead the anti-Vietnamese cause to the West, and concentrated on military action inside Cambodia. They quickly demonstrated that they were much more effective than the non-Communist groups.

The Khmer Rouge's war remained essentially one of ambushes and hit-and-run raids, but in 1983–84 its actions became more daring. In August 1983 Khmer Rouge guerrillas killed ten Soviet cotton experts in an ambush in Kompong Chhnang province. Following this, PRK authorities began refusing requests by aid workers and journalists to travel by road in rural areas, especially in the west of the country. It was in this context that the PRK launched the security crackdown on actual or suspected collaborators with the resistance noted in chapter 6.

The Vietnamese army responded to increased resistance activity with renewed attacks on the border base camps in 1983–84. It took Chea Chutt's camp at Nong Samet (KPNLF) in January 1983. By the end of March the Khmer Rouge camp at Phnom Chat (north of Aranyapratet) and Sihanouk's camp at O-Smach had also been overrun. This fighting was right on the border, and led to artillery exchanges and troop clashes between the Thai and Vietnamese armies all along the border north of Aranyapratet. During the battle for Phnom Chat the Thai napalmed a Vietnamese unit which had, they said, crossed the border onto Thai territory. This also coincided with a dramatic upsurge of clashes on the Sino-Vietnamese border. Since the resistance located military bases within civilian camps, the fighting displaced tens of thousands of refugees. These were relocated to new border camps, which were promptly used as military bases by the resistance. Many western commentators angrily condemned the Vietnamese for their ruthlessness in attacking civilian camps. They said little about the callousness of resistance military commanders who used civilian populations as a shield or the pusillanimity of aid organizations which were willing to underpin such abuses with 'humanitarian' relief.

The Vietnamese soon withdrew from the positions they had captured. It seemed that, in reality, the resistance groups had been saved in 1983 less by their own capabilities than by Sino-Thai military intervention. But CGDK spokesmen declared any setbacks temporary, and promised more offensives in the future. More arms were shipped to the border, and preparations began.

In the 1983 rainy season both the Khmer Rouge and the KPNLF stepped up attempts to infiltrate troops into the interior. They were operating from their border base camps, but both groups were hoping to extend their range of operations by establishing bases in the swamps and jungles around the Tonle Sap in the centre of Cambodia. The Vietnamese countered this with increased patrolling in these areas. But, rather than pull back to the border when the rains eased, the Khmer Rouge now tried to sustain military activities in the interior through the dry season. In January–February 1984 forces under Ta Mok's command attacked the provincial capitals of Kompong Thom, Siem Reap, and Pursat. Reports from Thailand suggested that by blowing up bridges and planting landmines, the Khmer Rouge had virtually sealed off road access to Siem Reap. A jubilant Sihanouk proclaimed this to be the 'turning point' in the war. Now, he argued, the Vietnamese were so bogged down by guerrilla harassment inside Cambodia that they could no longer attack the border camps.[10]

Within two weeks, Sihanouk's claim was shown to be wildly wrong. Vietnamese troops responded to these raids with attacks on the Khmer Rouge's main military headquarters on the northern section of the border. This was known as Base 1003, and was located in the Dangrek Mountains near the ancient temple of Preah Vihear. It was run by Son Sen and Ta Mok. A frontal assault in January failed, largely due to the difficulty of the terrain. The Vietnamese captured the camp with a second attack in March, but most of the Khmer Rouge (including, of course, the top commanders) escaped.

Base 1003 straddled the border, and this operation once again bought the Vietnamese into direct conflict with the Thai army. Meanwhile, the Chinese vented their displeasure through artillery bombardments on the Sino-Vietnamese border. After holding on to the camp for ten days, the Vietnamese pulled out. The Vietnamese reporter Le Ba Thuyen published a description of Base 1003 in *Nhan Dan* in May 1984. It was a sophisticated installation with a perimeter stretching ten to fifteen kilometres along the border, and it extended ten kilometres back from the border. It was the starting point of a supply corridor, along which Chinese trucks ferried supplies for Khmer Rouge forces. The Vietnamese destroyed the base before pulling out.

They also launched attacks on other resistance positions on the southern section of the Thai–Cambodian border. They captured small Khmer Rouge base camps in the Ta Sanh and Samlaut areas. They drove the Sihanoukists out of the camp they had been relocated to in 1983 (Tatum), and attacked both the Khmer Rouge headquarters at Phnom Malai and the KPNLF headquarters at Ampil. The Chinese responded angrily: there was a wave of artillery exchanges and troop clashes along the Sino-Vietnamese border, and Beijing issued ominous threats of a 'second lesson' if Hanoi did not desist.

With the onset of the rains in May, the Vietnamese broke off their attacks at Ampil and Phnom Malai. Thai analysts pounced on this as evidence that Hanoi's military capability was crumbling. One Bangkok-based reporter declared that this was 'the first time the Cambodian resistance forces have thrown back the Vietnamese in a set-piece battle'. But this was a triumph of wishful thinking.

The Vietnamese operations had inflicted considerable losses both in men and supplies on the resistance. The withdrawal from Ampil and Phnom Malai was a response to the opening of the rainy season rather than to military defeats. It was consistent with the basic strategy the Vietnamese had followed since 1979. However, Paul Quinn-Judge reported that ASEAN sources 'seem satisfied with the performance of their proteges this dry season and say the Sihanoukists and the KPNLF can expect more military supplies and training in the near future.'[11] The Chinese resupplied the Khmer Rouge, providing them with 85-millimetre artillery pieces as well as an abundance of small arms. Both China and Singapore shipped AK-47s and rocket-grenade launchers to the KPNLF and the ANS. The USA was providing 'non-lethal' aid to the non-Communist resistance groups, but in June 1984 refused a direct request to provide 'lethal' assistance.

The Vietnamese had been hoping that once Pol Pot's forces had been decisively defeated, the world would come to accept the installation of the PRK as a *fait accompli*. They promised that when this happened they would withdraw their troops. The Vietnamese did not seem particularly alarmed by the formation of the CGDK in 1982. 'A corpse is just a corpse, no matter how dressed up', commented *Nhan Dan* at that time. But following the Khmer Rouge raids on provincial capitals in January 1985, Le Duc Tho and Vo Chi Cong flew to Cambodia to assess the situation. When Quinn-Judge visited Hanoi in May 1984 Vietnamese military leaders told him that they were considering changing strategy in Cambodia.[12]

The new strategy was set out in an article by General Le Duc Anh, the commander of Vietnamese forces in Cambodia.[13] All Vietnamese personnel in Cambodia were required to make themselves thoroughly familiar with this article. Anh reasserted the strategic importance of Cambodia in Vietnamese eyes, but set the objective of withdrawing Vietnamese troops even without a settlement with ASEAN and China. The key to this was consolidating an independent but friendly government in Phnom Penh.

In response to the overthrow of Pol Pot, wrote Anh, the Chinese had forged an alliance with the USA, Thailand, and 'Khmer reactionaries of all stripes' to destroy the 'Khmer people's revolution'. Beijing maintained its 'hegemonist and expansionist ambitions' towards the three Indochinese countries, and saw Cambodia as the 'weakest link'. Thus the threat posed by Chinese policies was ultimately a threat not only to the independence of Cambodia, but to that of all three Indochinese countries. This made an alliance between them a 'law of survival'.

Anh implicitly criticized previous Vietnamese policy for its passivity. He called for a much more aggressive military policy towards the resistance groups: 'We must destroy them by military attacks, raze their bases, build and consolidate our defence lines.' But Anh knew he could not achieve a total military victory, despite Vietnam's military supremacy. The resistance groups could avoid annihilation by retreating into Thailand. The objective of an offensive was rather to secure control of the border for the Vietnamese/PRK side. This would reduce the ability of the CGDK groups to infiltrate back and organize 'rebellious and subversive activities' in the interior. As Anh saw it, the war in Cambodia was being fought on two fronts – on the border, and in the interior. The interior, where the mass of the population lived, was where the struggle would ultimately be decided.

Anh argued that Vietnamese battlefield successes would count for nothing in the long run if they did not enable the PRK to stand on its own feet. 'Our duty cannot be termed as fulfilled', he wrote, 'if we destroy a lot of enemy troops but fail to create conditions for the local people to gain mastery and for our friends to reach maturity and undertake all activities by themselves.' Success was not to be measured by anything the Vietnamese themselves were doing in Cambodia, but by the 'maturity and mastery' of their Cambodian allies.

Some Vietnamese believed that the Cambodians could not be trusted, and that Vietnam should retain control. Anh (and presumably, the Hanoi Politburo) knew that this was playing into the hands of the CGDK propagandists. Anh argued that, although in the past the Cambodian people had been deceived and misled by a succession of regimes, since 1979 they had 'clearly proved' their capacity to rebuild and defend their country. Vietnam, he warned, would never achieve its objectives if it adopted an attitude of 'big-nation chauvinism' – the Cambodians were 'very sensitive about their sovereignty', and the Vietnamese approach must be 'to help the Cambodian people decide their own destiny and carry out their own revolutionary cause'.

Thus a border offensive by the Vietnamese must be accompanied by accelerated efforts to build up the PRK administration, the party (the PRPK), and the PRK armed forces. The latter should combine a 'back-bone' of regular units of full-time professionals with a body of local militia. They should combine combat duties with propaganda, popular mobilization and 'economic and social welfare missions'. They would thus become a 'people's revolutionary army', deeply embedded in Cambodian society rather than standing over it as an alien force. Whereas previously the military high command had been Vietnamese, a 'unified command' which shared responsibility with Cambodians should be established. As the PRK armed forces gained in strength and experience, they would be able increasingly to take over the responsibility for national defence in Cambodia.

Although the struggle would be 'long and complicated', this would enable the Vietnamese to withdraw their troops and leave the PRK in control. Anh did not set a time-frame for carrying out this strategy. But it was at this time that Vietnamese diplomats began saying that Vietnam aimed at pulling its troops out by the end of 1990, even if there was no political settlement. With a political settlement, they could be out earlier. Most western commentators refused to take the suggestion seriously.

Over the 1984 rainy season the Vietnamese shipped large quantities of arms into Cambodia. With the coming of the dry season, the Vietnamese army (joined by large numbers of PRK troops) launched the biggest military operation in Cambodia since 1979. General Anh's campaign opened with an assault on Nong Chan in November. By the time it ended in April, all major resistance bases were in Vietnamese/PRK hands: the KPNLF headquarters at Ampil fell in January; the Khmer Rouge headquarters at Phnom Malai in February, the ANS headquarters at Tatum in March.

The CGDK groups escaped the offensive by retreating into Thailand. Anthony Paul visited the border in the aftermath of this operation, and described its impact:

The last time I was on the border was to witness Sihanouk receiving the credentials of a brace of ambassadors. Under substantial bamboo-and-thatch struc-

tures at Phnom Thmei, a sort of resistance-style Club Med run by the Khmer
Rouge on Cambodian territory south of Thailand's Aranyapratet border town,
the Prince sipped champagne and presided over elaborate diplomatic banquets.

Last week the scene was different. With Lt-Gen Pichit Kullavanich, Thai
First Army Commander, I clambered to a Thai Army outpost atop a rocky
borderline escarpment not far north of Aranyapratet.

Phnom Thmei, beyond our horizon, had been put to the torch; the greater
part of a Vietnamese battalion squatted in its ruins. At the Thai outpost, a
trooper pointed to a tiny speck some 3 km distant. No more Club Med. Amongst
the sparse trees and shrubs on the still-dry plain was a small lean-to braced
as best it could for the rains. 'The resistance', said the Thai.[14]

Phnom Penh Radio claimed that 5,000 resistance troops were put out
of action. The Khmer Rouge claimed that the Vietnamese suffered nearly
8,000 casualties.

The Vietnamese offensive destroyed the whole infrastructure of border
camps on which CGDK operations had been based. Some 230,000 people,
virtually the entire population of the camps, were forced into Thailand.
Aid donors met in May, and decided to support the construction of a
new network of camps. This time they were on the Thai side of the border,
and an attempt was made to distinguish between civilian and military
camps.

Each of the resistance groups was allowed to rebuild its separate fief-
dom. One hundred and forty thousand people from the KPNLF camps
were relocated at Site 2, sixty-five kilometres north of Aranyapratet and
only three or four kilometres from the border. Eight thousand people
from the KPNLF camp at Sok Sann were relocated in camp in Trat
province. Thirty thousand people were housed at Site 8, to the south
of the Phnom Malai area. This was the main 'open' Khmer Rouge Camp,
to which outsiders were allowed access. An additional 55,000 people were
in 'closed' camps at other points along the border. Thirty-two thousand
people were housed at the Sihanoukist camp of Site B (also known as
Green Hill). This was close to the old Sihanoukist camp at Tatum, but
was further back from the border.

Following their offensive, Vietnamese and PRK troops dug in along
the border. They also used Cambodian corvée labour to build access
roads to the border, to dig trenches, clear firing zones and plant mine-
fields. According to Vice Foreign Minister Kong Korm there were 10,000
people engaged in this at the peak of the operation. It was arduous work
in often dangerous circumstances. There were many casualties due to
malaria and land-mines. CGDK propagandists naturally made great play
on the suffering this involved. They ridiculed the PRK's new defence
perimeter as a new 'Maginot line' but made no major effort to disrupt
its construction.

What used to be an open buffer zone along the border, where resistance forces operated more or less freely, was brought under effective PRK/ Vietnamese control. Their troops stayed there throughout the year, rather than pulling back to less vulnerable bases during the rainy season. In 1986 Radio Hanoi described the new front line, as seen from the Vietnamese side: 'During the rainy season, forward bases look like small, desolate islands surrounded on all sides by dense jungle. All the trails leading to them seem to be impassable.' The infantry defending these posts were 'dressed in rags, puritanically fed, mostly disease-ridden and devoid of news from the rear'.[15]

The Resistance after 1985

The Khmer Rouge claimed that the 1984–85 fighting had ended in 'total defeat' for Vietnam. By concentrating troops along the border, it was allowing resistance forces greater freedom of action in the interior. There would be a dramatic upsurge in guerrilla activity in the rainy season. 'The loss of the border camps has forced the Khmer resistance movements to fight deeper inside Cambodia', argued the Thai. For Vietnam 'the enemy, suddenly, is everywhere'.[16]

The enemy was not 'everywhere', but in Thailand. The Khmer Rouge set up camps along the border in Chantaburi and Trat provinces. Pol Pot and the other top leaders reportedly lived in a fortified camp near Nerm Po village, in Trat. Other camps were established in the Dangrek mountains along the northern border. The non-Communist resistance groups operated from satellite military camps near their main civilian camps at Site 2 and Site B.

Vietnamese and PRK troops blocked most of the key supply routes into Cambodia. While the resistance groups could still get men and matériel across the border, it had become a much more difficult and dangerous exercise. In the 1985 rainy season, Paul Quinn-Judge observed, the Khmer Rouge was having difficulty getting army recruits even in camps under its direct control. The rank-and-file were uncomfortably aware that they were 'being sent into a meat-grinder'. Even battle-hardened veterans were 'less keen to go back into combat this year', he reported.[17] In 1986 the Khmer Rouge did not attempt its usual rainy-season offensive. Nor did the Vietnamese launch a dry-season offensive in 1986–87. There were no longer any targets for them to hit in Cambodia. As Nayan Chanda noted, the usual seasonal cycle of fighting had been 'broken'.[18] The Thai–Cambodian border became relatively peaceful after the 1984–85 offensive ended.

The most serious fighting occurred at Chong Bok pass, in the Dangrek

Mountains, in early 1987. But here the Vietnamese were attacked, not by CGDK forces, but by the Thai army.

After the 1984–85 offensive, Khmer Rouge military commander Son Sen established his new base near Chong Bok, on the Thai side of the border. The Vietnamese blocked the pass and captured several hilltops which overlooked it. These hills straddled the border, so the Vietnamese positions were intruding into Thailand. In January 1987 the Thai decided to push the Vietnamese off the strategic hilltops. They found that the Vietnamese were well dug in, with a complex of tunnels and trenches along the hilltops, and had strewn the approaches with thousands of mines. Five months and hundreds of deaths later, the Thai called the attack off. The Vietnamese still held most of the strategic hills, but Bangkok declared itself satisfied that a Thai military presence had been 'established' in the area.

The Vietnamese offensive of 1984–85 had destroyed the resistance camps along the border, pushing the CGDK forces into Thailand, and securing the border perimeter for the time being. The editor of the Vietnamese army newspaper, General Tran Cong Man, told a western reporter that it had been more successful than Hanoi had expected. But the Khmer Rouge had not been eliminated. It was able to regroup and reorganize, this time on Thai soil, and renew its struggle. Thus, Man remarked, in the final analysis the Cambodia conflict could only be settled by political and not military means.[19]

The Chinese were dismayed by the loss of the resistance border camps, and of the large quantities of supplies they had provided. They were especially upset by the fall of Phnom Malai, and a few days after the Khmer Rouge abandoned it a Chinese military delegation arrived in Bangkok demanding an explanation. Pol Pot himself was called to the Thai capital, and provided the Chinese with an upbeat account of the fighting. In May 1985 he returned to give the Thai army deputy chief of staff, General Chaovalit Yongchaiyut, a briefing.

In July the Voice of Democratic Kampuchea broadcast a spirited defence of Pol Pot's achievements, declaring him to be a great patriot who had thwarted Vietnamese plans to gobble up Cambodia. It would seem that the Chinese and the Thai had cast doubt on his accomplishments. Six weeks later, it was announced that Pol Pot had relinquished the post of supreme commander of the DK armed forces to Son Sen. However, he would actively remain in the field as a military commander. Both the Thai and the Chinese welcomed the change, playing up Khieu Samphan as political leader and Son Sen as military leader of a new-look Khmer Rouge.

This suggests that the Chinese and Thai had finally decided that Pol Pot was more of a liability than an asset, and they pressured the Khmer

Rouge into removing him from the leadership. When Pol Pot paid a visit to China in November 1986, his hosts spread false reports that he was dying of cancer and thus had no future role in Cambodia. But Khmer Rouge spokesmen, pressed on the point, continued to praise him as a great leader and affirmed he was in charge.

There were also reports of increased bickering among Pol Pot's underlings after 1985. Ta Mok, who was the most powerful military commander, was resistant to Chinese–Thai pressures and contemptuous of the Khmer Rouge's nominal allies in the CGDK. At the same time Khieu Samphan, Son Sen, and Ieng Sary were supposed to have been in favour of accepting Chinese–Thai guidance and returning to power through a continued alliance with Sihanouk, who had by now managed to rally considerable international support for the CGDK. Pol Pot's retirement was taken by some observers as the triumph of 'moderate' Khmer Rouge over the 'radicals' responsible for the débâcle of 1975–78. But both groups upheld 1975–78 as the best period in all of Cambodia's two-thousand-year history, and both were believed to defer to Pol Pot's decisions.

The Khmer Rouge leaders continued to claim that there was intense fighting in Cambodia, and that their troops were advancing ever closer to victory. In fact, at about this time the Khmer Rouge leaders instructed their soldiers to avoid military confrontations with the Vietnamese and the PRK armed forces. Instead, they were to infiltrate villages, spread propaganda, and prepare for an uprising when the Vietnamese had gone. They aimed at getting control of between 1,000 and 1,300 of Cambodia's 10,000-odd villages. By mid-1988, according to defectors to the non-Communist resistance groups, the Khmer Rouge had succeeded in infiltrating some 700 villages, but had won control of none.[20] At the same time they began shifting Chinese military supplies across the border into the mountains south of Aranyapratet.

Internationally, the Khmer Rouge tried to present itself as moderate and selflessly patriotic. But its propaganda campaign inside Cambodia revealed a different face. A reporter quoted a verse which its propaganda teams were daubing on village walls in 1988:

> When you eat from a small pot,
> Remember the big pot.
>
> When you wear a flowery silk sampot
> Don't forget the thick black material you once wore.
>
> When the Vietnamese are gone,
> Each pit will hold 100 corpses.[21]

The Khmer Rouge was relying on memories of the terror of 1975–78 to intimidate the peasantry into collaborating with it.

An article by a Vietnamese officer described the Khmer Rouge's new tactics of 'psychological warfare' as 'very dangerous'.[22] But, he argued, they were best dealt with by Cambodian rather than Vietnamese forces. A Vietnamese official in Phnom Penh explained in 1987:

> The important battles are now in the villages – small group encounters. Really, our troops are of little use in such a war. They can't speak the language, they don't know the people, so it is possible to withdraw our troops without ill-effect.

The Khmer Rouge remained the most powerful of the resistance groups. The KPNLF, the favourite of western anti-Communists, went into a spiral of self-destruction after 1984–85. After the Vietnamese/PRK forces drove them out of their bases, they promised to wage intensified guerrilla war in the interior. They admitted that, in the past, they had confined themselves to protecting their border camps, but without these they would now be free to step up their attacks. They did make some efforts, but the results were meagre. They re-established military base camps along the border once again, but they had little success in the interior. At Sok Sanh, a tattooed soldier told a western reporter:

> I don't trust anyone in Cambodia. Most villages we come across are inclined towards the Heng Samrin government. In each village there is at least one Heng Samrin agent. ... We never stay long in villages, and we never enter them at night. It's too dangerous.[23]

In 1986 the KPNLF was crippled by factional disputes as political leaders and military commanders blamed each other for their setbacks. Most of the military commanders on the border favoured greater cooperation with the Sihanoukists. Others, including Son Sann and most of the KPNLF's overseas supporters, were opposed to this. Sann attempted to dismiss Dien Del, Sak Sutsakhan, and other KPNLF military commanders. But they refused to accept this, and declared that they were taking control of the KPNLF. The military decided to keep Son Sann on as a figurehead president while dismissing commanders on the border who remained loyal to him. But they, in turn, refused to accept dismissal. Son Sann supported them, for almost two years the KPNLF military command refused to allow Sann or his son, Son Soubert, near the border. The split 'paralysed' the KPNLF and caused the Thai 'deep frustration', according to John McBeth. He reported that the Thai were 'by-passing' the KPNLF leadership and giving money and weapons 'directly to field commanders for specific missions which had been approved beforehand'.[24] On at least some operations, KPNLF troops fought under the command of Thai officers in disguise. The USA tightened the pressure on the Son

Sann loyalists by withholding funds from them until the dispute was resolved.

Some of these troops turned to banditry and extortion. Refugees were 'robbed, raped and held until their relatives abroad could send ransoms'.[25] Troops under the command of Chea Chutt and Liv Ne were supposedly responsible for most of these activities. They were, reportedly, the most corrupt military commanders on the border. But they also happened to be the main ones supporting Son Sann. By late 1986, the Thai were pushing to have their units disbanded. In 1987 the Thai army set up a special unit to suppress Khmer 'banditry' in Buriram and Prachinburi provinces, where Chea Chutt and Liv Ne's forces were based. An unknown, but considerable, number of 'bandits' were killed over the next few months.

Finally, in February 1988 Son Sann agreed to the removal of Chea Chutt and Liv Ne from the border. They were reportedly bought to Bangkok, and kept under house arrest. In return, Sann was promised the dismissal of two of his opponents, Dien Del and Hing Kuthon.[26] But Sann no longer had any bargaining power on the border, and this was soon forgotten. The Thai expressed the hope that, with the internal dispute resolved, Sak Sutsakhan would now be able to rebuild the KPNLF as an effective fighting force.

The Sihanoukists also went through a round of recriminations in the wake of the 1984–85 fighting. The ANS commander-in-chief, Teap Ben, was accused of 'corruption, incompetence, and failing to understand how to wage guerrilla war'. Sihanouk replaced him with one of his own sons, Prince Rannarith. The USA was pleased with this, and expanded funding to the Sihanoukists. France and the UK joined in trying to build them up as an alternative to both the Phnom Penh government and the Khmer Rouge.

Rannarith proved a capable spokesman, with many of his father's mannerisms. It soon became clear that Sihanouk was grooming him as his successor. Rannarith's capabilities as a military commander were not so clear. The ANS stepped up its activities under Rannarith's direction, and by 1988 was able to carry out occasional missions well inside Cambodia. But it concentrated mainly on propaganda rather than military activity. In 1988 Rannarith's strategy was reported as preparing his forces for a showdown after the Vietnamese withdrew in 1990.[27]

Often, the misfortunes of the KPNLF were the Sihanoukists' gains. Their camp, Site B, was more comfortably located, better administered, and seemingly free from the gangsterism plaguing Site 2, the KPNLF camp. Most of the trickle of new refugees arriving on the border preferred to go there, and there were requests for transfers from refugees in the KPNLF and even the Khmer Rouge camps.

The final phase of Vietnam's military withdrawal from Cambodia took place in 1988–89. In May 1988, it was announced that the number of Vietnamese troops in Cambodia would be cut by half by the end of the year, and those that remained were put under Cambodian command. Arriving back in Saigon in June 1989, General Le Kha Phieu, who had served as deputy commander of the Vietnamese forces in Cambodia, released casualty statistics that summed up the course of the war for the Vietnamese. Thirty thousand Vietnamese troops had been killed in the years 1977–79, and another 15,000 in 1980–81, and 10,000 over 1982–88. Approximately equal numbers were injured. These figures made it clear that the heaviest fighting was in the earliest stages of the war, when the Khmer Rouge still held state power. Contrary to much western mis-interpretation ('Vietnam's Vietnam' once again), they did not show Vietnam under growing military pressure in Cambodia.

As well as pulling a further half of its troops out in May 1988, Vietnam also pulled its remaining troops back thirty kilometres along most of the border (the main exception was the tri-border junction, where Son Sen's troops were active). From that point on, it was Cambodians in the front line against the CGDK forces. Vietnam's hope was that by agreeing to the demand for withdrawals, it would create the climate for a political settlement, with Hanoi able to move towards a *rapprochement* with Beijing while Phnom Penh negotiated with the Cambodian resistance groups from a position of strength. But at the same time, this provided the Khmer Rouge with the best chance it was ever likely to have of fighting its way back to power.

The Khmer Rouge went onto the attack again in June 1988, and unnamed diplomats in Bangkok were quick to inform reporters that its campaign was a 'surprising success'. The attack was three-pronged. In the north, three Khmer Rouge divisions launched offensives down out of the Dangrek Mountains. In the southwest, another two divisions, supported by batteries of 120-millimetre mortars attempted to recapture their old base area at Phnom Malai and to capture the gem-mining town of Pailin. At the same time the infiltration of armed propaganda units into the interior was stepped up.

By September the assault on Phnom Malai had failed. The Khmer Rouge took only a few pockets of land on the Cambodian side of the border, failed to penetrate the PRK defence perimeter, and suffered heavy casualties at the hands of government artillery gunners. Nor, despite reports from Thailand, was Pailin captured. The defence perimeter held in the north as well.

Only the infiltration operation seemed to yield positive results for the Khmer Rouge. An increase in hit-and-run raids, some of them deep inside the country, was reported. Mines were planted, village heads assassinated, youths press-ganged into the Khmer Rouge army. From the fragmentary and conflicting reports available it is impossible to determine how wide-spread this was. But, most probably, it was in these obscure battles for the villages rather than the big battles on the border that the destiny of Cambodia was being decided.

As it launched its troops back into battle, the Khmer Rouge also began transferring people out of refugee camps to transit points on the border, with the intention of moving them back into Cambodia once 'liberated zones' had been secured. Two-thirds of the people at the Na Trao camp, run by Ta Mok, were trucked to the border in vehicles belonging to Task Force 838, 'a shadowy Thai military unit responsible for relations with the Cambodian guerrillas'.[28] They were taken to remote, malaria-ridden areas, housed in thatch-covered bunkers, and used as forced labour carrying supplies to combat troops, or felling timber for the Khmer Rouge to sell in Thailand. A number managed to escape, and made their way to the KPNLF's Site 2. Months later, after the failure of the military offensive, those refugees who survived were allowed to return to the camps run (and funded) by the UN. In 1988 the Khmer Rouge thus had little success in taking advantage of major Vietnamese withdrawals.

A decade after the fall of Pol Pot's government, the three resistance groups were better organized than they had been in the early 1980s. But the CGDK still looked like a coalition of lost causes, the surviving rumps of former regimes brought into an unlikely alliance by Chinese and Thai diplomats, and surviving in protected fiefdoms on Thai soil. Few thought that they could fight their way back to power. If they were to return to Phnom Penh, it would most likely be as the result of a deal brokered by their great-power patrons.

The Anti-Communist Resistance in Laos and Vietnam

There were also anti-Communist resistance movements in Laos and Viet-nam itself. By the early 1980s they were in an even more parlous state than their Cambodian counterparts. Unlike the Cambodian groups, they were unable to attract significant international patronage.

Yet the notion that Laos was languishing under an oppressive foreign occupation led some commentators to claim that Lao anti-government forces enjoyed (potentially, if not yet in actuality) a substantial nationalist appeal. In the only detailed account of anti-government activity in Laos (written in 1983) Geoffrey Gunn concluded:

Clearly it is the Soviet-backed, armed Vietnamese domination of the Indo-chinese peninsula that supplies the raison d'être of resistance movements in

Laos and Cambodia. The corollary is that as long as Hanoi pre-empts by military suasion alternative political arrangements or alignments in Laos or Cambodia, the popular appeal of these resistance fronts can only expand.[29]

Even at the time this article appeared, this judgement was not supported by the available evidence. The main opposition to the government in Vientiane after 1975 was based on local rather than class or national loyalties. Its backbone was the Hmong hill tribes of central Laos, who had traditionally resisted lowland Lao control. Many of them had served with General Vang Pao's CIA-funded 'secret army' prior to 1975, and were fearful of Communist retaliation. Government attempts to encourage the hill tribes to resettle in the lowlands, confused attempts at collectivization, and a series of poor harvests all helped fuel Hmong resentment of the Pathet Lao government. But this resentment found expression in flight into Thailand rather than in armed resistance inside Laos. And the tribal loyalties that gave the movement some basis among the Hmong severely restricted its appeal to other sections of the population.

There was some military resistance to the new regime after 1975, but on an ever-diminishing scale. The number of Vang Pao supporters who remained in Laos after 1975 is unclear, but it was probably no more than a few thousand. The organizational framework of the old 'secret army' had disintegrated, and they were totally disorganized. Scattered fighting was reported throughout 1976 and 1977, and in the closing months of 1977 there was a major clash with government forces in the vicinity of Phu Bia, near the Plain of Jars. This battle appears to have broken the back of what resistance there was, and many of the remaining Vang Pao supporters either fled to Thailand, turned to simple banditry, or returned to their villages.[30] Since then, there have been few major Pathet Lao military operations. As Gunn put it, the main opposition to Vientiane was a 'constellation of rightists' drawing their support from 'the refugee population in the camps in the north and the northeast of Thailand' – not from inside Laos at all.

The scale of Hmong resistance hardly warranted resort to drastic measures such as the use of poison gas, as was claimed by the US State Department. This prompted accusations of genocide against the governments in Vientiane and Hanoi, and sceptics were denounced as apologists for mass murder. But a UN investigation in 1982 failed to find any hard evidence in support of these claims. A further examination revealed that the samples of 'toxic agents' touted by the State Department were no more than bee-droppings. US government scientists subsequently admitted that politically motivated officials had put constructions on their findings which had never been justified by evidence.[31]

There were scattered rumours of resistance from other parts of the

country in the late 1970s and early 1980s. A resistance movement based
on the Yao hill tribe and led by one Chao La was supposed to be active
in Luang Nam Tha, in northern Laos. A 'General Champa' was said
to be leading a guerrilla army in Phong Saly province. But very few details
of their operations ever emerged – if indeed these groups really did exist.

After the Vietnamese invasion of Cambodia in December 1978, the
Chinese began providing supplies to the Hmong and Yao guerrillas.
'General Champa's' group was said to be Chinese-trained and Chinese-
directed. In 1981 it was reported that the Chinese were running a training
camp in Yunnan province, where Thai right-wingers (many of whom
had earlier fought with the 'secret army') trained Lao insurgents.

Yet these efforts by the Chinese had little impact. Gunn suggests that
this is because the Chinese have provided 'less support than might be
expected', Beijing being reluctant to cut all ties with Vientiane. The ferocity of Chinese polemics against the 'puppets of Le Duan' in both Phnom
Penh and Vientiane make this unlikely. Two other considerations are
probably more relevant. In the first place, the hill-tribe resistances always
had a very limited base, and militarily their backbone had been broken
before 1979. While the Chinese doubtless wished to encourage them to
continue the struggle, there was little point in sinking money into lost
causes. Second, and more importantly, Beijing may have been wary of
encouraging separatist tendencies among the hill tribes of northern Laos,
because with many (including the two key groups, the Hmong and the
Yao) the majority of their population lived in China, not Laos. An upsurge
of tribal separatism could have uncontrollable consequences for China
itself.

There were also some reports of resistance in the southern parts of
the country, a traditional stronghold of aristocratic rivals to the royal
house of Luang Prabang. Appealing to lowland Lao, the southern Lao
resistance had a potentially wider basis than an ethnic minority movement.
This 'White Lao' resistance had disintegrated by mid-1977, but revived
in early 1980. In September 1980 the formation of a Lao People's National
Liberation Front (LPNLF) was announced.

The revival of the southern resistance in 1980 was partly a result of
the dissaffection produced by the bungled collectivization drive by the
Pathet Lao in 1978–79, but the White Lao appear to have had little success
in linking their cause to local peasant grievances, or recruiting inside
Laos. Their reinvigoration appears to have been largely a result of the
support they got from the Khmer Rouge, via Son Sen's base near the
junction of the Thai, Lao and Cambodian borders. Gunn quoted reports
that up to 1,500 Lao were being trained by the Khmer Rouge. 'While
there is no unified command structure', he writes, 'liaison between the
Lao guerrillas and the DK forces is said to extend to the organizational

and supply requirements of the Lao maquisards as far north as Savan-nakhet'. Or, to put it somewhat differently, the White Lao were so weak that throughout their entire field of operations they depended heavily on Khmer Rouge backing.

This could hardly have enhanced their appeal to Lao peasants. Nor did it overcome the endemic factionalism among right-wing Lao. Chinese- and DK-encouraged efforts to bring about a united front of all anti-Vietnamese resistance groups had little result. Despite Gunn's claim that joining forces with the Khmer Rouge was a 'landmark event' in the development of the southern Lao resistance, the White Lao movement sank out of sight once more after 1980.

The Lao resistance groups could, as a rule, count on the support of sympathetic Thai government and army officials in the provinces. But Bangkok would have nothing to do with these groups, despite its support for the Khmer resistance. Apparently encouraged by the enthusiastic reception given to the Cambodian coalition, a former Royal Lao Government prime minister, Phoumi Nosovan, announced that he would establish an anti-Communist liberation government in Laos in October 1982. But the Thai quickly declared that they would neither recognize nor support such a government. Bangkok sought to pressure the LPDR into pursuing a course more independent of the Vietnamese, not to overthrow it. Nosovan's 'government' was ignored even by those journalists who hung on every word of spokesmen for the CGDK. By the time of Nosovan's death in 1985 it had been largely forgotten even among Laos-watchers. It took eight months for the 'government' to get around to issuing a statement saying that it intended to elect a successor.

The Lao resistance found some friends among the extreme Right in the USA. In 1982–83 'Bo' Gritz, who had served as a lieutenant-colonel in US Special Forces (the famous Green Berets) in Vietnam, twice led a party of American mercenaries and Lao resistance guerrillas into Laos in search of servicemen missing in action (MIAs). Gritz's first expedition returned to Thailand after a shootout with a Lao border patrol, and the second was captured. Gritz claimed his operation was CIA-backed. But he was promptly disowned by the CIA, and seems to have funded his operation by selling the film rights of his story to actors Clint Eastwood and William Shatner. The members of his party were each fined US$150 and given a suspended sentence by a Lao court, and expelled from the country. When he attempted to organize a third raid in May 1983, the Thai in turn kicked him out. In the end, Eastwood and Shatner apparently did not feel that this was material for a Hollywood epic.

In May 1985 unnamed Lao resistance figures made a brief reappearance, to assert that Vietnamese policies in Laos were 'no different' to those they followed in Cambodia. The Hanoi authorities were said to 'have

sent over 3 million Vietnamese nationals' into Laos as settlers. The Vietnamese were seeking to 'exterminate the Lao race' by impregnating Lao
women and thus creating a 'half-breed' people. This anonymous fantasy
was broadcast by the Khmer Rouge army radio station, and discounted
by outside observers.

None of this adds up to a very impressive resistance. Even in the early
years, most of those who opposed Pathet Lao rule chose to leave the
country rather than to take up arms. Such armed resistance as there
was had largely ended by 1980, and subsequent efforts by the Chinese
and the Khmer Rouge to revive it seem to have been completely ineffective.
Nothing has happened since 1983 to support Gunn's scenario of mounting
popular resistance to the Communist government in Vientiane.

The Khmer Rouge had also tried to build up links with the main armed
resistance inside Vietnam, the 'Front Uni pour la Lutte des Races Oppri-
mées' (FULRO). This operated among the hill tribes of the central highlands of Vietnam, exploiting their resentment at political control by
lowlanders. The tribes that provided the main basis of FULRO, the Rhade
and the Jarai, spread over the border into Cambodia's Ratanikiri and
Mondulkiri provinces, so it is plausible that Khmer Rouge groups operating in northeastern Cambodia had established links with them.

Little is known of FULRO's activities after 1975. Visitors to the Central
Highlands in 1981 reported that the local Vietnamese authorities still
faced serious security problems. FULRO forces 'and other armed groups'
frequently extorted money from passengers on local buses, and from time
to time Vietnamese army vehicles were ambushed on remote roads. On
the whole, however, fighting appears to have been small-scale and
infrequent, certainly by comparison with the pre-1975 period.

In September 1982 the Vietnamese paper *Saigon Giai Phong* published
an account of the demise of FULRO. According to this source, FULRO
had been weakened by a series of purges and assassinations associated
with an internal power struggle in 1976–78. In 1980 the Khmer Rouge
began claiming that it had joined forces with FULRO. Other sources
reported that Chinese weapons were being channelled to FULRO via
launching a series of military operations against FULRO's forces. By
mid-1981 its forces were said to have been broken, and a number of
the movement's leaders captured. But several key figures had evaded the
Vietnamese, so the victory was by no means total.

From time to time in the early 1980s Hanoi announced military operations against 'bandits' in the mountains of northern Vietnam. An article
in *Nhan Dan* in 1981 asserted that in Son La and Lai Chau provinces
'the Chinese reactionaries have colluded with and instigated former bandits to form reactionary groups in an attempt to stir up anti-revolutionary
rebellion'. Some officials in border provinces were accused of 'double-

dealing' – professing loyalty to Hanoi, but secretly coming to terms with the Chinese.

The background to this was a decision by Hanoi in 1976 to abandon the autonomous zones for minority peoples in these strategic areas. While this strengthening of central authority was motivated by security concerns, it apparently created local dissatisfaction, which the Chinese have been doing their best to exploit. But there is nothing to suggest that the problem was on such a scale as to be a major worry for Hanoi. Once again, the localized basis of these groups ensures that they have little wider class or national appeal.

The main area of mass dissatisfaction with Communist rule in Vietnam is in the south, especially in Saigon. There were many complaints of economic mismanagement and political high-handedness. But any organized resistance was effectively decapitated by sending the leading figures of the old regime to 're-education camps'. And a considerable part of the constituency for such a movement subsequently fled the country as 'boat people'. Some ARVN units supposedly went underground in 1975, to continue the struggle, but nothing has been heard from them since.

For all practical purposes, then, the bourgeois opposition in Vietnam became an *émigré* opposition. Most Vietnamese refugees arriving in countries such as France, the USA, Canada and Australia were hostile to the government in Hanoi. But only a few of them were interested in trying to continue the war lost in 1975. Some were, however, and made efforts to instigate uprisings in Vietnam.

Lam Van Phat, a former lieutenant-colonel in the South Vietnamese army who escaped to Singapore in July 1984, said that resistance groups in Vietnam 'were too weak and fragmented to mount a full-scale campaign against the communist regime without outside assistance'. He went on: 'I intend to mobilise support for the Vietnamese cause. I believe resistance in Vietnam is feasible, but it cannot continue without support from countries like China. Once we get going, I am sure the US could be persuaded to revive its interest in Indochina.'[32] Unfortunately for Phat, US interest in supporting insurrection in Indochina was limited to Cambodia.

In December 1984 Saigon authorities arrested about 120 people, and seized 70 tonnes of arms and ammunition. Those arrested, most of them former officers in the South Vietnamese military, were accused of attempting to organize an armed insurrection. The leader of the uprising, which was allegedly backed by Chinese, Thai and US 'reactionaries', escaped arrest. Three of the accused were executed, and the rest were given long jail sentences.

The biggest *émigré*-organized operation took place in 1987. The National United Front for the Liberation of Vietnam (NUFLV), the largest and best organized of the militant anti-Communist *émigré* groups, organized a 200-strong guerrilla force to launch an uprising inside Vietnam. The plan was to cross secretly from Thailand through Laos, with the help of the Lao resistance and weapons provided by the Khmer Rouge, and establish a base in southern Vietnam.

But the NUFLV group was apprehended by Lao security forces shortly after crossing the Thai border. The leader of the expedition, Houang Qu Vinh, a former rear-admiral in the South Vietnamese navy, and chairman of the NUFLV, was killed in the fighting. Seventy-seven guerrillas were captured. They were extradited to Vietnam, and tried in December. Five agreed to cooperate fully with the prosecution, and were exempted from prosecution. The others were given jail terms ranging from three years to life imprisonment. During the trial, the prosecution submitted evidence that Thai military intelligence officers had helped organize the operation.

To sum up, there is little sign of a nationalist resistance to Vietnamese influence in Laos, or of organized opposition to Communist rule within Vietnam. Such resistance as exists is atomized. Often, it is a matter of traditional communities resisting the encroachments of the centralizing state, rather than a modern nationalist movement. Failure to recognize this point underlies most of the exaggerated assessments of their potential strength. While the Chinese and the Khmer Rouge have given some support to these groups, the ASEAN countries have kept their distance.

But the chief problem has not been, as *émigré* leaders sometimes assert, the lack of external support. It has been the lack of a popular constituency within Laos or Vietnam. The failures of the Communists have been many, but the defeated right wing has not developed a credible alternative. In both countries, the sources of change have been those who sought to reform the new governments from within, not those who sought to overthrow them from without. Cambodia has remained the principal focus of the hopes of those hoping for the triumph of violent counter-revolution in Indochina.

Notes

1. This section draws heavily on two papers by Steve Heder, although reaching very different conclusions from the evidence. See his *Kampuchea: Occupation and Resistance*, Asian Studies Monograph no. 027, Chulalongkorn University, Bangkok, January 1980, and the unpublished 1981 paper 'The Democratic Kampuchea Military'.

2. Quoted by Heder, 'The Democratic Kampuchea Military'.

3. Henry Kamm, *New York Times*, 25 November 1980.

4. Quoted by Nayan Chanda, *Brother Enemy: The War after the War*, San Diego 1986, p. 394.

5. Elizabeth Becker, 'The Quiet Cambodian', *New Republic*, 20 January 1982.

6. Nayan Chanda, *Far Eastern Economic Review*, 6 March 1981.

7. *Far Eastern Economic Review*, 7 November 1980.

8. John McBeth, *Far Eastern Economic Review*, 24 January 1985.

9. Almerigo Grilz and Gian Micalessin, *Bangkok Post*, 12 November 1984.

10. John McBeth, *Far Eastern Economic Review*, 16 February 1984.

11. Paul Quinn-Judge, *Far Eastern Economic Review*, 14 June 1984.

12. Paul Quinn-Judge, *Far Eastern Economic Review*, 17 May 1984.

13. *Tap Chi Quan Doi Nhan Dan*, December 1984.

14. Anthony Paul, *Asiaweek*, 29 March 1985.

15. Radio Hanoi, 14 August 1986.

16. 'The Military Occupation of Kampuchea', *Indochina Report* (Singapore), no. 3, July–September 1985, p. 22. This article was prepared 'by a team of analysts led by a prominent journalist based in Bangkok'. Both the information and the delusions in it suggest that the 'team of analysts' worked closely with Thai military intelligence.

17. Paul Quinn-Judge, *Far Eastern Economic Review*, 4 July 1985.

18. Nayan Chanda, 'Cambodia in 1986: Beginning to Tire', *Asian Survey*, vol. 27, 1987, pp. 115–16.

19. Marcel Barung, *South*, March 1986, p. 20.

20. *Asiaweek*, 29 July 1988.

21. James Pringle, *Far Eastern Economic Review*, 25 February 1988.

22. Colonel Nguyen Huu Dinh, *Tap Chi Quan Doi Nhan Dan*, July 1987.

23. Francis Deron, *Australian*, 1 August 1985.

24. John McBeth, *Far Eastern Economic Review*, 6 March 1986.

25. Murray Hiebert, *Far Eastern Economic Review*, 19 March 1987.

26. *Asiaweek*, 25 March 1988.

27. *Asiaweek*, 15 April 1988.

28. Murray Hiebert, *Far Eastern Economic Review*, 1 December 1988.

29. Geoffrey C. Gunn, 'Resistance Coalitions in Laos', *Asian Survey*, vol. 28, 1983, pp. 337–8.

30. For details see 'The Rise and Fall of the Secret Army', in Grant Evans, *The Yellow Rainmakers*, London 1983.

31. For an early critical discussion of the issue, see Grant Evans, *The Yellow Rainmakers*. The decisive scrutiny of the physical evidence provided by the State Department was Thomas D. Seely, *et al.*, 'Yellow Rain', *Scientific American*, September 1985, and J. Robinson, J. Guillemi and M. Meselson, 'Yellow Rain: The Story Collapses', *Foreign Policy*, vol. 86, 1987.

32. Quoted by Michael Richardson, *Age* (Melbourne), 14 December 1984.

9

The Great-Power Triangle
and Indochina

The conflict in Indochina after 1975 was a multi-dimensional one, with developments at a local and regional level constantly interacting with the changing relations between the great powers. This continued to be the case in the 1980s. In the early years of the decade, the deteriorating relations between the great powers made almost any attempt to settle regional conflicts such as those in Indochina futile. But when great-power relations began to improve once more after 1983, this enabled a shift to take place from confrontation to negotiation over the Indochina conflict to take place.

This trend raised hopes of peace in Indochina. But there was still a long way to go. An outbreak of good will was by itself not enough to end contention. Real conflicts of interest remained, and real sacrifices had to be made somewhere. Attempts at conflict resolution were often attempts to win at the negotiating table what had been lost on the battlefield, and in the late 1980s hopes frequently ran ahead of realities. As has often been the case, the further away from the problem people were, the easier it looked.

The Great-Power Triangle in the 1980s

In the USA the election of Ronald Reagan as president in 1980 consolidated the trend towards renewed Cold War in US–Soviet relations. Reagan declared that, as far as he was concerned, 'the Soviet Union is at war with the United States'. He blamed US setbacks in the Third World in the 1970s on American 'weakness' in the face of the menace of Soviet military power. Describing the Soviets as 'liars and cheats', he placed little value on diplomacy and saw American strength as the key to a peaceful world. The core of Reagan's policies was to restore US military supremacy over the Soviets, and to roll back Soviet gains in the Third World.

In Southeast Asia Reagan made no attempt to reverse the retrenchment of US forces from the mainland that took place as a result of defeat in Vietnam. But forces at Clark Air Base and Subic Bay in the Philippines were upgraded for rapid deployment throughout the region, from the North Pacific to the Persian Gulf. The US naval build-up in the Gulf following the collapse of the Shah's regime in Iran and the outbreak of the Iran–Iraq war in 1980 depended on the Philippines bases. This also made unrestricted transit through the Straits of Malacca, Sunda and Lombock vital to US strategy, and a united, pro-US ASEAN was one of the pillars of American policy in the region.

The restoration of American supremacy was expected to yield political dividends in the Third World. By 1985 Reagan was proclaiming the USA the leader of a world-wide 'democratic revolution', morally obligated to support 'freedom-fighters' battling to topple pro-Soviet regimes. 'We must stand by our democratic allies', Reagan proclaimed in his State of the Union address. 'And we must not break faith with those who are risking their lives – on every continent, from Afghanistan to Nicaragua – to defy Soviet-supported aggression and secure rights which have been ours from birth. ... Support for freedom-fighters is self-defence.' A US official explained what this meant for American policy in the Third World: 'We're talking about getting involved in insurgency now – rather than what we did in the '60s, which was mainly counter-insurgency. Socialism is not irreversible.'[1]

Zbigniew Brzezinski had made China the second pillar of US policy. By encouraging Chinese hostility to the Soviet Union and drawing China into the US economic and military orbit, the USA hoped to block Soviet diplomatic advances in the Far East. Moscow watched with undisguised alarm as Washington moved rapidly towards not only normalizing relations with Beijing, but towards helping with China's economic and military modernization. But this policy foundered under the Reagan administration. Reagan repeatedly attacked the Brzezinski policy as a betrayal of Taiwan, declaring: 'We do not believe that to make one friend, we should discard a long-term ally and friend – the people of Taiwan.' To the anger of Beijing, he expanded American arms sales to Taiwan. Reagan was also unhappy at the prospect of Communist China emerging as a regional power in its own right. As a State Department spokesperson put it in 1981: 'We are not asking China to be the regional policeman. We want to play an active role here.' American policy began to place more emphasis on Japan and, to a lesser extent, South Korea and the ASEAN countries, as the main US allies in the region.

Both pillars of US policy converged in support for an ASEAN–China hard line against the Vietnamese in Cambodia. Brzezinski later explained his approach: 'I encouraged the Chinese to support Pol Pot. I encouraged the Thai to help [Democratic Kampuchea]. ... Pol Pot was an abomination. We could never support him but China could.'[2] The Carter administration left China to organize the military campaign to topple the new government in Phnom Penh, while it took the lead in orchestrating attempts to isolate and economically cripple Vietnam. The only changes brought about by the new administration were summed up by one analyst as follows: 'The Reagan administration's effort to punish Vietnam is much more comprehensive and systematic than similar efforts by the Carter administration.'[3]

The Reagan administration's covert operations were largely focused on Central America and the Middle East. Reagan's CIA chief, William Casey, also pushed Cambodia. The idea of renewed US involvement in Indochina initially 'stood hair on end' inside the CIA. In 1982 – once they agreed to join a coalition with the Khmer Rouge – the non-Communist resistance groups were provided with $5 million a year.[4] As enthusiasm for the 'Reagan Doctrine' spread in Washington, liberal Democrat Stephen R. Solarz accused the administration of not doing enough to help the non-Communist resistance in Cambodia, and persuaded Congress to vote a further $5 million a year for it. In response to an inquiry in 1986, the US Congressional Information Service said Washington had provided the Khmer Rouge with over $80 million worth of aid, but Reagan administration officials strenuously denied this and none of the threads of the Irangate scandal led to Cambodia.

Central to American thinking in the early 1980s was the assumption that the Sino-Soviet split could not be undone. Beijing had turned to the West to safeguard itself against the Soviet threat, and would therefore have little choice but to yield to American pressures. As late as 1984, one American academic argued that the pressure of Soviet–Vietnamese encirclement had forced China to abandon its view of Southeast Asia as a Chinese sphere of influence. He endorsed the view of 'many observers' that China had become 'a willing instrument or surrogate of United States foreign policy in Southeast Asia'.[5] Thus policies which strengthened China's position in Indochina were pursued under the illusion that this was strengthening the position of the USA.

This, of course, quickly turned out to be a major miscalculation. China had ambitions of its own. Beijing began to stress the 'independent' character of Chinese policy. It dropped criticism of Soviet policy in the non-Asian Third World, and began criticizing US policies. It was stressed that such disagreements did not stand in the way of developing Sino-American cooperation. This also seemed to imply that Chinese disagreements with Soviet policies in Asia might not stand in the way of growing Sino-Soviet relations.

The Soviets had always looked forward to an eventual reconciliation between the two Communist great powers. This seemed out of the question while Mao dominated Chinese politics. After his death the Soviets were disappointed when the Chinese responded to their overtures by reaffirming Mao's view of the Soviet Union. But by 1981 articles in the Chinese press made it clear that Mao's critique of the Soviet Union had fallen into as much disfavour in Deng Xiaoping's China as his views on domestic policy. The significance of this was not lost on Moscow. In March 1982 Brezhnev appealed to Beijing for a full normalization of Sino-Soviet relations, declaring that 'there has not been and there is no threat to the People's Republic of China from the Soviet Union'. Soviet officials visited Beijing in May, and negotiations resumed in October 1982. But deep suspicions remained.

Yet the conflict was no longer about ideological principles, but about specific regional issues. The Chinese demanded 'deeds, not words' from the Soviets on three areas of conflict – the Sino-Soviet border, Afghanistan, and Indochina – before they would agree to normalization. They insisted that the Soviets withdraw their troops from the Chinese border, and agree to a renegotiation of the border. They demanded that the Soviets withdraw from Afghanistan. On Indochina, they demanded that the Vietnamese withdraw from Cambodia unconditionally, and that the Soviet navy quit Cam Ranh Bay.

These 'three obstacles', as the Chinese called them, embodied the clash of strategic interests between the Soviets and the Chinese, neatly summed up by Thomas Robinson:

> No amount of negotiation and agreement will eliminate the fact that the Soviet Union has accumulated many new interests in Asia stemming from its newly projectable power there or that latter-day modernization has enabled China to assert itself around its periphery and, with increasing conviction, in the Middle East and in the global strategic realm.[6]

The Soviets could not meet China's demands in full without ceasing to be a great power in Asia.

They objected to the Chinese attempting to dictate Soviet relations with Mongolia, Afghanistan and Vietnam as part of their bilateral relationship. *Pravda* complained that 'the piling up of all sorts of preliminary conditions bordering on ultimatums' showed that the Chinese were 'not yet' serious about normalizing relations. And so the Soviets rejected the Chinese demands outright. As Yuri Andropov put the Soviet view in

1983: 'We proceed firmly from the premiss that Soviet–Chinese relations must be built in such a way that they do not harm third countries. We expect the same from the Chinese side.' The talks soon stalled.

For the next couple of years political paralysis in Moscow, as old and ailing leaders succeeded each other, prevented any major Soviet initiative. But relations improved steadily. Trade, cultural and sporting exchanges between China and the Soviet Union multiplied. There were no border incidents, and in 1983 sections of the Sino-Soviet border were opened for the first time since the early 1960s. In July 1984 China signed a border agreement with the government in Ulan Bator, silently abandoning Mao's claims to Mongolia. Xinhua reported that the Sino-Mongolian border was now 'peaceful and friendly'.

A major review of military policy by Beijing in 1983 decided that there was little danger of an invasion of China itself by the Soviets or any other power. The People's Liberation Army could be cut from 4 million to three million, releasing resources for economic development. At the same time, it was decided Mao's 'people's war' doctrines were not relevant for China in the 1980s, emerging as a great power. The Sino-Vietnamese war had demonstrated that China lacked the capability to deploy forces effectively beyond its borders. Thus, while reducing the overall size of the army, China would set about acquiring the modern weaponry, logistics and communications technology needed for this. As well as modernizing the army, the navy was to be transformed from a coastal to a blue-water force.

While the Chinese were contemplating how they could achieve this, the Reagan administration attempted to salvage the Brzezinski strategy. In early 1984 the Americans agreed to supply weapons for China's military modernization, to lift restrictions on the export of American high techno-logy (including nuclear technology) to China, and to allow more Chinese exports into the US market. They made no secret of what they expected in return. When Premier Zhao Ziyang came to Washington in February, Reagan stressed that China and the USA 'stand on common ground' in 'opposing expansionism and interference in the affairs of independent states'. Before arriving in Beijing two months later, Reagan said he wanted to re-enlist the Chinese in 'opposing expansionist aggression by the Soviet Union'. Invited to give an interview on Beijing television, Reagan denounced the Soviet threat to China and proclaimed Sino-American unity in opposition to 'military expansionism'.

The Chinese were happy to buy weapons from the USA, but were unresponsive to Reagan's anti-Soviet line. 'We shall never attach ourselves to any country or group of countries', General Secretary Hu Yaobang told him. When US officials complained that the Chinese had censored Reagan's television interview, they were told that it was 'not appropriate' for the Chinese media to 'publicize the comments of President Reagan on a third country'. Reagan had restored Sino-American cooperation, but it no longer served American strategic purposes – if, indeed, it ever had.

In March 1985 the Soviet Union emerged from its leadership crisis with the ascendancy of Mikhail Gorbachev. He was convinced that the conduct of Soviet foreign policy needed drastic change, and quickly replaced Foreign Minister Andrei Gromyko with one of his own associates, Eduard Shevardnadze. Shevardnadze and Gorbachev knew that military parity with the USA sought by Brezhnev had been achieved at a heavy cost to the Soviet economy. And it was now crumbling in the face of further technological advances on the US side and a faltering economy on the Soviet side. Unless something was done to deal with this, Moscow was facing another dangerous period of strategic inferiority. In dealing with the USA, Gorbachev tried to turn Soviet military weaknesses into diplomatic strengths, and to capitalize on the widespread fears created by Reagan's bellicose posture. He also had to undo the US–Chinese alliance which pitted the Soviets both against China in the east and NATO in the west.

Gorbachev thus set out to redefine the USSR's role as a world power. He began arguing that the military dimension of superpower relations had been overstressed at the expense of diplomacy and economic cooperation. He called for 'new thinking' emphasizing 'global security' rather than unilateral advantage, and showered Reagan with proposals for summits and nuclear disarmament. The Americans were unprepared for this Soviet 'peace offensive', and uncertain how to respond.

To the surprise of many, Reagan decided to react positively. The result was a series of Reagan–Gorbachev summits, beginning in November 1985. At the 1988 Moscow summit, Reagan described Gorbachev as 'a friend'. By the end of the Reagan presidency, commentators were speculating about the 'end of the Cold War'. The Americans made major concessions on disarmament, hoping that this would lead to Soviet concessions on regional conflicts. Some experts argued that the Soviets were ready to sacrifice their Third World allies in order to obtain improved US–Soviet relations.[7]

In 1988–89 the Soviets agreed to withdraw their troops from Afghanistan, to a withdrawal of Cuban troops from Angola, and to cut supplies of arms to the government in Nicaragua. Reagan presented this as a US triumph. But in each case the settlement left in office a pro-Soviet government which the Reagan administration had spent years trying to destroy. Not only did the South Africans agree to end their intervention in Angola, they agreed to independence for Namibia as well. The Nicaraguan contras were to be disbanded.

The real test came in Afghanistan. Here US officials initially saw events as a rerun of their own humiliation in Vietnam. They equated the withdrawal of Soviet troops with the abandonment of Afghanistan. They assumed that Gorbachev would accept the destruction of the Kabul government in the name of improved relations with Washington. Believing that the 'puppet' regime in Kabul lacked staying power, they stepped up supplies to the mujahideen and pushed them to drive for total military victory. But the government in Kabul did not collapse, and as the fighting escalated the Soviets airlifted arms and supplies to their Afghan allies. By September 1989 the mujahideen were in disarray and the CIA had sacked the officer in charge of its Afghan operations. This did not mean the war was over, however. A senior Bush official was quoted as saying that the Kabul government had committed the 'original sin' of establishing a Marxist regime, and that the USA would continue to work for its overthrow. If the Soviets continued to support the government, he said, 'one could see a military struggle going on for some time'.

Gorbachev was keen to see negotiated settlements to regional conflicts, and Soviet diplomacy became more flexible than under Brezhnev. But Gorbachev was not about to sacrifice Soviet allies and interests to the ambitions of other powers if he could help it. The Soviets hoped the 'end of the Cold War' would usher in a period of 'peaceful coexistence', in which the great powers continued to have differences and conflicts of interest but settled them by negotiation rather than by military means. If the Bush administration sees the 'end of the Cold War' as a continuation of Reagan's rollback policies, the military confrontations will continue.

Gorbachev believed that Brezhnev had placed too much emphasis on bilateral Soviet–American relations. He became much more active in dealing with the Europeans, and he was 'fascinated by Asia, and appalled at the diplomatic difficulties [the Soviet Union] faced there'.[8] The key here was China, and shortly after he came to power Gorbachev declared: 'We would like a serious improvement of relations with the Chinese People's Republic and believe that, given reciprocity, this is quite possible.'

An Eastern-bloc diplomat explained that Gorbachev, in contrast to his predecessors, 'intends to treat China like a world power'. This was an approach to which the Chinese warmed, and they soon began referring to Gorbachev as 'comrade'. Within months, Sino-Soviet relations were 'infused with a degree of cordiality unparalleled since the heyday of the Sino-Soviet alliance in the early 1950s'.[9] Both sides cut troop numbers on the Sino-Soviet border, and the Chinese softened their stance towards the Soviet presence in Indochina. 'Even if the Vietnamese don't withdraw from Cambodia,' Deng Xiaoping declared, 'the Soviets can still have relations with Vietnam. They can still have the base Vietnam gave them.' As Richard Nations noted, the Chinese had for the first time separated the issue of Vietnamese troops in Cambodia from the issue of the Soviet–Vietnamese alliance and the Soviet presence in Cam Ranh Bay.[10]

Welcome as these moves must have been to Gorbachev, they were fiddling at the margins rather than resolving the basic issues of the Sino-Soviet dispute. Gorbachev set out a comprehensive statement of Soviet policy in the Asian-Pacific region in his speech at Vladivostok on 28 July 1986, in which he dealt with all of these. The development of the Soviet Union's Far Eastern territories and its vast natural resources lay at the heart of his argument. The dynamism of the USA's west coast economy, said Gorbachev, had ensured the role of the USA as 'a great Pacific power' with 'important and legitimate economic and political interests'. He argued that the development of the Soviet Far East would ensure a similar role for the USSR.

Gorbachev thus asserted the Soviet Union's role as an Asian-Pacific power, more forcefully than any previous Soviet leader. But at the same time he stressed that he was not advancing a 'claim for privileges and a special position, or an egotistic attempt to strengthen our security at someone else's expense, or a search for advantages at the expense of others'. The Soviet Union, he said, wished to develop cooperative and mutually advantageous relations with countries in the region, not one based on military domination. He blamed the USA for the continuing arms race, and called for the disbanding of military alliances, the renunciation of military bases, and the withdrawal of troops from the territories of other countries in the Asian-Pacific region. The import of this was that the Asian-Pacific region should not be carved into exclusive spheres of influence by the great powers. Gorbachev's speech was, in essence, a recognition of the interests of both the USA and China in the region, linked to a demand for the reciprocal acceptance of Soviet interests and a call for the demilitarization of great-power relations.

Gorbachev stated his desire to expand ties with the non-Communist countries. But he stressed the importance of socialism as a force in Asian politics, and said the Soviet Union would seek to strengthen relations with friendly governments in Mongolia, North Korea, Vietnam, Laos and Cambodia. He emphasized the common ideals and interests of post-Maoist China and the USSR – in particular, their need for a peaceful international environment in order to focus on economic development – and called for talks 'at any time and any level' to establish 'an atmosphere of good-neighbourliness'. His aim was not to banish China, despite disagreements between Moscow and Beijing, but to include it in what a Singapore diplomat termed 'an expanded Asian socialist community'.[11]

Gorbachev knew he could not reunify the socialist world by Stalinist-style diktat. His hope was to restore it on the basis of mutual consent and shared interests. In his speech to the 27th Congress of the Communist

Party of the Soviet Union (CPSU) in February 1986 Gorbachev had stressed the Soviet Union's 'unconditional respect in international practice for the right of every people to choose the paths and forms of its own development'. Effectively burying the 'Brezhnev doctrine', he said: 'unity has nothing in common with uniformity, with a hierarchy'. Instead he spoke of the need to 'solve problems ... avert crisis situations ... and find mutually acceptable solutions to even the most difficult problems'.

The Chinese welcomed Gorbachev's acceptance of diversity among socialist countries, but remained wary of the idea of an Asian socialist community. They preferred the freedom of manoeuvre available to an independent great power courted by the leading powers of both the capitalist and socialist worlds. Like the Soviets themselves, they wanted their relations with the industrially advanced countries of the capitalist world to expand more than their relations with the more backward countries of the Soviet bloc. Both sides made it clear that Sino-Soviet reconciliation would not involve a return to the military alliance of the 1950s. Consequently both sought to assure the West that it had nothing to fear from such a development, militarily or economically.

Gorbachev also addressed himself to the 'three obstacles' to Sino-Soviet *rapprochement*, and made concessions to China on two of them. He said a withdrawal of Soviet troops from Mongolia was being considered, and called for discussions on reductions of ground forces on both sides of the Sino-Soviet border. He proposed that the Sino-Soviet border run along the main ship channel of the Amur and Ussuri Rivers, rather than the Chinese bank. He announced that the Soviets would begin withdrawing troops from Afghanistan. On the third 'obstacle', Cambodia, Gorbachev agreed for the first time to put the subject on the agenda of Sino-Soviet discussions. But he offered Beijing nothing – a settlement, he said, here would not be decided in 'far-away capitals'; it depended on the Cambodians themselves, and on the normalization of Sino-Vietnamese relations.

Deng Xiaoping's response came in an interview on American television a month after the Vladivostok speech. He was ready for a summit with Gorbachev, but the Soviets would have to take a 'solid step' towards a Vietnamese withdrawal from Cambodia. Without Soviet backing, said Deng, 'the Vietnamese cannot go on fighting in Cambodia for a single day.' Cambodia was now elevated to the status of being the 'main obstacle' to Sino-Soviet normalization. Deng was seeking to persuade the Soviets that Hanoi's 'intransigence' was the principal obstacle to Sino-Soviet normalization, and that Gorbachev should pressure Vietnam into accepting a settlement of the Cambodian issue on China's terms. But if Gorbachev did force Hanoi into accepting a return of the Khmer Rouge regime, that would surely spell the end of the Sino-Vietnamese alliance, and of

Soviet influence in Indochina. The belief that Gorbachev would accept this as the price of improved relations with China was, as Leszek Buszynski has commented, 'an ill-founded hope rather than an accurate assessment'.[12] Gorbachev had rejected such a course at Vladivostok. He reiterated that Sino-Soviet normalization would not be at the expense of a third country (Vietnam), and he included Cambodia among the socialist countries with which the Soviet Union intended to expand its relations. He also opposed attempts to return Cambodia to its 'tragic past' and said that 'by its sufferings' Cambodia had 'earned itself the right to choose its friends and its allies' – a clear rejection of China's attempts to restore the Khmer Rouge to power and dictate the foreign policy orientation of the government in Phnom Penh.

While Moscow and Beijing remained at odds over Indochina, they made rapid progress in dealing with the other issues. By 1987 basic agreement had been reached on the Sino-Soviet border, and a detailed survey was under way. The Soviet withdrawal from Afghanistan was completed in January 1989. Meanwhile, Sino-Soviet trade expanded, with Chinese and Soviet authorities signing trade contracts worth about $3.25 billion in 1988. This made the Soviet Union China's fifth-largest trading partner. Chinese workers were allowed to go to work in the Soviet Far East for the first time in 1988, and in 1989 Xinhua reported plans for 10,000 Chinese labourers to work on agricultural, forestry, fishing and mining projects in the Soviet Union. They will presumably work alongside Vietnamese 'guest workers', but there were no denunciations of China for 'exporting slave labour'.

Since Beijing proclaimed Cambodia the 'main obstacle' to Sino-Soviet relations, many western commentators assumed that China's principal motivation in dealing with Moscow was to isolate Hanoi from its patron. This was one factor, but far from the only – or even the most important – one. Within China the expansion of Sino-Soviet relations has been pushed by a coalition of disparate interest groups – foreign trade and central planning officials, western provincial authorities, and cultural conservatives fearful of 'spiritual pollution' from the West – none of whom had any real interest in the Cambodia dispute.[13] That seemed to be a preoccupation of the top party leaders, above all Deng Xiaoping. But changes in Chinese politics after 1986 steadily strengthened the hand of the coalition favouring improved Sino-Soviet relations.

Thus, with much foot-dragging from Deng, Sino-Soviet relations steadily warmed, despite – from China's point of view – the lack of progress on Cambodia. In June 1987 Premier Zhao left Beijing for a tour which marked the full normalization of relations between China and Poland, East Germany, Hungary and Bulgaria. As for relations with the Soviet Union, as Gerald Segal wrote in 1988, 'there has been an obvious healing in every major dimension of the original split.... For all intents and purposes Sino-Soviet relations are already normalised.'[14]

Gorbachev moved to take advantage of these developments. In an interview which the Chinese magazine *Liaowang* published in January 1988, Gorbachev said a summit meeting would be a 'logical development' of Sino-Soviet dialogue. Deng's response came quickly. On January 12 the Chinese Foreign Ministry issued a statement saying that China's 'elder statesman' had made it 'quite clear' that the Soviets must pressure Vietnam into withdrawing from Cambodia before he would consent to a summit with Gorbachev.

After an interval of eight months, Chinese officials diluted this down to a demand that the Soviets take a 'constructive approach' to the problem. Following the US–Soviet summit in May 1988 the Chinese became concerned that Moscow might sew up a deal on Cambodia along Afghanistan lines, through negotiations with Washington and the ASEAN countries, bypassing China altogether.[15] In November 1988 Li Peng reduced China's demands to insistence on a 'definite timetable' for a Vietnamese withdrawal. In December, Qian Qichen flew to Moscow, where he agreed to begin direct talks with Hanoi if Vietnam announced a complete and unconditional withdrawal of its troops from Cambodia. In January 1989 Hanoi declared it would pull its troops out by the end of September, and the Chinese agreed to a Deng–Gorbachev summit.

Shevardnadze arrived in Beijing in February 1989 to prepare for Gorbachev's visit. He said his aim was to create 'a new type of relationship with China'. 'At one time a lot was said about various "triangles", "quadrangles" and "pentangles" of great powers', he explained. 'It was automatically assumed that the improvement of relations between the two sides would inevitably lead to a loss for a third side. The time of such "political geometry" has gone for good.' Lengthy negotiations between lower-level officials followed. At the same time, Sino-Vietnamese talks were held in Beijing. The Chinese and the Soviets remained at odds over Cambodia, but despite this the summit went ahead.

Gorbachev arrived in Beijing on 15 May 1989, and met Deng the next day. They officially announced the full normalization of Sino-Soviet relations. According to Xinhua's account, Deng 'reviewed the years when China had suffered invasion, oppression and territorial cession by foreign powers, as well as the period when relations between the two countries experienced a tortuous path'. Gorbachev said that Deng's views were 'not groundless', but the historical issues were 'very complicated' and the Soviet side had 'different views' on some issues. They agreed to let bygones be bygones, and to look forward rather than backward. Deng and Gorbachev had a 'detailed discussion' on Cambodia, and 'shared some viewpoints' but 'failed to reach a complete agreement'. The meeting, which went for half an hour longer than the two hours planned, was held, said Xinhua, 'in a warm and friendly atmosphere'.

The Soviets had consistently said that Sino-Soviet detente would not be at the expense of a 'third country'. It is true that they pressed the Vietnamese to speed up their troop withdrawals, but that was a concession of timing rather than substance. At the same time they pushed China into beginning the process of Sino-Vietnamese normalization. But they were still unable to agree on a settlement in Cambodia.

An article in *Beijing Review* on the eve of the meeting stressed that the normalization of relations would be based on applying the principle of peaceful coexistence to relations between socialist countries, as well as to relations between capitalist and socialist countries. 'China and the Soviet Union have the same social system', the author declared, 'but they also have their respective national interests. To handle the different national interests of the two countries properly, the only feasible way in dealing with each other is to strictly adhere to the Five Principles of Peaceful Co-existence.' There would be no return to the military alliance of the 1950s, which was a response to US hostility and military deployments. Beijing's entry into an alliance with Moscow 'was a choice that was forced on China by the US policy towards China'. This would not recur in the 1980s, for China's position in world affairs was 'quite different'.[16]

The Americans watched Sino-Soviet *rapprochement* with little enthusiasm. The *Washington Post* commented: 'The Sino-Soviet split, while it lasted, was a great break for the West. It forced the Kremlin to divide its resources to protect itself from China, as well as from the United States.' Had it occurred earlier, this *rapprochement* would have been a 'strategic disaster' for the USA. But as Washington thought Communism was in decline in the 1980s, it was able to view the detente with 'relative calm'.

As Sino-Soviet ties grew, US hopes of playing China against the Soviet Union evaporated. Following Deng's response to Gorbachev's Vladivostok speech, the USA concluded it was time to distance itself from China's policies. By 1988 one Washington official explained: 'The time when China policy was formulated in the context of a global strategy has given way to a situation where a variety of concerns – like weapons proliferation, diversion of technology and human rights – drive the [USA's] China policy.' As Beijing warmed to Moscow, Washington became increasingly vocal over China's poor human rights record in particular, while Beijing rejected this as 'interference in China's internal affairs'.

When George Bush became US president in January 1989, there were hopes in Washington that this would reverse the deterioration of Sino-American relations. Bush made a quick trip to Beijing. His aim was to demonstrate Sino-American friendship on the eve of the Deng–Gorbachev summit. He was greeted in the *People's Daily* as an 'old friend', but the visit was marred by a spat with the Chinese over dissident Professor Fang Lizhi. The Chinese agreed to let US warships dock in Shanghai while Gorbachev visited Beijing; but when the Soviets insisted that this would be inappropriate, the Chinese agreed to postpone it until after Gorbachev's visit.

The crisis in Beijing in June 1989, when troops shot down demonstrators in the streets and General Secretary Zhao Ziyang was purged, plunged Sino-American relations to an all-time low. Bush bitterly condemned the actions of the Chinese government, and ordered a halt to military co-operation. 'We thought we were on a real roll with China, and look what happened', said one US official. 'Now our 35-year relationship with Japan takes on more importance.' In contrast, Moscow felt no compulsion to lecture the Chinese on human rights issues. It treated the Beijing crisis as regrettable, but purely an internal Chinese affair, and as Sino-American relations declined, Sino-Soviet relations continued to improve. Despite Shevardnadze's disclaimer, it seemed as if great-power diplomacy still followed a triangular pattern.

It has been a common western view that the Sino-Soviet thaw is occurring because China's 'rock-hard' resistance has finally caused the Soviets to abandon their 'expansionist' ambitions in Asia. This is a delusion. The thaw marked Chinese acceptance of a Soviet role as a great power in Asia, with the abandonment of China's 1970s claim to exclusive hegemony in the region, and also Soviet acceptance that Communist China had achieved great-power status. It marked the acceptance that these two vast neighbours had more to gain from co-operation than from continued antagonism, and that this would not prevent clashes of interest over particular issues.

The Deng–Gorbachev detente marked the acceptance of a plurality of great powers in the Far East, and an end to exclusive spheres of influence. For the Soviet Union, the impact of this will be greatest in Eastern Europe rather than in Asia. But it does mean allowing China a role in Indochina. However, it was China which adopted the most rigidly Stalinist exclusivism in this region, and Chinese attitudes which will have to undergo the greatest revision. This has, in fact, already begun with China's reluctant acceptance of Vietnam's Soviet alliance in 1985. The great-power pluralism propounded by Deng and Gorbachev also has major repercussions for US policy in Asia.

For the USA, it will mean the final collapse of the policy of 'containment of Communism', and the acceptance of the legitimacy of both the Soviet Union and China as great powers. In fact, this was already happening before the summit. In the 1970s China had, with US blessing, normalized relations with most countries in Southeast Asia. Now countries such as Thailand and the Philippines began to open up relations with the Soviets as well, while India and China warmed to each other, and Indonesia normalized relations with both China and the Soviet Union. Expanding relations with the Communist great powers was made easier in most cases because domestic Communist movements had been decisively defeated. But even in the Philippines, it was generally recognized that the insurgency was an indigenous problem and not an instrument of Soviet (or Chinese) subversion.

Indochina was the region where all this fine rhetoric was put to its first test. Here the interests of the Soviets and the Chinese clashed most directly, while the USA was angling to re-establish a role for itself. The local allies of all three powers were still fighting each other, and a settlement seemed beyond immediate reach.

Vietnam: Economic Crisis and Reform

Fourteen years after the end of the American war, and ten years after the overthrow of the Pol Pot regime, Vietnam was still under siege. Its economy was still in a parlous state, and refugees still streamed out of the country. However it had managed a political succession, successfully withstood Sino-American pressure, and by the late 1980s the isolation imposed on it was beginning to crumble.

The leadership of the Vietnamese Communist Party (VCP) passed from the 'Dien Bien Phu generation'. After leading the VCP for nearly thirty years, Le Duan died on 10 July 1986. The party's 6th Congress six months later continued the 'renovation' of the party leadership begun in 1982. Truong Chinh, Pham Van Dong and Le Duc Tho all resigned their positions 'on the grounds of advanced years and failing health'. Truong Chinh died on 30 September 1988. Three other members of the old Politburo failed to be re-elected, including Defence Minister General Van Tien Dung.

The Congress elected a fourteen-member Politburo, with five new members. Nguyen Van Linh, the leader of the southern reformers, was elected general secretary. His associates Vo Van Kiet and Vo Chi Cong also shot up the Politburo ranking. So did General Le Duc Anh, the former commander of Vietnamese forces in Cambodia, who replaced Dung in the Defence Ministry a few weeks after the Congress. Pham Hung, the last of the old guard, was number two in the Politburo hierarchy, and replaced Pham Van Dong as premier. When he died in March 1988, Vo Van Kiet was widely tipped to take the premiership. Instead it went to Do Muoi, who was seen as a more conservative figure.

The Political Report was presented to the 6th Congress by Truong Chinh, who stood in as general secretary after Le Duan's death. Once again, the party leadership was highly critical of its own performance. It was preoccupied largely with Vietnam's massive economic problems. The party leadership, Truong Chinh told the Congress, had failed to achieve the objectives set by the 5th Congress in 1982. Then the party had called for the emphasis to be shifted from heavy industry to light industry, agriculture, and exports. This had not happened, the report said, because they had continued to rely on a 'bureaucratic-centralist, subsidy-based' system. That system would have to be abandoned in favour of 'economic accounting and socialist business methods' emphasizing decentralized management and enterprise profitability rather than centralized resource allocation.

The first instalment of economic reform had already taken place. In September 1985 the government tried to overhaul wages, prices and the currency system. The results proved disastrous. Prices skyrocketed, speculation and corruption became rife. Never before, said Nguyen Van Linh in April 1987, 'has inflation worsened so fast, prices increased so unexpectedly, and the lives of wage-earners and members of the armed services become so much more difficult'. Indeed, Vietnam was struggling not with mere inflation, but with hyper-inflation; by 1987 prices were rising by 700–1,000 per cent per year.

Economic growth slumped from 6 per cent in 1985 to 2 per cent in 1987, barely keeping pace with the growth of population.[17] Reporting to the National Assembly in December 1987, Vo Van Kiet said that while the figures for industrial growth were good, the quality of output was poor and productivity was actually declining. Exports continued to grow, but the government had discovered that 'inappropriate prices and rates of exchange ... resulted in a situation where the more we exported the bigger the losses we suffered'.

Most serious of all was the situation in agriculture. Grain production stagnated at just over 18 million tonnes in 1985–86 and then declined to 17.6 million in 1987. As the population continued to grow rapidly this meant that per capita food production, having shown healthy rises in the early 1980s, fell sharply – from 304 kilograms per person in 1985 to 280 kilograms in 1987.

In early 1988, it emerged that the situation in agriculture was even worse than Kiet's analysis indicated. In three northern provinces, 8 million people faced serious food shortages. Hundreds of impoverished people descended on Hanoi, to make a living begging on the streets, but the authorities rounded most of them up and returned them to their home provinces. Rice was hastily shipped in to relieve the situation, and a campaign was launched to plant fast-growing crops. Even so, twelve people reportedly starved to death. There had been typhoons, pests and floods. But these problems were compounded by the inability of the government to provide farmers with fertilizer and insecticides, and provincial authorities had concealed the gravity of the situation from Hanoi until it became overwhelming. Hanoi had appealed to the international community for emergency food assistance for the stricken provinces. Australia, France, and the UN World Food Program provided some, while Sweden offered some fertilizer. But most western countries refused to help, maintaining the policy of keeping Vietnam isolated.

Many outside analysts concluded that the Sino-American policy of economic strangulation was at last working. But that was not the way the problem was seen in Hanoi. Vietnam had recovered from the worst effects of economic blockade in the early 1980s. The crisis in the mid-1980s was not so much the fruit of Sino-American policy, but the result of bad policies and inept administration in Vietnam. The only remedy, Nguyen Van Linh argued, was to lift Vietnam out of the 'quicksand of bureaucratic centralism and subsidization' into which it had fallen.

This meant pushing ahead with reform. In 1987–88 Hanoi passed a great deal of reform legislation – encouraging the formation of private 'family enterprises', and restructuring the management of state enterprises. Agricultural cooperatives were downgraded, and land was returned to peasants who had been coerced into joining them. The system of central directive planning, and the controls that went with it, was dismantled. A drastic austerity programme was introduced to reduce the budget deficit and bring inflation under control. These included plans to cut military expenditure, and in 1988 the government announced plans to cut its army by half. The 1977 Foreign Investment Code was replaced with one which provided even more generous terms to attract foreign capital in Vietnam.[18] In another move aimed at western creditors, loan repayments to the IMF (suspended in 1981) were resumed.

Nguyen Van Linh also liberalized the official stance towards old-regime intellectuals, and the Catholics and Hoa communities. Most of these people, said Linh in October 1986, were patriotic, hard-working and competent. It was the duty of the Vietnamese government to adopt 'satisfactory policies' towards them so that they may 'rid themselves of the conviction that they are being discriminated against and, especially, may see their children's future under the socialist regime'.

Ten thousand re-education camp inmates were released in 1987–88. Radio Hanoi declared that although 'millions of puppet army and administrative personnel of the old regime had committed crimes against the people', only 90,000 had been sent to the camps after 1975. In February 1988, Deputy Minister of Information Phan Quang said there were only 159 old-regime officials left in detention. They still needed more time 'to ponder over the past and prove their repentance for the crimes they perpetrated against their own people'.

Linh launched a campaign of *do moi* – 'transformation' or 'rejuvenation'. In 1987 he himself led the way in the liberalization of the Vietnamese media with a column in *Nhan Dan*, largely devoted to attacks on 'negative phenomena' in government. This attracted a flood of letters, many voicing complaints about abuses of power and incompetence. Others warned that Linh was 'blackening the government' with his exposés. Over the next couple of years, writers tested the limits of government tolerance. By 1989 Linh was trying to rein in the more outspoken critics, urging the press to avoid a 'one-sided point of view'.

The aim of *do moi* was not to do away with the 'leading role' of the VCP, but to renovate it. The Vietnamese leadership was alarmed by developments in Eastern Europe, especially Poland. 'They don't like some of the things they see in Eastern Europe the anarchy, the talk of a multi-party system', said a Communist diplomat in Hanoi.'They've decided the political side isn't so important now. They look to their neighbours like Singapore and see you don't need to liberalize politics to achieve economic progress.' In September 1989 Nguyen Van Linh warned that the USA and other imperialists would exploit anarchy and disorder in socialist countries, and rejected 'limitless democratization': 'The VCP is the leader, initiator and pace-setter in renovation', he said. 'We shall not allow any force to work against the people and socialism.'

But the VCP itself was experiencing considerable difficulties, for official corruption seemed to grow in parallel with the market economy. 'The relationship between the party and the masses has eroded, and the party's prestige has waned', warned *Nhan Dan* in August 1988. 'Bureaucratism and alienation from the masses, theft of public property and bribe-taking remain prevalent, especially among a number of cadres who abuse their position and power'. Many officials were arrested in an anti-corruption drive, and the leadership launched a campaign to restore discipline and unity within the party's ranks. This resulted in many expulsions which, combined with more stringent vetting of new recruits, led to a fall in the membership of the VCP by 20 per cent in 1988.

By 1989 the limited nature of political reform in Vietnam had become clear. As David Marr has pointed out, the stratum of professionals and intellectuals that underpinned Gorbachev's perestroika (and the reform movement that was crushed in China in June 1989) was small in Vietnam. But so was the stratum of industrial and white-collar workers dependent on subsidized food, housing and services. Thus, if the pressure for reform was weaker, so was the opposition to it.[19] In what remained an overwhelmingly peasant society, authoritarian rule persisted. However, the economic reforms had been pushed through. One observer wrote in 1989:

After the changes of the past 12 months, it can fairly be argued that no other communist country has moved so far in the direction of market-oriented economic reform. ... Market forces – albeit rather primitive ones – ... now guide the flow of resources through most of the economy.[20]

By 1989, Vietnam was emerging from its economic crisis. In December 1988 Vo Van Kiet was able to report an overall growth rate of 5.4 per cent for the year. For the first time, agricultural production was on target, at 19 million tonnes. Industrial output was up 9 per cent, and for the first time, the composition of output was in line with government priorities, with consumer goods and exports leading the industrial sector. By 1989 inflation had fallen to 10 per cent per month or less. Vietnam's foreign trade grew by a massive 21 per cent in 1988. Increasing numbers of Japanese, Thai, and other foreign businessmen were to be seen in Ho Chi Minh City. By April 1989 agreements bringing some $450 million worth of western capital into Vietnam had been signed, mostly in offshore oil and gas exploration, and in food-processing for export. To the surprise of many, Vietnam emerged as a major exporter of rice in 1989, selling to Africa, India, the Philippines and even China.

The transition from bureaucratic centralism to market socialism was not, however, painless. Kiet said that the country's transport infrastructure was deteriorating, and austerity measures had resulted in 'the degradation of some public health, education, information and cultural, physical education and sports establishments'. Unemployment had risen to an estimated 20 per cent of the workforce.

In the late 1970s the Americans and the Chinese had been predicting that by isolating Vietnam economically they would 'break' Hanoi. Vietnam had certainly suffered, but it had not been broken. By the end of the 1980s its isolation was ending. In actions, if not in words, China appeared to be accepting this.

The Regional Dimension: More Boat People

The crisis that hit Vietnam in the mid-1980s had an important regional dimension, as it provoked a new outpouring of boat people. By 1986, the number of people departing illegally from Vietnam had fallen to 19,500, less than 10 per cent of the 1979 figure. Then the trend was reversed, with the number of Vietnamese illegal arrivals in neighbouring countries jumping to 45,000 in 1988 and 50,000 in the first half of 1989. Most of these came from northern Vietnam, where the food crisis had hit hardest, and they headed for Hong Kong, or even Japan. But departures from the south for Thailand and Malaysia also increased.

This new outflow undermined the arrangements thrashed out at the 1979 Geneva Conference on Indochina Refugees. Then the USA and China were determined to make Vietnam bleed, but Southeast Asian countries were alarmed at the outpouring of boat people. The outcome was that western countries persuaded Hong Kong and the Southeast Asian countries to open their borders to the boat people by promises that they would resettle all of them. In the rush to help the victims of Vietnamese Communism, the criteria normally applied to refugees were swept aside in the case of the boat people. 'Do you remember that ten years ago UNHCR officials suggested submitting boat-people to the standards and procedures laid down in regulations and applied elsewhere?', an official recalled in 1989. 'At the time it was politically unacceptable.'[21]

Thus the problem was resolved, at least for the time being. Hanoi continued to be ostracized. Hong Kong and the Southeast Asian countries agreed to accept as a 'refugee' everybody who left Vietnam illegally by boat. And, rather than being resettled in the region, as is the case with most refugees, the boat people were virtually guaranteed resettlement in the West. This set up a pipeline for moving people from one of the world's most impoverished countries to the most affluent, and people continued to flow through it long after the 1979 crisis passed.

No comparable arrangement existed for Lao or Cambodians, or for Vietnamese land people. Most of the latter had crossed the border to southern China, and were resettled there. The Lao who arrived in Thailand were screened, and only those who met the criteria for a refugee under international law were resettled abroad. The 'residuals' were classified as illegal entrants, and repatriated to Laos after an agreement between Bangkok and Vientiane. More Cambodians were accepted for resettlement than Lao, but the bulk were destined to be repatriated once they had outlived their politico-military usefulness.

It was known in the early 1980s that most Vietnamese arriving in countries of first asylum were better described as 'economic migrants' than as 'refugees'. But as Vietnam was recovering from the economic and political crisis of the late 1970s, the dangers of the open oceans were enough to deter many. The number of new arrivals declined each year, and was exceeded by the number resettled. By the middle of the decade, the problem seemed to be largely over. By 1984 the number departing via the UNHCR-sponsored Orderly Departure Programme exceeded illegal departures. The countries of final settlement began to wind down their refugee resettlement programmes. At the same time, they restricted emigration under the Orderly Departure Programme largely to relatives of those already abroad.

Then came the new economic crisis and the resultant upsurge in illegal departures. The resettlement countries refused to take the bulk of the latest arrivals, whom they classified as 'economic migrants'. It was increasingly recognized that the prospect of resettlement in the affluent West was actually a factor generating the outflow. In that sense, it was argued, the resettlement scheme was part of the problem, not the solution. With only half of the pipeline set up in 1979 still operating, the countries of first asylum were saddled with a crisis. The two countries most affected, Thailand and Hong Kong, moved to deter them from coming.

In January 1988 the Thai authorities began 'redirecting' boat people. This was 'a unilateral, methodical and tough policy of driving refugees back'. A Bangkok diplomat summed up the policy: 'All boats which can be driven back into the sea must be driven back. The luckier ones, those who have enough food, and don't fall into pirates' hands, end up in Malaysia.' Those boat people who did make it ashore in Thailand were not allowed to apply for resettlement. This policy was widely criticized for its harshness, and its failure to provide asylum to genuine refugees. But it was successful in that the number of boat people arriving in Thai waters fell by half in 1988.

Thailand's policies shifted part of the burden to Malaysia, which responded by setting a deadline before it adopted the same approach. After receiving refugees at the Pulau Bidong camp for ten years, the Malaysians announced that it would be closed in April 1989, and from that date boat people would be 'shooed away' from Malaysia as well as Thailand. In mid-1989 it was reported that Malaysian authorities had forced some 900 boat people into Indonesian waters. Others were said to have been given life jackets, compasses and directions to Australia. The government denied these reports.

In June 1988, the Hong Kong authorities stopped giving illegal arrivals from Vietnam automatic refugee status. They began a screening programme to distinguish the 'genuine' refugees from 'economic migrants'. They found that over 90 per cent of arrivals fell into the latter category. As these were not eligible for resettlement, the only solution was repatriation to Vietnam. Hong Kong was already turning back thousands of illegal entrants from mainland China. But repatriation required Vietnam's cooperation.

The British began discussions with Hanoi, and in December 1988 they agreed to repatriation on a voluntary basis. The UNHCR agreed to provide $50 for each adult and $25 per child to assist in resettlement, and was to ensure that those who went back did not suffer retribution from the authorities. By the end of June 1989, a total of 148 people had returned and an additional 180 had volunteered, out of a total of 26,000 refugees. The authorities hoped that more would follow, once they realized the only alternative was rotting away in what were prison-camp conditions in Hong Kong. Said one of the returnees: 'We were encouraged by friends who wrote and told us of the freedom and opportunities here. We had no idea about the screening policy and were shocked by the harsh conditions. We don't want to spend our lives here. It's worse than home.'

The boat people were travelling along the Chinese coast to reach Hong Kong, and the Chinese authorities had been helping them 'in the interests', they said, 'of human rights'. But in September 1989 'reliable sources' reported that China had agreed to turn them back. Apparently they had no intention of inheriting a boat-people problem when they took over Hong Kong in 1997.

The ASEAN governments adopted the Hong Kong approach in March. Then, on 13–14 June 1989 – ten years after the 1979 conference – another international conference was held in Geneva. The Philippine foreign secretary, Raul Manglapus, told the gathering: 'Not only has the problem of Indochinese refugees remained unsolved – it has worsened and degenerated into a most serious threat to peace and stability in Southeast Asia.'

The resettlement countries agreed to accept all the boat people who had arrived before screening procedures were introduced. Some 55,000 people were to be resettled over the next five years. It was agreed to allow legal emigration from Vietnam to be expanded. All those who left the country illegally would be screened, and only those who qualified as genuine refugees would be resettled. Hanoi agreed to launch a crackdown on people organizing illegal departures, and a propaganda campaign emphasizing the dangers faced by those leaving illegally and the fact that they had little chance of being resettled.

There was disagreement over what should happen to those who still left illegally, did not qualify as refugees, and would not agree to voluntary repatriation. The countries of first asylum pushed for compulsory repatriation. Both Hanoi and the USA objected to this. The Vietnamese government said it would only accept back those who returned voluntarily. It agreed to 'urgent discussions' with Hong Kong, Thailand and Malaysia to try and resolve their differences. But the USA argued that it was inhumane to force anyone back to Vietnam. It proposed a regional holding centre, where boat people could be detained indefinitely.

The West's willingness to absorb large numbers of Vietnamese refugees was a necessary corollary of Sino-American efforts to keep Vietnam the sick man of Asia. That willingness made it possible to absorb the outpouring of illegal emigrants in the late 1970s and early 1980s without having to seek Hanoi's cooperation. But once western countries tired of absorbing the continuing outflow, that was no longer possible. Vietnam's second economic crisis meant a boat-people crisis for the region, and this time Hanoi's cooperation was needed for its resolution.

The Geneva Conference had little to say about the state of the Vietnamese economy, but this was generally acknowledged to be the root of the problem. It was easy, but not particularly helpful, to castigate Hanoi over this. Nor was it helpful to seek to punish Hanoi while seeking its cooperation. The real question that was being avoided at Geneva was whether regional interests were well served by policies aimed at keeping a nation of 65 million people in isolation and poverty.

Hanoi and the Great Powers

If Sino-Soviet detente was not aimed principally at increasing the pressure on Hanoi, Beijing certainly hoped that this would be one of the by-products. If Moscow could be persuaded that Hanoi's stubbornness was the principal obstacle to Sino-Soviet normalization, Beijing might achieve through great-power diplomacy what it had been unable to achieve at a regional level through diplomatic, economic and military pressure. But Moscow had no intention of abandoning its role as an Asian power. And as China was unable to enforce its will in Indochina, even with the help of the USA and ASEAN, Moscow had no real reason to abandon its role there. From Moscow's point of view the best course was to hold firm over Indochina while pursuing detente with China.

As Moscow began pushing for detente with Beijing after 1981, it gave Hanoi repeated assurances that this would not be at its expense. Initially, the Soviets declared that they would not even discuss the affairs of 'third countries' with the Chinese. If China wanted to negotiate over Cambodia, therefore, it should talk to the Vietnamese or the Cambodians. The consequence of this stance was that the Soviet Union refused to play any role in settling the Cambodia dispute. Since China refused to do this, there was no diplomatic solution in sight.

The first test of Moscow's commitment to Hanoi came in April 1984. On the eve of Reagan's visit to Beijing, the Chinese announced that Soviet First Deputy Premier Ivan Arkhipov, the man who had overseen the Soviet aid programme in China in the 1950s, would be visiting Beijing shortly. Then they launched the largest attacks on the Sino-Vietnamese border since 1979, and sent the Chinese navy's southern fleet to the disputed Spratly Islands. As Chanda observed, for Arkhipov to go to Beijing under these circumstances would have meant Moscow's 'acceptance of Chinese rules of the game' and a willingness to sacrifice Hanoi in particular.[22]

The Soviets refused to do this. Shortly after Chinese troops crossed the Vietnamese border, Soviet marines landed on the Vietnamese coast near Haiphong in a 'joint exercise'. Moscow condemned China's 'military provocations' and postponed the Arkhipov visit. Chinese diplomats professed to be 'shocked' by this reaction. Vice Foreign Minister Qian Qichen flew to Moscow for unscheduled discussions, and the Soviet and Chinese foreign ministers met for lengthy discussions at the UN in September. As a consequence, it was decided to go ahead with the Arkhipov visit in December. He was greeted as 'an old friend', met many of the top Chinese leaders (but not Deng Xiaoping), and signed three agreements on economic and technical cooperation.

This time it was China which was put to the test. Shortly before Arkhipov arrived, the Soviets deployed more planes to Cam Ranh Bay, and the Vietnamese launched their 1984–85 offensive against the Cambodian resistance camps on the Thai border. The Chinese professed not to notice what was happening until after Arkhipov had left. After the Arkhipov visit *Nhan Dan* ran an article by Soviet Vice Foreign Minister Mikhail Kapitska declaring that Moscow was a 'loyal friend' of Vietnam's. The article expressed full support for Vietnamese policies in Cambodia, and reaffirmed the 'wish of both the Soviet Union and Vietnam to normalize relations with China': 'Our two countries cannot accept that we must "pay a price" for the normalization of relations with China by downplaying our relations with faithful friends.'

The Chinese threatened to teach Vietnam 'another lesson' if it continued its onslaught against the Cambodian resistance camps. But the Vietnamese ignored this, and pressed on with their attacks. As the Khmer Rouge were driven out of the Phnom Malai area, Sihanouk publicly appealed to the Chinese to 'fight now', saying that the resistance forces 'would not be able to win alone'. 'Is China willing to save us or not?', he asked.[23] Beijing's response was to lecture him on the virtues of self-reliance.

A few months later it was reported that a highly-classified western intelligence analysis

maintains that sometime between mid-December and March, the Chinese leadership decided it could afford to launch a major military campaign against Vietnam, even though China's prestige as a regional power was at stake, and failure to 'punish' Vietnam after highly publicised threats could undermine China's credibility with ASEAN.[24]

It was also in the wake of these talks that Deng announced that the Soviets could continue to have relations with Vietnam, and to use Cam Ranh Bay.

This particular round seemed to go quite clearly to the Soviets and the Vietnamese. And this, it must be remembered, occurred in the context of rapidly improving Sino-Soviet relations. Watching Beijing's deeds rather than its words suggested that the pace of the Moscow–Beijing thaw was, in fact, largely independent of the Moscow–Hanoi relationship. But this was the result of pre-Gorbachev diplomacy.

The conventional western view is that since the advent of Gorbachev the Sino-Vietnamese relationship has been deteriorating steadily as Sino-Soviet relations improved. A Rand Corporation analyst, Jonathan Pollack, argued that Vietnam has lost out in the reorientation Gorbachev bought to Soviet diplomacy. Gorbachev wanted to cut back on 'the open-ended burdens imposed on his country by Vietnam's pervasive economic requirements'. He wanted to develop relations with China and the ASEAN states, and has found Vietnam to be the main obstacle. While seeking to 'avoid the impression' of a Sino-Vietnamese rift through 'ostentatious' displays of solidarity, Gorbachev has relentlessly tightened the economic screws and pressured Hanoi to abandon its 'goal of hegemony in Indochina'. The election of Nguyen Van Linh had 'bought Vietnam additional time', but in the late 1980s time was once more running out.[25]

This is yet another triumph of half-truths and wishful thinking over objective analysis. It is without doubt true that, like most marriages, the Sino-Vietnamese relationship was not made in heaven. In the early 1980s Soviet officials privately complained about pouring their money into Vietnam without seeing any gain, and Vietnamese officials complained about the poor quality of Soviet goods, and the inappropriateness of much of their aid. When the Soviets increased their presence in Cambodia and Laos, they were supposedly trying to squeeze the Vietnamese out. These difficulties, real and imagined, led knowledgeable journalists to write of the impending collapse of the alliance. They were wrong.

Contrary to some western claims, Moscow and Hanoi were not increasingly at ideological odds after the ascendancy of Gorbachev. When Nguyen Van Linh visited Moscow in 1987, he and Gorbachev both spoke of the need for 'restructuring', disarmament and detente, and normalization of relations with China. The Soviets, reported Sophie Quinn-Judge, 'clearly feel happy' with the new leadership in Vietnam.[26]

Gorbachev did not cut Soviet aid to Vietnam. Instead, he increased it. But Gorbachev did seek to change drastically the nature of Moscow's aid programme. This did not set him fundamentally at odds with the Vietnamese, however. In fact, a change was long overdue. By the mid-1980s, both Moscow and Hanoi were deeply disenchanted with how the bulk of previous Soviet aid had worked. The problem was not so much one of the Vietnamese exploiting the Soviets (as Pollack argued) or of the Soviets exploiting the Vietnamese (as anti-Communist Vietnamese are prone to claim). It was rather one of incompetence all round. The Vietnamese admitted that they had squandered much of what they had received, blaming the 'bureaucratic centralist' system. The Soviets admitted that they had reinforced these tendencies. A Soviet economist said in 1988:

Before we didn't have co-operation – we just advanced money. ... No one on either side answered for this money, billions of roubles. Now many of our long-term construction projects are just standing there. Some work at 50% capacity.

Vietnam, she said, had needed a new Lenin-style, market-orientated economic policy. Instead the Soviets had encouraged the Vietnamese to pursue Stalin-style crash industrialization, concentrating on 'chemical plants, large hydro-electric plants'.

In the early 1980s Soviet-bloc aid to Vietnam had begun to shift away from grants and big construction projects to joint ventures which paid for themselves by exporting some or all of their output. One example was a textile factory opened in Saigon with Hungarian assistance, which within a few years was supplying about a third of the shirts sold in Hungary. Gorbachev was accelerating this shift.

Following the Gorbachev–Linh meeting in 1987, Moscow and Hanoi drew up an agreement on setting up joint ventures in Vietnam. A commentator in the army newspaper described this as a 'turning point' in the Sino-Vietnamese relationship. Vietnam would stop 'relying on one-way aid' and operate on the principle of 'mutual benefit and mutual need'. By doing away with the 'mentality of dependency', this would enhance Vietnamese sovereignty.[27] It paralleled the investment code Vietnam had drawn up for western companies, and was also congruent with the thrust of domestic economic reform in both the Soviet Union and Vietnam.

However, the new system soon brought out areas where Soviet and Vietnamese interests did not coincide. The Vietnamese complained that the Soviets paid below world-market prices for their goods. The Soviets complained that Vietnamese goods were not of world-market quality, and were often delivered late. There was justice to both complaints, which probably cancelled each other out. A more serious problem underlay these disagreements. The Vietnamese began to emphasize that if they were to compete on world markets, they needed access to modern technology. And this the Soviets often could not provide. Interviewed by Radio Moscow, a Vietnamese visitor to a shoe factory in the Ukraine in 1988 noted that the production line was 'unchanged since Lenin's time'. Not only was the equipment obsolete, he went on, the management was incompetent and working conditions were poor. Unless they wished to retreat to Pol Pot-type autarchy, with all its consequences, the only solution (for Moscow as well as Hanoi) was trade with and investment from the capitalist West. Furthermore, by the late 1980s, both Moscow and Hanoi were well aware that Vietnam's 'natural' trading partners were the East Asian countries – other Southeast Asian nations, Japan, Australia, China, the Soviet Far East – rather than Eastern and Soviet Europe. But while Vietnam remained a nation under siege, it had little choice in this.

By the tenth anniversary of the Soviet–Vietnamese friendship treaty in 1988, the relationship between Moscow and Hanoi had undergone major changes. But it had been put on a basis that, while far from perfect, was of greater advantage to both sides than the earlier arrangements. It seemed far from the point of collapse that western analysts were hoping for, although both Moscow and Hanoi would have welcomed a breakthrough in Vietnam's relations with the West, and in its region.

The sticking point here was Cambodia. While the Chinese clearly beat a retreat in 1984–85 on the question of Soviet–Vietnamese relations, Deng raised Cambodia to the status of being the main 'obstacle' to Sino-Soviet normalization. As Pollack, and many others, have seen mounting tension between Moscow and Hanoi over Cambodia since the ascent of Gorbachev, it is necessary to look more closely at the Soviet position on this issue.

Gorbachev gave his basic position in his Vladivostok speech. He showed more flexibility towards China by agreeing to include Cambodia in Sino-Soviet negotiations. That was the easy bit, although it is still worth noting that the issue was discussed with the Vietnamese first. Since some western commentators have claimed that Hanoi opposed Gorbachev's Vladivostok initiative, it is worth stressing that they gave it full endorsement. Their main concern was to tell the world that it was the Chinese, not Vietnam, which was opposed to Sino-Vietnamese normalization. Vientiane and Phnom Penh also gave their blessing to the Soviet leader's initiative.

In his Vladivostok speech Gorbachev declared that the Soviet Union would not impose on its allies, as China was demanding. He said the solution of Cambodian problems was a matter for the Cambodians themselves. He went on:

> Here, as with other problems of Southeast Asia, much depends on the normalization of Sino-Vietnamese relations. It is a sovereign matter of the governments and leaderships of the two countries. We can only express our interest in seeing the border between these two socialist states become again a border of peace and good-neighbourly relations, in seeing friendly dialogue resumed, and the unnecessary suspicion and mistrust removed. It seems that the moment is right, and all Asia needs this change.

While the Chinese insisted that settling the Cambodian issue was the key to Sino-Soviet normalization, Gorbachev was proposing that normalizing Sino-Vietnamese relations was the key to the Cambodia conflict.

As with Sino-Soviet relations, all depended on what the priorities were in Beijing.

The Vladivostok speech was followed by a round of diplomatic activity by the Soviets. Cambodia was included on the agenda at the ninth round of Sino-Soviet talks in October 1986, and at each session thereafter. Although these negotiations took place in an increasingly friendly atmosphere, 'serious differences' over Cambodia remained. The Soviets rejected Chinese demands to impose on Vietnam. In March 1987 Shevardnadze visited Thailand, Australia, Indonesia, Laos, Cambodia and Vietnam – the first visit to this region by such a high-level Soviet leader since the Khrushchev era. In Laos, after his discussions with ASEAN leaders, he reiterated the position Gorbachev had laid out at Vladivostok: 'We have stressed everywhere that the solution to the Cambodian problem is the affair of the Cambodian people themselves. In Cambodia there is a legitimate government which has gained support.'

But for Pollack and his co-thinkers, who were legion, repeated statements of the Soviet position was mere 'ostentation'. They knew – though they could not document it – that the 'real' position of Gorbachev was to force Hanoi into abandoning its expansionist objectives in Cambodia. As a 'pragmatist' Nguyen Van Linh was reluctantly willing to go along with this. But the fact is that Vietnam initiated a determined effort to patch up relations with China and the USA in December 1984 – before the ascendancy of either Linh or Gorbachev.[28]

At its Congress in December 1986, the Vietnamese Communist Party dropped all explicit criticism of China and declared:

We hold that the time has come for the two sides to enter into negotiations to solve both immediate and long-term problems in the relationship between the two countries. Once again we officially declare that Vietnam is ready to negotiate with China at any time, at any level and in any place to normalise the relations between the two countries, in the interests of the two peoples, and of peace in Southeast Asia and the rest of the world.[29]

But at bottom the Vietnamese did not change the basic thrust of their policy towards China. The Congress reaffirmed that the main objectives of Vietnamese foreign policy were 'to defend the homeland, maintain political security, defeat the multi-faceted war of sabotage waged by the enemy, and continue our internationalist duty towards Cambodia and Laos'. Nobody in Beijing would have failed to recognize who Hanoi meant by 'the enemy'. The Congress also reaffirmed that 'solidarity and all-round cooperation' with the Soviet Union was the 'keystone' of Vietnamese foreign policy.

There had been some hopes that Beijing would soften its attitude towards the new leadership in Hanoi, but these hopes were disappointed. A Chinese commentator wrote in 1987:

> In foreign policy, Nguyen Van Linh is following the lead of Le Duan. ... Vietnam has taken no practical steps towards resuming normal relations with China ... and stubbornly clings to its position on the Cambodia problem, which is the main obstacle to normal relations between the two countries.[30]

There were four issues which had set Beijing at odds with Hanoi in 1978 – Cambodia, Vietnam's alliance with the Soviet Union, the status of the Hoa, and the South China Seas. The issue of the Hoa disappeared in 1980 when China renounced dual citizenship, abandoning any claim to the loyalties of the overseas Chinese. Beijing thus abandoned Hua Guofeng's aggressive stance on this issue in favour of the more conventional approach originally adopted by Zhou Enlai. As China moved towards detente with the USSR in 1985, it ceased to object to Hanoi's alliance with Moscow. This cut the areas of disagreement to two.

There were signs of a thaw in Chinese attitudes to Vietnam. The Vietnamese began to recall in public the support China had given them during the American war. The Chinese Embassy in Hanoi renewed contacts with the Vietnam–China Friendship Society, enabling it to engage in what the Vietnamese called 'people's diplomacy' even while spurning state-to-state contacts. In January 1989, when Vietnam proposed to pull its troops out of Cambodia, China agreed to negotiations with Vietnam at a vice-ministerial level. Tensions relaxed on the Sino-Vietnamese border, the last major clash occurring in 1986. By early 1989 cross-border trade had revived, and shops in Hanoi were once again stocked with many goods from China. By mid-1989 traders were crossing the border in their thousands. Markets were again booming in towns like Lang Son, where a decade before there had been only a wasteland of charred rubble. Hanoi was hopeful that these favourable trends would continue. The rhetoric of 'two thousand years of struggle' in favour in 1979 had been buried. In early 1989 one official said to us: 'The last ten years is a short time in the long history of friendship between our two peoples.'

China moved to restore its relations with Hanoi's Lao allies. In 1986 China responded positively to proposals from Laos to agreed to restore normal state-to-state relations. Laos expressed particular pleasure at China's agreement to end the support it had been giving to anti-government rebels in Laos since 1979. Hanoi responded by withdrawing its troops from Laos. In September 1989 party-to-party relations were normalized, and Kaysone visited Beijing in October. Deng Xiaoping greeted him, and said that China had improved relations with the Soviet Union and with Laos. 'Only Vietnam is left', said Deng. 'I don't understand why

Vietnam is against China.' He said that Vietnam had appealed to Beijing for an early normalization of relations. 'We have always held that the two countries will finally improve their relations, but there is a problem which is easy to solve', said Deng. 'That is, Vietnam withdraws its troops completely and thoroughly from Cambodia. We have no other demands. ... We are willing to improve our relations with Vietnam, but only when it withdraws its troops completely and thoroughly from Cambodia can we say "the past is ended".'[31]

But China also remained at odds with Vietnam over the South China Seas. In 1987 China proclaimed its right to recover the Spratlys 'at a suitable time'. Following a series of naval exercises, the Chinese began landing troops on two islands in the Spratlys in January 1988. Fighting erupted seven weeks later. The Vietnamese claimed that six Chinese war-ships attacked three Vietnamese freighters, sinking one of them, badly damaging two, and causing the loss of seventy-four men. The Chinese claimed that the Vietnamese had started the fighting, and that they them-selves fired only in self-defence. The Vietnamese called for negotiations to resolve this dispute. On 24 March the Chinese dismissed calls for nego-tiations as 'hypocrisy', saying China's sovereignty was 'indisputable'. The issue flared up again in April 1989, when Chinese forces occupied a further atoll.

China probably had three reasons for pressing this issue at this time. First, as it developed a blue-water naval capability both Beijing's interest in and ability to assert its control over the South China Sea islands was enhanced. According to Jerry Cushing:

A major objective for naval planners in Beijing is to build up adequate naval forces to secure China's interests all the way to the [Persian] Gulf from what is seen in Beijing as a rising potential threat from India's navy and from what is viewed as an ever-present Soviet threat.[32]

In this perspective the Spratlys must appear as assets of considerable strategic significance.

Second, the Chinese had to enforce their claim while Vietnam was still an international pariah, which meant before a Cambodia settlement, in order to minimize the reaction from the ASEAN countries. As it was, an ASEAN statement in July expressed concern that a fundamental change in the balance of power in the region would result if China conti-nued its military build-up. And, finally, it was a way of stepping up pres-sure on Vietnam at a time when serious negotiations were beginning on Cambodia. It is scarcely coincidence that the Chinese action in the Spratlys began on the day (20 January 1988) talks opened between Hun Sen and Sihanouk in Paris.

While the Vietnamese reiterated their claims to both the Paracels and the Spratlys, and pushed for negotiations, they did not attempt to drive the Chinese off the islands they had taken. A Vietnamese official later said that Hanoi did not wish to inflame the situation, and that in reality the Chinese were more flexible than their propaganda indicated. If relations between Hanoi and Beijing could be improved, that would open the way to a settlement of issues such as the Spratlys. 'In a friendly relationship a big problem becomes a small one,' he said. 'In a hostile relationship a small problem becomes a big one.'

The Soviets were also low-key in their response to the 1988 Spratlys crisis. This has led some western commentators to say that they refused to support the Vietnamese. In fact, the Soviets called for negotiations – which was the Vietnamese position. In addition, they were 'quietly helpful to the Vietnamese' during the crisis: 'The Soviets have provided Hanoi with aerial and satellite reconnaissance of Chinese naval movements, enabling the Vietnamese to beef up their defences'.[33] Gorbachev, trying to cut back on the big-spenders in the Soviet navy, can hardly relish the prospect of Chinese naval expansion any more than Hanoi does.

By the late 1980s, US policies showed little sign of change. After the Vladivostok speech, the Reagan administration feared that a Sino-Soviet detente would largely exclude US influence from mainland Southeast Asia. It began cautiously to distance itself from Chinese policy, while at the same time still trying to counter Soviet influence. This led to a decision to move quietly towards normalizing relations with Hanoi. Vietnam welcomed this enthusiastically. 'The USA has an important role to play to bring about peace and stability in Southeast Asia', declared Radio Hanoi. 'The Vietnamese people are prepared to turn a new chapter of history and to facilitate the development of relations of friendship and co-operation between the two peoples.'

But little came of this. The outstanding problem, for many Americans, was the servicemen missing in action. A retired general, John Vessey, was sent to Hanoi in August 1987 as a special presidential emissary to negotiate the matter. He signed an agreement in which the Vietnamese promised to cooperate in the search for MIAs, and the USA expressed willingness to 'address certain urgent humanitarian concerns of Vietnam'. However the USA would not establish diplomatic relations with Vietnam until it pulled its troops out of Cambodia. Fourteen years after the end of the Vietnam war US trade with Vietnam was still banned under the Trading with the Enemy Act.

A few businessmen complained that they were losing a potential market to their less ideological competitors. A few Republicans complained that Washington's rigid attitude meant it was squandering a chance to coax an important nation out of the Soviet orbit. But these were isolated voices.

At the end of the Reagan presidency US policy towards Vietnam remained, in the words of a conservative critic, mired in a 'sterile mixture of spite, bitterness and guilt' which was not 'worthy of a superpower'.[34] The Bush administration brought little change to this in 1989. It preferred to make support for the 'democratic revolution' in Cambodia the centre-piece of its Indochina policy.

For Hanoi, then, the situation it faced as the 1980s came to a close was bearable – if necessary. But a decisive breakthrough depended on a resolution of the Cambodian issue.

Notes

1. Quoted by Doyle McManus, *Age* (Melbourne), 17 June 1985.
2. Quoted by Elizabeth Becker, *When the War Was Over*, New York 1986, p. 440.
3. John W. Garver, 'The Reagan Administration's Southeast Asian Policy', in James C. Hsiung, ed., *US–Asian Relations: The National Security Paradox*, New York 1983, p. 114.
4. Bob Woodward, *VEIL: The Secret Wars of the CIA*, New York 1987, pp. 215–16.
5. John F. Cropper, 'China and Southeast Asia', *Current History*, December 1984, pp. 405–6.
6. Thomas W. Robinson, 'The New Era in Sino-Soviet Relations', *Current History*, September 1987, p. 242.
7. For a useful summary of debates in Moscow and Washington on these matters, see David E. Albright, 'The USSR and the Third World in the 1980s', *Problems of Communism*, March–June 1989.
8. Martin Walker, *The Waking Giant: The Soviet Union under Gorbachev*, London 1987, pp. 116–17.
9. Gregory D. Knight, 'China's Soviet Policy in the Gorbachev Era', *Washington Quarterly*, vol. 9, 1985, p. 97.
10. Richard Nations, *Far Eastern Economic Review*, 30 May 1985.
11. Quoted by Carlyle A. Thayer, 'Kampuchea: Soviet Initiatives and Regional Responses', in Ramesh Thakur and Carlyle A. Thayer, eds, *The Soviet Union as an Asian Pacific Power*, Boulder 1987, p. 187. The full text of the Vladivostok speech is included as an appendix to this volume.
12. Leszek Buszynski, 'Soviet Foreign Policy and Southeast Asia: Prospects for the Gorbachev Era', *Asian Survey*, vol. 26, 1986, p. 597.
13. David Lampton, 'China's Limited Accommodation with the USSR: Coalition Politics', *AEI Foreign Policy and Defence Review*, vol. 6, 1986.
14. Gerald Segal, 'Sino-Soviet Relations: the New Agenda', *World Today*, June 1988, p. 95.
15. Robert Delfs, *Far Eastern Economic Review*, 3 November 1988.
16. Yu Gang, 'World Impact of Sino-Soviet Normalisation', *Beijing Review*, 8–14 May 1989.
17. Economist Intelligence Unit, *Indochina: Vietnam, Laos, Cambodia: Country Report*, no. 1, London 1989, p. 2.
18. See 'Vietnam's Quest for Foreign Investment: A Bold Move', *Indochina Issues*, no. 80, March 1988, for the text of the code and a commentary.
19. David Marr, *Far Eastern Economic Review*, 3 November 1988.
20. Adam Fforde, *Far Eastern Economic Review*, 14 September 1989.
21. Quoted by Roland Pierre Paringaux, *Guardian Weekly*, 26 March 1989, reprinted from *Le Monde*. For good overviews of the boat people problem, see Alexander Casella, 'The Refugees from Vietnam: Rethinking the Issue', *World Today*, August–September 1989,

and Carlyle A. Thayer, 'Vietnamese Refugees: Why the Outflow Continues', in Amin Saikal, ed., *Refugees in the Modern World*, Canberra 1989.

22. Nayan Chanda, *Far Eastern Economic Review*, 14 June 1984.

23. *Bangkok Post*, 16 February 1985.

24. Richard Nations, *Far Eastern Economic Review*, 30 May 1985.

25. Jonathan D. Pollack, *Far Eastern Economic Review*, 22 September 1988.

26. Sophie Quinn-Judge, *Far Eastern Economic Review*, 4 June 1987.

27. Le Tinh, *Quan Doi Nhan Dan*, 13 October 1987. The Vietnamese–Soviet Agreement on Basic Principles for Setting up Joint Entities was published in *Nhan Dan*, 23 November 1987.

28. Nayan Chanda, *Far Eastern Economic Review*, 31 January 1985.

29. *6th National Congress of the Communist Party of Vietnam (15–18 December 1986): Documents*, Hanoi 1987, p. 128.

30. Ji Wen, *Beijing Review*, 20 July 1987.

31. Xinhua, 7 October 1989.

32. Jerry Cushing, *Far Eastern Economic Review*, 5 May 1988.

33. *Far Eastern Economic Review*, 24 March 1988.

34. John Le Boutillier, quoted by George Black, 'Good Morning Vietnam: Republican Overtures to Hanoi', *Nation*, 4 June 1988.

10

Towards the Golden Peninsula?

Like Vietnam, Thailand had reacted to the great-power polarization of the early 1980s by aligning its policies closely with those of its great-power allies and protectors (in this case, the USA and China). As the tensions of the New Cold War eased, Thailand began to inch back towards the policy of 'balance' between the great powers that it had pursued before the Cambodia crisis of 1978–79. As it did so, relations with Laos warmed dramatically. Relations with Vietnam also improved as Hanoi progressed towards a withdrawal from Cambodia.

Thailand Changes Tack

In the late 1980s Thai leaders were much more confident about their nation's security than they had been a decade earlier. The whole international political climate was more relaxed, the Communist insurgency in Thailand was dead, Vietnamese troops in Laos were going home. The Thai economy was booming. Claims that Thailand was the 'next domino' lost much credibility. As a middle-ranking regional power, Thailand could once more seek to advance its interests by developing multi-polar relationships. Indeed, only part of the balanced foreign policy of the 1970s had been destroyed by the Cambodia crisis; Bangkok had continued to develop relations with China through the decade without sacrificing its relationship with the USA. As both Beijing and Washington were already moving towards detente within Moscow, Thailand was hardly being adventurous in deciding it could follow suit. And as Moscow came to be seen in less Manichaean terms, its local allies likewise appeared less menacing. As before the collapse of the 1970s detente, some Thai leaders tried to turn their country's relations with the Communist countries of Indochina from Cold War confrontation into a more constructive engagement.

There were economic as well as political motives for such a turn in the Thai approach to Indochina. Influential Thai businessmen were eyeing the natural sources, markets and investment opportunities that the Indo-chinese countries could offer, especially as Thailand's forest and marine resources were being depleted rapidly. Such thinking was encouraged by Vietnam's economic reforms. The Thai also noted that the Indonesians were taking advantage of the opening door in Vietnam, and feared that unless they joined in they would be left behind.

However, such a shift in Thai policy went against established policies and deeply entrenched attitudes in Bangkok. General Prem Tinsulanond, prime minister since 1980, had left foreign policy to his foreign minister, Siddhi Sawetsila. Siddhi and his ministry were firmly wedded to the hard-line anti-Vietnamese approach. So were many army officers whose whole careers had been moulded by the struggle against Communism.

Shevardnadze's visit to Bangkok in early 1987 was well received, and Siddhi and the commander-in-chief of the armed forces, General Chaovalit Yongchiyudh, followed up with visits to Moscow. Siddhi seems to have remained steadfastly unimpressed with the Gorbachev–Shevard-nadze approach to policy. But before he left for Moscow in November 1987 Chaovalit declared that the army rejected the Foreign Ministry view that conflicts within Cambodia had been a mere pretext for an aggressive Vietnam to invade. He said that the 'correct perception' of the Cambodian conflict was that it was a 'civil war' between two Cambodian Communist factions. The Soviet Union would inevitably play a role in finding a solu-tion, he said, implying that it had established its position as a great power in the region.

For those unaware of how swiftly great-power relations were evolving, this was real heresy. 'Chaovalit cannot be serious!' spluttered an editorial writer for the Bangkok *Nation*. The Thai Foreign Ministry declared that Chaovalit was only expressing a 'personal view', and Siddhi warned that his statement could 'confuse' ASEAN on the Cambodia issue. Over the next couple of years, it often seemed that Thailand was running two foreign policies simultaneously – Siddhi's and Chaovalit's. While he was in Moscow, Chaovalit discussed the Cambodian conflict, the US war-reserve stockpile in Thailand, and Cam Ranh Bay with Soviet military leaders. On his return to Bangkok, Chaovalit declared that he was pulling Thai troops back from the Cambodian border, except in sensitive regions. A couple of weeks later, Hanoi announced its plan to pull Vietnamese troops back from the border as well.

Prime Minister Prem followed this up by visiting Moscow in May 1988. The Soviets told him of Vietnam's planned troop withdrawal from Cambo-dia, and Prem returned, it was reported, with a radically new perception of the Cambodian problem, and a conviction that the Soviets were genuinely trying to resolve the issue.[1] By this time, however, Prem was in political trouble at home. He dissolved parliament in April, and called an early election for July, and refused to serve a further term as prime minister. When the Thai parliament opened in August 1988, Major-General Chatichai Choonhavan became the new prime minister. Chatichai's government was at first shaky, but quickly consolidated its position. This accelerated the shift in Thai policy. Chatichai kept Siddhi on as foreign minister (his was a coalition government, and he needed Siddhi's support in parliament); but he made it clear that he would play an active role in setting Thailand's course in foreign policy. Chatichai supported Chaovalit's initiatives, and made a famous speech declaring that his objective was to turn Indochina 'from a battleground into a market'.

In a speech on 25 January 1989 Chaovalit set out an even more ambitious vision. As peace and stability were established in mainland Southeast Asia, Bangkok was strategically placed to serve as the main business centre not only for Thailand, but for Indochina and Burma as well. Thai capital could help build mainland Asia into a region of prosperity as well as peace, into a 'Golden Land'. To some observers, in Bangkok as well as in neighbouring capitals, there were unpleasant echoes of the 'pan-Thai' military expansionism of the 1930s and 1940s in Chaovalit's vision. This was especially so as, under Chaovalit, the Thai military had developed an offensive military capability; it no longer aimed to deter an attack from Indochina by border defences, but by counter-attacking across Laos into central Vietnam. But Chaovalit and Chatichai stressed that their purposes were defensive, and they had no expansionist ambitions. 'Our aim', said Chaovalit's deputy, General Pat Akkanibutr, on 9 February 1989, 'is to bring peace and prosperity to peoples in this region. Thailand will not dominate other countries but rather it will serve as a centre for them all.'

Siddhi had spurned talks with Vietnamese Foreign Minister Nguyen Co Thach unless he had 'something concrete' to offer on the Cambodian conflict. When Vietnam announced a major troop withdrawal from Cambodia in May 1988, Siddhi invited Thach to Bangkok for talks which lasted two days – the first time that Thailand and Vietnam had engaged in substantive discussions, rather than point-scoring, since 1979. For the first time the Vietnamese and the Thai said they had found 'common ground' on Cambodia.

Towards the end of 1988 Chaovalit proposed to follow through Thach's successful visit to Bangkok by visiting Hanoi himself. Siddhi persuaded him that this was a job for the foreign minister, and so it was Siddhi who made the historic trip to Hanoi in January 1989. The number of businessmen who accompanied him nonetheless underscored the shift in

Thai orientation from ideological–military concerns to a search for economic opportunity.

A detente between Bangkok and Hanoi, admittedly tentative, thus flowed from the easing of Cold War tensions. It was not Vietnam – let alone Cambodia – which was the first beneficiary of this development, but Laos.

Laos between Vietnam and Thailand

Lao foreign policy options remained as restricted as ever. Vientiane clung to its alliance with Vietnam, and looked for signs of improvement in relations in Thailand, China and the West. At last, this began to happen.

The 'special relationship' between Vietnam and Laos remained strong. Party-to-party consultations, military cooperation, trade and economic assistance continued as before. When Vietnam and Laos finally signed a border delimitation agreement, there were the usual assertions that Hanoi had annexed large slabs of Lao territory. As usual, no evidence was presented to support these claims.

The agreement flowed from a commitment to finalizing their borders made in Article 4 of their 1977 treaty of friendship. The negotiations were reported to be tough and occasionally heated,[2] which hardly supports the claim of abject servility on the Lao part. However, the basic reason for the length of the process of border determination seems to have been the fact that it runs through some of the most rugged territory in the region, making accurate surveying a lengthy business. The key point about these negotiations was that there was no disagreement on basic principles. Both sides accepted the original French maps as the basis for defining the border. The agreement signed was one which delineated the border, while demarcation of an area approximating 1,000 square kilometres along the 2,000-kilometre border remained outstanding. Thus in June 1987 the two sides signed a memorandum on border demarcation, and a supplementary protocol on the delineation of the border in areas where rivers and streams form the boundary was agreed in 1987. The Lao had every reason to be satisfied with the negotiations. Not only were they conducted according to shared principles, but they also took place at the highest levels of government. The Vietnamese approach to these matters contrasted favourably with that of the Thai, with whom the Lao had continuing border problems.

By early 1986 Vientiane was soft-peddling its difficulties with Bangkok in an attempt to improve trade between the two countries. Significant economic liberalization in Laos partly depended for its success on improved market exchange with Thailand and foreign markets generally.

Business groups in the Thai northeast and also in Bangkok responded by lobbying the Thai government for improved business opportunities along the border where, in 1985, the value of smuggled goods was reported to be far in excess of official Thai exports to Laos.[3]

In March the Thai Foreign Ministry refused requests from two border provinces to open trading posts with Laos, but it did allow the easing of quotas on some items. Simultaneously, however, the hardline secretary general of Thailand's National Security Council, Prasong Soonsiri, accused the Lao government of producing heroin and opium and smuggling it to Thailand. The Lao rejected the charges, claiming they were a device to 'cause Lao–Thai relations to remain tense'. But growing formal and informal trade across the border could not be ignored in Bangkok, and following bilateral talks in November Thailand agreed to cut its list of banned 'strategic items' from 273 to 61. In return Laos allowed Thai businessmen to cooperate with state industries in lieu of a code on foreign investment. Part of the background to the warming of relations between the two countries was the fall in May 1986 of army strong-man Arthit Khamlang-Ek, who had presided over the three-villages dispute.

But in early 1987 relations between the two countries stalled. In March Lao Deputy Foreign Minister Soubanh Srithirath visited Bangkok in an attempt to negotiate all outstanding issues between the two governments. But, as Soubanh told one of the authors just before his visit, the problem of the 'three villages' was the 'key problem for Laos'.[4] Lao national security was undermined by a situation in which the Thai refused to define the border and applied military pressure selectively in disputed parts. But the Thai refused to acknowledge the importance of this. They were thus shocked when Soubanh publicly accused them of not negotiating seriously. The Thai were stung by such precociousness from their Lao 'little brother', and the talks broke up amid recriminations.

The importance of the border issue was soon underscored by the most serious Thai–Lao border dispute since World War II, when Bangkok had taken advantage of the Japanese occupation of Indochina to seize Sayaboury province from Laos. The dispute was once again on the land border between Sayaboury province and Thailand's Phitsanalok province. It occurred around the headwaters of the Nam Heung River, a remote and rugged area inhabited largely by former Hmong members of the Communist Party of Thailand, and where there was much illegal logging. The immediate causes of the conflict are murky and have not been investigated on the ground, although they were tied up with illegal Thai logging in Lao forests. According to reports from Bangkok, Thai foresters had stopped paying protection money to local Lao soldiers, and began using either Thai soldiers or the paramilitary Hmong for protection. According to the Lao side 'warlords of the Thai Third Army Region' were protecting

Thai who were illegally logging in Sayaboury province. Whatever the reason, in May 1987 Lao soldiers had a shoot-out with Thai rangers, destroyed logging equipment, captured five Thai loggers, and occupied the village of Ban Rom Klao. The Lao called on the Thai to acknowledge that this village was part of Laos. The Thai refused. Soon all the unresolved issues previously associated with the 1984 three-villages dispute resurfaced.

The Lao called for negotiations in August but received no response from Thailand until 25 December. Meanwhile, on 4 September the Thai Foreign Ministry released a 'clarification' of its understanding of the border, claiming that the evidence clearly showed the disputed area was in Thailand and that 'the problem regarding the border incident between Thailand and Laos in the Phitsanalok and Loei border area has ended'. But nothing had been agreed on a government-to-government basis, and both sides continued to reinforce their troops in the area. In early November the Thai launched 'Operation Phu Soi Dao' to retake key hills controlled by Lao forces. When initial attempts failed, the Thai side escalated the fighting, bringing in aircraft to bomb Lao positions in December.

The Thai army had boldly promised that it would throw the Lao out of the disputed territory in a few days, but after weeks of fighting they had not achieved this. Embarrassed, the Thai claimed that Hanoi was behind the dispute and that Vietnamese soldiers were involved in the fighting. No evidence was furnished to prove this charge. By early January 1988 around seventy Thai soldiers and an unknown number of Lao had died in the clashes. Right-wing demonstrators in Bangkok and the provinces, and much of the Thai press, were by then clamouring for the expulsion of the Lao 'intruders'.

As the dispute mounted, the Lao side accused 'ultra-rightist reactionaries in Thai ruling circles' of 'pan-Thai' ambitions. Soubanh called the clashes the most serious since the Communist victory. Vientiane called for unconditional negotiations, but the Thai side insisted that the Lao first withdraw from the disputed area, and said Soubanh was not acceptable as a negotiator for the Lao. Vientiane rejected the idea that Bangkok could veto whom it put forward to negotiate with the Thai. With passions running high on both sides and diplomacy deadlocked, a head-on confrontation was inevitable. For the first two weeks of February 1988 the Thai and Lao armies were engaged in artillery duels and fierce fighting, including air-strikes by Thai planes, something they had never done on the Cambodian border. This still failed to dislodge the Lao troops. Casualties among Thai soldiers, and embarrassment among their commanders, were rising rapidly.

Lao Prime Minister Kaysone Phomvihane issued a direct appeal to General Prem for discussions between the opposing military commanders, thus bypassing the diplomats. Delegations led by General Sisavat Keobounphan on the Lao side and Chaovalit on the Thai side quickly negotiated a ceasefire and a mutual withdrawal from the disputed territory, coming into effect on 19 February. Sisavat implied that the Lao were not as certain of their border claims as they had been over the three villages when he said: 'Laos has few people and much territory. We don't need additional territory.' Chaovalit said of the ceasefire: 'The result of this meeting is the basis for a historic change in Thai–Lao relations.'

Since this intense border dispute, Thai–Lao relations have rapidly improved. Why is this so? The three-villages dispute in 1984 was less bloody. The propaganda war between Bangkok and Vientiane was intense, and emotions were inflamed on both sides. On the Thai side, even a moderate figure like the former prime minister, Kukrit Pramoj, was moved to urge that Thai troops cross the Mekong and put Vientiane to the torch; to associate with Laos, he said, is 'like raising an untamed gibbon. It will turn on its owner unexpectedly while he is hugging it.' Exuding the worst Thai arrogance towards Laos, he went on: 'Laos does not think that deeply. They are very backward and make simple statements and have no sense of formality.'[5] And articles in the Thai press showing most of Laos and parts of Cambodia as areas lost by Bangkok as a result of 'unequal treaties' can only have aggravated Lao fears of 'pan-Thaism'.[6] Despite all this, the rapidly changing regional diplomacy, and internal political changes taking place in Bangkok, ensured a settlement.

For a start, the Lao were careful never to suggest that Thailand was in collusion with China, as it had charged in the earlier dispute. Behind this there lay the fact of improving Sino-Lao relations since 1986. Following Gorbachev's Vladivostok speech, Vientiane had – like Hanoi, but with greater success – appealed for improved relations with Beijing. In December the Chinese deputy foreign minister, Liu Shuqing, visited Vientiane to lay the basis for full normalization in November 1987 during the visit of a Lao delegation to the Chinese capital. Vientiane was especially pleased when China dropped its support for the anti-government insurgents in Laos. At the end of 1988 Laos and China agreed to grant each other most favoured nation status and drew up their first trade agreement since the early 1960s. Cross-border trade began to boom.

The Sino-Lao *rapprochement* was followed immediately by withdrawals of Vietnamese troops from Laos. As it was seen in Vientiane, with the 'Chinese threat' evaporating, Vietnamese forces were no longer needed in Laos. Vientiane also had reason to be satisfied with the performance of its own army in fighting the Thai to a stand-off on the Nam Heung River. On 25 February 1988 the Lao government announced that Vietnam had begun pulling out more than half of the 40,000 troops it had stationed in Laos. 'The Vietnamese troops, who are here in accordance with a bilateral agreement, are leaving because we are increasingly able to defend ourselves', said a Lao spokesman. By the end of the year the Lao government announced that all Vietnamese troops had been withdrawn.

This made things difficult for those who argued that the Lao People's Democratic Republic (LPDR) was a 'government under guard' with the Vietnamese army there to enforce Hanoi's 'ultimate control' of Laos. There was neither a popular uprising against the LPDR nor any changes in its leadership as the 'Vietnamese grip' on Laos relaxed. In contrast to both Vietnam and Cambodia, the LPDR in the late 1980s was controlled by the same elite as in 1976–77. Stuart-Fox has claimed that the Lao are now 'less willing to accept Vietnamese advice'.[7] But there is no sign of any real political dissonance between Hanoi and the LPDR leaders. Close party-to-party consultations have continued.

The chief divergence was that Laos carried through market-socialist reforms more quickly, more thoroughly, and more successfully in the early 1980s than Vietnam. So far as one can tell, they were applauded in Hanoi for this.[8] Vientiane's growing self-confidence saw it conduct its first nation-wide elections in 1989. As external pressures relaxed, the government sought to consolidate its internal legitimacy, but this led to no recognizable policy divergence from Hanoi.

Since the Thai had seen the Vietnamese military presence in Cambodia as the principal threat to their national security, the withdrawal greatly pleased the Thai. By comparison, the bloody dispute on the Nam Heung suddenly seemed only a minor irritant. Bilateral relations between Thailand and Laos had always taken place in the shadow of China, and the thaw in Beijing's relations with Vientiane immediately spilled over into improved Thai–Lao relations. Those in Bangkok who saw a sinister Vietnamese hand behind every manifestation of Communist nationalism in Laos were suddenly disarmed.

Laos became a testing ground for overall regional attempts to lower tensions and work towards a resolution of the Cambodian conflict. Made possible by relatively independent developments in Sino-Lao and Thai–Lao relations, the withdrawal of Vietnamese troops from Laos was also a confidence-building measure *vis-à-vis* Vietnam's promises to withdraw all its troops from Cambodia.

Internal developments in Thailand also sped up the improvement in relations with Laos. Chaovalit began promoting the expansion of Thai–Lao ties, and when Chatichai came into office in mid-1988 Laos was an obvious target of his policy of turning battlefields into markets. The rapid warming of relations was consolidated when Chatichai visited Vientiane in late November, the first visit by a Thai prime minister since Kriangsak's visit in 1979. During these talks they agreed on mechanisms for resolving their border problems, agreed to exchange military attachés, and on the need to build a bridge across the Mekong to facilitate trade. The Mekong River was to become, they declared, a 'border of peace and development'. New trading points along the Thai–Lao border were being opened in 1988–89. The volume of Lao–Thai trade grew by a staggering 26 per cent in 1988. The list of items whose export to Laos was banned by Thailand, which had stood at over 250 in the early 1980s, was finally abolished in a Thai–Lao trade agreement signed on 6 October 1989.

In April 1988 the LPDR passed a foreign investment law modelled on Vietnam's. There was a rush of Thai businessmen to Vientiane to check out the opportunities there. This did not always go well. Among them were some unscrupulous operators whose aim seemed to be to fleece the Lao before they had a chance to become worldly-wise. The noted Thai social critic Sulak Sivaraksa commented: 'The apparent haste to tap our neighbouring countries' rich natural resources smacks of the exploitative nature of the Japanese and South Koreans.' And Chatichai himself felt it necessary to warn businessmen to 'avoid unilateral exploitation' and to seek 'two-way' deals which would serve the interests of all parties. Signs of Lao discontent with Thai entrepreneurs emerged in mid-year with a broadcast that seemed to open old wounds: 'Having failed to destroy our country through their military might, the enemy has now employed a new strategy in attacking us through the so-called attempt to turn the Indochinese battlefield into a marketplace ... because their armed provocations were ineffective.' The Lao response, however, has not been to freeze its new ties with Thailand but to try to diversify its foreign sources of capital and trade.

Lao relations with Vietnam remained strong, however. At long last Route 9, from Savannakhet to Da Nang, was virtually completed in 1988, with the final asphalting to be completed in 1989. While this route will not reduce Lao use of Klong Touey port in Bangkok, it ensured Laos greater all-round access to world markets. Furthermore, as Thai relations with Indochina improved this road was seen less as a threat, and more as a potential route into the Vietnamese market from Thailand.

The tenth anniversary of the Lao–Vietnamese friendship treaty was duly celebrated in 1987, but as the era of confrontation and threats receded, it was of diminishing relevance to both Hanoi and Vientiane. This is not to say it was collapsing. Vietnamese and Lao officials both stressed that their alliance had served them well, and would continue – but for both countries the emphasis would be on diversifying their foreign relations rather than bloc alignments, and on economic relations rather than ones based on military security considerations. A number of committees devoted to encouraging cooperation among the Indochinese countries were wound down as opportunities for wider multilateral relations opened up. But when Nguyen Van Linh made his first state visit to Laos in July 1989 neither side thought it incongruous to affirm once again 'the fine development of the time-honoured special relations between the LPRP and the VCP, and the PRP of Kampuchea'.

One of the keys to improved relations with the West for Laos is its relationship with the USA. Here there was no significant movement under the second Reagan administration or the first year of the Bush administration. American attentions were focused elsewhere. Fitful discussions of the issues concerning missing US servicemen (MIAs) continued, and some excavations were carried out. The Lao requested, with increasing irritation, that the humanitarian concerns of the Lao as well as of the Americans be recognized as well. The USA finally promised in late 1987 to give some aid 'within the limits of its capabilities', but the begrudging tone of this pledge warned the Lao not to expect much.

In May 1988 relations took a turn for the worse when the US State Department accused the LPDR of trafficking in narcotics 'as a matter of policy'. When the Lao government brought fifty drug traffickers (Thai nationals and Lao from the northern province of Oudomsay) to justice in August, the Americans claimed that it had done this only in response to US diplomatic pressure. Yet, after these grave allegations, the State Department admitted 'we don't have the smoking gun' on LPDR involvement in the drug trade. For what it is worth, most independent observers believe that – since the collapse of Vang Pao's 'secret army' – the vast bulk of heroin produced in the 'Golden Triangle' originates in Burma, and most of the rest in northern Thailand. The fact that only a trickle is believed to originate in Laos suggests that what narcotics trafficking does occur there does not enjoy government support.[9]

The evolution of Laos's relationship with Vietnam underscores a central argument of this book: relations between modern states are best understood in terms of shifting historical conjunctures, and not ancient enmities or friendships, or secretive plans for 'federations' hatched in dramatically different historical contexts. This myth-mongering has made for colourful propaganda, but has only obstructed understanding of how the alliance between the governments of Communist Indochina actually operated in the 1980s – and of how it changed as the context changed as well.

Strengthening the Phnom Penh Government

Nowhere has this had more tragic consequences than in Cambodia. Propagandists of the Coalition Government of Democratic Kampuchea (CGDK) depicted the administration in Phnom Penh as a puppet regime

which has overseen the eclipse of Cambodian independence. Unfortunately many western writers who should know better have rehashed this
propaganda line. Elizabeth Becker asserts: 'Each year ... has produced
humiliating orders from the Vietnamese overlords.' She argues that the
Khmer Rouge has been the 'undeserving benefactors' of Vietnam's
occupation policies, thus conveniently distracting criticism from those
who have actively supported the Khmer Rouge.[10] Nayan Chanda recognized that Hanoi's policy was not to destroy Cambodian cultural and
political life, as the CGDK claimed, but to create 'a new Khmer state,
a government and party institutions'. Chanda asserted that this meant
'consolidating Vietnamese control'.[11] The logic of this is evident only
to those who equated an independent Cambodian state exclusively with
one of the *ancien régimes* represented by the CGDK. Most importantly,
however, Chanda implied that this effort to build a new state in Cambodia
would fail in the face of the remorseless campaign of disruption by guerrillas backed by Beijing and Bangkok.

We saw in chapter 8 that although the CGDK insurgency was serious,
it was much weaker than many western commentators suggested. The
key to the strategy set out by General Anh was to take advantage of
this to allow a friendly government to consolidate its position, so that
it could stand on its own and enable Vietnam to withdraw.

We can consider the success of this attempt at regime-building in terms
of the economic base, and the political and military capability, of the
government Vietnam was backing: the People's Republic of Kampuchea
(PRK) – which changed its name to the State of Cambodia in 1989.

Lack of statistics prevents a precise description of the course of economic developments under the PRK. However, the basic pattern seems
clear. A high birth rate meant that the population recovered rapidly from
the demographic catastrophe of the 1970s. By the late 1980s the population
had reached 8 million, while that of Phnom Penh had risen to around
800,000. In the early 1980s, production increased more rapidly than population, but then slowed. Agriculture accounted for most of the Cambodian
economy, and here output rose rapidly in the early 1980s, as villagers
struggled to secure their basic subsistence requirements. Once that had
been achieved in most of the country, the forward movement slowed.
Productivity was low, and the peasants had little incentive to produce
a surplus over their subsistence requirement. In the simplest terms, after
1983 a subsistence economy grew as the population grew.

The reality was, of course, more complicated than this. As government
officials stressed, growth was hampered by shortages of draft animals,
fertilizer, irrigation, and able-bodied men. The ability to overcome these
problems was reduced as western aid wound down. In the northwest,
near the Thai border, continued fighting, and the planting of land-mines

in particular, disrupted agriculture. But the core of Cambodia's economic problem was the failure to advance beyond a basic subsistence economy.

This left the towns and the government itself with a precarious economic base. Towns in Cambodia had traditionally been market centres, but they were limited in the extent to which they could fulfil this function. The government adopted a laissez faire approach to private trade, but transport and communications were very poor. Internationally, most governments tried to punish Cambodia as well as Vietnam for the overthrow of Pol Pot's government. The PRK was denied normal commercial as well as diplomatic relations with western countries.

Government officials tried to boost production by working to restore the irrigation infrastructure, and providing fertilizers and other inputs. They tried to squeeze a surplus out of the peasant economy by introducing a land tax in 1983, and compulsory deliveries of produce to the state in 1984. By 1987 it seemed clear that these administrative means had not provided a satisfactory solution to these problems.

Nevertheless a slow, if unsteady, recovery was occurring. Drought badly affected the harvest in 1987. But in 1988 the rice harvest (2.5 million tonnes) exceeded the pre-war (1969) harvest for the first time. This was less impressive than it appeared, since the harvest had now to feed a population 20 per cent larger. If Cambodia still appeared run down and shabby by comparison with the pre-war years, life had improved considerably from the desperate years immediately after 1979 – not to mention the charnel-house years that preceded them. People were visibly better dressed and fed than they had been in the early 1980s, and, at least in the towns, they were better housed. Food and consumer goods were available in the markets. Wages were low, but the riel held its value well. Cambodia was not affected by the hyper-inflation that racked Vietnam in 1985–88.

But there were still many problems. The poorest provinces still suffered serious food shortages. In the provinces near the Thai border, notably Pursat and Battambang, fishing and farming were seriously disrupted by guerrilla activities. The indiscriminate spreading of anti-personnel land-mines by CGDK forces seemed to be aimed more at economic disruption and terrorizing civilians than at achieving any discernible military objective. Everywhere public health conditions were poor. The country's infrastructure was in a state of disrepair, but the government was unable to tackle this problem. It had difficulty paying adequate salaries to its public servants. Probably half the state budget was eaten up by defence.

As administrative measures failed to provide the government with a secure economic base, it had to rely on market forces. In the early 1980s the Cambodians had not built up a Soviet-type command economy – PRK policies were then markedly more liberal those of Vietnam. In the late 1980s they re-emphasized the importance of market forces. In June

1988 the government announced further measures of liberalization, and began issuing legal titles to land and property. This stimulated substantial growth, at least in the commercial and handicraft sectors. There was some apprehension that this might lead to peasants mortgaging their land to merchants and moneylenders, and falling into a 'debt trap'.

Cambodia's 'official' foreign trade was with Soviet-bloc countries. The Soviet Union itself accounted for over 80 per cent of Cambodia's foreign trade. Imports expanded rapidly in the early 1980s, exports much more slowly. Most of the country's supply of fuel, automobiles, irrigation equipment and its textiles came from Soviet-bloc countries. After 1985 the tendency was for imports from Soviet bloc countries to stop growing, while Cambodian exports to them (mostly of rubber) continued to grow. Even so Cambodia faced a large deficit and was dependent on Soviet aid to finance it.

Under Gorbachev the Soviet Union continued to provide aid worth $130 million a year to Cambodia. In April 1986, the USSR and the PRK signed a new aid agreement covering the years 1986–90. But, as with Vietnam, Gorbachev sought to reorientate Soviet aid from grants towards projects which would pay their way with produce. For all the propaganda about Vietnamese domination, in the late 1980s the Soviet presence was more obvious to visitors than the Vietnamese presence. There was little sign that the Soviet Union intended to pull out of Cambodia – though there were plenty that it would welcome western countries joining in Cambodia's post-war reconstruction.

While trade with Cambodia was officially proscribed by most countries outside the Soviet bloc, a large volume of international trade was carried on 'unofficially' across the Thai–Cambodian border. In the early 1980s this was largely centred on the sector of the border north of Aranyapratet. It was tolerated partly because the resistance groups were able to build themselves up by 'taxing' the trade, but mainly because business interests in Thailand found it profitable. Many of these goods were re-exported from Cambodia, and in the early 1980s many western consumer goods on sale in Hanoi had found their way to the Vietnamese capital via the Thai–Cambodian border.

The Vietnamese/PRK military offensive of 1984–85 shattered the institutional basis of this trade. It did not dry up, however, but simply relocated and became a maritime trade. Thai merchants began shipping goods to the Cambodian port of Koh Kong. This had the happy consequence of eliminating the dubious middlemen who had controlled the land-border trade, and quickly proved a mutually satisfactory arrangement for both the Thai and the Cambodians. By the late 1980s a rapidly increasing volume of Cambodian seafoods, spices and timber products was being exported to ASEAN countries by this 'unofficial' route. By 1989 some observers thought that the value of this two-way trade might be $20 million.

The PRK established a tourism service in 1986, and hoped it would be able to attract an increasing number of foreign visitors as the country returned to normal. To develop a tourist industry, however, it needed foreign investment. Here it has had some successes. The Soviets began refurbishing the Cambodian Hotel, a luxury hotel whose construction had been started in 1968 and suspended in 1970. But the Soviets stepped aside when a businessman and former movie star from Hong Kong, Huy Kung, proposed to complete the construction and refurbish the hotel in return for a twenty-year lease. Businessmen from Japan, Thailand, Singapore and South Korea were also quietly sounding out investment opportunities in Cambodia by 1987–88, and in July 1988 the Phnom Penh government decided to draw up a foreign investment code similar to Vietnam's.

The Phnom Penh government was thus slowly securing a stronger economic base. Its administrative capacity was also improving. In 1979 small groups of overworked and inexperienced officials had struggled to create a government out of chaos. The acute shortage of capable personnel was met only with the help of Vietnamese advisers. By the mid-1980s almost all of these had been withdrawn. They left behind a core of Cambodian officials who had learnt on the job, buttressed by a steady stream of Cambodians returned from higher education and training in the USSR and Eastern Europe. In 1986 a Bangkok observer wrote:

> Should one day a national reconciliation government be formed ... the core of the ministries would have to come from the PRK, with a few people from [the Democratic Kampuchea (DK) regime, the Front Uni National pour un Cambodge Indépendant, Neutre, Pacifique et Cooperatif (FUNCINPEC) and the Khmer People's National Liberation Front (KPNLF)].... [The resistance groups] have few men as dedicated as some of the young PRK ministers working in Phnom Penh.... [The CGDK] is hardly a government at all, and ... there is little space for well-intentioned individuals to do anything of substance.[12]

Even so, the PRK has been anxious to obtain technical assistance and training from western countries. Most have refused to provide it.

The Communist Party formed under the new regime has expanded. By 1985 the membership of the People's Revolutionary Party of Kampuchea (PRDK) had risen to 7,500, and to 10,000 by the end of 1986.[13] It was reported to be nearly 20,000 by mid-1988, but this may be an overstatement.[14] By comparison with Vietnam and Laos, the party's penetration of society was still weak, but it was considerably stronger than the Communist Party of Kampuchea's had ever been.

In early 1979 the vast majority of the Cambodian population had notionally lived under the authority of the PRK, but vast areas had little or no contact with the government. Since then, despite the attempts of guerrillas to disrupt it, the provincial and district administration has been strengthened. PRK control appeared firm in the central rice-growing areas (with perhaps two-thirds of the population), though less firm in the settled uplands. As a rough guess, 7 million out of the 8 million Cambodians were firmly under its control, compared to 300,000 people controlled by the CGDK groups in their camps in Thailand. The periphery of Cambodia, the outlying, sparsely populated areas of jungles, mountains and swamps was a no man's land over which the PRK, like all previous Cambodian governments, had difficulty securing control. The areas immediately adjacent to the resistance border camps were another no man's land. It was in these areas that the contest between government forces and guerrillas was focused in the late 1980s.

With the Khmer Rouge army still lurking across the border in Thailand, the key to the survival of the Phnom Penh government lay in its military capability. Most western analysts have contemptuously dismissed the PRK armed forces. In the US Department of Defense's estimate, in 1989 they were made up of 'inexperienced troops and largely unqualified officers'. By contrast, in the Vietnamese view the PRK armed forces had developed from 'a few work-teams and battalions operating in coordination with Vietnam army volunteers' in the early days to a 'rather strong army with divisional army groups including infantry, naval and technical services under a close command' by 1987. All young adult men in Cambodia have been declared liable for military service, and local officials are assigned conscription quotas to fill – which they often did by very arbitrary methods. By 1989 the government's regular forces had been built up to between 45,000 and 50,000 troops.

The US Department of Defense saw the Phnom Penh government as allowing itself to become 'preoccupied' with the development of village militia. About 100,000 men served in these on a part-time basis. Most western analysts dismissed this as a 'Dad's army' exercise. It seems they had managed to forget entirely the grief that Communist-organized village militia had brought to US and ARVN forces in South Vietnam twenty years earlier. They were part-time soldiers, rather than professionals. But they were fighting to protect their homes and families from a hated marauder. Some, at least, meant business: James Pringle reported that in Kampot province they went out to hunt down Khmer Rouge bands in the mountains at night, which surely demands both courage and motivation. Pringle wrote: 'The old syndrome of hunkering down in a village bunker while the enemy controls the night, as happened to the pro-Western regimes in south Vietnam and Cambodia in an early war, are not part of the scenario.'[15]

The PRK armed forces were also not as inexperienced as many thought.

They had borne an increasing share of the burden of the fighting since 1982. They participated fully in the 1984–85 offensive, and garrisoned large parts of the border thereafter. A Vietnamese diplomat said in 1985 that 50 per cent of military operations were then being undertaken by the PRK armed forces. Throughout this period they were still under the supervision of a joint command, but by the late 1980s they were a more experienced and battle-hardened force than many outsiders allowed for. In 1988 the Vietnamese pulled their forces thirty kilometres back from the Thai border, except those facing Son Sen's forces around the Thai–Lao–Cambodian border junction. By the time the Vietnamese pulled their last troops out in September 1989, PRK troops under a Cambodian command had held the front line against the resistance for a year and thrown back a major Khmer Rouge offensive.

In early 1989, a PRK official said to one of us:

> Ten years ago we had nothing, absolutely nothing. We started from scratch. Today, our forces are young, but they are strong. Their patriotic spirit, their hatred of the Khmer Rouge, is strong. Even in 1985, there were still many Vietnamese soldiers. Most are gone now, and the rest will go soon. We will be standing on our own. So what pretext can the reactionaries use to attack us then? But if we have to fight, we will. We are determined never to allow this country to be taken back to the Pol Pot times. On that our people, our government, and our army are united as one.

Many pundits in the West and the ASEAN countries were convinced that this was all bluff and bluster, and that the Phnom Penh government would collapse like a house of cards as soon as the Vietnamese left. They contemplated the 'power vacuum' that would then exist in Cambodia, and debated whether it would be filled by Pol Pot or by Prince Sihanouk. Dogmatic prejudice against the PRK had slowly grown into a monumental miscalculation, which finally wrecked the whole strategy on which western diplomacy over Cambodia was based.

From the Battlefield to the Conference Table

In the early 1980s Hanoi had pushed hard to win international acceptance of the PRK, offering to withdraw its forces once the danger of a Khmer Rouge comeback had been averted. Such a deal was rejected by China, the ASEAN countries and the West. They thought that time was on the side of the CGDK groups, and that the Vietnamese/PRK side would be forced to capitulate on Chinese–ASEAN terms. But after General Anh's 1984–85 blitz, the prospect of military successes for the CGDK receded. At the same time, the Vietnamese/PRK side could not eliminate the CGDK groups without major incursions into Thailand, which would probably have meant a major regional war.

Under these circumstances, the emphasis shifted from the battlefield to the conference table. It took a protracted effort to bring this about. Once that had been achieved, however, it seemed that all that had been achieved was to reveal the gulf that separated the antagonists. Of the regional conflicts of the 1970s which fuelled the New Cold War in the early 1980s, the Cambodian conflict proved the most intractable.

As part of the new Cambodia strategy Vietnam embraced in 1984, Hanoi had adopted a new diplomatic approach. In October of that year Nguyen Co Thach called for an international conference to work out a settlement based on a Vietnamese withdrawal, the elimination of the Khmer Rouge, and negotiations between the PRK and the non-Communist resistance groups. This was reiterated by the Indochinese foreign minister's meeting in Ho Chi Minh City (Saigon) in January 1985. As Vietnamese troops took the offensive on the Thai–Cambodian border, the meeting emphasized that negotiations were the 'best way' to settle the conflict. It proposed that these could lead to the formation of a new government based on general elections under international supervision. At the same time, both Vietnamese and PRK officials began hinting that Prince Sihanouk could head the new government.

After talking to the Vietnamese, UN Secretary General Perez de Cuellar, thought that 'modest progress' had been made. The Australian foreign minister, Bill Hayden, thought likewise. But the Thai Foreign Ministry said there was 'nothing new' in Vietnam's position, and the Chinese reiterated their demand that Vietnam withdraw its troops unconditionally before any negotiations take place. When Hayden said that Vietnam was offering significant concessions, he was dismissed as naive. The 1984–85 border offensive was cited as proof that Vietnam's proposals for negotiations were not sincere, although anyone who knew anything of the diplomacy of the Vietnam war knew that Hanoi's strategy then was 'to negotiate while fighting'. And so it was in the 1980s.

Even so, the ASEAN states also began talking about 'national reconciliation'. This envisaged some role for the PRK in a power-sharing arrangement. But they insisted that there must also be a role for the Khmer Rouge as well. It must be a quadripartite government. The Khmer Rouge rather reluctantly accepted this position. It agreed to a role for the PRK. But Khieu Samphan said: 'We can agree to its participation in a government only on condition that the Samrin group declares its opposition to the Vietnamese and agrees to join us in fighting the Vietnamese and the Soviets.' This was the old Khmer Rouge view of the 1970s reasserted: peace between Cambodians comes through war with Vietnam.

Hanoi and Phnom Penh made their next move at the Foreign Ministers'

Conference in Phnom Penh in August 1985. They set 1990 as a target for completing the withdrawal of Vietnamese forces from Cambodia. At a press conference Hun Sen explained that the success of the 1984–85 dry-season offensive had improved PRK security, making the withdrawal possible. However, he added, if the peace and security of Cambodia were threatened, 'appropriate measures' would be taken. The CGDK side dismissed the planned withdrawal as a cunning deceit to conceal Vietnam's plans to colonize Cambodia, and countered with an eight-point proposal in March 1986. This proposed the withdrawal of Vietnamese troops under UN supervision, as the result of negotiations between the CGDK and Vietnam. A quadripartite coalition government would then be set up headed by Sihanouk, with Son Sann as prime minister, to organize elections, again under UN supervision.

Both sides were now proposing 'national reconciliation', but they were closer on form than substance. Phnom Penh demanded the exclusion of the 'Pol Pot clique', although it hinted that it might be ready to talk to lesser figures in the Khmer Rouge, ones without such a bloody past. The CGDK side insisted on the inclusion of the Khmer Rouge in the government and the exclusion of the PRK from the negotiations, although it promised the PRK a minority position in the ensuing government. As a consequence, even while speaking of compromise the opposing sides still refused even to talk to each other.

This situation led to increasing disagreements among the ASEAN states. The hardline states, Singapore and Thailand, argued that Vietnam was cracking. They argued that ASEAN should keep up the pressure, to force it into accepting the CGDK's demands. Malaysia and Indonesia were frustrated by the fact that, for all the moves and counter-proposals, there were still no meaningful negotiations under way. In April 1985 the Malaysians put forward a proposal for 'proximity talks'. As the two Cambodian sides refused to talk to each other directly, perhaps they could use go-betweens to exchange ideas. When the ASEAN foreign ministers met in July 1985, they endorsed this idea. But, at the insistence of the Thai, they proposed that these be talks between the CGDK on one side and the Vietnamese on the other; the PRK could participate as part of the Vietnamese delegation. Hanoi rejected this, arguing that the internal affairs of Cambodia – such as details of a new government – must be settled by negotiations between the Cambodians. Privately, Vietnamese officials saw the Thai proposal as a calculated insult to the PRK.

No further progress was made in 1986. However, Sihanouk was showing signs of increasing frustration. Vietnamese and PRK officials were talking of him returning to Phnom Penh as head of state. He wanted to discuss this proposal with them, but his Chinese patrons and his CGDK partners opposed the move. Late in 1985 Sihanouk proposed a 'cocktail party' in Paris, where members of the Cambodian groups could hold informal discussions, without pre-conditions or a fixed agenda. But the idea was buried by the Thai foreign minister – 'From Bangkok, Paris is too far to come just for a cocktail or a glass of champagne.'

In May 1987 Sihanouk announced that he was 'standing down' from the CGDK for a year. At the time, he said that this was in protest at the murder of some of his soldiers by Khmer Rouge troops. But his real aim was to open the way for talks with Phnom Penh. As the Vietnamese would not do a deal over the head of the PRK, continued refusal to talk to Phnom Penh would 'only prolong the conflict'. In July Indonesian Foreign Minister Mochtar went to Hanoi, and found the Vietnamese receptive to talks, although they still insisted that these should be between the Cambodian groups, rather than between the CGDK and Vietnam. This was acceptable to Mochtar, but when the ASEAN foreign ministers met in August 1987, Thailand and Singapore were not willing to allow it. The Chinese were dismayed when Sihanouk broke ranks with his CGDK partners. Sihanouk went to Beijing in August, where he was warned by Deng Xiaoping himself not to agree to national reconciliation while there were Vietnamese troops in Cambodia, and not to accept a government 'based on' the PRK. Sihanouk responded: 'There is no way for us to go into the illegal state in Phnom Penh. They must join us in a national reconciliation government.'

But in September Sihanouk wrote to Hun Sen, proposing a meeting. Hun Sen quickly accepted. The PRK began preparing for what they hoped would be the decisive breakthrough. On 8 October, it put forward a new five-point peace proposal which formally offered Sihanouk a 'high position' in the resulting government. It accepted the participation of all opposition groups 'except Pol Pot and some of his close associates' in elections. Hun Sen said he was willing to meet Khieu Samphan; but his government still refused to bargain with the 'criminals' responsible for the mass killings of 1975–78. Asked to name the particular individuals he meant, Hun Sen said that this was an issue which would have to be dealt with by a tribunal.

Sihanouk and Hun Sen met at Fere-en-Tardenois in France on 2–4 December 1987. Sihanouk declared he would only return to Phnom Penh to head a quadripartite coalition 'in the framework of a new Cambodian state … a Cambodia which shall be neither "popular" nor "democratic", nor Communist, nor socialist, but which will have a parliamentary system of "the French style" and a multi-party system'. He called for a '100 per cent independent' Cambodia, condemned the PRK for aligning itself with Vietnam, and called for it to be dismantled. Hun Sen praised the prince's rule before 1970, and blamed Cambodia's misfortunes on the Lon Nol and Pol Pot regimes. But he denied the accusation that the

PRK had betrayed Cambodia's independence, rejected the demand that it be dismantled and called for the disarming of the Khmer Rouge. He later added in an interview that he was not opposed to Sihanouk's demand for French-style democracy 'if all the factions and the people accept it'.

The outcome of the meeting was a four-point agreement:

1. The conflict in Cambodia must inevitably go through a political solution.

2. The Cambodian problem must necessarily be solved by the Cambodian people themselves, between all the parties in conflict, by means of negotiations in order to end the war, the bloodshed, and to rebuild a peaceful, independent, democratic, sovereign, neutral and non-aligned Cambodia.

3. As soon as an agreement is obtained by the Cambodian parties, an international conference will be summoned to guarantee this agreement, to safeguard the independence of Cambodia, peace and stability in Southeast Asia.

4. The two parties agreed to meet again during January 1988 at Fere-en-Tardenois (France).

This deviated considerably from the CGDK six-point programme, and Sihanouk was bitterly attacked for putting his name to it. Son Sann said the talks were a Vietnamese trick to 'divert the world's attention from their invasion of Cambodia' by promoting the 'false notion' that there 'exists a civil war between the Khmers'. The Khmer Rouge dismissed them as just a 'new manoeuvre' by Hanoi, and declared that the task was still to force the Vietnamese to accept CGDK terms for negotiations. The Chinese were likewise unhappy. Pressed for comments on Sihanouk's endeavour, all Chinese diplomats would say was that they 'respected' his efforts to find a settlement; they refused to say they supported it. The only thing they could find to approve was his refusal to join the PRK.

Sihanouk's response to these pressures was to send a telegram to Hun Sen abusing him for coming to Paris 'with empty hands', and accusing Vietnam of being 'arrogant' because it sent its 'valet' (Hun Sen) to Paris instead of talking to him itself. He cancelled the next round of talks. Then, when this drew criticism from those hoping to see the negotiations continue, he reinstated the scheduled talks. As usual, there was much comment on Sihanouk's 'mercurial' personality and his 'erratic' behaviour. There was much more to it than this. Sihanouk was engaged in a desperate effort to balance opposing forces against each other to his own advantage. But, lacking a strong power-base of his own, he was swept along by forces he was unable to control.

The second round of Hun Sen–Sihanouk talks began in Saint-Germain-en-Laye, near Paris, on 20 January 1988. These soon broke down over the key problems that had emerged the previous November – the dismantling of the PRK and the disarming of the Khmer Rouge. Then the prince flew to Beijing, for talks with Zhao Ziyang and Khieu Samphan. Sihanouk pushed the Chinese to agree to the disarming of the Khmer Rouge. But they would not accept this.[16] So Sihanouk abruptly changed tack. He dispatched a telegram to Hun Sen cancelling their next round of talks. 'I have decided to go on fighting against Vietnam', he declared. 'Hanoi only understands the language of force.' Next, he announced his decision to make permanent his previously 'temporary' resignation as president of the CGDK. This decision he made 'after mature reflection and numerous nights of insomnia', because of the 'unceasing' hostility of the Khmer Rouge and the KPNLF towards him. This was 'irrevocable and irreversible', but after being pressured by the Chinese for a month, Sihanouk declared he was resuming the presidency of the CGDK.

Sihanouk's performance at this point merits a closer examination than the usual clichés about a 'mercurial personality' permit. It indicated the gulf separating the opposing Cambodian sides. In the first place, although he had been out of power for almost two decades, Sihanouk had not been able to shed the royal absolutist attitudes into which he had been bred. What Sihanouk found most attractive about the French system was not its parliamentarism, but the powers it bestowed on the head of state. He explained in a 1987 interview:

I have always been a royalist.... When we were a kingdom, Cambodia was great. Even without Sihanouk, when we were a kingdom, we were great. A king is not a political *chef de parti*. For a king, there is only one party – the country, the homeland. The Republicans, they think in terms of parties, political plans and so on. They don't think of the superior interests of the country. So even if we did not have Sihanouk, but instead my son installed as king of Cambodia, I am sure that Cambodia would be great again. We need a king, not a republic. As a republic, we lost our national dignity; we lost everything. Sssssss, just like that – dirt, mud.... The poor, humble people of Cambodia don't criticise me. They don't resent anything, because they feel they are like me. Some intellectual refugees say that the prince dances, sings, and plays music while our people suffer. But at the same time, the people dance.[17]

But Sihanouk no longer had the power-base inside Cambodia to sustain this vision. Each of the three regimes that had followed his rejected it, albeit in different ways. The KPNLF, the Khmer Rouge and the PRK were all prepared to exploit what they could of his 'god-king' reputation, and to get this they were all prepared to go through the motions of deference, but none wanted to grant him the sort of powers he demanded. Some of their followers did not bother to conceal their contempt for what they regarded as the antics of an ageing prima donna.

Sihanouk's response was to seek the backing of powerful patrons abroad. When his little kingdom was cast loose in the world of nations in 1954, circumstances led him to pin his faith on Communist China. But in the 1970s and 1980s, Beijing bestowed its favours on the Khmer Rouge. Since he was unwilling to break with China, this locked Sihanouk into unhappily supporting them. Rannarith summed up his father's views on why the Khmer Rouge had to be brought into government in Phnom Penh as follows:

I and my family, like all Cambodians, have been the victims of the Khmer Rouge. However, first of all, how do we eliminate the Khmer Rouge? For the past eight years Vietnam's forces, numbering between 140,000 and 160,000 men and now totalling 140,000, have been unable to eliminate the Khmer Rouge. What can I, Sihanouk, do? Secondly, I have told our great friend, the PRC, that following the Vietnamese troop withdrawal, we should lay down our weapons – or at least, all Cambodian forces should be equal and that no Cambodian party should have the ability to threaten the Cambodian people or threaten another party with force or arms. The PRC refused to agree. This means that China will not allow the Khmer Rouge to be eliminated at any cost. So what can I do?[18]

But Hun Sen believed that it was madness to allow the Khmer Rouge to return to power and bring its army back into Cambodia, in the hope that it would be a benign ruler. He thought Sihanouk overrated its strength, and saw no reason for subservience to China. According to Hun Sen:

To us, to dismantle the PRK is to commit suicide and to allow an easy return of the Khmer opposition forces including the Polpotists who have, over the past nine years, failed to control a single inch of the Cambodian territory in spite of their all-out endeavours in the military, political and diplomatic fields. For our part, we have made great efforts to defend our homeland and take a firm control of the whole territory with the people's power established across the country.[19]

The PRK was prepared to fight, rather than surrender to the Khmer Rouge in advance, as Sihanouk was advocating. The initial efforts of Hun Sen and Sihanouk to reach a compromise turned over the next few months into a bitter test of wills. In this contest, most western countries chose Sihanouk's side, with little comprehension of the consequences. It was not Sihanouk but Pol Pot who was the main beneficiary of this.

From the Barrel of a Gun

The collapse of the Sihanouk–Hun Sen talks was followed by a sustained burst of low-key but high-level diplomatic activity. For five months Soviet, Indian, US, Vietnamese and ASEAN diplomats consulted each other over the Cambodian question. Igor Rogachev spent five weeks touring Asia. The Indonesians agreed to host talks between all the Cambodians in Jakarta, which were scheduled to begin in July 1988.

In May 1988 the Vietnamese also agreed to withdraw half their forces from Cambodia by the end of the year. This decision was the result of extended Soviet–Vietnamese discussions over the previous two months. But it is unlikely that this was forced on an unwilling Hanoi by an impatient Moscow. Rogachev said: 'Some countries asked us to exert pressure on Vietnam. Each time we've responded that Vietnam is a sovereign country. No one has the right to impose his will on the Vietnamese leaders.'[20] Hanoi's strategy had been aimed at withdrawing from Cambodia in 1990; Moscow, at most, persuaded Hanoi to speed the process up by a few months. Vietnam had implemented all the basic planks of General Anh's strategy, but the decisive test for the opposing Cambodian sides would come only when Vietnam did withdraw. The hints of improved relations with China, Thailand and the USA after the withdrawal probably helped tilt the balance.

The 26 May statement was carefully timed to give impetus to the search for a diplomatic settlement: the Soviets were able to tell Thai prime minister Prem during his historic visit to Moscow; it came on the eve of the Gorbachev–Reagan Moscow summit, and two months before the Cambodian groups were scheduled to meet in Indonesia. Statements from both Phnom Penh and Hanoi emphasized that the main obstacle to a political settlement in Cambodia was no longer the Vietnamese presence, but the Khmer Rouge.

'Nobody', responded the Voice of the National Army of Kampuchea, 'is so stupid as to believe the endless deceiving lies of the Vietnamese enemy aggressors.' But reporters in Cambodia found that the withdrawal was real, and seemed to be occurring even more rapidly than the Vietnamese had indicated. The Chinese appeared to be caught off guard; then they supported the Khmer Rouge position. Beijing accused Vietnam of resorting to the 'same old tricks' and 'entirely deceptive talk'.

But within a few weeks Beijing quietly came to accept that Hanoi was indeed pulling out of Cambodia. It responded by softening its stance, although it was still far from abandoning the Khmer Rouge. On 1 July 1988, the Chinese Foreign Ministry issued a statement setting out a new position on Cambodia. The most interesting aspect of the Chinese statement was the proposal that each of the group would only put forward candidates acceptable to the others. This was the first time that China had ever suggested a formula which would allow Cambodians to reject Pol Pot and his henchmen. But in return the Khmer Rouge would be granted the right to veto all other candidates for government, a power they would presumably use to remove the PRK leadership. The Chinese proposal also implied that any new government in Cambodia would be worked out by high-level negotiations before granting voters a token opportunity to register their approval. It is notable that the Khmer Rouge failed to endorse this until September, weeks after the Cambodian groups met in Jakarta.

Vietnam's withdrawals were also welcomed in Bangkok. Fresh from his visit to Moscow, Prem abandoned the hardline stance pushed by Siddhi and began pushing the parties towards a resolution of the conflict. In 1987 Bangkok had helped scuttle Mochtar's initiatives because they would involve talking to the PRK. A year later they were willing to let the PRK participate, and Hanoi agreed that once the Cambodians were talking to each other Vietnam would join other 'interested parties' in discussing the external aspects of the problem. The road was suddenly open to serious negotiations.

Singapore found itself the leading spokesman of the ASEAN hardliners. If Bangkok's antagonism to the Vietnamese presence in Cambodia was inspired by a mixture of concern for Thailand's military security and ideological hostility to Communism, Singapore's was fuelled purely by ideological animosity. In the Singaporean view Hanoi's motivation in overthrowing Pol Pot was doctrinally motivated military expansionism. In Singaporean eyes, Hanoi's willingness to negotiate was merely a sign of weakness; and the only proper response was to step up military, diplomatic and economic pressure. Seeking an accommodation with Hanoi was moral cowardice, a 'new Munich'; it would only result in ASEAN snatching defeat from the jaws of victory.

The great worry of the hardliners was the weakness of the non-Communist resistance groups. After all the support lavished on them for a decade, they were still no match for either Phnom Penh or the Khmer Rouge. Now the ASEAN hardliners played for enough time for the non-Communists to develop into a credible alternative. It was unclear how long that would take, but to the anti-Communist ideologues nothing else was acceptable. A Sihanouk–Hun Sen compromise had to be averted, and so they pushed for a quadripartite government – knowing that Khmer Rouge participation was unacceptable to Phnom Penh. Just as the Khmer Rouge despised the non-Communists but found them useful, the ASEAN anti-Communist ideologues loathed the Khmer Rouge but found them useful.

The USA threw itself behind the ASEAN hardliners. Washington was, in the words of Secretary of State George Schultz, 'unalterably opposed' to the Khmer Rouge returning to power – even while it demanded their inclusion in the government, with their army to back them up. The reasoning was that they would be eliminated at the ballot box; in the meantime, Sihanouk could be relied on to keep them under control. Extravagant praise was lavished on Sihanouk, and his ability to bring all Cambodians together in harmony. There had been little evidence of this in the last twenty years, and none at all in the past twelve months. Ignoring this, western policy-makers piled illusion on illusion in an attempt to avoid making a hard decision about Cambodia.

Amid this fog of obstruction and delusion, the Cambodians leaders met to bring peace to their country. It is scarcely surprising that they failed. The first Jakarta Informal Meeting (JIM-1) was held at Bogor Palace, near Jakarta, on 25–28 July 1988. The Cambodian delegations met alone in the morning sessions, and were joined by representatives of 'interested parties' (the other Indochinese and the ASEAN states) in the afternoon sessions.

Two weeks earlier, Sihanouk resigned from the CGDK. He claimed he had been insulted in an article in the Thai press. He told some journalists that he was seeking to isolate the Khmer Rouge. But he sent Rannarith to Bogor, where he did nothing to isolate the Khmer Rouge. At the invitation of President Suharto, Sihanouk consented to visit Jakarta while the talks were on. But if he was hoping that the delegates at Bogor would humbly petition him to assume leadership of 'his' nation once more, Sihanouk was sorely disappointed.

At the Bogor conference each group restated its established proposals, and made no concessions to its opponents. The Sihanoukists differed from the Khmer Rouge and the KPNLF in demanding that the dismantling of the PRK should be carried out 'gradually and meticulously' rather than immediately and unconditionally. Rannarith tried to present this as showing flexibility and a willingness to compromise; but Hun Sen remained unimpressed. The talks ended with the Indonesian foreign minister optimistically noting a 'convergence of views' and a 'common understanding' between the two sides, based on the need to work for an independent, non-aligned Cambodia, and the linking of the Vietnamese withdrawal to preventing a recurrence 'of the genocidal policies and practices of the Pol Pot regime'. Predictably, Khieu Samphan protested angrily that this was not a view accepted by the Khmer Rouge at all. Indeed, the Khmer Rouge objected to anything that smelt of compromise. Later, Hun Sen claimed the talks failed because of Khieu Samphan's attitude. He told Marcel Barung:

These last few years, I assessed him wrongly. I thought he had a conciliatory position. But now I realise that Khieu Samphan is really a Polpotist, and not a person to compromise. He sabotaged all that was being conceded by Samdech Sihanouk, Son Sann's group and myself.[21]

Yet ASEAN and the USA were also doing their best to encourage the intransigence of the Sihanoukists and the KPNLF.

The most substantial outcome of JIM-1 was the decision to continue the negotiations. A working party met in October, and the top leaders in November. This time, Sihanouk agreed to attend. But the Khmer Rouge dragged its feet – it failed to attend the working party session at all, and sent a low-level official to the meeting of leaders. Hun Sen and Sihanouk met first, and were joined by Son Sann. Once again there was no breakthrough, but another Jakarta meeting (JIM-2) was planned for February 1989, to be followed by an international conference to guarantee settlement between Cambodian groups.

The anti-Communists were worried by the increasingly prominent role that Hun Sen was playing in the negotiations, and by hints that Sihanouk might decide to cut a deal with him. The ASEAN Foreign Ministers' Conference in January 1989 demanded a 'comprehensive and durable political solution'. The insistence on an all-or-nothing solution was aimed at obstructing any attempt at compromise. At their next conference, in July, the ASEAN foreign ministers warned of the dangers of a 'partial' settlement. As Singapore's foreign minister, Wong Kan Seng, argued in 1989:

> A settlement that leaves the regime installed by the Vietnamese in Phnom Penh will make a mockery of the results of ASEAN's 10 years of solidarity and collective effort to undo the Vietnamese invasion of Cambodia. It would be a moral and political tragedy. By handing the prize to the aggressor after 10 years of denying what the Vietnamese regard as a fait accompli, we would have created a dangerous precedent in Southeast Asia: the precedent that aggression pays.[22]

These warnings were directed above all at the Chatichai government in Bangkok. As the threat to Thailand's security (real or imagined) posed by Vietnamese troops in Cambodia and Laos evaporated, the Thai revealed an alarming tendency to live and let live with their Communist neighbours – worse, even to cooperate with them, where it seemed to Thailand's advantage.

Nothing the hardliners did, however, seemed to stop the rot. After Siddhi's visit to Hanoi in January 1989, Chatichai issued an invitation for Hun Sen to come to Bangkok as his 'private guest'. Hun Sen quickly accepted, and visited Bangkok on 25–27 January 1989. Siddhi spluttered that this would be 'misunderstood' by the ASEAN countries, while other right-wingers were harshly critical. 'Why should we hold talks with Hun

Sen? He is merely a mouthpiece of Vietnam. He is a postman', said Prasong Soonsiri. Chatichai dismissed these critics as 'dinosaurs and million-year-old turtles'.

But there were a lot of dinosaurs. Sihanouk denounced Chatichai for talking to 'the quisling, the collaborator' and said he would boycott JIM-2. The USA was reportedly 'displeased' by Chatichai's 'naive' move, and threatened that Thailand 'would have to pay a price' if it abandoned the Cambodian resistance: 'Thailand should consider whether the total value of any new Indochinese trade would even cover the US trade access privileges it gets under the Generalised Special Preferences', said one administration official.[23]

There was movement elsewhere, however. Following JIM-1, China further softened its stance. In September 1988 Zhao Ziyang said: 'The Khmer Rouge should not be allowed to assume exclusive power, and the Heng Samrin regime, a *fait accompli* created by Vietnam, must not be allowed to continue in power. I think both dangers should be removed.' Beijing commentators now conceded that due to Cambodia's 'tragic past' (significantly, perhaps, the phrase used by Gorbachev in his Vladivostok speech) it was 'understandable' that some people would be worried by Khmer Rouge attempts to return to power. This perception was rather belated, but still welcome.

By this time the Khmer Rouge had fallen into line with China's July statement on Cambodia. In a statement on 15 August 1988 the Party of Democratic Kampuchea offered to accept international supervision and other measures to prevent any one group dominating a coalition government. Khieu Samphan was now obliged to devote his considerable talents to explaining why Cambodians should accept into government people from whom they needed to be protected by international guarantees. By November, the obvious foot-dragging on the part of the Khmer Rouge over negotiations earned it a public rebuke from Thailand and China. Khieu Samphan hastened to assure them that he would attend JIM-2.

Meanwhile, Sihanouk set about rallying western support after JIM-1, with considerable success. Japan, France, and the UK all affirmed him as their choice for Cambodian leader. Sihanouk was very optimistic about the chances for a non-Communist Cambodia, if only the resistance groups were given enough money. 'From now on we are going to the end of the tunnel', he proclaimed in September 1988. Washington announced it was tripling its aid to the non-Communist resistance, and Sihanouk visited Washington to be received by President Reagan himself.

JIM-2 took place on 16–21 February 1989. Once again Ali Alatas heroically managed to extract a 'consensus statement' from the meeting. This endorsed the view that the two key issues were, first, a Vietnamese withdrawal 'within the context of an overall political solution'; and second, preventing a 'recurrence of the genocidal policies and practices of the Pol Pot regime' and ending 'foreign interference' and external arms supplies to the Cambodian groups. These were seen as linked. It was agreed that an international control mechanism, 'equipped with the necessary arms for self-defence' – but no more – be established to oversee the Vietnamese withdrawal. But this was agreed to by the Cambodians in an atmosphere of recrimination and bitterness, while Singapore attacked Thailand's new-found willingness to truck openly with the enemy.

Following this Rannarith went to Washington and called for the USA to boost the non-Communist resistance until it was 'able to call the shots through military pressure' in Cambodia, and did not have to 'negotiate under the domination of the two Communist factions'. Son Sann also came to Washington, also asking for more funds, and for military aid. According to Chanda, the Bush administration let itself be persuaded that within a year 'the non-Communist resistance forces could be strengthened enough to dominate the country'. Inspired by this delusion, it stepped up supplies to the Armée Nationale Sihanoukiste and the KPNLF – as did China 'at Washington's urging'.[24]

Despite this, Vietnam pushed ahead with its withdrawal. On 5 April 1989 the three Indochinese countries issued a joint statement announcing that all Vietnamese troops were to be withdrawn from Cambodia by 30 September regardless of whether a settlement was reached. They called for an end to military aid to the resistance. Xinhua declared there was 'nothing new' in this statement, and said that China would cut off its supplies to the resistance only when the last Vietnamese soldier had left Cambodia. Sihanouk's response was to declare that he 'diametrically rejected all decisions, conditions and agreements made by Vietnam, Laos and the foreign lackey Phnom Penh regime'. China endorsed this statement.

The PRK also moved to accommodate some of the demands of its opponents. In late March a special committee was set up to revise the 1981 Constitution, and the changes were endorsed by a special session of the National Assembly on 29–30 April. The title 'People's Republic', with its Communist connotation, was dropped in favour of the neutral 'State of Cambodia', as Sihanouk had demanded. A new flag and national anthem were adopted as well. On 24 April Hun Sen announced that general elections would be held in Cambodia in November.[25] The CGDK leaders professed outrage. Sihanouk condemned the State of Cambodia as a 'creature of Vietnam' which had 'no right' to hold elections. The CGDK Foreign Ministry also condemned Hanoi for making these changes without its permission.

There was little doubt that Phnom Penh intended to continue fraternal relations with Hanoi. The tenth anniversary of the Vietnam–Cambodia friendship treaty was duly celebrated in both capitals. *Nhan Dan* declared: 'Reality in the past ten years has vindicated the importance of the Treaty.' On 20 July SPK reported that the changes being written into the Cambodian constitution included a declaration of neutralism. It gave no indication of how this affected the treaty with Vietnam. As with Laos, however, the ability of Cambodia to pursue such a policy depended on its acceptance by more powerful states.

Hun Sen, Sihanouk and Son Sann met once more at Bogor on 2–3 May 1989. Before he left Phnom Penh, Hun Sen said that this would be Sihanouk's 'last chance', but he was optimistic. 'Now is the time for Sihanouk to play his hand', said a senior western diplomat in Bangkok. 'If he doesn't he risks having the PRK accepted as the *de facto* government of Cambodia.' With a Sino-Soviet summit pending, Beijing and Hanoi talking to each other again, and Thailand seeking improved relations with the Indochinese countries, the diplomatic position of the CGDK side had weakened visibly. If the Vietnamese really did pull their troops out in September, the CGDK would lose its *raison d'être*. But the State of Cambodia was in power, and the CGDK was not.

However, while the Chinese appeared to be softening their stance towards Vietnam, they were still implacably opposed to the Phnom Penh government. So too were the USA and ASEAN hardliners, who hoped that fear of the Khmer Rouge would lead the Phnom Penh government to cave in to the non-Communist resistance. But Hun Sen believed that would be folly because the non-Communist groups were incapable of controlling the Khmer Rouge.

It was impossible to reconcile these opposing perspectives. Unless some agreement could be reached by September, the Vietnamese pullout would be followed by intensified fighting between Cambodians. Major concessions would have to be made, but which side would make them?

In May Sihanouk made a serious effort to come to terms with Hun Sen. On his arrival at Bogor, Sihanouk said he was ready to compromise: 'I have to be realistic.' He made conciliatory statements about Hun Sen, praised the constitutional amendments, and dropped his demand for the dismantling of the government. They agreed that after the Vietnamese troops had left they would stop accepting arms from outside supporters. Sihanouk accepted Hun Sen's international control mechanism proposal, and that an international conference would be held in Jakarta. On 3 May, Sihanouk said he would be prepared to return to Phnom Penh in October–November 1989 – if the Vietnamese withdrawal had been internationally verified, if a multi-party system were enshrined in the constitution, and if a ceasefire were in force. And – crucially – he said he was ready to abandon the Khmer Rouge if it alone blocked a negotiated settlement.

On his way back to Phnom Penh, Hun Sen stopped in Bangkok for
further talks with Chatichai. He proposed that Thailand should assume
a special role in supervising the Vietnamese withdrawal, and Chatichai
called for a ceasefire in Cambodia. Thai leaders were reported as saying
that 'all external aid to the resistance will cease – but only after the last
. . . Vietnamese troops leave Cambodia'.[26] Everything seemed to be falling
into place.

But the harsh fact was that, for all the rhetoric in Washington and
elsewhere, Sihanouk did not have the power to do a deal. As he explained,
this would need the approval of Son Sann, and of Khieu Samphan.[27]
Son Sann was uncooperative, insisting that the constitutional changes
proposed by Hun Sen were unacceptable; he demanded an entirely new
document drafted jointly by all four groups. But diplomats in Jakarta
were confident that Son Sann would soon fall into line. No one was
positive that the Khmer Rouge would do likewise. There was nothing
in the proposed agreement for it – and the absence of Khieu Samphan
from the talks was itself silent testimony as to what it thought of the
negotiating process.

The conflict within the Khmer Rouge deepened as the Chinese applied
pressure. Pol Pot was taken to Beijing at the beginning of 1989 – allegedly
for medical treatment, although the Khmer Rouge said his health was
robust. A Khmer Rouge official said: 'There is disunity among our leaders.
Those who adopt a hard line want to go on fighting, but others are interested in the peace process. We have lost our orientation and there is
soul searching going on.' From Beijing, Pol Pot sent the party leadership
a letter resigning from all his official posts on 4 March, but saying he
would stay on as a 'researcher' until the Vietnamese left Cambodia. Three
months passed before the Khmer Rouge leadership accepted this.[28] Ieng
Sary was reported to favour negotiations, but the formidable Ta Mok
was leading a group wanting a 'fight to the death' with the other Cambodian groups.[29] Ta Mok's group apparently had the upper hand, and
the ASEAN hardliners provided it with the excuse it needed. On 8 May
Khieu Samphan responded to Chatichai's call for a ceasefire by demanding a comprehensive settlement first.

The Chinese supported the Khmer Rouge position, and sent it a large
shipment of arms just after the May meeting. In July, Li Peng told
Sihanouk that Vietnam was 'playing a trick' in its withdrawal, leaving
130,000 soldiers behind in disguise and a million settlers. Li Peng said
that China would continue to supply the resistance even after September.
The ASEAN Foreign Ministers' Conference that month again warned
of the dangers of a 'partial' settlement, and was considering continuing
military aid to the resistance after the Vietnamese withdrawal. Both China

and ASEAN assumed that the impending withdrawal of Vietnamese troops would seriously weaken the position of the State of Cambodia. As there was no sign that Hun Sen would submit to diplomatic pressure for the dismantling of the State of Cambodia, military force would have to be applied as well.

Sihanouk was in no position to resist such pressures, and he abandoned his search for a settlement. 'There is no way to stop the war against Vietnam,' he said after his meeting with Li Peng. 'There will not be a civil war. There will be a continuation of the war against Vietnamese colonialism.' He denounced Hun Sen as a lackey of the Vietnamese, and said he would refuse to shake his hand. He predicted that the conference on Cambodia scheduled to meet in Paris a few weeks later would be a failure.

Khieu Samphan, Hun Sen, Sihanouk and Son Sann met in Paris for the first round of discussions on 24–25 July. They got nowhere. 'We disagreed on everything but the menu', said Sihanouk. Actually, they disagreed even here. Hun Sen preferred Cambodian to French food, and Sihanouk related that he had a special repast prepared for the 'lowly born' Hun Sen while the others enjoyed the *haute cuisine* of Paris.[30]

The main conference got under way on 30 July 1989. It opened with star appearances by James Baker, Eduard Shevardnadze and Qian Qichen, and some people still had high hopes. One western diplomat explained:

These days nobody has an axe to grind in the international arena. The Khmer Rouge have served their purpose for China, this conference gives China an honourable way out.... China can put the Khmer Rouge up at the polls, they aren't likely to poll well and then will be seen to have failed on their own.

But the conference was a failure from day one. Each side reiterated its established position, and conceded nothing. Khieu Samphan objected to all attempts to establish working parties to examine the technical aspects of a settlement. Then Qian Qichen took him out to dinner, and next morning all the objections had disappeared. The working parties put in a month's labour on the details, but there was no agreement at all about the overall framework of a settlement. The basic issues were the usual ones. The CGDK groups demanded they each get equal shares in a new government (reducing the existing State of Cambodia to a minority grouping) before elections were held. Hun Sen was willing to accept them into a governmental council to oversee a ceasefire and national elections, but not to grant them political power before the elections.

The Khmer Rouge denied that Hanoi was withdrawing at all, saying that many thousands of Vietnamese soldiers remained, in disguise, along with hundreds of thousands of settlers. Hun Sen invited the conference to send a team of observers to Cambodia to verify that these claims were untrue. But the Khmer Rouge vetoed this, and declared it would continue the war against the 'puppet' regime. Sihanouk dutifully supported the Khmer Rouge on all of these issues. He said that the Phnom Penh government 'doesn't exist, but by the imperialist, colonialist, and dictatorial will of the Socialist Republic of Vietnam' and that 'final victory' in the war would go to the resistance.

Sihanouk obviously felt that he had no choice but to do the bidding of the Khmer Rouge and China in Paris. But before the meeting reconvened, he made one forlorn effort to break the deadlock. Sihanouk declared he would break with the Khmer Rouge 'even if China is against it' if an 'overwhelming majority' of other countries would support him.[31] There was no support for this from ASEAN and the West. Instead, they pushed a French–Indonesian proposal in which the State of Cambodia would be dissolved, and Hun Sen given the prime ministership in a quadripartite government. Both the Cambodian sides rejected this idea immediately.

With the deadlock obviously unbroken, the US secretary of state, and the Soviet, Chinese, and UK foreign ministers declined to turn up at all for the closing session on 28–30 August, as did UN Secretary General Perez de Cuellar. 'It was all very depressing', said one who stuck it out to the grim end, Australian Foreign Minister Gareth Evans.

Sihanouk was the greatest loser at Paris. The Americans had apparently expected that it would be his hour of triumph. Elizabeth Becker wrote: 'Paris conference leaders expected Prince Sihanouk to rise to the occasion and bring his countrymen together.... [Sihanouk] seemed to embody Cambodian nationalism, abroad and at home.' After watching his performance at Paris, she wrote, 'some diplomats ... have begun to wonder if Prince Sihanouk's day has not passed'.[32] US diplomats were dismayed by his obvious subservience to the Khmer Rouge, but continued to back him.

In May Sihanouk had said: 'Time is working against the Khmer Rouge, so the Khmer Rouge must launch a big offensive, a blitzkrieg against Phnom Penh.' It had already launched a new offensive on the southern section of the border in April. The fighting was little reported, but government/Vietnamese counter-attacks drove 10,000 people out of Khmer Rouge camps on the border in the heaviest fighting since 1985.

In June the Khmer Rouge began preparations for a bigger offensive. It took 4,000 refugees from Ta Luen camp to border restaging posts. These people were pressed into the army, or forced to work as porters. Several hundred managed to escape, and sought sanctuary in the KPNLF camp at Sok Sanh; Thai officials returned them to the Khmer Rouge, saying they had to uphold the principle that 'refugees belong to their leaders'.[33] In July western relief workers said 23,000 people had been removed from Khmer Rouge camps over the last year.

Following the Paris conference Pol Pot re-emerged, according to Thai sources, as the man in overall control of the Khmer Rouge.[34] Ta Mok moved some of his forces from the northern to the southwestern border. As the Vietnamese withdrew their troops, the Khmer Rouge launched a major offensive in the Cardamon Mountains, in the long-contested hills around Pailin in the first instance. The Khmer Rouge claimed to have captured Pailin on 22 October, and was reported to be preparing to swoop down from the mountains into Battambang province. Guerrillas also stepped up hit-and-run attacks elsewhere in the country. Their radio broadcasts exhorted government soldiers and officials to come over to the Khmer Rouge side immediately if they wanted to stay alive.[35] To stay in the game the non-Communist resistance also had to go on the offensive. The KPNLF seized a string of government outposts along Route 69, running north from Sisophon to Banteay Chhmar. The ANS also claimed to have overrun government posts in Oddar Meanchey province, to the north.

It was probably always inevitable that the negotiations would fail. The idea that the Khmer Rouge leaders would meekly lay down their arms if they were rejected by the voters in nation-wide elections was probably as ill founded as the idea that Sihanouk could control them. For most western statesmen, it seemed, diplomacy was the art of compromise and the Pol Pot army was just one more bargaining chip. But the Khmer Rouge leaders were raised on the conviction that political power grows out of the barrel of a gun.

And so the fighting resumed. This time the State of Cambodia was standing alone against the CGDK forces. Both sides were aided and supported by outside allies, but this was a civil war of Cambodian against Cambodian. In essence it always had been a civil war, ever since Sirik Matik and Lon Nol overthrew Sihanouk in 1970. This had been obscured by the way the Vietnamese, the Americans, the Chinese and the Thai had all been drawn into it in varying ways. Now it was being fought out to the bitter end.

Pol Pot's Last Stand?

The terms on which the Cambodians fought each other had always been heavily influenced by outside forces, and this continued to be the case in 1989. The Vietnamese had gone, but they left a well-equipped army of 50,000 troops and 100,000 village militiamen behind. The Soviets continued to supply arms to Phnom Penh. China, ASEAN and the USA

continued to support some 40,000 CGDK troops, about half of them
Khmer Rouge, operating from secure sanctuaries in Thailand. But with
the Vietnamese gone, with US–Soviet and Sino-Soviet detente, and with
Thailand seeking to mend fences with the Indochinese countries, fuelling
the conflict no longer served any useful purpose to anyone but the ideological hardliners in Singapore and Bangkok.

The policy of the Americans seemed to be in complete disarray after
the Paris conference. They had seen the Reagan 'democratic revolution'
taking place in Cambodia through the non-Communist resistance groups.
Now they looked as if they were mere cat's-paws for the Khmer Rouge.
There was a growing awareness that the USA's ability to influence the
outcome of events was really marginal.

The publicity given to Sihanouk's performance in Paris sparked the
first significant public debate about the administration's Cambodia policy.
Assistant Secretary of State Richard Solomon explained that the US
government continued to be 'absolutely opposed' to Khmer Rouge participation in government, and wanted to ensure that 'there are no more
killing fields in Cambodia'. But Sihanouk, said Solomon, was 'our horse
in this race' – and Sihanouk supported the inclusion of the Khmer Rouge
in the government. It would be, he added, 'self-delusional' to ignore the
Khmer Rouge. This, said one critic of the administration, Democrat Con-
gressman Chester Atkins, was 'the most twisted and distorted logic that
I've ever seen in foreign policy'.

The USA joined China in blaming the failure to make peace at Paris
on the 'intransigence' of Hanoi. The proof of this was Hun Sen's refusal
to accept the Khmer Rouge into government. Because of this, declared
Deputy Assistant Secretary of State David F. Lambertson:

> In the present situation we plan to steadfastly maintain our support for the
> diplomatic and economic isolation of Vietnam as a reminder ... that attempts
> to manipulate international opinion will not provide a real basis for improved
> relations with other countries.

An IMF team which visited Hanoi in mid-year praised the Vietnamese
economic reforms and recommended that Vietnam be permitted to re-
enter the international economic community, and provided with a struc-
tural adjustment loan to assist in this. The USA and Japan – the latter
in response to US pressure – insisted on blocking this.

Vietnam went ahead with its troop withdrawal as planned on 20–26
September 1989. General Vo Nguyen Giap hosted a reception for the
officers, and spoke of the proud achievements of the People's army of
Vietnam. One of the returning officers said that Vietnam was able to
withdraw because it had achieved its objectives in Cambodia once the

Cambodian people were able to defend themselves. 'The difficulties which our Division faced in the Cambodian war were very minor compared to those we faced in the war with America', he said. 'In the American war, we had the philosophy that one doesn't win because of equipment and supplies, but because one's cause is just. I think the Cambodian people also have a just cause in trying to prevent the return of the Khmer Rouge.' A young soldier took a more prosaic view. Asked his opinion on the withdrawal, he said: 'It's nice to talk to Vietnamese girls again.'

China and the CGDK had been demanding that Vietnam withdraw from Cambodia unconditionally. Now the withdrawal was condemned because it was not part of a 'comprehensive settlement'. The *People's Daily* quoted Sihanouk saying Vietnam's withdrawal was a 'sham' and that Vietnam was 'cheating'. Declaring that China would continue to send arms to the Khmer Rouge, a Foreign Ministry spokesman said on 28 September: 'Clearly there has been no change in Vietnam's basic scheme for keeping Cambodia under its control and creating an Indochina Federation.'

Reporters who visited Cambodia, however, said that the withdrawal was genuine. So did the US Department of Defense. CGDK groups continued to issue claims of vast numbers of Vietnamese in Cambodian uniforms. 'I have heard many reports of Vietnamese disguised as Phnom Penh soldiers', said a military analyst in Thailand. 'I am not saying it isn't happening, but we have no proof.' In Washington Secretary Lambertson continued to blame Hanoi's intransigence for the slide into 'the military option', and called for Moscow to cut off arms to Phnom Penh. Shevardnadze responded with a proposal that all outside powers stop supplying arms to Cambodian factions.

Bangkok definitely did not want an escalating civil war on its border. Chatichai tried to arrange a ceasefire, and invited Hun Sen to Bangkok. Hun Sen readily agreed to a ceasefire, but urged Chatichai to stop allowing arms to pass through Thai territory, and to stop giving sanctuary to the Khmer Rouge. According to Hun Sen, Chatichai responded: 'We need a ceasefire agreement and then we will tell all the superpowers to stop sending arms to Cambodia.' But Rannarith and Son Sann rejected this.

At Chatichai's urging, Hun Sen agreed to talk to Sihanouk once again. Chaovalit then flew to Beijing for discussions with Sihanouk. The Chinese said that Sihanouk had refused categorically to talk to Hun Sen, and that this was 'justifiable' because Vietnam 'lacks sincerity'. But arriving back in Bangkok, Chaovalit gave a different version of his discussion with Sihanouk. He said that the prince had agreed to talks 'as soon as possible', but he could not say when that would be. It seemed that Sihanouk was not in any position to decide such issues for himself.

The Chatichai government was still not willing to close military supply routes through its territory without a settlement – that would be in defiance of both China and the USA. 'We would like to see a lead against the Khmer Rouge taken by the US before we close the Chinese supply route', said a Thai official. No such lead was forthcoming. Indeed, Thai officials said, 'despite its publicly expressed revulsion towards the Khmer Rouge, the US has been quietly aiding the Khmer Rouge war for several years.'[36]

Everything seemed to depend on the Chinese. In essence, neither the Thai nor the Americans and their allies were willing to upset Beijing by dumping the CGDK and coming to terms with the State of Cambodia. And in late 1989, at least for the time being, the Chinese were letting themselves be guided by their Cambodian allies. But the Khmer Rouge leaders could not be sure how long Chinese support for them would last. The Chinese had no fondness for the Khmer Rouge itself (at least in post-Gang of Four times), but had found it useful as a way of bashing the Vietnamese. With Hanoi's troops out of Cambodia, it was not doing that any more. Nor was it obvious what China would really gain if the Khmer Rouge replaced the State of Cambodia in Phnom Penh.

The pattern of Chinese policy in the past had been to go along with Khmer Rouge propaganda initially, then to make a concession and, finally, to force the Khmer Rouge into line. In dealing with the USSR, Vietnam and Laos, the Chinese had also moved quietly to restore economic ties before normalizing political relations. It seemed possible that this pattern would be repeated after the Vietnamese withdrawal from Cambodia. In his meeting with Kaysone in October 1989, Deng had said that Sino-Vietnamese relations would 'finally improve' if Vietnam 'withdraws its troops completely and thoroughly from Vietnam. We have no other demands.' He made no mention of dismantling the Phnom Penh government, or sharing power with the Khmer Rouge. Furthermore, after Vietnam set its September withdrawal date, Chinese merchants began visiting Phnom Penh.

The Chinese were evidently impressed with what they saw. A Chinese journalist who visited Phnom Penh wrote in a Shanghai newspaper that Cambodia had 'risen from the grave' under the Heng Samrin government. The new round of war in Cambodia in 1989 thus cut against the grain of the wider trends. If the State of Cambodia proved capable of containing the Khmer Rouge offensive, this could easily turn out to be Pol Pot's last stand.

Notes

1. *Asiaweek*, 13 May 1988.
2. Martin Stuart-Fox, *Vietnam in Laos: Hanoi's Model for Kampuchea*, Essays on

Strategy and Diplomacy no. 8, May 1987, Kech Center for International Strategic Studies, p. 8.

3. Paisal Sricharatchanya, *Far Eastern Economic Review*, 19 September 1985.

4. Grant Evans, 'Thai–Lao Relations: "Three Villages" not Trade Is the Key', *Nation* (Bangkok), 22 February 1987.

5. *Bangkok Post*, 23 February 1988; *Age* (Melbourne), 6 April 1988. Kukrit later said: 'I want to destroy the relationship between Thailand and Laos because it does not benefit Thailand' (*Nation* [Bangkok], 13 August 1989).

6. Termsak C. Palanupap, 'Thai–Lao Border Conflict: Legacy of Colonialism', *Nation* (Bangkok), 21 February 1988.

7. Martin Stuart-Fox, 'Laos in 1988: In Pursuit of New Directions', *Asian Survey*, vol. 29, 1989.

8. For an extended discussion of Lao economic policy, see Grant Evans, 'Planning Problems in Peripheral Socialism: The Case of Laos', in Leonard Unger and Joseph J. Zasloff, eds, *Current Developments in Laos*, New York 1990. See also the series of articles on the Lao economy by Evans in the *Asian Wall Street Journal*, 14–15, 17–18 February 1989.

9. For a journalistic beat-up on the issue, see Alan Dawson, *Bangkok Post*, 7 February 1988. For an overview of the heroin trade in the region (including estimates of production by country) see Jon A. Wiant, 'Narcotics in the Golden Triangle', *Washington Quarterly*, vol. 8, 1985.

10. Elizabeth Becker, *When the War Was Over*, New York 1986, p. 444. See also her review article, 'The Hanoi Pact', *New Republic*, 20 October 1986.

11. Nayan Chanda, *Brother Enemy*, San Diego 1986, p. 372.

12. Jacques Bekaert, *Bangkok Post*, 27 December 1986, reporting the views of an unnamed, pro-CGDK diplomat.

13. Michael Vickery, *Cambodia: Politics, Economics and Society*, London 1986, pp. 78–9; Nick Cuming-Bruce, *Far Eastern Economic Review*, 25 December 1986.

14. Clayton Jones, *Christian Science Monitor*, 25–31 July 1988. This figure may include candidates as well as full members.

15. James Pringle, *The Independent* (London), 23 February 1989; cf. also H. H. S. Greenway, *Guardian Weekly*, 19 March 1989.

16. Prince Rannarith, reported in the *Australian*, 10 February 1988.

17. Sihanouk, interview by Debra Weiner, in *Playboy* (US edn), May 1987, pp. 71, 70, 62. We have changed the order but not the sense of the passages quoted.

18. Rannarith, on Voice of the Khmer, 7 February 1988.

19. SPK, the official Phnom Penh news agency, 1 February 1988.

20. *Asiaweek*, 10 June 1988.

21. Marcel Barung, *South*, October 1988.

22. Cameron Forbes, *Age*, 6 July 1989.

23. *Far Eastern Economic Review*, 2 March 1989.

24. Nayan Chanda, *Far Eastern Economic Review*, 2 March 1989.

25. The changes were reported by SPK, 1 May 1989. Western press reports said that Phnom Penh dropped 'Kampuchea' in favour of 'Cambodia'; but the original Khmer word remained unchanged.

26. Paisal Sricharatchanya, *Far Eastern Economic Review*, 11 May 1989.

27. United Press International, 30 April 1989.

28. Voice of Democratic Kampuchea, 5 June 1989.

29. Michael Field, Rodney Tasker and Murray Hiebert, *Far Eastern Economic Review*, 7 September 1989.

30. *Asiaweek*, 11 August 1989.

31. *Bangkok Post*, 20 August 1989.

32. Elizabeth Becker, *Age*, 3 September 1989, from the *Washington Post*.

33. *Age*, 28 June 1989.

34. Rodney Tasker and Murray Hiebert, *Far Eastern Economic Review*, 28 September 1989.

35. Voice of the National Army of DK, 24 October 1989.

36. Michael Field, Rodney Tasker and Murray Hiebert, *Far Eastern Economic Review*, 7 September 1989.

11

Red Brotherhood
in War and Peace

The Third Indochina War, which began with Democratic Kampuchea (DK) attacks on Vietnam in January 1977, was not the product of either 'proletarian internationalism' or of 'nationalist deviations'; still less was it the result of deep-buried 'traditional antagonisms'. The Communist movements of Indochina have their roots in the nationalist revolt against western colonialism, and the war had its basis in the dynamics of that revolt.

The main driving force for revolutionary change in Indochina as a whole was the cataclysmic upheaval in the most developed and populous country, Vietnam. It was inevitable that Vietnamese influence was deeply imprinted on the Communist movements of Laos and Cambodia. But as they developed a social and political base of their own, they adapted to different national political environments, and their paths diverged. This was true even of Laos which, while a close ally of Vietnam's, followed its own path on economic policy, for example. The presence of Vietnamese troops in Laos reflected tensions with China and, to a lesser extent Thailand, rather than the installation of a quasi-colonial Vietnamese 'garrison-state' as anti-Vientiane propagandists claimed.

The immediate catalyst of the Third Indochina War was not Hanoi's alleged expansionism, but the violent and provocative conduct of Pol Pot's regime. It is thus on the nature of the DK regime rather than on the alleged regional ambitions of Vietnam that we have to focus if we wish to understand the genesis of the Third Indochina War. In the chaos that followed the overthrow of Sihanouk, the Khmer Rouge rose from extreme isolation to state power in only five years. Its resort to terrorist methods of rule was a symptom of weakness and insecurity rather than a sign of strength. It resulted in a highly centralized military police state, headed by a family clique, which cultivated nationalist delirium in a des-

301

perate attempt to establish its legitimacy. As Anthony Barnett has pointed out, this is only one of a number of wars precipitated in the late 1970s and early 1980s by unstable dictatorships in an attempt to create internal unity, with similarly disastrous consequences, among them Somalia's invasion of Ethiopia, Uganda's invasion of Tanzania, Iraq's invasion of Iran and Argentina's occupation of the Falklands.[1]

The local conflict was compounded by the actions of the great powers, above all China. The Communist victories in Indochina in 1975 fundamentally recast the balance of power in the whole Southeast Asian region. With American power on the retreat, China aspired to establish itself as the dominant power in the region, and saw the USSR as its main rival. China's drive to open diplomatic and trade relations with Southeast Asian nations was highly successful. Ironically, it was in Communist Vietnam that China's demands met with the most resistance: there were few countries with more ties to Beijing, but Hanoi's leaders had long struggled to balance Chinese with Soviet patronage. The Lao followed suit. In Communist Indochina, only Pol Pot's regime aligned itself with China. Support for it provided Beijing with a way of increasing the pressure on Hanoi.

After 1975 China's increasing assertiveness made Hanoi's balancing act between Beijing and Moscow increasingly difficult. While the non-Communist countries of Southeast Asia were able to offset Chinese influence with American influence, this course was not open to Vietnam. As the Chinese stepped up their pressure, Hanoi had little choice but to align itself with Moscow, strengthen its alliance with Vientiane, and prepare to face Beijing's wrath. When the Vietnamese overthrew Pol Pot's regime, it was quick in coming. China was odds with Vietnam in the 1970s over a range of issues other than Cambodia. There was the question of the status of the Hoa in Vietnam, and the ownership of the Spratly and Paracel Islands.

But the most fundamental issue was Hanoi's alignment with Moscow, and it was this which bought the USA (and, in its wake, most western countries) into alignment with China over the Cambodia conflict during the early 1980s. The result was western support for the non-Communist resistance groups on the Thai border, and their alliance with the Khmer Rouge in the Coalition Government of Kampuchea (CGDK).

The CGDK was never able to pose an effective challenge to the Vietnamese. But with sanctuary in Thailand, it could not be eliminated either. This was a stalemate, but of a distinctive kind, for the People's Republic of Kampuchea was in effective control of most of Cambodia, and was able to consolidate its position. This was one factor which led Hanoi to move towards a withdrawal of its troops from Cambodia. The other factor was the Sino-Soviet thaw, which removed much of the original motivation of Beijing's anti-Hanoi policies and also widened the rift between the USA and China over Cambodia. The US response was to persuade itself that the non-Communist resistance groups it was backing would be the chief beneficiary of Sino-Soviet efforts to find a compromise. That was always fanciful, and by the end of the 1980s the USA was starting to awaken to how little influence it had on events in contemporary Indochina.

It is probable that – like other great powers before it – China has no permanent friends, only permanent interests. At least in the post-Gang of Four period, China's support for the Khmer Rouge has been based on their joint opposition to Vietnam rather on than any common ideological goal. And as China has slowly softened its anti-Vietnamese stance in the wake of Sino-Soviet detente, there have been clear signs that it is distancing itself from the Khmer Rouge.

In the 1970s, China's behaviour was that of an immature great power. It was both arrogant and insecure in its handling of Vietnam, and threw its weight behind a discredited cause in Cambodia. In the 1980s, Chinese diplomacy has become more mature. As relations with the Soviets improved, China felt confident enough to abandon the Stalinist assumption of exclusive spheres of influence in favour of a pluralism of powers in Southeast Asia. This led it quietly to soften its stance towards Vietnam and to fully normalize its relations with Laos. Beijing policy-makers knew that this would enable them to diversify their foreign relations, and that no threat was posed to China.

In this context, Chinese policy towards Cambodia became an embarrassing anachronism. China had committed itself strongly to the Khmer Rouge, but as it wound down its quarrel with Vietnam the strategic purpose was lost – especially once Vietnam had fulfilled China's demand to withdraw its troops from Cambodia. China can be defeated, but it cannot let itself be *seen* to have been defeated. It is thus not hard to envisage the shape of a Sino-Vietnamese *rapprochement*. Having achieved its objectives in Cambodia, Hanoi must apologise profusely. After a decent interval, China will then accept the reality of Vietnamese withdrawal and quietly distance itself from the Khmer Rouge. This opens the way for a possible settlement based on the Phnom Penh administration; suitably reorganized, perhaps renamed, and its mandate renewed through general elections.

The Third Indochina War was a pivotal moment in the disintegration of what in Stalin's time was supposed to be one single 'socialist camp'. To be sure, there had been crises before, notably as first Yugoslavia and then China went their own way. And Soviet and Chinese troops had fought each on the Sino-Soviet border in 1969. But this was the first full-scale war between Communist states. That was not supposed to happen. Mao had proudly told General Montgomery in 1961: 'We are Marxist-Leninist, our state is a socialist state not a capitalist state, therefore we wouldn't invade others in a hundred years or even ten thousand years.'[2] His successors had proved him wrong within three years of his death.

In closing, it worth reflecting on the broader implications of Communist nationalism. According to orthodox Marxist theory, the state is essentially an institution of class power. Hence the terminology of 'bourgeois states', 'proletarian states', and so on. Conflict between capitalist and Communist states is understood as a form of the class struggle. It is a systemic conflict, although the forms it takes may vary widely. On this, though not on its socio-economic roots, the anti-Communist militants are in full agreement. For orthodox Marxism, conflicts between capitalist states can also be explained readily enough, in terms of the anarchy and competition engendered by the global spread of the capitalist system. Conflicts between Communist states are not so readily explained.

A central part of our argument is that the motive force of the revolutions in Indochina has been state-building and political mobilization in which nationalism is not a 'deviation' but an expression of the central aspiration, the creation of a sovereign nation-state. Khieu Samphan was probably speaking for many Third World radicals when he declared in the early 1980s that socialism was only a means to this end. In recent years there has been much theorizing about the 'relative autonomy' of the state from its class base. Too often, this is a form of theoretical double-talk which allows recognition of the problem while evading giving an answer to it. Some writers, however, have developed the idea in a quite illuminating fashion. Theda Skocpol has observe that international state relations have a fundamental impact on the degree of state autonomy from internal forces:

> a state's involvement in an international network of states is a basis for potential autonomy of action over and against groups and economic arrangements within its jurisdiction — even including the dominant class and existing relations of production. For international military pressures and opportunities can prompt state rulers to attempt policies that conflict with, and even in extreme instances contradict, the fundamental interests of a dominant class.[3]

In the present context, such a perspective explains our primary concentration on international politics rather than domestic developments in the states of Indochina.

Such an approach can readily lead to the view that all states, Communist or not, are driven by the same basic logic of power politics.

Such an approach has much to recommend it in preference to utopian versions of socialist internationalism, the rhetoric of which often masks straightforward *raison d'état* - this was the case with the 'Brezhnev Doctrine' formulated in justification of the Warsaw Pact intervention in Czechoslovakia in 1968. But the pure realist approach overlooks the internal organizational and socio-economic coordinates of state power.

Marxist revolutionaries in the twentieth century found that their 'historical mission' was not so much leading the working class in advanced industrial capitalist societies, but state-building in underdeveloped countries. It is, therefore, hardly surprising to find that they are among the most strident promulgators of nationalist ideology. They more than anyone have been prepared to acquiesce in 'an international order which accepts as its basis the submersion of the rights of the individual in the rights of the nation'.[4] The dangers inherent in this are evident enough in the rhetoric pouring out of Beijing in the wake of the June 1989 repression. No criticism of such actions can be tolerated, on the grounds that they are an 'internal affair' of the Chinese people. Pol Pot, of course, took refuge in a similar rhetoric.

Against this background, it is perhaps not surprising that the forms of international organization that have existed among Communist states to date have usually been politically imposed or a product of military necessity. It has been an internationalism of bureaucrats, not of people. Hence their brittle character, as revealed by recent developments in Eastern Europe – not to mention the 'fraternal solidarity' between Vietnam and Democratic Kampuchea. But it may be premature to pronounce 'socialist internationalism' dead.

If the creation of nation-states in some sense involves the creation of 'imagined communities' at a national level, to use Ben Anderson's evocative phrase, then internationalism must involve the creation of an 'imagined community' on an international level. Are there forces pushing in the direction of such an international community? Gellner argues that the age of industrialism creates a universal culture, rather than one based on direct personal ties, and we live in a nationalist era because the state is the main agency for producing this culture.[5] But the process of universalization which he sees occuring across specific societies is also occurring across national boundaries, not least because of the increasing flow of people, commodities and information around the globe. This suggests that an organic – rather than an imposed – internationalism is most likely to emerge in those countries most fully integrated into the international economy of advanced industrialism.

The democratization of the Eastern European states is clearly linked to the process of European integration. Twenty years ago, the idea of a 'United States of Europe' was little more than a utopian fantasy. It is now rapidly becoming a reality, and it is no surprise that the most dynamic nations of Europe – the advanced capitalist ones, not the ones with centrally planned economies – are leading the way. From this perspective, many of the features of the 'socialist internationalism' that developed in the Stalinist era are actually barriers to the development of a genuine internationalism.

Talk of the 'death of Communism' often obscures as much as it reveals. It is true that the Gorbachev revolution is sweeping away the relics of Stalinism in the Soviet Union and Eastern Europe. It is much less clear what will take its place. As there are wide variations in historical circumstances, levels of economic development and social structures from one part of what was once a 'monolithic' Soviet bloc to another, it is unlikely that any single pattern will prevail. If pluralist democracy and a market-socialist economy seem most probable in the more developed countries, 'developmental-authoritarian' regimes are more likely in the most backward ones. At least a few of these regimes seem likely to decay into satraps ruled by family cliques in the style of the Mafia or some of the more notorious Latin American generals.

The agrarian Communist states of Indochina seem most likely to fall into the 'developmental-authoritarian' zone of this spectrum. This means that they will have more in common with the China of Li Peng than with, say, Hungary. Vietnamese diplomats are no doubt hastening to point this out whenever they meet their Chinese counterparts. But this does not mean that pure Stalinism is being upheld here. Both China and the Indochinese countries are committed to economic reform, and to opening up their economies to international trade and investment. Authentic versions of high Stalinism survive only in a few beleaguered outposts (Albania, North Korea and the surviving rump of Democratic Kampuchea). Both the Soviet Union and China are so vast and heterogeneous that this whole process is being felt as centrifugal forces within them. Assuming the central authorities retain control in both countries, neither will cease to be a great power, with its own particular regional and global interests to protect.

Under these circumstances, it is uncertain how much of Gorbachev's Vladivostok vision of a new 'socialist community' of nations, basing their relations on respect for national sovereignty and mutual benefits, will come about. Less rather than more, we suspect. The magnetic poles of the emerging world-order are based on economic rather than military strength, and are located in capitalist Europe and Asia, rather than in Moscow or Beijing (or Washington).

The idea that we are witnessing the 'end of the Cold War' is also both true and false. It is true that Gorbachev's diplomacy has succeeded in discrediting the Cold War rhetoric of the early 1980s. The speed with which he was able to do this shows how the rhetoric of the Cold War had already become obsolete, on both sides. But the Cold War was much more than an ideological contest. The Soviet Union and China remain great powers with their own particular interests – interests which conflict with, as well as overlap, those of the USA. If the Cold War began with the division of Europe into two opposing spheres of influence, the confrontation of the two blocs in Europe had become largely ritualistic long before Gorbachev. What did Soviet troops in East Germany (or US troops in West Germany) add to the security of Moscow (or Washington) when the real danger, militarily, was that of thousands of nuclear missiles raining down from the stratosphere?

From 1950 onwards, the real military conflicts of the Cold War have been fought out on the soil of Third World countries, above all in Asia. Political instability and regional conflicts, and the temptation of the great powers to intervene in them, have not disappeared because of the opening of the Gorbachev era. One has only to look at Washington's behaviour towards Central America to realize this. Indeed, one of the dangers of the 'post-Cold War' era is that the USA, buoyed up by the conviction that it has 'won' the Cold War, will adopt a stance that is more rather than less interventionist, although the reality is that Washington's ability to control world affairs has – like Moscow's – actually been in decline.

Vietnam and its neighbours were devastated by the military conflicts of the Cold War, and then hit hard by the emergence of China as a great power. But today, the prospects of dissolving the opposing blocs that have divided Southeast Asia and opening an era of regional co-operation are better than they have been for decades – not least because all the great powers have burnt their fingers badly through military intervention (the USA and China in Vietnam; the Soviets in Afghanistan) and will not lightly repeat their past blunders. This has ensured that the people of Indochina underwent a particularly traumatic initiation into the modern political world. Now, perhaps, as the region sets the conflicts of the Cold War era behind it, it may mean that a younger generation will have the chance to enjoy peace and even a measure of prosperity. Let us hope that the vision of mainland Southeast Asia as a 'golden land' is an idea whose time has come.

Notes

1. Anthony Barnett, 'Iron Britannia', *New Left Review*, no. 134, July–August 1982, pp. 65–6.
2. Quoted in Dick Wislon, *Mao: The People's Emperor*, Melbourne 1979. p. 362.

3. Theda Skocpol, *States and Social Revolutions*, London 1979. p. 31. See also Michael Mann, *The Sources of Social Power*, Cambridge 1986.

4. E. H. Carr, *Nationalism and After*, London 1945. p. 43.

5. Ernest Gellner, *Nations and Nationalism*, London 1983, pp. 35–9.

Bibliography

As a work of contemporary history, this book is based primarily on current investigations, and our own discussions with those involved in the events, rather than on published research. The best coverage is to be found in the Hong Kong weekly, *Far Eastern Economic Review*. In its *Asia Yearbook* the same office produces a valuable reference work. *Asiaweek*, also published in Hong Kong, is the *Review*'s main competitor. One publication which brings together information from a wide range of sources is the monthly *Keesing's Record of World Events* (formerly *Keesing's Contemporary Archives*), published in London. Many important statements are broadcast over radio, and are most accessible in the BBC's *Summary of World Broadcasts* (London).

We have also sought to keep abreast of scholarly publications in relevant fields. When the first edition of this work appeared, there were few dealing with post-1975 developments. With the passage of time, of course, the number of such works has multiplied rapidly. Here we list those we have found the most useful – or important. Other publications, from which we have used only particular points, are given in the relevant footnotes. William W. Sage and Judith A.N. Henchy, *Laos: A Bibliography* (Institute of Southeast Asian Studies Library Bulletin no. 16, Singapore 1986) provides a good guide to publications on one of the countries we are concerned with.

Ablin, David A. and Hood, Marlowe, eds, *The Cambodian Agony*, New York 1987.

Adams, Nina and McCoy, Alfred W., eds, *Laos: War and Revolution*, New York 1970.

Anderson, Benedict R., *Imagined Communities: Reflections on the Origins of Nationalism*, London 1983.

Barnett, A. Doak, *The Making of Foreign Policy in China: Structure and Process*, London 1985.

Becker, Elizabeth, *When the War Was Over: The Voices of Cambodia's Revolution and its People*, New York 1986.

Beresford, Melanie, *Vietnam: Politics, Economics and Society*, London and New York 1988.

Brown, MacAlister and Zasloff, Joseph J., *Apprentice Revolutionaries: The Communist Movement in Laos 1935–1985*, Stanford 1986.

Burchett, Wilfred G., *The Vietnam–China–Cambodia Triangle*, London 1981.

Buszynski, Leszek, *Soviet Foreign Policy and Southeast Asia*, London 1986.

——, 'Soviet Foreign Policy and Southeast Asia: Prospects for the Gorbachev Era', *Asian Survey*, vol. 26, 1986.

Chanda, Nayan, *Brother Enemy: The War after the War*, San Diego 1986.

Chandler, David P., *A History of Cambodia*, Boulder 1983.

—— and Kiernan, Ben, eds, *Revolution and its Aftermath in Kampuchea: Eight Essays*, New Haven 1983.

Chang, Pao Min, 'The Sino-Vietnamese Conflict over the Ethnic Chinese', *China Quarterly*, no. 90, 1982.

——, *The Sino-Vietnamese Territorial Dispute*, Singapore 1983.

——, *Kampuchea between China and Vietnam*, Singapore 1985.

Chen, King C., *China's War with Vietnam, 1979: Issues, Decisions, and Implications*, Stanford 1988.

Dommen, Arthur J., *Laos: Keystone of Indochina*, Boulder 1985.

Duiker, William J., *The Communist Road to Power in Vietnam*, Boulder 1981.

——, *Vietnam Since the Fall of Saigon*, revised edn, Athens, Ohio 1985.

——, *China and Vietnam: The Roots of Conflict*, Berkeley 1986.

Etcheson, Craig, *The Rise and Demise of Democratic Kampuchea*, Boulder 1984.

Elliott, David W.P., ed., *The Third Indochina Conflict*, Boulder 1981.

Evans, Grant, *The Yellow Rainmakers: Are Chemical Weapons Being Used in Southeast Asia?*, London 1983.

——, *Agrarian Change in Communist Laos*, Singapore 1988.

Fitzgerald, Stephen, *China and the Overseas Chinese: A Study of Peking's Changing Policy 1949–70*, Cambridge 1972.

Gellner, Ernest, *Nations and Nationalism*, London 1983.

Girling, John, *Thailand: Society and Politics*, Ithaca 1981.

Grant, Bruce, *The 'Boat People': An 'Age' Investigation*, Melbourne 1979.

Gunn, Geoffrey C., 'Resistance Coalitions in Laos', *Asian Survey*, vol. 23, 1983.

Harrison, Selig S., *China, Oil and Asia: Conflict Ahead?*, New York 1977.

Horn, Robert C. 'Vietnam and Sino-Soviet Relations: What Price Rapprochement?', *Asian Survey*, vol. 27, 1987.

Kiernan, Ben, *How Pol Pot Came to Power: A History of Communism in Cambodia 1930–1975*, London 1985.

——, 'New Light on the Origins of the Vietnam–Kampuchea Conflict', *Bulletin of Concerned Asian Scholars*, vol. 12, 1980.

—— and, Boua, Chanthou, eds, *Peasants and Politics in Kampuchea 1942–81*, London 1981.

——, *Pol Pot Plans the Future: Confidential Leadership Documents from Democratic Kampuchea, 1976–1977*, New Haven 1988.

Kim, Hong N. and Hammersmith, Jack L., 'US–China Relations in the Post-

Normalisation Era, 1979–1985', *Pacific Affairs*, vol. 59, 1986.

Kimura, Tetsusaburo, *The Vietnamese Economy: Reforms and International Relations*, Tokyo 1989.

Klintworth, Gary, *China's Modernisation: The Strategic Implications for the Asia-Pacific Region*, Canberra 1989.

——, *Vietnam's Intervention in Cambodia in International Law*, Canberra 1989.

Kubalkova, V. and Cruikshank, A.A., *Marxism and International Relations*, Oxford 1985.

Lampton, David M., 'China's Limited Accommodation with the USSR: Coalition Politics', *AEI Foreign Policy and Defence Review*, vol. 6, 1986.

Lawson, Eugene K., *The Sino-Vietnamese Conflict*, New York 1984.

Mason, Linda and Brown, Roger, *Rice, Rivalry and Politics: Managing Cambodian Relief*, Notre Dame 1983.

Marr, David G. and White, Christine P., eds, *Postwar Vietnam: Dilemmas in Socialist Development*, New York 1988.

Medvedev, Roy, *China and the Superpowers*, Oxford 1986.

Mei, Yan, 'The Maturing of Soviet–Chinese Relations', *Annals of AAPS*, vol. 481, 1985.

Mysliwiec, Eva, *Punishing the Poor: The International Isolation of Kampuchea*, London 1988.

Osborne, Milton, *Power and Politics in Cambodia: The Sihanouk Years*, Melbourne 1973.

——, *Before Kampuchea: Preludes to Tragedy*, Sydney 1979.

Pike, Douglas, *Vietnam and the Soviet Union: Anatomy of an Alliance*, Boulder 1987.

Ponchaud, François, *Cambodia Year Zero*, Harmondsworth 1978.

Porter, Gareth, 'Hanoi's Strategic Perspective and the Sino-Vietnamese Conflict', *Pacific Affairs*, vol. 57, 1984.

Prescott, J.R.V., Collier, D.F. and Prescott, D.F., *Frontiers of Southeast Asia*, Melbourne 1977.

Reynell, Josephine, *Political Pawns: Refugees on the Thai–Kampuchean Border*, Oxford 1989.

Robinson, Thomas W., 'The New Era in Sino-Soviet Relations', *Current History*, September 1987.

Ross, Robert S., *The Indochina Tangle: China's Vietnam Policy 1975–1979*, New York 1988.

Samuels, Marwan S., *Contest for the South China Seas*, London 1982.

Segal, Gerald, *Defending China*, London 1985.

——, 'Sino-Soviet Relations: The New Agenda', *World Today*, June 1988.

Shawcross, William, *Sideshow: Kissinger, Nixon, and the Destruction of Cambodia*, 2nd edn, London 1981.

——, *The Quality of Mercy: Cambodia, Holocaust and Modern Conscience*, London 1984.

Steele, Jonathan, *The Limits of Soviet Power: The Kremlin's Foreign Policy – Brezhnev to Chernenko*, revised edn, Harmondsworth 1985.

Stern, Lewis M., 'The Overseas Chinese in the Socialist Republic of Vietnam.

1979–82', *Asian Survey*, vol. 25, 1985.

Stuart-Fox, Martin, *Laos: Politics, Economics and Society*, London and Boulder 1986.

——, *Vietnam in Laos: Hanoi's Model for Kampuchea*, Claremont 1987.

——, ed., *Contemporary Laos: Studies of the Politics and Society of the Lao People's Democratic Republic*, St Lucia, Queensland 1982.

Sutter, Robert G., *Chinese Foreign Policy after the Cultural Revolution 1966–73*, Boulder 1978.

——, *Chinese Foreign Policy: Developments after Mao*, New York 1985.

Taylor, Jay, *China and Southeast Asia: Peking's Relationships with Revolutionary Movements*, New York 1974.

Thakur, Ramesh, and Thayer, Carlyle A., eds, *The Soviet Union as an Asian-Pacific Power*, Boulder 1987.

Toye, Hugh, *Laos: Buffer State or Battleground*, London 1968.

Tri, Vo Nhan, *Socialist Vietnam's Economy 1975–85: An Assessment*, Tokyo 1987.

Ungar, E.S., 'The Struggle Over the Chinese Community in Vietnam', *Pacific Affairs*, vol. 60, 1987–88.

Vickery, Michael, *Kampuchea: Politics, Economics and Society*, London 1986.

——, *Cambodia 1975–1982*, London and Sydney 1984.

Vien, Nguyen Khac, *Vietnam: A Long History*, Hanoi 1987.

Wain, Barry, *The Refused: The Agony of the Indochinese Refugees*, Hong Kong 1981.

Wolf, Eric, *Peasant Wars of the 20th Century*, London 1973.

Zasloff, Joseph J., ed., *Postwar Indochina: Old Enemies and New Allies*, Washington 1988.

Index

ABC News 157
Afghanistan 232, 234, 236, 237, 239,
    240, 241, 307
Africa 248
agriculture
    Cambodian 94, 95, 96, 154, 158, 159,
        164, 273–4
    Lao 68
    Vietnamese 8, 37, 38, 55, 147, 148,
        149, 245–6, 248
aid, foreign 156–60, 178 n18, 195, 198,
    201, 203, 216, 246, 252, 254
    see also specific agencies
Akehurst, Michael 189
Akkanibutr, Pat 265
Albania 70, 127, 306
Ali Alatas 289
Amin, Idi 191
Amnesty International 99, 112 n34,
    163, 179 n29
Anderson, Benedict 305
Andropov, Yuri 234
Angkor 6, 20, 84, 88
Angola 236
Anh, General see Le Duc Anh
ANS see Armée Nationale
    Sihanoukiste
Argentina 288, 302
Arkhipov, Ivan 252, 253
Armée Nationale Sihanoukiste (ANS)
    207, 213, 215, 221, 290, 295
Army of the Republic of Vietnam
    (ARVN) 46, 228, 277
Association of South East Asian

Nations (ASEAN) 39, 40, 41, 42,
    54, 57, 68, 109, 133, 140, 169,
    183–93, 201, 204, 208, 213, 214,
    229, 232, 233, 241, 251, 252, 253,
    254, 257, 259, 264, 275, 278, 279,
    280, 281, 286, 287, 288, 291, 292,
    293, 294, 295
Atkins, Chester 296
Australia 62, 177, 192, 195, 228, 246,
    250, 256, 257
Austria 155

Baker, James 293
Bali 185
Ban Noi Parai 102–3, 104
Bandung Conference (1955) 125
Bangladesh 193
Bao Dai 14, 16, 20
Barnett, Anthony 302
Barung, Marcel 287
Becker, Elizabeth 2, 20, 71, 81, 82, 83,
    85, 89, 96, 97, 107, 109, 111 n13,
    112 n33, 163, 206–7, 273, 294
Beijing Review 242
Black Book on Vietnamese Aggression
    82, 91
Black Paper 1, 86, 92, 101, 108, 136
boat people 53, 54, 183, 184, 228,
    248–51, 261 n21
    see also refugees
Brevie Line 83
Brezhnev, Leonid 174, 234, 236, 237
Brezhnev Doctrine 239, 305
Brown, MacAlister 177

Brzezinski, Zbigniew 44, 56, 141, 232, 233, 235
Bulgaria 240
Burchett, Wilfred 139, 147
Burma 3, 22, 66, 133, 265, 272
Bush, George 237, 242–3, 261, 272, 290
Buszynski, Leszek 178 n13, 240

Cam Ranh Bay 45, 55, 152–3, 178 n13, 178 n14, 234, 238, 253, 264
Cambodia 36, 59, 62, 229
   American policy on 27, 39, 42, 130, 141, 142, 233, 261, 296
   and ASEAN 183–7, 191, 193
   Chinese policy on 115, 118, 137, 139, 234, 237, 241, 252, 253, 258, 259, 298, 303
   famine relief in 156–60, 197
   French colonialism and 8, 9, 10, 14, 17–19
   kingdom of 2–4, 6, 7, 20–24, 26, 30
   and Laos 65, 66, 69–71, 168, 170, 175, 176, 177, 226
   Soviet relations with 238, 239, 240, 254, 256–7, 275
   and Thailand 103, 173, 181, 194–9, 264, 269
   Vietnamese relations with 1, 2, 35, 38, 54, 56, 57, 64, 73, 74, 76, 81–8 passim, 90, 102, 104, 107, 109, 119, 143, 147, 152, 160, 189, 190, 263, 265, 270, 290, 297, 301
   see also Coalition Government of Democratic Kampuchea; Democratic Kampuchea; Khmer Rouge; Norodom Sihanouk; People's Republic of Kampuchea; Pol Pot
Cambodian Democratic Party 18–19, 20
Canada 228
Cao Dai sect 16
capitalism 31, 34 n27, 81, 131, 239, 304
Carter, James 43, 44, 45, 56, 142, 156, 157, 233
Casey, William 233
Catholic Relief Service 195
Catholicism 16, 246
Central Intelligence Agency (CIA) 28, 101, 234, 237
Cham, General see Hoang Cham

Champa, General 225
Chanda, Nayan 51, 70, 108, 109, 217, 252, 273, 290
Chandler, David 32 n4, 164
Chanoff, David 167
Chao La 225
Chaovalit, General see Yongchaiyut, Chaovalit
Charandola, Harish 154
Chatichai, Major-General see Choonhaven, Chatichai
Chea Chutt 206, 211, 221
Chen, King C. 176
Ch'en Yi 128, 129
Chiang Kai-shek 11, 126
China, People's Republic of (PRC) 2, 4, 8, 11, 14, 176, 306, 307
   hegemony of, in Indochina 9–10, 186
   and Laos 60, 66, 74, 168–70, 174, 266, 269
   policy of, on Cambodia 21, 89, 108, 193, 202, 204, 208, 225, 282, 284, 285–6, 292–3, 295, 298, 303
   Soviet relations with 124–9 passim, 131–3, 192, 234–5, 237–8, 239–42, 252–3, 257, 258, 298
   and Thailand 182, 263
   and United States 44, 45, 127, 128, 129, 130, 134, 135, 137, 139, 141, 142, 143, 144 n13, 232–3, 235–6
   and Vietnam 1–2, 37, 39, 40, 41, 46–57 passim, 63, 65, 72, 73, 76, 77, 78, 115–24, 134–9, 141, 143, 147, 148, 151, 153, 155, 168, 185, 187, 190, 201, 212, 213, 227–8, 233, 248, 252–3, 256, 257–8, 259, 278, 279, 291, 297, 301, 302
China Pictorial 47
Chomanan, Kriangsak 74, 75, 100, 157, 170, 171, 182, 197
Choonhaven, Chatichai 265, 270, 288, 289, 291, 297, 298
Chowdry, Golam W. 145 n22
Chulalongkorn, King 22, 24
CIA see Central Intelligence Agency
Coalition Government of Democratic Kampuchea (CGDK) 209–16 passim, 218, 219, 222, 223, 272, 273, 274, 276–83 passim, 290, 291, 293, 295, 296, 297, 302
Cold War 26, 27, 44, 124, 125, 130,

143, 153, 155, 159, 181, 182, 231,
    236, 237, 263, 265, 279, 306–7
colonialism 4, 32, 33 n10, 85, 122, 185,
    301
    British 21
    French 7–14, 17, 18, 19, 20, 81, 86
    Vietnamese 59, 60, 79, 293, 294
Communism 3, 12, 21, 76, 126, 127,
    242, 264, 286, 306
    Cambodian 23, 81, 89, 90, 91, 102,
        161–3, 202, 301
    Chinese 120–25, 129, 131
    in Indochina 1, 14, 32, 39, 40, 181,
        182, 183, 198, 263, 272, 301, 302,
        304, 306
    in Laos 1, 26, 29, 31, 62, 67, 73, 74,
        223–4, 276, 301
    Thai 75, 76
    Vietnamese 11, 12, 13, 16, 17, 24–5,
        35–9, 50, 78, 86, 121, 123, 136,
        229, 249
Communist Party of China 117, 127,
    128, 133–4, 144 n13
Communist Party of Kampuchea
    (CPK) 90, 91, 92, 93, 96, 97, 98,
        99, 101, 107, 119, 137, 138, 195,
        202
Communist Party of the Soviet Union
    238–9
Communist Party of Thailand (CPT)
    75, 76, 172, 267
Confucianism 6, 8, 10, 11, 16, 62, 123
Corriere della Sera 116
Council for Mutual Economic
    Assistance (Comecon) 45, 56, 108,
        139
Cuellar, Perez de 279, 294
Cultural Revolution, Chinese 49, 128,
    129, 130, 131, 135
culture 4, 5, 10, 11, 305
Cushing, Jerry 259
Czechoslovakia 129, 305

democracy 12, 13, 16, 282, 283, 305–6
Democratic Kampuchea (DK) 66, 70,
    82, 84, 85, 86, 94, 96, 99, 100, 101,
        102, 105, 106, 107, 109, 111, 112
        n34, 119, 140, 141, 155, 160, 162,
        176, 184, 185, 187, 191, 192, 202,
        204, 207, 218, 225, 226, 233, 276,
        289, 301, 305, 306

Democratic Republic of Vietnam
    (DRV) 14
Deng Xiaoping 40, 41, 45, 48, 108, 115,
    116, 118, 127, 128, 130, 131, 133,
        140, 141, 142, 143, 182, 187, 197,
        204, 234, 237, 239, 240, 241, 242,
        243, 253, 256, 258–9, 281, 298
Deng Yingchao 139
Diem, Prime Minister see Ngo Dinh
    Diem
Dien Bien Phu 14, 16, 168, 169, 244
Dien Del 205, 206, 220, 221
Do Muoi 244
Doan Van Toai 167
Dommen, Arthur J. 59, 60, 64, 65
drug trafficking 272, 299 n9
Dudman, Richard 96
Duiker, William 151
Dy Lamthol 161

East Germany 240, 307
Economist 35, 36, 57
Ethiopia 302
Evans, Gareth 294
Evans, Grant 299 n8

Falkland Islands 302
Fall, Bernard 16
Fallachi, Oriana 116
Fang Lizhi 243
fascism 12, 13, 14
Faydang Lobliyao 27, 29
Fitzgerald, C. P. 121
Ford, Gerald 42, 43
France 44, 155, 221, 228, 246, 289
    as colonizer 7–14 passim, 17, 18, 19,
        26, 59, 61, 81, 87, 165, 172
Free French forces 14
Front Uni National pour un
    Cambodge Independent Neutre,
    Pacifique et Cooperatif
    (FUNCINPEC) 207, 276
Front Uni pour la Lutte des Races
    Opprimées (Fulro) 227

Gang of Four 48, 56, 133, 137, 144 n13,
    298
Gellner, Ernest 305
Geneva Conference
    1954   14, 15, 16, 19, 20, 21, 89, 121,
        125, 134, 135, 137, 144 n21

1961 28, 62
1979 54, 249
1989 251–2
George III 121, 122
Giap, General *see* Vo Nguyen Giap
Girling, John 181
Gorbachev, Mikhail 174, 236–43
    passim, 254, 255, 256, 257, 260,
    264, 269, 275, 285, 289, 306, 307
Gray, Denis 195
Great Britain 8, 175, 176, 192, 221,
    250, 289, 294
Great Depression 12
Great Han chauvinism 120, 123
Grieg, D. W. 189, 190
Gritz, Bo 226
Gromyko, Andrei 236
Gunn, Geoffrey 223–4, 225, 226, 227
Guomindang 11, 46

Hainan Islands 46
Han Nianlong 117
Hayden, Bill 279
Hender, Stephen 82, 84, 85, 104, 105,
    138, 203, 204
Heng Samrin 108, 109, 155, 156, 162,
    163, 205
  government 7, 99, 168, 186, 187, 190,
    192, 193, 220, 279, 289, 298
Hieu Seng 89, 93
Hing Kamthorn 206
Hing Kuthon 221
Hmong tribespeople 27, 28, 29, 64,
    224, 225, 267
Ho Chi Minh 11, 13, 14, 35, 36, 45, 59
Ho Chi Minh Trail 23, 62, 91
Hoa (ethnic Chinese) 48–53 *passim*, 73,
    137, 246, 258, 302
Hoa Hao sect 16
Hoang Cham 108, 109
Hoang Tung 106
Hoang Van Hoan 37, 135, 143 n5
Holbrooke, Richard 44, 56
Holdridge, John 175
Hong Kong 53, 75, 248, 249, 250, 251
Hou Yuon 96, 97
Houang Qu Vinh 229
Hu Nim 98
Hu Yaobang 235
Hua Guofeng 133, 138, 139, 141, 142,
    258

Huang Hua 48
Hun Sen 157, 161, 162, 166, 259,
    280–94 *passim*, 297
Hungary 240, 255, 306
Hurley, Patrick J. 144 n13
Huy Kung 276

Ieng Sary 83, 86, 89, 96, 97, 99, 101,
    107, 109, 110, 155, 168, 202, 204,
    208, 219, 292
Ieng Thirith 96, 110
In Sakhan 206
India 2, 120, 126, 141, 193, 244, 248,
    259, 285
Indochina 1, 5, 6, 31, 38, 54, 72, 73,
    74, 75, 76, 79, 86–7, 175, 177, 181,
    182, 183, 185, 197, 231, 264, 265,
    307
  China's interests in 137, 138, 140,
    173, 234, 252
  French 7, 8, 10, 12, 14, 18, 19, 35,
    46, 62, 81, 87, 135
  Japanese occupation of 13, 14, 267
  Soviet presence in 174, 237, 240
  United States engagement in 25, 37,
    59, 133, 136, 233
  see also Communism, in Indochina;
    specific countries
Indochina Federation 7, 8, 36, 59, 60,
    70, 86, 87, 118, 176, 177, 297
Indochina War
  First 14, 25, 26, 89
  Second 15, 87, 204
  Third 301–2, 303
Indochinese Communist Party (ICP)
    11, 13, 14, 70, 72, 86, 87
Indonesia 39, 46, 132, 133, 183, 184,
    244, 257, 264, 281, 285, 286, 287,
    288
International Mekong Committee
    (IMC) 176
International Monetary Fund (IMF)
    149, 150, 246, 296
Iran 232, 302
Irangate 233
Iraq 232, 302

Jakarta Informal Meeting (JIM)
  First 285–9 *passim*
  Second 288, 289, 291

Japan 13, 14, 18, 26, 47, 108, 128, 132, 147, 153, 189, 190, 191, 232, 243, 248, 256, 271, 276, 289, 296
Jarai tribe 227
Jenkins, David 150–51
Jiang Qing 133
Johnson, L. B. 130
Jukes, Geoffrey 132

Kam, Henry 204
Kampuchea Krom 84, 100, 101, 107
Kampuchea–Vietnam Friendship Treaty (1979) 165
Kampuchean National United Front for National Salvation (KNUFNS) 109, 164
Kapitska, Mikhail 253
Kaysone Phomvihane 60, 61, 62, 63, 71, 72, 73, 174, 258, 268, 298
Keo Meas 97
Khaing Gech Lev 98
Khang Sarin 164
Kieu Samphan 20, 89, 96, 99, 100, 102, 138, 202, 208, 209, 218, 219, 279, 281, 283, 284, 287–8, 289, 292, 293, 304
Khmer Issaraks 19, 20, 134
Khmer National Liberation Movement 206
Khmer People's National Liberation Front (KPNLF) 205, 206, 2–7, 210, 211, 212, 213, 216, 220, 221, 223, 276, 283, 287, 288, 290, 294, 295
Khmer People's Revolutionary Party (KPRP) 89, 162
Khmer Rouge 23, 25, 40, 55, 57, 70, 81, 82, 83, 84, 85, 86, 88, 91, 92–5, 97, 99, 100, 103, 105–11 passim, 115, 138, 139, 140, 147, 153, 154, 156, 159, 160, 162, 163, 165, 166, 182, 186, 189, 190, 192, 193, 194, 195, 196, 197, 199, 201–13 passim, 217–20, 222, 223, 225, 227, 229, 233, 239, 240, 253, 273, 277–98 passim, 301, 302, 303
Khmer Serei 102, 103, 205
Khrushchev, Nikita 126
Kiernan, Ben 111 n14
Kissinger, Henry 42, 43, 91, 136
    Years of Upheaval 35

Klintworth, Gary 192
KNUFNS see Kampuchean National United Front for National Salvation
Kohn, Hans 5
Kong, Korm 216
Kong Sileah 205, 206
Korean War 14, 116, 125
KPNLF see Khmer People's National Liberation Front
Kraivichien, Thanin 65, 67, 68, 74, 75, 182
Kriangsak, Prime Minister see Chomanan, Kriangsak
Kunming Documents 136

Lam Van Phat 228
Lambertson, David F. 296, 297
Lane Xang 6, 9, 69
Lang Son 115, 116, 258
Langer, Paul 61
Lao Issara 27
Lao People's Democratic Republic (LPDR) 6, 183, 299 n8
    and China 71–4, 118, 137, 143, 169–70, 258, 298
    relations with Cambodia 69–71, 81, 83, 85, 102, 168, 225, 291
    relations with Thailand 66–8, 75–6, 170–75, 249, 165, 167–9, 288
    and the Soviet Union 238, 254, 257
    and United States 174–5, 226, 272
    Vietnamese relations with 39, 57, 59–66, 77–9, 86, 88, 119, 176, 177, 187, 227, 229, 263, 266, 270, 271, 290
Lao People's National Liberation Front (LPNLF) 225
Lao People's Revolutionary Party (LPRP) 60, 73, 77, 78, 79, 92, 174
Laos (pre 1975) 3, 7, 8, 9, 10, 14, 17, 23, 26, 27, 28, 29, 30, 35, 36, 42, 61, 62, 86, 87, 89, 91, 127, 134, 135, 136, 181, 267
Le Ba Thuyen 212
Le Duan 15, 36, 37, 38, 39, 45, 46, 47, 55, 82, 121, 134, 135, 143, 149, 225, 244, 245, 261
Le Duc Anh 109, 214, 215, 244, 273, 278, 285

Le Duc Tho 55, 213, 244
Le Kha Phieu 222
League for the Independence of
    Vietnam *see* Viet Minh
Lenin, V. I. 126
Li Peng 241, 292, 293, 306
Li Xiannian 50
Liaowang 241
Lin Biao 128, 129, 130, 144 n13
Liu Shao-ch'i 127
Liu Shuqing 269
Liv Ne 221
Lochart, Greg 11
Lon Nol 20, 23, 24, 25, 28, 88, 91, 92,
    94, 95, 98, 101, 138, 193, 205, 206,
    207, 281, 295
LPDR *see* Lao People's Democratic
    Republic
Luang Prabang 9, 26, 169, 225

Malaysia 39, 46, 48, 56, 68, 133, 183,
    184, 185, 187, 248, 250, 251, 280
Malik, Adam 40
Manchini Daily News 210
Manglapus, Raul 251
Mao Zedong 45, 50, 55, 93, 117, 124,
    125, 126, 127, 128, 129, 131, 133,
    137, 144 n13, 145 n22, 173–4, 234,
    235, 304
Marcos, Ferdinand 40
Marr, David 247
Martin, Marie-Alexandrine 165–6,
    167
Marxist-Leninism 36, 62, 125, 304
Matkins, Sir Roger 190–91
McBeth, John 220
mercenaries 226
Missing In Action Servicemen (MIAs)
    42, 43, 44, 174–5, 260, 272
Mitr Don 206
Mochtar, Foreign Minister 281, 287
monarchism 21, 22, 23, 24, 26, 31, 283
Le Monde 67
Mongolia 120, 238
Montgomery, General 304
Moore, Barrington 4
Movement of National Liberation of
    Cambodia (Moulinaka) 205, 207
Murray, Martin J. 33 n10
Mussolini, Benito 191

Nakorn, Serm Na 74
Namibia 236
National Liberation Front of South
    Vietnam *see* Viet Cong
National United Front of Kampuchea
    (NUFK) 24, 25, 93, 94, 205
National United Front for the
    Liberation Of Vietnam (NUFLV)
    228–9
nationalism 5, 6, 31, 32, 48, 123, 301,
    304, 305
    Cambodian 1, 3, 17, 18, 19, 20, 24,
        25, 69, 92, 93, 166, 202, 204, 209,
        294
    Chinese 120, 122, 124
    Lao 26, 27, 28, 29, 31, 61, 174, 270
    Vietnamese 9–17 *passim*
Nations, Richard 177, 237
NATO *see* North Atlantic Treaty
    Organization
Navari, Cornelia 33 n7
New Economic Zones (NEZs) 55
Ngo Din Diem 16, 28, 48, 50
Nguyen Cao Ky 17
Nguyen Co Thach 56, 106, 196, 265,
    279
Nguyen Duy Trinh 41
Nguyen Van Linh 37, 150, 151, 244,
    245, 246, 247, 254, 255, 257, 258,
    272
Nguyen Van Thieu 46, 137
Nhan Dan 63, 82, 106, 151, 212, 213,
    227, 247, 253, 291
Nicaragua 232, 236
Nixon, Richard 42, 43, 44, 88, 130,
    133
Norodom Sihanouk 18–26 *passim*, 28,
    65, 66, 69, 87–93 *passim*, 96, 99,
    100, 101, 137, 138, 140, 155, 162,
    165, 167, 176, 205, 207, 208, 209,
    210, 211, 212, 215, 216, 220, 221,
    253, 259, 278, 279, 280–97 *passim*,
    301
Norodom Soriavong *see* Okthol,
    André
North Atlantic Treaty Organization
    (NATO) 177, 236
North Korea 47, 125, 127, 238, 306
NUFK *see* National United Front of
    Kampuchea
Nuon Chea 97, 98, 99, 140

Office of Strategic Services (OSS) 14,
    33 n13
Okthol, André 206
Osborne, Milton 2–3, 6, 32 n3
Oxfam 156

Pakistan 145 n22
Pao Min Chang 164, 165
Paolo Wai 82
Paracel Islands 46, 47, 48, 117, 137, 260
Paris Agreement (1973) 42, 62, 136
Parrot's Beak 109
Partial Test-Ban Treaty (1963) 127
Pathet Lao 27, 28, 29, 30, 31, 59, 61,
    62, 66, 68, 73, 81, 89, 90, 135, 224,
    225, 227
Paul, Anthony 215–16
peasantry 32
    Cambodian 21, 24, 90, 91, 93, 158,
        159, 164, 273, 274
    Lao 30, 226
    Thai 198
    Vietnamese 11, 12, 13
Peking Review 143 n5
Pen Sovan 162
Penn Nouth 65, 66, 96
People's Daily 47, 50–51, 125, 126, 139,
    143 n5, 168, 243, 297
People's Liberation Army (PLA) 115,
    116, 117, 169, 235
People's Republic of Kampuchea
    (PRK) 77, 154–68 *passim*, 171,
    176, 177, 187, 188, 190, 191, 192,
    197, 201, 203, 207, 208, 211, 213,
    214, 215, 216, 217, 219, 220, 222,
    273–84 *passim*, 286, 287, 290, 291,
    302
People's Revolutionary Council 284
People's Revolutionary Party of
    Kampuchea (PRPK) 89, 90, 161,
    164, 215, 272, 276
perestroika 247
Phak Lim 196
Pham Hung 244
Pham Van Dong 14, 42, 44, 50, 55, 57,
    76, 88, 108, 135, 140, 151, 161, 244
Phan Hien 41, 42, 44, 56, 57
Phan Quang 246
Phet Sarath 27
Philippines 39, 40, 41, 46, 108, 133,
    136, 183, 232, 244, 248, 251

Phoumi Nosovan 28, 226
Phoumi Vongvichit 65, 71, 73, 171
Phoune Sipraseuth 65, 69, 70
Phu Quoc Islands 82, 83
Pike, Douglas 151, 152–3, 178 n12
Pilger, John 155, 199
PLA *see* People's Liberation Army
Pol Pot 25, 57, 63, 71, 76, 77, 78, 82,
    89, 90, 91, 92, 93, 94–5, 97, 98,
    100, 101, 103, 106, 107, 108, 110,
    111, 112 n33, 118, 119, 138, 143,
    155, 156, 160, 162, 186, 202, 213,
    214, 218–19, 233, 286, 292, 295,
    298, 305
    regime of 1, 2, 3, 4, 5, 7, 45, 51, 56,
        69, 70, 83, 93, 96, 99, 102, 104,
        105, 137, 139, 140, 141, 142, 147,
        148, 153, 154, 161, 164, 166, 168,
        174, 176, 181, 183, 184, 188, 189,
        193, 196, 197, 200, 201, 204, 205,
        207, 208, 209, 244, 255, 274, 278,
        281, 284, 287, 290, 301, 302
Poland 240, 247
Pollack, Jonathan 254, 256, 257
Pracheachon 20, 89, 90
Pramoj, Kukrit 40, 100, 269
Pramoj, Seni 67
Pravda 169, 234
Prem, Prime Minister *see* Tinsulanond,
    Prem
Pringle, James 277
PRK *see* People's Republic of
    Kampuchea
Prom Sam Ar 98
Provisional Revolutionary
    Government (PRG), South
    Vietnamese 40, 46
PRPK *see* People's Revolutionary
    Party of Kampuchea
Prum Vit 210
Pushkin Pact 127

Quemoy–Formosa Crisis 126
Qian Qichen 241, 252–3, 293
Qianlong, Emperor 121, 122
Quinn-Judge, Paul 213, 217
Quinn-Judge, Sophie 254

Rajaratnam, Sinathamby 40, 54, 183,
    185
Rannarith, Prince 221, 284, 287, 290, 297

Reagan, Ronald 43, 44, 231–2, 233, 235, 236, 237, 252, 260, 261, 272, 285, 289, 296
Red Cross 156–7, 195, 198
Red Flag 127
refugees 193–200, 294–5
  see also boat people
revolution
  Chinese 11, 122
  Russian 11, 72
  Vietnamese 38, 39, 134
  world 60, 86
Rhade tribe 227
Richardson, Michael 195
RLG *see* Royal Laos Government
Robinson, Thomas 234
Rogachev, Igor 285
Ross, Robert 137
Roy, M. N. 32
Royal Laos Government (RLG) 27, 28, 29, 30, 61, 66, 67, 73

Sa Kaeo camp 196, 199
Saigon 8, 11, 15, 16, 17, 30, 46, 50, 53, 228
Saigon Giai Phong 227
Sak Sutsakhan 206, 220, 221
Sam Neua province 27, 62, 63
Samlaut Revolt 90
Sangkum Party 20, 89, 99
Savang Vatthana, King 30
Savetsila, Siddhi 171, 264, 265, 286, 288
Say Phouthang 162
Scandinavia 155
Schultz, George 286
SEATO *see* South East Asia Treaty Organization
Second International 34 n27
Segal, Gerald 240–41
Shawcross, William 155, 159, 178 n15
Shevardnadze, Eduard 236, 241, 243, 257, 264, 293, 297
Sieng Pasason 72
Sihanouk, Prince *see* Norodom, Sihanouk
Singapore 39, 53, 108, 133, 136, 183, 184, 185, 187, 213, 247, 276, 280, 281, 290, 296
Sirik Matik 24, 295
Sisavat Keobounphan 269

Sivaraksa, Sulak 271
Skocpol, Theda 304
So Phim 98, 99, 108, 112 n33
socialism 38, 39, 168, 202, 232, 238, 239, 304
  market 248, 255, 270, 306
Sokh Sanh camp 210–11, 294
Solarz, Stephen R. 233
Solomon, Richard 296
Sam Ngoc Minh 19, 20, 25
Somalia 302
Son Ngoc Thanh 18, 19, 25
Son Sann 205, 206–7, 209, 210, 211, 220, 221, 280, 282, 290, 291, 292, 293, 297
Son Sen 98, 99, 100, 139, 140, 212, 218, 219, 222, 225, 278
Soonsiri, Prasong 267, 289
Soubanh Srithirath 69, 267, 268
Soulivong Phatsihideth 171
Souphannavong, Prince 27, 30, 69, 70, 71, 72, 73, 168
South Africa 236
South East Asia Treaty Organization (SEATO) 21, 27, 39, 40, 41, 181, 183
South Korea 47, 232, 271, 276
South Vietnam 1, 6, 15, 16, 17, 21, 23, 24, 27, 28, 37, 40, 46, 50, 62, 82, 91, 100, 109, 135, 136, 183, 228, 229, 277
Souvanna Phouma 27, 28, 30, 73, 168
Soviet Union 11, 39, 41, 47, 70, 73, 74, 79, 119, 120, 182, 263, 306, 307
  and Cambodia 155–6, 159–60, 264, 275, 276, 285
  and China 124, 125, 126, 127, 128, 129, 131–3, 234–5, 237–8, 239–42, 252–3, 258, 302
  and Laos 174, 238, 254, 257
  and United States 126, 127, 132, 232
  Vietnamese policy of 45, 46, 55, 56, 65, 101, 108, 118, 140, 141, 142, 143, 144 n21, 151, 152, 175, 192, 252–7, 258, 259, 262 n27
Soviet–Vietnamese Friendship Treaty 108
Spain 155
Spratly Islands 46, 117, 252, 259, 260, 302
Stalin, Josef 125, 127, 132, 303, 306

state
  Confucian 6, 13
  federal 176–7
  Indian ideas of 2, 3–4
  Marxist theory of 304, 305
  nation 5, 31, 33 n7, 123, 124, 305
Stimson, Henry 191
Stuart-Fox, Martin 59, 60, 78, 79, 270
Suharto, President 287
Sukarno, Doctor 183
Summit Conference of the Peoples of
    Indochina (1970) 87, 88
Suslov, Mikhail 46

Ta Mok 98, 99, 101, 104, 212, 219, 223,
    292, 295
Taiwan 46, 47, 48, 53, 136, 141, 142,
    145 n22, 232
Tanzania 191, 302
Teap Ben 221
Tet offensive (1968) 17, 33 n16
Thailand 2, 3, 6, 7, 8–9, 10, 21, 22, 24,
    26, 29, 30, 37, 39, 40, 41, 57, 63–9
    passim, 75, 76, 77, 78, 85, 102–3,
    109, 110, 133, 136, 156, 157, 158,
    169, 170, 171, 172, 173, 174, 181–3,
    184, 185, 187, 193–9, 202, 210,
    211, 213, 216, 217, 218, 222, 223,
    224, 226, 229, 244, 248, 249, 250,
    251, 257, 263–72 passim, 276, 277,
    279, 280, 281, 285, 286, 288, 289,
    290, 291, 292, 296, 297, 298, 302
Thanarat, Sarit 181
Thang Reng 206
Thanin regime see Kraivichien, Thanin
Thayer, Karl 37
Theeravit, Khien 3, 32 n3
Therevada Buddhism 6, 16, 26
Thieu, President see Nguyen Van
    Thieu
Third World 232, 233, 236, 248, 304,
    307
Tho Chu Island 82
Tibet 126
Tinsulanond, Prem 171, 211, 264, 265,
    268, 285, 286
Tito, J. B. 125
To Huu 147
Tou Samouth 90
Touby Ly Fong 29
Toul Sleng 97, 98, 101

Tran Cong Man 218
Truong Chinh 151, 244, 245
Tyrell, Emmett 157

Uganda 191, 192, 193, 302
United Nations (UN) 42, 43, 60, 79 n4,
    130, 155, 157, 172, 176, 186,
    188–9, 191, 192, 194, 195, 207,
    223, 224, 246, 280
United Nations Development Project 68
United Nations Food and Agriculture
    Organization (UNFAO) 164
United Nations High Commission for
    Refugees (UNHCR) 197, 199,
    249, 250
United Nations Law of the Sea
    Conference (1974) 46, 47
Unicef 156, 157, 195
United States of America 40, 41, 42,
    119, 120, 176, 177, 185, 191, 213,
    307
  and Cambodia 24, 25, 100, 156, 157,
    191–2, 193, 204, 220, 221, 277,
    285, 286–7, 289, 290, 294, 295–6,
    298, 303
  and China 124, 125, 126, 128, 129,
    130, 141, 142, 143, 144 n13, 201,
    232–3, 235–6, 242–3
  and Laos 27, 28, 29, 30, 59, 60, 67,
    74, 174–5, 224, 226, 272
  opposition of, to Communism 14,
    15, 21, 39, 181, 243
  and Soviet Union 127, 231–2, 238
  and Thailand 26, 182, 263
  and Vietnam 1, 16, 17, 37, 39, 43, 44,
    55, 56, 57, 87, 88, 91, 116, 123,
    127, 134, 153, 155, 183, 186, 213,
    228, 232, 237, 244, 257, 260–61,
    285, 291, 296, 302

Van Tien Dung 109, 244
Vance, Cyrus 43, 44, 56, 156, 185
Vang Pao 28, 29, 30, 63, 224, 272
VCP see Vietnamese Communist Party
Vessey, John 260
Vickery, Michael 21, 22, 105, 112 n34,
    166, 199
Viet Cong 15, 16, 50, 100
Viet Minh 14, 15, 16, 17, 19, 20, 26,
    27, 29, 81, 86, 89, 100, 125, 135,
    144 n21

Vietnam 20, 37, 40, 54, 177, 244–8, 251, 282, 283, 296, 301, 307
 and China 2, 4, 45–53, 57, 73, 76, 135, 141, 142, 201, 241, 252–4, 258–60, 289, 292, 297, 302, 307
 communism in 13, 36, 38–9, 127, 228, 229, 276, 305
 French rule of 7, 8, 9, 10, 11, 12, 14, 15, 17, 33 n10, 35
 influence in Laos 26, 59–64, 66, 67, 68, 72, 74, 77, 78, 79, 81, 168, 171, 174, 269–70, 271
 relations with Cambodia 6, 69, 71, 83–90, 101, 140, 157, 160–62, 165, 173, 175, 176, 185, 189, 221–2, 273, 274, 279, 280, 281, 290, 291
 and Soviet Union 55, 56, 239, 255–7, 285
 and Thailand 75, 181, 182, 183, 263–6
 and United States 16, 23, 42, 43, 44, 91, 136, 233, 237, 261
Vietnam–Cambodia War 6, 72, 73, 74, 81–6, 102, 104–11, 115, 119, 120, 138, 139, 141, 153, 165, 182, 187, 189–90, 192, 217, 297
Vietnam Quoc Dan Dang (VNQDD) 11, 12
Vietnam Workers' Party 15
Vietnamese Communist Party (VCP) 1, 36, 37, 39, 51, 53, 55, 56, 60, 90, 92, 107–8, 138, 143 n5, 147–51, 155, 161, 244–5, 247, 257, 272
Vladivostok Initiative 256–7, 260, 269, 289, 306

Vo Chi Kong 213, 244
Vo Nguyen Giap 56, 86, 88, 100, 106, 296–7
Vo Van Kiet 37, 244, 245, 248
Vong Atichvong see Sarin
Vongvichit, Deputy Premier see Phoumi Vongvichit

Wan Sarin 205, 206
Wang Dong Xing 140
Washington Post 157, 242
Weber, Max 6, 21, 33–4 n22
West Germany 189, 190, 307
White Lao 225, 226
Wong Kan Seng 288
Woodcock, Leonard 43, 44
World War
 First 11
 Second 10, 12, 13, 14, 18, 48, 131, 173, 188, 189, 267

Xinhua 235, 240, 241, 242, 290

Yongchaiyut, Chaovalit 218, 264, 265, 269, 270, 297
Yugoslavia 303

Zasloff, Joseph 61, 77, 78, 79 n4
Zhao Ziyang 208–9, 235, 240, 243, 283, 289
Zhou Enlai 49, 128, 133, 138, 139, 144 n13, 145 n22, 158
Zorza, Victor 142